I0814340

THE FATHERS OF THE CHURCH

MEDIAEVAL CONTINUATION

VOLUME 23

THE FATHERS OF THE CHURCH

MEDIAEVAL CONTINUATION

ST. ALBERT THE GREAT

ON JOB, VOLUME 2

Translated by

FRANKLIN T. HARKINS

THE CATHOLIC UNIVERSITY OF AMERICA PRESS
Washington, D.C.

Printed in Canada

The paper used in this publication meets the minimum requirements of the American National Standards for Information Science—Permanence of Paper for Printed Library Materials, ANSI Z39.48–1984.

∞

ISBN 978-0-8132-3940-8

Library of Congress Cataloging-in-Publication Data is available from the Library of Congress.

To Angela and Joseph

CONTENTS

INDICES

ACKNOWLEDGMENTS

It is a pleasure to acknowledge a number of individuals and institutions whose assistance has enabled the following translation. First, I am indebted to the Boston College Clough School of Theology and Ministry (BC CSTM) and my faculty colleagues for their support in various ways, especially Dean Mick McCarthy, S.J. Second, I am grateful to Max Woolley and Walter Evans, who served as my Research Assistants in 2021–22 and 2023–24, respectively, for their many able and conscientious labors. Third, several librarians and scholars at research institutes generously assisted me in procuring digital images of several manuscripts of Albert's *Super Iob,* against which I was able to check Melchior Weiss's printed edition at various points. I am indebted to Drs. Elisabeth Dlugosch and Tamara Lust of the Department of Manuscripts, Rare Books, and Graphic Collection at University Library Erlangen-Nürnberg for providing me with scans of MS Erlangen UB 58 (fols. 1ra–58vb), including a high-resolution image of fol. 1r to serve as the frontispiece for volume 2. And I am grateful to BC CSTM for covering the cost of these digital scans. Thanks to Dr. Silvia Scipioni, Manuscripts Manager at the Laurentian Library (Biblioteca Medicea Laurenziana) in Florence, for her kind assistance with MS Florence Laur. Plut. 13,10. I am much obliged to Dr. Ruth Meyer and Prof. Hannes Möhle of the Albertus-Magnus-Institut in Cologne for granting me special access to the Institut's photographs of MS Koenigsberg UB 1308 (fols. 109ra–183va), a manuscript that unfortunately was destroyed in World War II. In addition, for Dr. Meyer's generous and expert assistance with several scholarly questions that arose in the course of my work on *Super Iob,* I remain very grateful. Fourth, a special thanks to Professors Irven M. Resnick and Brian P. Dunkle, S.J., who assisted me with various questions and bibliographical details related to this volume. Fifth, my heartfelt thanks to Dr. Carole Burnett, Staff Editor at The Catholic University of America Press, for her keen editorial eye and extraordinary skill with the Latin language, which served to improve my translation at various points, and for her gracious guidance regarding other aspects of the book's production. I would like to thank two very special people, Dr. Louis Caplan and Dr. Christopher Ogilvy, for all they have done for me: I am forever grateful. Finally and above all, I am profoundly grateful to my wife, Angela, and to our son, Joseph, for their enduring love and unfailing support, which together constitute the *sine qua non* of all my scholarly work. As a small token of my deep gratitude to Angela and Joseph, who have shared me so generously with Albert over the past several years, I lovingly dedicate this work to them.

ABBREVIATIONS

General Abbreviations

CCSL	Corpus Christianorum Series Latina
ch.	chapter
col(s).	column(s)
CSEL	Corpus Scriptorum Ecclesiasticorum Latinorum
Ep.	*Epistula*
FOTC	The Fathers of the Church
FOTC MC	The Fathers of the Church: Mediaeval Continuation
GO	*Glossa ordinaria (Biblia Latina cum Glossa ordinaria: Facsimile Reprint of the Editio Princeps Adolph Rusch of Strassburg 1480/81)*
Hom.	*homilia*
l(l).	line(s)
LCL	Loeb Classical Library
LXX	Septuagint
MS(S)	manuscript(s)
NETS	*A New English Translation of the Septuagint* (Oxford University Press, originally published 2000)
PG	Patrologia Cursus Completus. Series Graeca
PL	Patrologia Cursus Completus. Series Latina
v(v).	verse(s)
vol(s).	volume(s)
Vulg.	Vulgate

Abbreviations for Specific Works

Albert the Great

AL	*De animalibus*
Anim.	*De anima*
Caus. et proc.	*De causis et processu universitatis*
De min.	*Mineralium*
De somn. et vig.	*De somno et vigilia*
Eth.	*Ethica*
In Am	*In Amos prophetam Enarratio*
Intellec. intellig.	*De intellectu et intelligibili*
Lib. caus.	*Liber de causis proprietatium elementorum*
Met.	*De meteoris*
Metaph.	*Metaphysica*
NOA	*De natura et origine animae*
Ph.	*Physica*
QQ. AL	*Quaestiones super* De animalibus
ST	*Summa theologiae*
Super Ioh.	*Super Iohannem*
Super Matt.	*Super Matthaeum*
Top.	*Topica*
Veg.	*De vegetabilibus et plantis*

Ambrose

De fide	*De fide ad Gratianum Augustum*

Anselm of Canterbury

Conc.	*De concordia praescientiae et praedestinationis et gratiae Dei cum libero arbitrio*
Mon.	*Monologion*

Aristotle

APost.	*Analytica posteriora*
APr.	*Analytica priora*
Cael.	*De caelo*
Caus.	*Liber de causis*
De an.	*De anima*

De part. animal. — *De partibus animalium*
EN — *Ethica Nicomachea*
GA — *De generatione animalium*
GC — *De generatione et corruptione*
Metaph. — *Metaphysica*
Mete. — *Meteorologica*
Mund. — *De mundo*
Ph. — *Physica*
Pl. — *De plantis*
Pol. — *Politica*
SE — *De sophisticis elenchis*
Somn. — *De somno et vigilia*
SS — *De sensu et sensibili*
Top. — *Topica*

Augustine of Hippo

c. Acad. — *Contra Academicos*
c. Faustum — *Contra Faustum*
Civ. — *De civitate Dei*
c. Iul. — *contra Iulianum*
De coniug. adult. — *de coniugiis adulterinis*
De Gen. litt. imp. — *De Genesi ad litteram imperfectus liber*
En. Ps. — *Enarrationes in Psalmos*
mend. — *De mendacio*
pat. — *De patientia*
vid. Deo — *De videndo Deo* (*Ep.* 147)

Avicenna

Metaph. — *Metaphysics*

Basil the Great

HS — *De hominis structura*

Bernard of Clairvaux

Cons. — *De consideratione*

Boethius

CP *De consolatione philosophiae*

Trin. *De Trinitate*

Cato

Dist. *Disticha de moribus ad filium*

Cicero

ND *De natura Deorum*

TD *Tusculanae Disputationes*

Dionysius the Areopagite

CH *De coelesti hierarchia*

DN *De divinis nominibus*

Fulgentius of Ruspe

AM *Ad Monimum*

Galen

DM *Definitiones medicae*

IHH *In Hippocratis de humoribus*

Gregory the Great

Hom. eu. *In euangelia homiliae*

Mor. *Moralia in Iob*

Hippocrates

Prog. *Prognosticon*

Horace

AP *De arte poetica*

Sat. *Satirae*

Hugh of St. Victor

De sacr. *De sacramentis Christianae fidei*

Isaac Israeli

Def.	*Liber de definitionibus*

Isidore

Etymol.	*Etymologiae*

Jerome

In Hos	*Commentarium in Osee prophetam*
Vita S. Hil.	*Vita Sancti Hilarionis*

John Damascene

F.o.	*De fide orthodoxa*

Macrobius

CSS	*Commentarius in Ciceronis* Somnium Scipionis
Satu.	*Saturnalia*

Maximus the Confessor

Loc. comm.	*Loci communes*

Moses Maimonides

Dux	*Dux seu director neutrorum sive perplexorum*

Origen

In Ex	*In Exodum*
In Lam	*In Threnos seu Lamentationes Ieremiae*

Ovid

Ars amat.	*Ars amatoria*
Metam.	*Metamorphoseon libri*

Palladius

OA	*Opus agriculturae*

Peter Lombard

Sent.	*Sententiae in IV libris distinctae*

Plato

Parm.	*Parmenides*
Polit.	*Politeia*
Rep.	*Res publica* (*Republic*)
Ti.	*Timaeus*

Priscian

IG	*Institutiones grammaticae*

Ps.-Chrysostom

OIM	*Opus imperfectum in Matthaeum*

Suetonius

VC	*De vita Caesarum*

Thomas Aquinas

Exp. Iob	*Expositio super Iob ad litteram*

Virgil

Aen.	*Aeneis*
Georg.	*Georgica*

Abbreviations for Biblical Books

Old Testament

Genesis	Gn	2 Kings	2 Kgs
Exodus	Ex	1 Chronicles	1 Chr
Leviticus	Lv	2 Chronicles	2 Chr
Numbers	Nm	1 Esdras (Ezra)	Ezr
Deuteronomy	Dt	2 Esdras (Nehemiah)	Neh
Joshua	Jos	3 Esdras (1 Esdras)	Unabbreviated
Judges	Jgs	4 Esdras (2 Esdras)	Unabbreviated
Ruth	Ru	Tobit	Tb
1 Samuel	1 Sm	Judith	Jdt
2 Samuel	2 Sm		
1 Kings	1 Kgs		

Esther	Est
1 Maccabees	1 Mc
2 Maccabees	2 Mc
Job	Jb
Psalm(s)	Ps(s)
Proverbs	Prv
Ecclesiastes	Eccl
Song of Songs	Song
Wisdom	Wis
Sirach	Sir
Isaiah	Is
Jeremiah	Jer
Lamentations	Lam
Baruch	Bar
Ezekiel	Ezek
Daniel	Dn
Hosea	Hos
Joel	Jl
Amos	Am
Obadiah	Ob
Jonah	Jon
Micah	Mi
Nahum	Na
Habakkuk	Hab
Zephaniah	Zep
Haggai	Hg
Zechariah	Zec
Malachi	Mal

New Testament

Matthew	Mt
Mark	Mk
Luke	Lk
John	Jn
Acts of the Apostles	Acts
Romans	Rom
1 Corinthians	1 Cor
2 Corinthians	2 Cor
Galatians	Gal
Ephesians	Eph
Philippians	Phil
Colossians	Col
1 Thessalonians	1 Thes
2 Thessalonians	2 Thes
1 Timothy	1 Tm
2 Timothy	2 Tm
Titus	Ti
Philemon	Phlm
Hebrews	Heb
James	Jas
1 Peter	1 Pt
2 Peter	2 Pt
1 John	1 Jn
2 John	2 Jn
3 John	3 Jn
Jude	Jude
Revelation	Rv

SELECT BIBLIOGRAPHY

Primary Sources

Albert the Great

B. Alberti Magni O. Praed. Commentarii in Iob: Additamentum ad Opera Omnia B. Alberti. Edited by Melchior Weiss. Freiburg: Herder, 1904.

On Animals: A Medieval Summa Zoologica. Revised edition, translated and annotated by Kenneth F. Kitchell, Jr. and Irven Michael Resnick. Vol. 2. Columbus: The Ohio State University Press, 2018.

Opera Omnia. Edited by A. Borgnet. 38 vols. Paris: L. Vivès, 1890–99.

Opera Omnia. Edited by Bernhard Geyer (after t. 37/2 [1978]: Edited by Wilhelm Kübel). Monasterii Westfalorum: Aschendorff, 1951– .

Questions concerning Aristotle's On Animals. Translated by Irven M. Resnick and Kenneth F. Kitchell, Jr. FOTC MC 9. Washington, DC: The Catholic University of America Press, 2011.

Aristotle

The Book of Causes [*Liber de Causis*]. Translated by Dennis J. Brand. 2nd edition. Milwaukee: Marquette University Press, 1984.

The Categories, On Interpretation, Prior Analytics. Translated by Harold P. Cooke and Hugh Tredennick. LCL 325. London: William Heinemann Ltd, 1973.

Generation of Animals. Translated by A. L. Peck. LCL 366. Cambridge, MA: Harvard University Press, 1942.

The Metaphysics. Translated by John H. McMahon. Buffalo, NY: Prometheus Books, 1991.

Minor Works: On Colours, On Things Heard, Physiognomics, On Plants, On Marvellous Things Heard, Mechanical Problems, On Indivisible Lines, Situations and Names of Winds, On Melissus, Xenophanes, and *Gorgias.* Translated by W. S. Hett. LCL 307. Cambridge, MA: Harvard University Press, 1963.

Nicomachean Ethics. Translated by Terence Irwin, second edition. Indianapolis: Hackett Publishing Company, Inc., 1999.

On Sleep and Dreams. Translated by David Gallop. Warminster, UK: Aris & Phillips Ltd, 1996.

On Sophistical Refutations, On Coming-to-be and Passing-away, On the Cosmos. Translated by E. S. Forster and D. J. Furley. LCL 400. Cambridge, MA: Harvard University Press, 1955.

On the Heavens. Translated by W. K. C. Guthrie. LCL 338. Cambridge, MA: Harvard University Press, 1986.

Physics. Translated by C. D. C. Reeve. Indianapolis: Hackett Publishing Company, Inc., 2018.

Politics. Translated by Ernest Barker and revised by R. F. Stalley. Oxford: Oxford University Press, 1995.

Posterior Analytics, Topica. Edited and translated by Hugh Tredennick and E. S. Forster. LCL 391. Cambridge, MA: Harvard University Press, 1960.

The Works of Aristotle. Translated under the editorship of W. D. Ross. 12 vols. Oxford: Clarendon Press, 1908–1931.

Other Ancient and Medieval Authors and Works

Abraham ibn Daud. *The Exalted Faith.* Translated with commentary by Norbert M. Samuelson; translation edited by Gershon Weiss. Rutherford, NJ: Fairleigh Dickinson University Press, 1986.

Alexander Aphrodisias. *Alexandri Aphrodisiensis In Aristotelis Metaphysica Commentaria.* Edited by Michael Hayduck. Berlin: Verlag Georg Reimar, 1891.

Anselm of Canterbury. *Complete Philosophical and Theological Treatises of Anselm of Canterbury.* Translated by Jasper Hopkins and Herbert Richardson. Minneapolis: Arthur J. Banning, 2000.

Aspasius. *Aspasii in Ethica Nicomachea quae supersunt Commentaria.* Edited by Gustavus Heylbut. Berlin: Verlag Georg Reimar, 1889.

———. *Aspasius: The Earliest Extant Commentary on Aristotle's* Ethics. Edited by Antonia Alberti and Robert W. Sharples. Berlin: De Gruyter, 1999.

Avicenna. *Avicenna Latinus. Liber de anima seu Sextus de naturalibus.* Edited by S. Van Riet. 2 vols. Louvain: Peeters, 1968 and 1972.

———. *The Metaphysics of* The Healing. Translated by Michael E. Marmura. Provo, UT: Brigham Young University Press, 2005.

Basil of Caesarea. *Exegetic Homilies.* Translated by Sister Agnes Clare Way, CDP. FOTC 46. Washington, DC: The Catholic University of America Press, 1963,

Bernard of Clairvaux. *Five Books on Consideration: Advice to a Pope.* Translated by John D. Anderson and Elizabeth T. Kennan. Kalamazoo, MI: Cistercian Publications, 1976.

Biblia Latina cum Glossa ordinaria: Facsimile Reprint of the Editio Princeps Adolph Rusch of Strassburg 1480/81. Intro. Karlfried Froehlich and Margaret T. Gibson. 4 vols. Turnhout: Brepols, 1992.

Boethius. *The Consolation of Philosophy.* Translated by David R. Slavitt. Cambridge, MA: Harvard University Press, 2008.

Cicero, Marcus Tullius. *The Nature of the Gods and On Divination.* Translated by C. D. Yonge. Amherst, NY: Prometheus Books, 1997.

———. *Tusculan Disputations.* Translated by J. E. King. LCL 141. London: William Heinemann, 1927.

Euclid. *The First Latin Translation of Euclid's* Elements *Commonly Ascribed to Adelard of Bath, Books I–VIII and Books X.36–XV.2.* Edited by H. L. L. Busard. Toronto: PIMS, 1983.

Galen. *Definitiones medicae.* In *Clavdii Galeni Opera Omnia,* edited by C. G. Kühn, t. 19, 346–462. Hildesheim: Georg Olms Verlagsbuchhandlung, 1965.

———. *Exhortation à l'étude de la médecine: Art médical.* Edited and translated by Véronique Boudon, t. 2. Paris: Les Belles Lettres, 2000.

———. *Hippocratis de humoribus liber et Galeni in eum commentarii.* In *Clavdii Galeni Opera Omnia,* edited by C. G. Kühn, t. 16, 1–488. Hildesheim: Georg Olms Verlagsbuchhandlung, 1965.

Gregory the Great. *Moralia in Iob I–XXXV.* Edited by Marc Adriaen. CCSL 143, 143A, 143B. Turnhout: Brepols, 1979–1985.

Humbert of Romans. *Instructiones de officiis ordinis.* In *Opera de vita regulari,* vol. II, edited by Joachim Joseph Berthier, 179–371. Rome: A. Befani, 1889.

Isaac Israeli. "Isaac Israeli, *Liber de Definicionibus.*" Edited by J. T. Muckle. *Archives d'histoire doctrinale et littéraire du moyen âge* 11 (1937–38): 299–340.

———. *Isaac Israeli: A Neoplatonic Philosopher of the Early Tenth Century, His Works.* Translated by A. Altmann and S. M. Stern. Oxford: Oxford University Press, 1958. Reprint, Westport, CT: Greenwood Press, 1979.

Jerome. *Préfaces aux livres de la Bible.* Textes latins des éditions de R. Weber et R. Gryson et de l'abbaye Saint-Jérôme (Rome). Translated by Aline Canellis. Sources Chrétiennes 592. Paris: Cerf, 2017.

John Damascene. *De fide orthodoxa: Versions of Burgundio and Cerbanus.* Edited by Eligius M. Buytaert, OFM. St. Bonaventure, NY: The Franciscan Institute, 1955. English translation: *Saint John of Damascus: Writings.* Translated by Frederic H. Chase, Jr. FOTC 37, 165–406. New York: Fathers of the Church, Inc., 1958.

Macrobius. *Commentary on the Dream of Scipio.* Translated by William Harris Stahl. New York: Columbia University Press, 1952. Reprint, 1990.

Moses Maimonides. *The Guide of the Perplexed.* Translated by Shlomo Pines with an introductory essay by Leo Strauss. Chicago: University of Chicago Press, 1963.

Plato. *Parmenides.* Translated by Samuel Scolnicov. Berkeley: University of California Press, 2003.

———. *Timaeus, Critias, Cleitophon, Menexenus, Epistles.* Translated by R. G. Bury. LCL 234. Cambridge, MA: Harvard University Press, 1929. Reprint, 2005.

Pseudo-Dionysius. *The Complete Works.* Translated by Colm Luibheid. The Classics of Western Spirituality. New York: Paulist Press, 1987.

Ratherius of Verona. *The Complete Works of Rather of Verona.* Translated by Peter L. D. Reid. Binghamton, NY: Medieval & Renaissance Texts and Studies, 1991.

The Septuagint with Apocrypha: Greek and English. Edited and translated by Lancelot C. L. Brenton. Seventh printing. Peabody: MA: Hendrickson, 1998.

Thomas Aquinas. *Expositio super Iob ad litteram.* Edited by Antoine Dondaine. Editio Leonina 26. Rome: Ad Sanctae Sabinae, 1965.

Translation: *The Literal Exposition on Job: A Scriptural Commentary concerning Providence.* Translated by A. Damico. Interpretive essay and notes by Martin D. Yaffe. Atlanta: Scholars Press, 1989.
Voragine, Jacobus de. *De sancta Agatha virgine.* In Appendix I of Andrew M. Beresford, *The Severed Breast: The Legends of Saints Agatha and Lucy in Medieval Castilian Literature.* Newark, DE: Juan de la Cuesta, 2010.

Secondary Sources

Adamson, Peter. *Al-Kindi.* New York: Oxford University Press, 2007.
Anzulewicz, Henryk. "Metaphysics and its Relation to Theology in Albert's Thought." In *A Companion to Albert the Great: Theology, Philosophy, and the Sciences,* edited by Irven M. Resnick, 553–61. Leiden: Brill, 2013.
———."Pseudo-Dionysius Areopagita und das Strukturprinzip des Denkens von Albert dem Grossen." In *Die Dionysius-Rezeption im Mittelalter,* edited by Tzotcho Boiadjiev, Georgi Kapriev, and Andreas Speer, 251–95. Turnhout: Brepols, 2000.
Bazàn, Bernardo C. "Les questions disputées principalement dans les facultés de théologie." In *Les questions disputées et les questions quodlibétiques dans les facultés de théologie, de droit et de médecine,* edited by Bernardo C. Bazàn, John W. Wipple, Gérard Fransen, and Danielle Jacquart, 13–149. Turnhout: Brepols, 1985.
Blankenhorn, Bernhard, OP. *The Mystery of Union with God: Dionysian Mysticism in Albert the Great and Thomas Aquinas.* Washington, DC: The Catholic University of America Press, 2015.
Boureau, Alain. Introduction to *Petri Iohannis Olivi Postilla super Iob.* Edited by Alain Boureau, CCCM 275, pp. V–XXVII. Turnhout: Brepols, 2015.
Boyle, Leonard E., OP. "Notes on the Education of the *fratres communes* in the Dominican Order in the Thirteenth Century." In *Xenia medii aevi historiam illustrantia oblata Thomae Kaeppeli, O.P.*, 2 vols., edited by R. Creytons and P. Künzle, vol. 1, 249–67. Rome: Edizioni di storia e letteratura, 1978.
Brett, Edward Tracy. *Humbert of Romans: His Life and Views of Thirteenth-century Society.* Toronto: Pontifical Institute of Mediaeval Studies, 1984.
Burger, Maria. "Die Bedeutung der Aristotelesrezeption für das Verständnis der Theologie als Wissenschaft bei Albertus Magnus." In *Albertus Magnus and the Beginnings of the Medieval Reception of Aristotle in the Latin West,* edited by Ludger Honnefelder, 281–305. Münster: Aschendorff, 2005.
———. "*Fides et ratio* als Erkenntnisprinzipien der Theologie bei Albertus Magnus." In *Via Alberti: Texte—Quellen—Interpretationen,* edited by Ludger Honnefelder, Hannes Möhle, and Susana Bullido del Barrio, 37–58. Münster: Aschendorff, 2009.
———. "Das Verhältnis von Philosophie und Theologie in den Dionysius-

Kommentaren Alberts des Grossen." In *What is Philosophy in the Middle Ages?* edited by Jan A. Aertsen and Andreas Speer, 579–86. Berlin: de Gruyter, 1998.

Callus, Daniel M., OP. "The Writings of Albert the Great." *New Blackfriars* 13 (1932): 278–87.

Canty, Aaron. "Nicholas of Lyra's Literal Commentary on Job." In *A Companion to Job in the Middle Ages,* edited by Franklin T. Harkins and Aaron Canty, 225–53. Leiden: Brill, 2017.

Chenu, Marie-Dominique, OP. "The Revolutionary Intellectualism of St. Albert the Great." *Blackfriars* 19 (1938): 5–15.

Congar, Yves, OP. "St. Albert the Great: The Power and the Anguish of an Intellectual Vocation." In *Faith and Spiritual Life,* translated by A. Manson and L. C. Sheppard, 62–66. London: Darton, Longman & Todd, Ltd., 1969.

Courtenay, William J. "The Bible in Medieval Universities." In *The New Cambridge History of the Bible,* Vol. 2: *From 600 to 1450,* edited by Richard Marsden and E. Ann Matter, 555–78. Cambridge: Cambridge University Press, 2012.

———. *Schools & Scholars in Fourteenth-century England.* Princeton: Princeton University Press, 1987.

Dahan, Gilbert. *L'exégèse chrétienne de la Bible en Occident médiéval: XIIe–XIVe siècle.* Paris: Cerf, 1999.

Dreyer, Johan Ludwig Emil. *History of the Planetary Systems from Thales to Kepler.* New York: Cosimo, 2007.

Eisen, Robert. *The Book of Job in Medieval Jewish Philosophy.* Oxford: Oxford University Press, 2004.

Fauser, Winfried, SJ. *Die Werke des Albertus Magnus in ihrer Handschriftlichen Überlieferung. Teil I: Die echten Werke / Codices Manuscripti Operum Alberti Magni. Pars I: Opera Genuina.* Münster: Aschendorff, 1982.

Fehérvári, Géza. "Masterpieces of an Unknown Iranian Metalworker." *The Journal of Dar al-Athar al-Islamiyyah* 25 (2008): 2–8.

Fries, Albert. "Zur Entstehungszeit der Bibelkommentare Alberts des Grossen." In *Albertus Magnus, Doctor universalis: 1280/1980,* edited by Gerbert Meyer, OP, and Albert Zimmermann, 119–39. Mainz: Matthias Grünewald, 1980.

Ginther, James R. "A Scholastic Idea of the Church: Robert Grosseteste's Exposition of Psalm 86." *Archives d'histoire doctrinale et littéraire du moyen âge* 66 (1999): 49–72.

———. "There is a Text in this Classroom: The Bible and Theology in the Medieval University." In *Essays in Medieval Philosophy and Theology in Memory of Walter H. Principe, CSB: Fortresses and Launching Pads,* edited by James R. Ginther and Carl N. Still, 31–51. Aldershot: Ashgate, 2005.

Graham, William A. *Beyond the Written Word: Oral Aspects of Scripture in the History of Religion.* Cambridge: Cambridge University Press, 1987.

Hankinson, R. J., ed. *Cambridge Companion to Galen.* Cambridge: Cambridge University Press, 2008.

Harkins, Franklin T. "Christ and the Eternal Extent of Divine Providence in the *Expositio super Iob ad litteram* of Thomas Aquinas." In *A Companion to Job in the Middle Ages,* edited by Franklin T. Harkins and Aaron Canty, 161–200. Leiden: Brill, 2016.

——— and Aaron Canty, eds. *A Companion to Job in the Middle Ages.* Leiden: Brill, 2017.

Hellmeier, Paul D., OP. "Der *intellectus adeptus* und die Torheit der Philosophen. Philosophische Vollendung und christlicher Glaube in den Bibelkommentaren Alberts des Grossen." *Divus Thomas* 122 (2019): 144–84.

Hipp, Stephen A. *"Person" in Christian Tradition and the Conception of Saint Albert the Great: A Systematic Study of its Concept as Illuminated by the Mysteries of the Trinity and the Incarnation.* Münster: Aschendorff, 2001.

Honnefelder, Ludger. "Wisdom on the Way of Science: Christian Theology and the Universe of Sciences according to St. Albert the Great." In *Via Alberti: Texte—Quellen—Interpretationen,* edited by Ludger Honnefelder, Hannes Möhle, and Susana Bullido del Barrio, 13–36. Münster: Aschendorff, 2009.

Hossfeld, Paul. *Albertus Magnus als Naturphilosoph und Naturwissenschaftler.* Bonn: Albertus-Magnus-Institut, 1983.

Kovach, Francis J., and Robert W. Shahan, eds. *Albert the Great: Commemorative Essays.* Norman: University of Oklahoma Press, 1980.

Kugel, James L. *Traditions of the Bible: A Guide to the Bible as it Was at the Start of the Common Era.* Cambridge, MA: Harvard University Press, 1998.

Lawn, Brian. *Rise and Decline of the Scholastic* Quaestio disputata, *with special emphasis on its use in the teaching of medicine and science.* Leiden: Brill, 1993.

Legaspi, Michael C. *The Death of Scripture and the Rise of Biblical Studies.* Oxford: Oxford University Press, 2010.

Leinsle, Ulrich G. *Introduction to Scholastic Theology.* Translated by Michael J. Miller. Washington, DC: The Catholic University of America Press, 2010.

Levin, Leonard, R. David Walker, and Shalom Sadik. "Isaac Israeli." *The Stanford Encyclopedia of Philosophy.* Fall 2022. Edited by Edward N. Zalta and Uri Nodelman. URL: https://plato.stanford.edu/archives/fall2022/entries/israeli/.

Lienhard, Joseph T. "Reading the Bible and Learning to Read: The Influence of Education on St. Augustine's Exegesis." *Augustinian Studies* 27.1 (1996): 7–25.

Light, Laura. "French Bibles c. 1200–30: A New Look at the Origin of the Paris Bible." In *The Early Medieval Bible: Its Production, Decoration and Use,* edited by Richard Gameson, 155–76. Cambridge: Cambridge University Press, 1994.

———. "The Thirteenth Century and the Paris Bible." In *The New Cambridge History of the Bible.* Vol. 2, *From 600 to 1450,* edited by Richard Marsden and E. Ann Matter, 380–91. Cambridge: Cambridge University Press, 2012.

Martin, J. P. P. "Le texte parisien de la Vulgate latine." *Le Muséon* 8 (1889): 444–66; 9 (1890): 55–70, 301–16.

———. "La Vulgate latine au XIIIe siècle d'après Roger Bacon." *Le Muséon* 7 (1888): 88–107, 169–96, 277–91, 381–93.

Maurer, Armand, CSB. *Medieval Philosophy: An Introduction,* second edition. Toronto: Pontifical Institute of Mediaeval Studies, 1982.

Meyer, Gerbert, OP, and Albert Zimmermann, eds. *Albertus Magnus, Doctor universalis: 1280–1980.* Mainz: Matthias Grünewald Verlag, 1980.

Meyer, Ruth. "'Hanc autem disputationem solus Deus determinare potest': Das Buch Hiob als *disputatio* bei Albertus Magnus und Thomas von Aquin." In *Via Alberti. Texte—Quellen—Interpretationen,* edited by Ludger Honnefelder, Hannes Möhle, and Susana Bullido del Barrio, 325–83. Münster: Aschendorff, 2009.

———. "A Passionate Dispute over Divine Providence: Albert the Great's Commentary on the Book of Job." In *A Companion to Job in the Middle Ages,* edited by Franklin T. Harkins and Aaron Canty, 201–24. Leiden: Brill, 2017.

Möhle, Hannes. *Albertus Magnus.* Münster: Aschendorff, 2015.

———. "Zum Verhältnis von Theologie und Philosophie bei Albert dem Grossen." In *Rheinisch—Kölnisch—Katholisch. Beiträge zur Kirchen- und Landesgeschichte sowie zur Geschichte des Buch- und Bibliothekswesens der Rheinlande. Festschrift für Heinz Finger zum 60. Geburtstag,* edited by Siegfried Schmidt, 147–62. Cologne: Erzbischöfliche Diözesan- und Dombibliothek, 2008.

———, Henryk Anzulewicz, Maria Burger, et al., eds. *Albertus Magnus und sein System der Wissenschaften. Schlüsseltexte in Übersetzung. Lateinisch—Deutsch.* Münster: Aschendorff, 2011.

Moonan, Lawrence. "What is a Negative Theology? Albert's Answer." In *Albertus Magnus: Zum Gedenken nach 800 Jahren: Neue Zugänge, Aspekte und Perspektiven,* edited by Walter Senner, OP, Henryk Anzulewicz, et al., 605–18. Berlin: Akademie Verlag, 2001.

Mulchahey, M. Michèle. *"First the bow is bent in study . . .": Dominican Education before 1350.* Toronto: Pontifical Institute of Mediaeval Studies, 1998.

Noone, Timothy B. "Scholasticism." In *A Companion to Philosophy in the Middle Ages,* edited by Jorge J. E. Gracia and Timothy B. Noone, 55–64. Malden, MA: Blackwell Publishing, 2003.

Olszewski, Mikołaj. "The Nature of Theology according to Albert the Great." In *A Companion to Albert the Great: Theology, Philosophy, and the Sciences,* edited by Irven M. Resnick, 69–104. Leiden: Brill, 2013.

Prügl, Thomas. "Thomas Aquinas as Interpreter of Scripture." In *The Theology of Thomas Aquinas,* edited by Rik van Nieuwenhove and Joseph Wawrykow, 386–415. Notre Dame: University of Notre Dame Press, 2005.

Resnick, Irven M. "Albert the Great: Biographical Introduction." In *A Companion to Albert the Great: Theology, Philosophy, and the Sciences,* edited by Irven M. Resnick, 1–11. Leiden: Brill, 2013.

———, ed. *A Companion to Albert the Great: Theology, Philosophy, and the Sciences.* Leiden: Brill, 2013.

——— and Kenneth F. Kitchell, Jr. *Albert the Great: A Selectively Annotated Bibliography (1900–2000).* Tempe: Arizona Center for Medieval and Renaissance Studies, 2004.

Reynolds, Philip Lyndon. *Food and the Body: Some Peculiar Questions in High Medieval Theology.* Leiden: Brill, 1999.

Riché, Pierre, and Guy Lobrichon, eds. *Le Moyen Age et la Bible.* Paris: Éditions Beauchesne, 1984.

Senner, Walter, OP. *Alberts des Großen Verständnis von Theologie und Philosophie.* Münster: Aschendorff, 2009.

Smalley, Beryl. *The Study of the Bible in the Middle Ages.* Notre Dame: University of Notre Dame Press, 1964.

Smith, Lesley. *The* Glossa Ordinaria: *The Making of a Medieval Bible Commentary.* Leiden: Brill, 2009.

———. "Hugh of St. Cher and Medieval Collaboration." In *Transforming Relations: Essays on Jews and Christians throughout History in Honor of Michael A. Signer,* edited by Franklin T. Harkins, 241–64. Notre Dame: University of Notre Dame Press, 2010.

———. "Job in the *Glossa Ordinaria* on the Bible." In *A Companion to Job in the Middle Ages,* edited by Franklin T. Harkins and Aaron Canty, 101–28. Leiden: Brill, 2017.

Söder, Joachim R. "Albert the Great, 'The Astonishing Wonder.'" In *Albert the Great: Theologian and Scientist. Bibliographic Resources and Translated Essays,* edited and translated by Thomas F. O'Meara, OP, 26–28. Chicago: New Priory Press, 2013.

Straw, Carole. "Job's Sin in the *Moralia* of Gregory the Great." In *A Companion to Job in the Middle Ages,* edited by Franklin T. Harkins and Aaron Canty, 71–100. Leiden: Brill, 2017.

Theodossiou, Efstratios Th., Milan S. Dimitrijevic, Vassilios N. Manimanis, and Th. Grammenos, "*Hydor* from Ancient Greek Cosmogonies to Modern Astrophysics." *Transdisciplinarity in Science and Religion* 1 (2007): 137–52.

Tugwell, Simon, OP. "Introduction: I. The Life and Works of Albert." In *Albert & Thomas: Selected Writings,* edited and translated by Simon Tugwell, OP, 3–39. New York: Paulist Press, 1988.

Twetten, David, and Steven Baldner. "Introduction to Albert's Philosophical Work." In *A Companion to Albert the Great: Theology, Philosophy, and the Sciences,* edited by Irven M. Resnick, 165–72. Leiden: Brill, 2013.

Van Steenberghen, Fernand. "Saint Albert le Grand, Docteur de l'Église." *Collecteana Mechliniensia* 21 (1932): 518–34.

Wéber, Édouard-Henri. "La relation de la philosophie et de la théologie selon Albert le Grand." *Archives de Philosophie* 43 (1980): 559–88.

Wei, Ian P. *Intellectual Culture in Medieval Paris: Theologians and the University, c. 1100–1330.* Cambridge: Cambridge University Press, 2012.

Weijers, Olga. *La 'disputatio' à la Faculté des arts de Paris (1200–1350 environ): Esquisse d'une typologie.* Turnhout: Brepols, 1995.

———. "The Various Kinds of Disputation in the Faculties of Arts, Theology, and Law." In *Disputatio 1200–1800. Form, Funktion und Wirkung eines Leitmediums universitärer Wissenskultur,* edited by Marion Gindhart and Ursula Kundert, 21–32. Berlin: de Gruyter, 2010.

Weisheipl, James A., OP. "Albertus Magnus." In *Dictionary of the Middle Ages,* vol. 1, edited by Joseph R. Strayer, 126–30. New York: Scribner, 1982.

———. "The Life and Works of St. Albert the Great." In *Albertus Magnus and the Sciences: Commemorative Essays 1980,* edited by James A. Weisheipl, OP, 13–51. Toronto: Pontifical Institute of Mediaeval Studies, 1980.

ON JOB, VOLUME 2

University Library Erlangen-Nürnberg, MS 58, fol. 1r.
Reproduced by permission.

CHAPTER 22

BUT ELIPHAZ THE *Temanite responded and said.*

This response is divided into two parts. In the first, Eliphaz refutes blessed Job; in the second, he calls him back to penance in this place:[1] *Submit, therefore, to Him.*

The first part is subdivided into two: for he refutes him first in particular, [and] second in general in this place:[2] *For you have taken away the pledge.*

In the first [of these subdivisions], there are three points, namely: that a human is not comparable to God; that what has been done by a human can confer nothing on God, on account of the fact that the good of a human is not able to increase divine perfection; and that God can punish nothing in a human except sins.

And that is: ***But Eliphaz,*** which means "old age alone" on account of the gray hair of the mind, ***the Temanite,*** who was experienced in the study of letters. Wis 4:[3] *The understanding of a man is his gray hair.* Bar 3:[4] *The children of Agar who search for the wisdom that is of the earth, the merchants of the land and of Teman, the speakers and those who inquire into wisdom and understanding.* ***responded and said,*** as the corrector of falsehood, of course. Aristotle, in the first book of *On Sophistical Refutations,*[5] says: The work of the wise man is twofold: certainly not to deceive anyone concerning things about which he knows, and to be able to reveal one who is deceiving [others].

And therefore that man [Eliphaz], in the first place revealing

1. Jb 22.21.
2. Jb 22.6.
3. Wis 4.8.
4. Bar 3.23.
5. Aristotle, *SE* 1.6.

one who is deceiving, so it seems to him, says: [2] ***Can a human be compared to God.*** The same [interlocutor] had said this above in chapter 4,[6] and he said that it was revealed to him: *Can it be that a human will be made righteous in comparison to God, or will a man be purer than his Maker?* And this is what he adds: ***even if he were to have perfect knowledge?*** namely, by the perfection of the knower, not by the perfection of what is knowable. No one has perfect knowledge of divine matters except God. 1 Cor 13:[7] *We know in part, and we prophesy in part.* But the perfection of knowledge consists in the human knowing perfectly according to the human mode. Jn 15:[8] *A student is not above his teacher.* But every student will be perfect if he is like his teacher. And Eliphaz intends [to say] that God has such perfect knowledge of these inferior things that He sees and examines and looks upon the human in his thoughts and words and actions more effectively than the human is able to see his very self. Sir 23:[9] *The eyes of the Lord are far brighter than the sun, looking around and seeing all the ways of men.* Heb 4:[10] *The discerner of the thoughts and intentions of the heart. And there is no creature invisible in His sight.*

Then Eliphaz continues by demonstrating that God does not punish anything in him except sins. For if He were punishing something else, He would be doing so on account of some benefit [to Himself] and not with a view to justice. And Eliphaz removes this possibility, saying: [3] ***What benefit is it to God if you are just?*** as if to say: "Nothing, but it is a benefit to you yourself." Ps:[11] *You do not need my good works.* Gregory says: As long as He [namely, God] delights in Himself, He needs no good work.[12] ***or what do you confer on Him,*** namely, by adding to His goodness, ***if your way is spotless?*** For we do not confer [anything] on Him, but He confers on us, so that we might be good. 1 Chr, at the end:[13] *All things that are in heaven and on earth are yours—all things; and we*

6. Jb 4.17.
7. 1 Cor 13.9.
8. Cf. Jn 15.20: *A servant is not greater than his master.*
9. Sir 23.28.
10. Heb 4.12–13.
11. Ps 15.2. Psalm numbering in this volume is that of the LXX.
12. Gregory, *Mor.* 16.2.2.
13. 1 Chr 19.11, 14.

have given to you what we have received from your hand. Ps:[14] *Blessed are the spotless in the way, who walk in the law of the Lord.*

And he excludes the false response that could be given. For it could be said that God had struck Job in order to impede him, lest Job be made equal to [God] Himself. And that is: **[4]** ***Can it be that He will accuse you on account of fear,*** as if to say: "No." Indeed, God fears you in nothing because in nothing can He be impeded from His own goodness. Est 13:[15] *All things have been established in your power, and there is no one who can resist your will.* Rom 9:[16] *Who resists His will?*

And concerning the reason for his own punishment, he adds: ***and,*** supply: can it be that ***He will come with you into judgment?*** supply: in order that He may be judged with you, regarding whether He acts justly or unjustly concerning you, as if to say: "No." Ps:[17] *You may prevail when you are judged.* Jb 9:[18] *If I should wish to justify myself, my own mouth would condemn me; if to show myself innocent, He will confirm that I am perverse.* **[5]** ***And not,*** that is: is it not ***on account of your manifold wickedness,*** supply: He will reprove you. And Eliphaz calls sin that is committed not on account of weakness or ignorance, but on account of wickedness alone, "wickedness"; and he says "manifold" because it is multiplied in the formation of a habit. Jer 2:[19] *Your own wickedness will reprove you, and your apostasy will rebuke you.* ***and your infinite iniquities?*** which you have committed in your work, of course. Indeed, "iniquities" are "infinite" because they are neither limited nor toward a limit. 2 Chr, at the end:[20] *My iniquities are multiplied beyond the grains of sand of the sea.* Ps:[21] *For my iniquities have gone over my head.*

[6] ***For you have taken away.***

Here Eliphaz refutes [Job] in particular, and he says two things: first, he specifies the sin with the punishment; second, he

14. Ps 118.1.
15. Est 13.9.
16. Rom 9.19.
17. Ps 50.4.
18. Jb 9.20.
19. Jer 2.19.
20. Text not found, though similar language is found in texts such as Is 59.12 and Jer 15.8.
21. Ps 37.5.

sets forth the reasons advanced to the contrary, in that place:[22] *Can it be that you do not think.* To this point in the first [section] there are two things: the rebuking of the sin; and the threatening of the punishment, in that place:[23] *Therefore, you are surrounded.* He rebukes three sins in the first [section]: those of avarice, violence, and hostility. [He rebukes the sin] of avarice in a twofold way, in pillaging and in withholding.

And that is: ***For you have taken away the pledge of your brothers,*** supply: in certain things that are necessary for them, namely, in clothing and furniture, ***without cause,*** supply: [the cause] of justice, just as tyrants make exactions on the poor, establishing [exactions] and taking away their pledges. Ex 22:[24] *If you take a garment from your neighbor as a pledge, you shall return it to him before sunset. For that is the only thing with which he is covered, the clothing of his flesh; nor does he have anything else in which to sleep.* By way of rebuke, Am 2 says to the children of Israel:[25] *They sat down upon the garments taken as a pledge.* And elaborating on this, he adds: ***and the naked,*** that is, the nude, namely, those clothed insufficiently, ***you have stripped of clothing.*** Jb 24:[26] *They send men away naked, taking away their garments.*

And, concerning avarice in withholding, he adds: **[7]** ***You have not given water,*** that is, what is potable, ***to the weary one,*** that is, to the one who must be thirsty. Mt 25:[27] *I was thirsty, and you did not give me to drink.* The weary one is thirstier than another person. Is 21:[28] *Running to meet the thirsty one, bring him water.* ***and you have taken bread,*** that is, what is edible, ***from the hungry.*** Mt 25:[29] *I was hungry, and you did not give me to eat.* Is 21:[30] *With bread run to meet the one fleeing.* 1 Jn 3:[31] *He who possesses the wealth of this world, and sees his own brother suffering in poverty, and closes his heart to him: how is the love of the Father in him?*

22. Jb 22.12.
23. Jb 22.10.
24. Ex 22.26–27.
25. Am 2.8.
26. Jb 24.7.
27. Mt 25.42.
28. Is 21.14.
29. Mt 25.42.
30. Is 21.14.
31. 1 Jn 3.17.

And concerning violence, he adds: [8] ***In the strength of your arm,*** that is, with the force of violence, ***you possessed the land,*** that is, you have violently subjugated others' borders. Jdt 1:[32] *He* [*Nebuchadnezzar*] *sent to all who live in Cilicia and Damascus and Lebanon,* in order that they might subject themselves to him, and he subjected them by the power of Holofernes. And according to Judith, those who had been overthrown said to him:[33] *Let all that we have be subject to your law. We and our children are your servants. Come to us as a peaceable lord, and we will serve you happily.* And being the most powerful, you occupied it, that is, by the violence of your power and not by any right. Am 6:[34] *We have taken horns to ourselves by our own strength.* Jdt 1:[35] *He gloried as a mighty one in his own power.*

And concerning the vice of hostility, he adds: [9] ***You have sent widows away empty,*** namely, by robbing them and not judging in their favor. Is 1: *They do not judge in favor of the orphan, and the cause of the widow does not come to them.* ***and the arms of orphans,*** that is, the strength of orphans, ***you have broken into pieces.*** A "widow" (*vidua*) is so called from *viro idua,*[36] that is, a woman who has been separated [from her husband]; an "orphan" does not have a father to protect him. And by these, every kind of pitiable person, who has not encountered compassion in God's presence, is understood. Ps:[37] *They have destroyed the widow and the foreigner, and they have killed the orphan.* At the end of Lam:[38] *We have become orphans without a father; our mothers are as widows.*

He threatens punishment for these faults: [10] ***Therefore, you are surrounded by snares,*** that is, by tribulations, as snares holding you. Ps:[39] *Their foot has been caught in the very snare that they hid.*

And he rebukes [Job] because in such great sins he was hoping for impunity. And that is: ***and sudden dread,*** which you had

32. Jdt 1.7.
33. Jdt 3.4–6.
34. Am 6.14.
35. Jdt 1.4.
36. See Macrobius, *Satu.* 1.15.17: "Iduare enim Etrusca lingua dividere est: unde vidua, quasi valde idua, id est valde divisa: aut vidua, id est a viro divisa."
37. Ps 93.6.
38. Lam 5.3.
39. Ps 9.16.

not expected, but which you deserve, of course, ***confounds you.*** Dionysius [says] to the monk Gaius:[40] "What is contrary to expectation happens suddenly." Is 30:[41] *His destruction will come suddenly, when it is not expected, and he will be crushed to pieces.* **[11]** ***And did you think,*** existing in such great sins, ***that you would not see darkness,*** that is, the darkness of unanticipated tribulations, which was presumption. Wis 5:[42] *The hope of the wicked is as down, which is blown away by the wind.* Ps:[43] *He has established me in darkness, just like the dead of old.* And he explains this, adding: ***and that you would not be overwhelmed,*** that is, that you were not going to be overwhelmed, namely, by the fury, for you were able to know that such great fury was going to overwhelm you, ***by the fury of flooding waters?*** that is, of the swelling of tribulations. Lam 3:[44] *The waters have flooded over my head. I said: I have died.* Jon 2:[45] *All of your whirlpools and your floods have passed over me.*

Then Eliphaz sets forth two reasons advanced to the contrary, and that is: **[12]** ***Can it be that you do not think that God is higher than heaven,*** supply: and so removed from our actions, that is to say, that God does not see [them]. He explains this, adding: ***and is elevated,*** and thus rules the celestial realm, which is not accessible to the gaze of our eyes, ***above the highest point of the stars,*** that is, [above] the poles around which the stars revolve. **[13]** ***And you say,*** supply: because of this: ***For what does God know?*** concerning our actions, of course. The same [is said in] Ezek 8:[46] *For they say: The Lord does not see us, the Lord has forsaken the earth.* Jb 11:[47] *He is higher than heaven, and so how will you know?* And he explains this, adding: ***and He judges as if through mist,*** supply: concerning our actions. "To judge through mist" is to orient oneself to voluntary and casual and accidental realities not with an absolute consideration, but to weigh carefully each of the things that happen frequently through necessary realities, and, by means of neces-

40. Dionysius, *Ad Gaium* 3 (PG 3:1069).
41. Is 30.13–14.
42. Wis 5.15.
43. Ps 142.3.
44. Lam 3.54.
45. Jon 2.4.
46. Ezek 8.12.
47. Jb 11.8.

sary and frequent realities, to judge in whatever way something of voluntary and casual realities. Sir 23:[48] *Who sees me? Darkness envelops me, and the walls completely cover me, and no one sees me: whom do I fear? The Most High will not remember my transgressions.*

And this is what he adds: [14] ***The clouds are His hiding place,*** that is, His providence extends no further than to the clouds alone. Ps:[49] *He has made darkness His hiding place.* And this is what follows: ***and He does not consider our things,*** namely, our deeds and words and thoughts. And, according to the letter, this was the opinion or error of certain philosophers,[50] that God's providence does not extend beyond the motion of the heavens and does not come to lower things except through another and accidentally (*per aliud et per accidens*): through another, namely, through portions of a period; and accidentally because through the accidental actions of lower things. And both Alexander [Aphrodisias][51] and Averroes[52] and certain others of the Peripatetics seem to be in agreement on this error.

And this is what he adds: ***and He walks,*** namely, by providing for and ordering things that are constituted in one way, ***among the poles of heaven,*** within which the celestial bodies are moved, of course. Ps:[53] *The heaven of heaven is the Lord's; but the earth He has given to the sons of men.*

Then he introduces a second reason advanced [to the contrary]: [15] ***Can it be that you wish to keep,*** so that you might pursue, as it were, the fancies of error and the desires of the senses, as if he were saying: "You should not." ***the path of the ages,*** namely, the broad [path] that leads to death. Mt 7:[54] *Broad is the way that leads to death, and many there are who walk in it.* Jer 2:[55] *Have they walked after vanity, and have they become vain? And they have not said:*

48. Sir 23.25–26.
49. Ps 17.12.
50. See Alb., *Metaph.* 9.2.4.
51. See Alexander Aphrodisias, *Comm. in Metaph. Arist.* Λ.6.1071b.3 (*Alexandri Aphrodisiensis In Aristotelis Metaphysica Commentaria,* ed. Michael Hayduck [Berlin: Verlag Georg Reimar, 1891], p. 685); cf. Alb., *Metaph.* 11.2.10.
52. Cf. Alb., *Metaph.* 11.2.21.
53. Ps 113.16.
54. Mt 7.13.
55. Jer 2.5–6.

Where is the Lord? ***which wicked men,*** namely, those going astray and those driving them into error, ***have trod?*** 2 Tm 3:[56] *Evil men grow worse and worse, going astray and driving into error.* Is 59:[57] *Their paths have become crooked to them; all who tread in them do not know peace.*

And he adds how God has punished them: **[16]** ***Who were taken away before their time.*** Ps:[58] *Bloody and deceitful men will not live out half their days.* Is 38:[59] *While I was still beginning, He cut me down.* ***and a flood,*** namely, of divine indignation, ***has overthrown their foundations,*** that is, the places into which they were pouring their intentions and errors. Mt 7:[60] *The floods came, and the winds blew, and they beat upon that house, and it fell, and great was its destruction.* Sir 10:[61] *God has destroyed the thrones of proud princes.*

Then he adds the reason: **[17]** ***who,*** because they [were] in error and in [wicked] act, of course, ***said to God: Go away from us,*** that is, depart lest you consider our affairs. Jb 21:[62] *They said to God: Go away from us; we refuse to have knowledge of your ways.* ***and judged the Almighty as if He could do nothing,*** supply: with regard to those inferior things. Jb 21:[63] *Who is the Almighty that we should serve Him? And what does it profit us if we pray to Him?* But the contrary is written in Lk 1:[64] *No word will be impossible with God.*

And he adds that because of this they became ungrateful and went astray: **[18]** ***Although He had filled their houses with good things,*** which they could receive only from God, of course. Jb 12:[65] *The tents of robbers overflow, and audaciously they provoke God, whereas He Himself has given all things into their hands.* ***may their way of thinking be far from me!*** In this he seeks to vindicate himself. Ps:[66] *I have not sat with the council of vanity; and I will not go in with those doing unjust things.*

56. 2 Tm 3.13.
57. Is 59.8.
58. Ps 54.24.
59. Is 38.12.
60. Mt 7.27.
61. Sir 10.17.
62. Jb 21.14.
63. Jb 21.15.
64. Lk 1.37.
65. Jb 12.6.
66. Ps 25.4.

After making clear the destruction of the wicked on account of their errors, to which he does not consent, Eliphaz presents those in agreement with himself and he describes them, and that is: [19] ***The just will see,*** namely, that vengeance has been taken on the wicked, ***and will rejoice.*** Ps:[67] *The just man will rejoice when he sees the vengeance.* ***and the innocent one,*** supply: I, as it were, ***will mock them.*** Prv 1:[68] *I will laugh at your destruction, and I will mock you when what you feared comes upon you.* He shows that it is so, moreover, through the effect. And he adds: [20] ***Has not their,*** namely, of the wicked in every time, ***exaltation been cut down?*** Jb 40:[69] *Look on all who are proud and confound them, and crush the wicked in their place.* Ps:[70] *When they were lifted up, you have thrown them down.* ***and has not fire devoured their remains?*** namely, [their] successors and imitators. Jb 20:[71] *A fire that is not kindled will devour him.*

[21] ***Submit, therefore.***

Here Eliphaz calls Job back to penance, and he says three things. For, first, he calls him back; second, he promises many good things to the one who returns, in that place:[72] *If you will return;* third, he adds the reason, in that place:[73] *For he who has been humbled.*

In the recall there are two things, namely, the recall and the form of the recall.

And that is: ***Submit, therefore, to Him,*** namely, to God, who is striking you, in order that you may turn back to Him, of course, through conformity of the will, ***and be at peace,*** for then He will not pursue you any more. Hence the opposite is said in Is 9:[74] *His hand is still stretched out; and the people have not turned back to the one striking them.* Concerning peace, Phil 4:[75] *May the peace of God, which surpasses all understanding, guard your hearts and your minds.* ***and by this,*** namely, that you submit to Him, ***you will have the best fruit,*** namely,

67. Ps 57.11.
68. Prv 1.26.
69. Jb 40.7.
70. Ps 72.18.
71. Jb 20.26.
72. Jb 22.23.
73. Jb 22.29.
74. Is 9.12–13.
75. Phil 4.7.

the consolation of virtue and the refreshment that is introduced through discipline. Heb 12:[76] *Indeed, all discipline in the present certainly seems not to be a source of joy, but rather of sorrow; afterwards, however, it will yield to those who have been trained by it the most peaceful fruit of justice.* Ps:[77] *Your rod and your staff, they have comforted me.*

And concerning the form of the one who is going to return, he adds: **[22]** ***Receive the law from His mouth,*** namely, in precepts and judgments. Sir 45:[78] *He gave him a heart for precepts, and the law of life and discipline.* Is 8:[79] *Bind the testimony, seal the law among my disciples.* ***and lay up His words,*** by which understanding may be formed toward the truth, of course, ***in your heart.*** Lk 2:[80] *But Mary kept all these words, pondering them in her heart.* Ps:[81] *Your words I have hidden in my heart, that I may not sin against you.*

Then he promises many good things to the one who returns, in riches, in delights, in favorable answers to prayers, and in the success of vows. And that is: **[23]** ***If you will return*** through penance ***to the Almighty*** God, who is able to raise the fallen, ***you will be built up,*** supply: in all good things. Ex 1:[82] *Because the midwives feared God, He built houses for them.* The Gloss says:[83] "houses of the virtues." Jer 4:[84] *If you will turn back, O Israel, says the Lord, turn back to me; if you will remove your stumbling blocks from my sight, you will not be troubled.*

And that is: ***and you will put iniquity far from your tabernacle,*** so that neither you nor anyone living with you may be wicked, of course. Ps:[85] *He who works pride shall not live in the midst of my house.*

[24] ***He will give flint for earth,*** that is, abundantly; just as [he

76. Heb 12.11.
77. Ps 22.4.
78. Sir 45.6.
79. Is 8.16.
80. Lk 2.19.
81. Ps 118.11.
82. Ex 1.21.
83. Although Weiss was unable to find this reference in the PL edition of the *Glossa ordinaria,* it does appear as an interlinear gloss on Ex 1.21 in the Editio Princeps: see *Biblia Latina cum Glossa Ordinaria: Facsimile Reprint of the Editio Princeps, Adolph Rusch of Strassburg 1480/81* (Turnhout: Brepols, 1992), vol. 1, p. 114.
84. Jer 4.1.
85. Ps 100.7.

gives] the earth, [he gives] a precious stone, which he calls "flint" here. Indeed, he specifies this first because flint is among the most precious stones. Ezek 28:[86] *Every precious stone was your covering.* Ezek 27:[87] *Your merchants, with all the best spices and precious stones.* ***and for flint,*** supply: by including ***torrents of gold,*** that is, gold abundantly, as if a torrent were flowing forth. Is 60:[88] *All shall come from Saba, bringing gold and frankincense.*

[25] ***And the Almighty will be against your enemies.*** Is 11:[89] *The enemies of Judah will perish.* ***and gold,*** which is valuable for exchange, ***will be heaped up for you,*** as if in many piles. Bar 3:[90] *They hoard silver and gold, in which humans put their confidence.* Hos 2:[91] *I have multiplied her silver and gold.*

And he adds concerning delights: **[26]** ***Then in the Almighty,*** supply: helping you, ***you will abound in delights.*** Eccl 2:[92] *I said in my heart: I will go, and I will abound in delights and enjoy good things.*

Then, concerning favorable answers to prayers, he adds: ***and you will lift up your face to God,*** namely, in prayer. 2 Chr 20:[93] *This alone remains for us, that we should turn our eyes toward you.* **[27]** ***You will pray to Him,*** concerning everything that you want, of course, ***and He will hear you.*** Is 58:[94] *Then you will call, and the Lord will hear; you will cry out, and He will say: Behold, I am here.* ***and you will pay your vows,*** which you make from the will. Augustine:[95] To make a vow pertains to the will, but to pay it pertains to necessity. Is 19:[96] *They will make vows to the Lord and perform them.* Ps:[97] *I will pay my vows, which my lips have uttered.*

And, concerning the success of vows, he adds: **[28]** ***You will decide upon something*** lawful and good, whatever you wish, ***and it will***

86. Ezek 28.13.
87. Ezek 27.22.
88. Is 60.6.
89. Is 11.13.
90. Bar 3.18.
91. Hos 2.8.
92. Eccl 2.1.
93. 2 Chr 20.12.
94. Is 58.9.
95. See Augustine, *De coniug. adult.* 1.34.30 (PL 40:468) and Epist. 127.8 (PL 33:486).
96. Is 19.21.
97. Ps 65.13–14.

come to you. 2 Sm 23:[98] *He is my entire salvation, and there is nothing that does not sprout forth from it.* Ps:[99] *Delight in the Lord, and He will grant you the petitions of your heart.* ***and light,*** namely, of grace and truth, ***will shine in your ways,*** that is, your works. Is 58:[100] *Your light will break forth as the morning, and your health will speedily arise.*

He sets forth the reason of all these things: **[29]** ***For he who has been humbled,*** supply: in penance, ***will be in glory.*** Lk 14:[101] *He who humbles himself will be exalted.* Prv 29:[102] *Glory will uphold the humble of spirit.* Jas 4:[103] *God resists the proud but gives grace to the humble.* ***and he who bows down his eyes,*** not raising them to evil things, of course, and modest with regard to shameful things. Sir 26:[104] *The fornication of a woman [will be known] by the haughtiness of her eyes.* Ps:[105] *Turn away my eyes, that they may not see vanity.* ***he will be saved.*** 1 Tm 2:[106] *Who wills that all humans be saved and come to the knowledge of His name.* **[30]** ***The innocent one will be saved,*** for no one except the sinner is killed. Ps:[107] *In the morning I killed all the sinners of the land.* Dn 13:[108] *You shall not kill the innocent and the just.* ***and he will be saved by the cleanness,*** that is, according to the cleanness, ***of his hands,*** that is, of his works. Is 3:[109] *Say to the just man that it is well, for he shall eat the fruit of his doings.* Ps:[110] *His right hand has wrought salvation for Him, and His arm is holy.* At the end of Proverbs:[111] *She has wrought it by the action of her hands.*

98. 2 Sm 23.5.
99. Ps 36.4.
100. Is 58.8.
101. Lk 14.11.
102. Prv 29.23.
103. Jas 4.6.
104. Sir 26.12.
105. Ps 118.37.
106. 1 Tm 2.4.
107. Ps 100.8.
108. Dn 13.53.
109. Is 3.10.
110. Ps 97.1.
111. Prv 31.13.

CHAPTER 23

T*HEN JOB responded and said.*

This response of Job is divided into two parts. In the first part, he shows that according to the scales of human justice he will be found just; in the second part, that the injustice of wicked men is not found in him. And this [second part] begins below, in this place:[1] *From the Almighty times are not hidden.*

In the first part, there are two divisions: first, Job seeks the scales of human justice; second, he points out in which things he is just, in this place:[2] *His footprints my foot has followed.*

The first of these divisions is further subdivided into two. In the first, Job seeks to be judged as a human; in the second, he denies that he should be judged as God or some other godlike being or as being superhuman, in that place:[3] *I wish that He would not [contend with me] with great strength.*

There are three paragraphs in the first of these subdivisions. In the first paragraph, Job responds to the one questioning him; in the second, to the line of questioning itself, asking that his own action might come to judgment; in the third, he makes clear how he will set forth his own case.

And that is: ***Then Job responded and said,*** namely, to the one questioning him and to the line of questioning. Jb 14:[4] *You will call me, and I will answer you.* Sir 5:[5] *If you have understanding, answer your neighbor.* **[2]** ***Now also,*** since I ought to have been laid bare on account of your consolations, of course, ***my speech is in***

1. Jb 24.1.
2. Jb 23.11.
3. Jb 23.6.
4. Jb 14.15.
5. Sir 5.14.

bitterness. Indeed, because of your insulting reproaches I have been dragged down into bitterness. Jer 2:[6] *How have you turned to bitterness, O strange vineyard?* ***and,*** that is, because ***the hand,*** that is, the blow, ***of my scourge is made heavier,*** namely, because of your insulting reproaches, ***than my groaning,*** that is, than my suffering, about which I groan. Jb 16:[7] *All of you are burdensome comforters.* Ps:[8] *They have added to the pain of my wounds.* Lam 1:[9] *They have heard that I groan, and there is no one to comfort me.*

Then Job adds that he desires a judge: **[3]** ***Who will grant to me,*** this is a sign of his desire. Gregory says:[10] When the elect see anything whatsoever done contrary to a vow, they return to the hidden things of God in order to consider it according to these things, because what seems to be inordinate on the outside is not disposed inordinately within.

But Job seeks to know Him through signs; and that is: ***that I might know*** and [be able] to find Him through the truth, and that is: ***and find Him.*** Song 3:[11] *When I had passed by them a little, I found Him whom my soul loves.* And because he desires a judge, he adds: ***and come all the way to His throne,*** that is, a distinguished and fair judgment? Jer 14:[12] *Remember the throne of your glory; do not break your covenant with us.* Is 16:[13] *His throne will be prepared in mercy, and He will sit upon it in truth in the tabernacle of David, judging and quickly rendering what is just.* Jb 16:[14] *For behold, my witness is in heaven, and my confidant is on high.*

And he adds how he sets forth his case: **[4]** ***I would set judgment,*** of my case, ***before Him,*** supply: so that He Himself by the presence of His light may thoroughly scrutinize it, of course. Ps:[15] *Judge me, O God, and discern my case.* Jb 10:[16] *Show me why*

6. Jer 2.21.
7. Jb 16.2.
8. Ps 68.27.
9. Lam 1.21.
10. Gregory, *Mor.* 16.27.34.
11. Song 3.4.
12. Jer 14.21.
13. Is 16.5.
14. Jb 16.20.
15. Ps 42.1.
16. Jb 10.2.

you judge me in this way. ***and I would fill my mouth with complaints,*** reproving myself, of course, concerning the things in which I may be found blameworthy. Prv 18:[17] *From the beginning of the debate, the just person is the accuser of himself.* For it is just for a human to reprove himself concerning the things of which God accuses him. Jer 31:[18] *After you showed me, I struck my thigh. I am confounded and ashamed because I have borne the reproach of my youth.*

[5] ***so that I might know the words that He,*** namely, God, the just judge, ***would respond to me.*** Something similar is in the Psalm:[19] *I spoke with my tongue: Enable me to know my end, Lord, and what the number of my days is, so that I might know what is lacking in me.* ***and might understand,*** namely, within, through reasoning, ***what He would say to me,*** condemning or justifying me, of course. Hab 2:[20] *I will stand on my watch, and I will fix my foot on the fortification; and I will watch to see what will be said to me, and what I might respond to the one who accuses me.*

Then, refuting the judgment that he is superhuman, he adds, and that is: [6] ***I wish that He would not contend with me with great strength,*** supply: of His justice, which is superhuman. Jb 9:[21] *If he wishes to contend with Him, he will not answer one word for a thousand.* Ps:[22] *Do not enter into judgment with your servant, because in your sight no living thing will be justified.* ***nor overwhelm,*** that is, crush, ***me with the weight of His greatness,*** that is, the immeasurable excellence of His justice. So, indeed, in human affairs nothing is just, because everything has been polluted either by negligence or weakness or ignorance or the desires of the body. Is 64:[23] *All of our righteousness is, as it were, the rag of a menstruating woman.*

[7] ***Let Him show impartiality toward me.*** Chrysostom says that impartiality is justice tempered with the sweetness of mercy.[24] That is, let Him judge me according to what is fair, given human

17. Prv 18.17.
18. Jer 31.19.
19. Ps 38.5.
20. Hab 2.1.
21. Jb 9.3.
22. Ps 142.2.
23. Is 64.6.
24. See Chrysostom, *In Ps.* 142.1 (PG 55:448) and *In Matth.* 18.1 (PG 57:265).

weakness. Jb 16:[25] *And if only a man were to be judged by God in the same way that the son of man is judged by his fellow man.*

and let my judgment come to victory, namely, such that I am not punished for evils deserved. Jb 13:[26] *If I will be judged, I know that I will be found just.* Moreover, Job states the reason why he resists the excellence of greatness, and it is supplied, but the sense is: supply: "I am not able to come to His clear judgment" because **[8]** ***If I go to the east,*** examining whatever arises (*oritur*) on earth, ***He does not appear,*** namely, manifest in nature, for by eternity He exceeds everything that arises. 1 Tm 6:[27] *He dwells in inaccessible light,* which surpasses every beginning of light, of course. ***if to the west,*** namely, examining everything that perishes (*occidit*) on earth, ***I will not understand Him,*** for the lack of an end exceeds everything that perishes. Eccl 1:[28] *The sun rises* (oritur) *and goes down* (occidit), *and it returns to its place.* And similarly all those things that are generated and corrupted according to the sun's orbit.

[9] ***If to the left* (sinistram),** supply: I go, examining how the power of life and of motion comes to an end, ***what will I do?*** namely, in order to comprehend Him, as if to say: "nothing." For in Him absolutely nothing comes to an end and nothing is improper (*sinistrum*), and He is similar to nothing that comes to an end. Ps 101:[29] *You are always the same, and your years will not come to an end.* And this is what follows: ***I will not grasp Him.*** Prv 3:[30] *Length of days is in her right hand, and in her left hand, riches and glory.* ***if I turn myself to the right,*** namely, examining everything that is perfect among creatures, ***I will not see Him.*** For by the immensity of His own perfection He exceeds every perfect thing among creatures, and therefore He will not be able to be contemplated completely from creatures unless standing a long way from them. Jb 36:[31] *All see Him, everyone looks from far away.* Is 30:[32] *The name of the Lord comes from afar.*

25. Jb 16.22.
26. Jb 13.18.
27. 1 Tm 6.16.
28. Eccl 1.5.
29. Ps 101.28.
30. Prv 3.16.
31. Jb 36.25.
32. Is 30.27.

[10] ***But He,*** whom I do not comprehend, of course, and I do not see clearly, ***knows*** by the knowledge of perfect comprehension and manifestly ***my way,*** that is, my life. Sir 23:[33] *The eyes of the Lord are far brighter than the sun, looking around and seeing all the ways of men.* Ps:[34] *He who has formed their hearts one by one, and who understands all their works.* ***and has tried me,*** that is, He has shown that I have been tried by tribulations, ***as gold that passes through the fire.*** Sir 2:[35] *For gold and silver are tried in the fire, but acceptable men in the furnace of humiliation.* Ps:[36] *Prove me, O God, and try me; burn my reins and my heart, and see if the way of iniquity is in me.*[37]

[11] *His footprints.*

Here Job points out in what he is found to be just, and in what he comes to victory in his trial, and in what he has been tried, as gold. And he says four things. First, that he has followed in the ways of justice; second, that he was bound to do this; the third is that God has not dealt with him unjustly; [and] fourth, that he has not lost hope because of misfortunes.

The first section is divided into two. For, first, he offers an analogy, and, second, he explains it. And that is: ***His footprints.*** Signs of the divine will, of which there are five—namely, precept, prohibition, permission, counsel, and operation—are here called "footprints." ***my foot,*** that is, my disposition (*affectus*), ***has followed,*** because he has done what God has taught, he has put away what God has forbidden, he has patiently suffered what God has permitted, he has carried out what God has advised, and he has taken what God has done as an example. Is 26:[38] *In the path of your judgments, we have patiently waited for you; your name and your remembrance are the desire of the soul.* Ru 2:[39] *She collected the remaining ears of grain, following the footprints of the reapers. She has been in the field from morning until now and has not gone home even when admonished.*

33. Sir 23.28.
34. Ps 32.15.
35. Sir 2.5.
36. Ps 25.2.
37. This final phrase, *et vide si via iniquitatis in me est,* is not part of Ps 25.2, but rather Ps 138.24. Doubtless working from memory, Albert here conflates the two passages, which have a common theme.
38. Is 26.8.
39. Ru 2.7.

I have kept His way, that is, His law. Prv 6:[40] *The commandment is a lamp, and the law a light, and the reproof of discipline is along the way of life.* ***and I have not turned aside from it.*** Nm 20:[41] *We march along on the royal way, turning aside neither to the right nor to the left.*

Then he sets forth an analogy, adding: **[12]** ***I have not departed from the commandments of His lips,*** that is, of Scripture or of His revelation. Ps:[42] *I have run the way of your commandments, seeing that you have enlarged my heart.* ***and I have hidden the words of His mouth,*** which words, of course, He Himself has proclaimed through the saints, that is, I have pondered them secretly so that they might be the form of life for me. ***in my bosom,*** that is, in the hidden depth of my heart. Ps:[43] *That I should do your will: O my God, I have desired it, and your law at the center of my heart.*

Moreover, Job adds that he was bound to do this: **[13]** ***For He alone is,*** that is, He possesses the name of true essence (*verae essentiae*), which the whole world ought to seek. Dt 32:[44] *See that I alone am, and there is no God besides me.* Ex 3:[45] *HE WHO IS sent me to you.* ***and no one can divert His intentions,*** that is, His purposes, supply: such that they might not be done. Gregory says:[46] God does not change His purpose. Is 46: *My purpose shall stand, and my entire will shall be done.* ***and whatever His soul,*** that is, the innermost depths of His will, ***has willed,*** by the will of His good pleasure, of course, ***this He has done.*** Est 13:[47] *There is no one who can resist your will.* Rom 9:[48] *Who resists His will?* Ps:[49] *Everything whatsoever He has willed, He has done, in heaven and on earth and in the sea and in all the deeps.*

Then he adds that God has not committed an injustice by striking him, because there is no injustice in His presence. And that is: **[14]** ***When He has fulfilled His will,*** namely, which He is

40. Prv 6.23.
41. Nm 20.17.
42. Ps 118.32.
43. Ps 39.9.
44. Dt 32.39.
45. Ex 3.14.
46. Gregory, *Mor.* 16.37.46.
47. Est 13.9.
48. Rom 9.19.
49. Ps 134.6.

able to fulfill in every one of His own creatures, ***in me.*** Rom 9:[50] *Does not the potter have power over the clay?* 1 Sm 3:[51] *It is the Lord; let Him do what He wills.* Jer 18:[52] *As clay in the hand of the potter, so are you in my hand, O house of Israel, says the Lord.* ***many other similar things,*** namely, with which He may strike me and do His will with regard to His work, ***are ready,*** that is, prepared, ***for Him.*** Jb 6:[53] *He may untie His hand and cut me down. And let this be a consolation to me, that He who afflicts me with pain would not spare me, and I would not contradict the words of the Holy One.*

[15] ***And therefore,*** supply: because He is so excellent, and there is no inequity in Him, ***I am troubled by His presence,*** that is, by the presence of His blows. Ps:[54] *I was troubled, and I did not speak.* ***and when,*** that is, because, ***I consider Him,*** that is, His excellence and justice, ***I am disturbed by fear,*** fearing, of course, that He might punish something in me that I do not see. Is 21:[55] *I shuddered when I heard it; I was disturbed when I saw it. My heart failed.*

But if anyone should ask by whom that fear is [caused], Job responds, adding: [16] ***God has softened my heart,*** namely, by fear and by love. For something that easily gives way to one touching it and does not resist is soft. 2 Sm 23:[56] *He was like the softest little woodworm.* Indeed, a woodworm is so soft that it does not even perceive touch because it resists nothing.

And this is what follows: ***and the Almighty,*** whom nothing resists, of course, ***has confounded me,*** supply: for the purpose of penance. 2 Cor 7:[57] *For you were confounded according to God, that you might suffer loss in nothing because of us.* [17] ***For I have not perished,*** supply: through despair, ***on account of the darkness,*** namely, of tribulations, ***hanging over me.*** Jb 13:[58] *Even if He should kill me, I will hope in Him.* ***and the gloom,*** which may hide the light of rea-

50. Rom 9.21.
51. 1 Sm 3.18.
52. Jer 18.6.
53. Jb 6.9–10.
54. Ps 76.5.
55. Is 21.3–4.
56. 2 Sm 23.8.
57. 2 Cor 7.9.
58. Jb 13.15.

son, ***has not covered my face,*** namely, my mind and reason. Mi 7:[59] *When I sit in darkness, the Lord is my light.* And after a few words:[60] *He will bring me forth into the light. I will see His justice.*

59. Mi 7.8.
60. Mi 7.9.

CHAPTER 24

**ROM THE *Almighty*.**

In this chapter Job makes clear that the injustice of evil men is not found in him, and it is divided into two parts. In the first of these, he shows that he has not done evil things; in the second, that he has detested these things and cursed those who perform such evil deeds, in that place:[1] *Cursed is his portion.* In the first part there are two things: the confession of the truth; and the acquittal of iniquity, in that place:[2] *Some have removed landmarks.* And that is: ***From the Almighty,*** whose providence extends even to particular things, ***times are not hidden,*** that is, particular things that are done in time. At the end of Job:[3] *I know that you can do all things, and no thought is hidden from you.* Ps:[4] *He who has formed their hearts one by one, who understands all their works.* And so all of our things are known to God. Heb 4:[5] *All things are naked and manifest to His eyes, to whom we must give an account.*

Although all of our things are known to God, nevertheless His things are not known to us. And this is what Job adds: ***but those who know Him,*** immeasurable and excelling all created things, of course, ***do not know His days,*** that is, illuminations of wisdom whereby and how He knows things, which illuminations the human person cannot comprehend. Ps:[6] *Your knowledge has become astonishing to me; it has grown very high, and I cannot reach*

1. Jb 24.18.
2. Jb 24.2.
3. Jb 42.2.
4. Ps 32.15.
5. Heb 4.13.
6. Ps 138.6.

up to it. Wis 7:[7] *This [wisdom] is more beautiful than the sun, and above the entire order of the stars; compared to the light, it is found before it.* Jb 36:[8] *Remember that you do not know His work, about which men have sung.*

Then Job adds [a treatment] of the acquittal of sin, and it has two parts. First, he shows how evil is perpetrated in works by evil men; second, how it is opposed to the light of understanding, in that place:[9] *They have been rebellious to the light.* The first part is subdivided into two: first, indeed, he describes the sin of those who seize things that belong to someone else; second, the sin of those who do evil without restraint, in that place:[10] *Others, like wild asses.* In the first subdivision, he first describes [the sin of usurpation] in general; second, he describes it in particular in a twofold way.

And that is: [2] ***Some have removed landmarks,*** namely, by usurping the property of others. Hos 5:[11] *The princes of Judah have become as those who take up landmarks. I will pour out my wrath upon them like water.* Is 5:[12] *Woe to you who join house to house and connect field to field, all the way to the end of the territory.*

Then Job explains it [namely, the sin of usurpation] in particular: first, with regard to ordinary people; second, with regard to miserable people. And that is: ***they have plundered flocks.*** Ezek 34:[13] *My flock has been plundered because there was no shepherd.* Job also says "plundered" because someone carried off part [of the flock] according to his own desire. Ezek 34:[14] *You consumed the milk, and you clothed yourself with the wool, and you slaughtered what was fat.* ***and have fed them,*** that is, they have pastured them. Mi 3:[15] *Do you violently remove their skin from them, and their flesh from their bones?*

And he adds concerning miserable people, from damage to

7. Wis 7.29.
8. Jb 36.24.
9. Jb 24.13.
10. Jb 24.5.
11. Hos 5.10.
12. Is 5.8.
13. Ezek 34.5. Cf. Bar 4.26.
14. Ezek 34.3.
15. Mi 3.2.

whose property no compassion drew them away: [3] ***They have driven off the ass of orphans.*** The "ass," a beast of burden that is also unclean, signifies every animal created for the purpose of aiding in work; and "orphans" signifies miserable people who do not have a patron and protector. Is 33:[16] *Woe to you who prey on others! Will you yourself not also be preyed upon?*

and have taken the cow of the widow, who does not have a husband as a protector; and "cow" signifies every animal created for labor and for food, ***for a pledge;*** and those who impose oppressive taxes are understood by "for a pledge." Dt 24:[17] *When you demand of your neighbor something that he owes you, you shall not go into his house to take it away as a pledge; rather, you shall stand outside, and he will bring what he has out to you. But if he is poor, you shall not keep the pledge overnight.* For when her cow has been taken away and eaten and used as an aid in labor, the widow is left destitute.

[4] ***They have subverted the way of the poor.*** Augustine says:[18] The poor man is not self-sufficient. And the "way" is said to be "subverted" when, because the necessities have been taken away, one cannot find the way of life. Sir 34:[19] *The bread of the needy is the life of the poor; whoever deprives them of it is a murderer.* ***and have oppressed equally,*** that is, all ***the meek of the earth.*** Augustine says:[20] A person who neither provokes another by his own injustices nor is provoked by another's [injustices toward him] is meek. And on account of religion and the love of virtue, these people have refused to avenge themselves. Ps:[21] *They have humiliated your people, O Lord, and they have harassed your inheritance. They have destroyed the widow and the foreigner, and they have killed the orphans.*

And, reproaching the sin of license to do evil, namely, that they commit sin without restraint, Job adds: [5] ***Others, like wild asses,*** untamed asses, of course, ***in the desert,*** that is to say, on the plain of license without restraint, namely, [the restraint] of reason, of the law, and of virtue, ***go forth to their work,*** namely,

16. Is 33.1.
17. Dt 24.10–12.
18. See Augustine, *Civ.* 7.12 (PL 41:204).
19. Sir 34.25.
20. See Augustine, *En. Ps.* 33.5 (PL 36:310).
21. Ps 93.5–6.

of violence and robbery. Jb 11:[22] *A vain man is roused toward pride, and he thinks that he was born free as the colt of a wild ass is.* Jer 2:[23] *A wild ass, accustomed to being alone in the wilderness, in the desire of its soul drew in the wind of the love of itself. None will turn it away.* Concerning their works, Is 59 says:[24] *Their works are useless works, and the work of iniquity is in their hands.*

Then he adds an explanation of this, first in general, second in six particular cases, and that is: ***being vigilant for prey,*** that is, vigilantly exploiting prey, ***they prepare,*** supply: from the spoils, ***bread,*** that is, refreshment, ***for their children,*** who imitate them in wickedness. Prv 1:[25] *Let us lie in wait for blood, let us hide traps for the innocent.* And after a few words:[26] *We will obtain every precious substance; we will fill our houses with spoils.*

And he adds in particular first concerning what is edible: **[6]** ***They reap the field that is not their own,*** that is, the fruit of the field that is not their own. 1 Sm 23:[27] *The Philistines are attacking Keilah, and they are robbing the threshing floors.*

Second, he adds concerning what is potable: ***and harvest grapes from the vineyard of the one whom they have oppressed by violence,*** that is to say, with violence they have taken the vineyard away from him. 1 Kgs 21[28] provides the example of the vineyard of Naboth, whom Jezebel caused to be killed and of whose vineyard she took possession.

Third, he adds concerning clothing: [7] ***They send men away naked,*** that is, stripped naked; and he adds how this happened: **taking away**, that is, stealing, ***the garments.*** Lk 10:[29] *They stripped him of his clothes, and, having wounded him, they went away, leaving him half dead.* Song 5:[30] *The guards of the city walls took away my cloak.* Mi 2:[31] *You have taken away the cloak on top of the tunic.* And

22. Jb 11.12.
23. Jer 2.24.
24. Is 59.6.
25. Prv 1.11.
26. Prv 1.13.
27. 1 Sm 23.1.
28. 1 Kgs 21.11–16.
29. Lk 10.30.
30. Song 5.7.
31. Mi 2.8.

he expands on this, adding: ***of those who have no covering in the cold,*** namely, by which they may protect themselves. Gn 31:[32] *Day and night I was burned with heat and with frost.* [8] ***whom the showers of the mountains,*** which are cold and snowy, ***make wet.*** 1 Cor 4:[33] *We hunger and thirst, and we are naked.* ***and having no covering,*** namely, of clothing, ***they embrace the stones,*** that is, because of the shame of nakedness they hide themselves under the stones. Heb 11:[34] *Wandering in deserts, among mountains and in dens, and in caves of the earth.*

Fourth, concerning miserable people who do not have a protector, he adds: [9] ***They have used force,*** that is, they have inflicted violence, ***to plunder orphans,*** not being dissuaded by compassion, ***and they have robbed the poor among the common people,*** that is, the ordinary people, so they cannot plead ignorance as an excuse. Is 10:[35] *To oppress the poor in judgment and to do violence to the humble among my people: that widows might be their prey, and that they might rob orphans.*

Fifth, concerning the poorest people, he adds: [10] ***From the naked,*** that is, the bare, ***and,*** that is, ***those who go without clothing*** or are dressed in rags, for clothing is a decent garment, ***and from the hungry,*** those not having sufficient food, of course, ***they have taken,*** that is, they have stolen, ***the ears of grain,*** which they collected by following behind the reapers. Ru 2:[36] *I will go into the field and collect the ears of grain that have escaped the hands of the reapers, wherever I will have found grace with heads of households who are merciful to me.* 1 Chr 22:[37] *Behold, in my poverty I have prepared the expenditures of the house of the Lord.* For the Lord loves the very poor.

Then he expands further on this: [11] ***They have taken their noonday nap among the stores of those,*** that is, they have prepared lunches at midday. For it is typical to eat lunch at midday, when many things are prepared for eating and when, of course, the sun, ascending to its highest point, calls forth the nutrients of

32. Gn 31.40.
33. 1 Cor 4.11.
34. Heb 11.38.
35. Is 10.2.
36. Ru 2.2.
37. 1 Chr 22.14.

an earlier meal from the place of digestion to the limbs. Hence in Gn 43,[38] when Joseph was going to eat with his brothers, it is said that he came in to eat at midday. Song 1:[39] *Show me, you whom my soul loves, where you feed, where you lie down at midday.* An example of this is observed among tyrants, who, in the homes of the poor, force them to prepare lunch for them and satisfy themselves from the stores of the poor. Expanding on their poverty, Job adds: ***who, after treading the wine presses, are thirsty,*** on account of the fact that the wine produced from the wine press is not sufficient to quench their thirst. Is 16:[40] *The voice of those who tread is rushing in on the produce of your vineyard and on your harvest.*

Sixth, he adds that they have harassed not only the poor, but also their fellow city-dwellers (*civiles*). For Aristotle says that the country person (*rusticus*) is neither good nor evil on account of the fact that he is uncivilized, that is, not disposed to virtue.[41] And such are the poor people about whom Job has spoken, but they are not limited to this.

[12] ***From the cities they have made men groan,*** that is to say, eager for places of refinement or cities and for civil power, they have confounded and robbed them. Concerning this city it is said in a Psalm:[42] *Glorious things are said of you, O city of God.* Jeremiah deplores this in Lam 1:[43] *All her gates*[44] *are destroyed, her priests sigh, her virgins are squalid, and she is oppressed with bitterness.* ***and the souls of the wounded,*** namely, of the poor and the city-dwellers, ***will cry out,***[45] demanding vengeance. Rv 6:[46] *I saw under the altar the souls of those who were slain on account of the word of God and on account of the testimony that they held. And they cried out with a loud voice, saying: How long, O Lord, holy and true, will you not avenge our*

38. Gn 43.25–26.
39. Song 1.6.
40. Is 16.9.
41. See Aristotle, *Pol.* 2.3.3.
42. Ps 86.3.
43. Lam 1.4.
44. Here I read *portae* with MSS F and M, rather than the *viae* of Weiss's edition.
45. The Vulgate text, as it has come down to us, has the perfect-tense *clamavit* here, rather than Albert's future-tense *clamabunt.*
46. Rv 6.9–10.

blood and judge those who dwell on the earth? ***and God does not permit it to go unpunished.*** Dt 32:[47] *I will repay my enemies with vengeance.* Dt 18:[48] *In time I will come forth as the avenger.* Ps:[49] *The Lord is the God of vengeance.*

Then he adds how they were rebellious against the light of all true understanding, and he speaks of two things, namely: [their] hatred of the light or daylight, and [their] love of darkness. And that is: [13] ***They have been rebellious against the light,*** namely, to the understanding of the truth. Jn 3:[50] *The light has come into the world, and humans have loved darkness more than the light.* ***and they have not known*** by giving approval to ***its ways,*** that is, of the light, the ways of which lead to works of justice, of course. Prv 4:[51] *The path of the just is as a light shining brightly and growing into perfect day.* ***neither have they returned,*** supply: through penance, ***by its,*** that is, the light's, ***paths.*** Jn 12:[52] *While you have the light, believe in the light, that you may be children of the light.*

And he adds how they have loved the works of darkness, namely, murder, adultery, and theft. And that is: [14] ***First thing in the morning,*** being watchful for prey, of course, ***the murderer,*** thirsty for blood, ***arises,*** that is, he grows in the power of perception and in strength, and ***he kills the needy,*** he who wanders around in front of doorways is "needy," ***and the poor man,*** who is not self-sufficient. Gn 49:[53] *In the morning he will devour the prey, and in the evening he will divide the spoils.* Ps:[54] *They have not known nor understood: they walk in darkness.* ***but during the night he,*** namely, who was a grave robber in the daylight, ***will be as a thief*** **(fur)**, in the dark (*in furvo*), that is, carrying away in darkness. Jn 10:[55] *A thief does not come except to steal and to kill and to destroy.*

And, concerning adultery, he adds: [15] ***The eye of the adulterer,*** uniting itself to another man's wife, ***watches for darkness,***

47. Dt 32.41.
48. Dt 18.19.
49. Ps 93.1.
50. Jn 3.19.
51. Prv 4.18.
52. Jn 12.36.
53. Gn 49.27.
54. Ps 81.5.
55. Jn 10.10.

in which, of course, he may carry out his wicked will. Ps:[56] *Let their way become dark and slippery.* ***saying: No eye will see me;*** indeed, such a sin loves darkness. Prv 7:[57] *At dusk, when the day is drawing toward evening, in the darkness and obscurity of the night, a woman dressed as a prostitute runs to meet him, prepared to deceive souls.* ***and he will conceal his face.*** Gregory says: The adulterer, lest he be recognized.[58] Sir 23:[59] *The man who violates his own bed, despising his own soul, and saying: Who sees me? Darkness envelops me, and the walls completely cover me, and no one sees me.*

And concerning both, namely, adulterers and thieves, he adds: **[16]** ***They break into houses in the dark,*** in order secretly to advance upon the head of the household, of course. 2 Tm 3:[60] *These are the sort who invade houses and lead weak little women laden with sins away captive.* ***just as they,*** namely, the adulterer and the adulteress, ***had plotted for themselves during the day.*** Dn 13:[61] Indeed, they had plotted for themselves that they would come at the same time. ***and they have not known the light.*** Jer 13:[62] *Give glory to the Lord your God before it becomes dark and your feet stumble on the foggy mountains.*

[17] ***If dawn suddenly appears,*** that is, some degree of light illuminating their wicked works, ***they consider it,*** supply: those causing pain in this way, ***the shadow,*** that is, the image, ***of death.*** Gregory says: Because those who act perversely fear being punished, they are unwilling to be corrected.[63] Jn 3:[64] *He who does evil hates the light, and he does not come to the light, in order that his works may not be reproved.* And that is: ***and thus they walk in darkness,*** that is, in dark works, ***as if in the light,*** that is, they are advancing in

56. Ps 34.6.

57. Prv 7.9–10.

58. Gregory, *Mor.* 16.61.75.

59. Sir 23.25–26.

60. 2 Tm 3.6.

61. See Dn 13.12–14. Although Weiss sets the following words in quotation marks, they are not taken verbatim from Dn 13. Rather, this appears to be Albert's brief summary describing the two elders who planned, according to Dn 13.12–14, to return to Joakim's orchard at a certain time in order to watch his beautiful wife, Susannah, while she was alone there.

62. Jer 13.16.

63. Gregory, *Mor.* 16.63.77.

64. Jn 3.20.

punishments. 2 Tm 3:[65] *Evil people proceed to more wicked things.* Eph 5:[66] *Refuse to have fellowship with the unfruitful works of darkness, but rather reprove them. For the things that are done by them in secret, it is shameful even to speak of.*

And concerning the mildness of this sin, he adds: **[18] *He is slight,*** namely, the adulterer and the fornicator, ***on the surface of the water,*** which is pushed down by any wind whatsoever. Gregory says: Because, whatever wind of temptation strikes this [sinner], it pushes him down without the slowness of hesitation.[67] Hence about the adulterer Reuben it is said in Gn 49:[68] *You have been poured out like water, you shall not increase; because you have climbed into your father's bed and have defiled his couch.* Eliphaz has imposed all these things on Job, and therefore here Job has justified himself concerning all these things; and he shows that he detests such things by cursing them.

Cursed.

This part is divided into two. In the first, Job shows that such [wicked] people are cursed and that he detests them. In the second, he shows that, even if he were such a person, it could not be proven by those who upbraid one another, in that place:[69] *And if it is not so.* In the first part, he sets forth a curse through punishments—first, of loss; second, of sense perception; and third, he repeats the offense—so that the punishment might be more just.

And that is: ***Cursed is his portion on earth,*** that is, which he possesses on earth. For this [portion] is cursed inasmuch as it is the cause of someone's being cursed. Gn 3:[70] *Cursed is the earth in your work.* And Gn 4:[71] *Cursed shall you be upon the earth.* For he deserved the curse in earthly riches, delights, and honors. Indeed, in these things he deserved the curse. And according to this, it is said to all such people in Mt 25:[72] *Go, accursed ones!*

65. 2 Tm 3.13.
66. Eph 5.11–12.
67. Gregory, *Mor.* 16.65.79.
68. Gn 49.4.
69. Jb 24.25.
70. Gn 3.17.
71. Gn 4.11.
72. Mt 25.41.

Wis 12:[73] *It was a cursed seed from the beginning.* For a curse is the assignment of the evil of punishment; indeed, punishment is evil, as Augustine says, inasmuch as it is contrary to the nature of the good.[74] And he specifies property: ***may he not walk through the way of the vineyards.*** Metaphorically "the way of the vineyards" is [the way] of joys and delights. For by its shoots the vine produces pleasantness and relief even for servants;[75] by its fruit, moreover, it produces joy and gives the human a healthy hope. Jgs 9:[76] *The vine said: I cannot abandon my wine, which delights God and humans.* Is 16:[77] *In the vineyards there shall be no rejoicing.*

Then he adds the punishment of sense perception and of damnation: **[19]** ***To excessive heat,*** namely, of burning hell on account of the boiling of desire. Is 30:[78] *The breath of the Lord, like the burning of brimstone, sets it on fire.* ***may he cross over,*** namely, by a succession of punishments, ***from the waters of snow,*** whereby he is poured out, of course, by the lethal cold, on account of the fact that through desire for earthly things the little flame of charity in him became cold. Mt 24:[79] *And because iniquity has abounded, the charity of many shall grow cold.* Concerning this cold, it is said of the good wife at the end of Proverbs:[80] *She shall not fear for her house in the cold of the snow, for all the members of her household are clothed with double garments,* that is, with love of God and of neighbor. And it[81] is miserable, because in this life there is no passing over from the very cold into the very hot except through a mean (*medium*), which is temperate. In hell, however, one passes over from the excess (*excellentia*) of lethal cold to the boiling of burning fire, which will never be in a mean. And this is so because, in the case of sins, they [that is, sinners] have passed over from the cold of cupidity to the boiling of desire without ever coming

73. Wis 12.11.
74. See Augustine, *En. Ps.* 40.9 (PL 36:460).
75. Alb., *De veget.* 6.35.236.
76. Jgs 9.13.
77. Is 16.10.
78. Is 30.33.
79. Mt 24.12.
80. Prv 31.21.
81. Namely, the crossing over from the waters of snow to the excessive heat described here.

into contact with the mean (*medium*) of virtue. For Aristotle says that vice is in excess (*excellentia*), but virtue is in the mean (*medio*).[82] On account of these two punishments,[83] it is said in Mt 25 and Mt 8:[84] *There will be weeping and gnashing of teeth*—weeping because of the fire, gnashing because of the frost. ***and his sin all the way to hell,*** supply: may he cross over through impenitence. Jn 8:[85] *You shall die in your sins.*

And because suffrages can be made for him, which nevertheless are of no benefit for the damned, he adds: **[20]** ***May mercy,*** of the suffrages, of course, ***forget him.*** Jas 2:[86] *Judgment without mercy will come about for him who has not shown mercy.* Wis 6:[87] *To the little one mercy is granted; but the mighty will suffer torments mightily.* ***may worms,*** namely, of a gnawing conscience, ***be his sweetness,*** through antiphrasis, that is, bitterness. At the end of Isaiah:[88] *Their worm will not die, and their fire will not be extinguished.* Sir 10:[89] *When a man dies, he will inherit serpents, and beasts, and worms.* Bernard says: I shudder at the gnawing worm, the burning fire, and the weight of chains, of the hissing, burning [fires] that nevertheless do not consume.[90] ***may he not be remembered,*** namely, for the good, neither by God nor by angels nor by humans. At the end of Isaiah:[91] *Prior things will not be remembered, nor will they come upon the heart.* ***but be broken to pieces,*** that is, may he be worn out by various punishments, ***as an unfruitful tree,*** which has borne nothing but poisonous fruit. Lk 3:[92] *The ax is laid to the root of the tree. Therefore, every tree that does not bear good fruit will be cut down and thrown into the fire.* Lk 13:[93] *Look, for three years I have sought fruit on this fig tree, and I have found none. Cut it down, then. Why does it still occupy the ground?*

And so that the punishment might be more just, he repeats

82. See Aristotle (attrib.), *Magna moralia* 1.22.1.
83. Namely, of sense perception and of damnation.
84. Mt 25.30 and Mt 8.12.
85. Jn 8.24.
86. Jas 2.13.
87. Wis 6.7.
88. Is 66.24.
89. Sir 10.13.
90. See Bernard of Clairvaux, *De consideratione* 5.12.25.
91. Is 65.17.
92. Lk 3.9.
93. Lk 13.7.

the offense of adultery first, then of oppression. And that is: **[21]** ***For he has terrified,*** supply: for his desires, ***the barren one,*** that is, the adulteress, in whom nothing except barren desire is sought, ***who does not give birth,*** supply: does not produce an heir from a proper marriage. Sir 23:[94] *The woman who leaves her husband and brings in an heir by another marriage sins.* Hence, if she gives birth, she does not give birth by her own husband. ***and he has done no good to the widow.*** Here "the widow" is said with a wide signification of a proper spouse separated from the marriage bed, to whom he who is united to an adulteress "has done no good." Mal 2:[95] *The Lord has been a witness between you and the wife of your youth, whom you have despised; but she was your partner, and the wife of your covenant.*

Then, concerning the sin of oppression, he adds: **[22]** ***He has dragged down the strong,*** namely, the saints, who are truly strong. Gn 32:[96] *If you have been strong against God, how much more will you prevail against humans?* Is 40:[97] *Those who hope in the Lord will renew their strength.* **in his might,** that is, in the vigor of worldly power. Jas 2:[98] *Do the rich not oppress you with their power, and do they not drag you before the judgment seats?* ***and,*** supply: therefore, ***when he stands up,*** with the status of worldly power, of course, ***he will not trust in his life,*** that is, he will not be safe. Wis 17:[99] *Whenever wickedness is fearful, it is attributed to the condemnation of the ungodly.* Jb 15:[100] *The sound of terror is always in his ears; and when there is peace, he always suspects treachery.*

(On the dream of Scipio, Macrobius says:[101] Dionysius, the harshest occupant of the court of Sicily, wished to show a certain household servant of his, who thought that the only happy life was the life of the tyrant, how miserable he always was on

94. Sir 23.32.
95. Mal 2.14.
96. Gn 32.28.
97. Is 40.31.
98. Jas 2.6.
99. Wis 17.10.
100. Jb 15.21.
101. Macrobius, *CSS* 1.10.16. Weiss added this paragraph, which appears in parentheses both in his Latin edition and in this translation, from MSS F and M.

account of constant anxiety and how full of dangers his life was. So Dionysius ordered an unsheathed sword hanging by its handle from a thin thread, with the sword's point dropping low, to threaten the head of that servant between courses [of a banquet]. And when that servant also might have been separated from the wealth of Sicily and tyrannical power by the present danger, Dionysius said, "Such is the life that you thought happy; in this way we always see death threatening us. Consider when someone who never ceases to fear will be able to be happy.")

But because God accepts everyone who repents, Job shows that this person[102] was not penitent, and that is: **[23]** ***God has given him a place for penance,*** supply: and a time, just as He provided before the flood at the beginning of the world. Gn 6:[103] *And his days shall be a hundred and twenty years.* Mt 4:[104] *Do penance, for the kingdom of heaven is at hand.* ***and he squanders it in pride,*** by which, of course, he disdains to make himself subject to God and to His precepts through the humility of penance. Is 16:[105] *We have heard of the pride of Moab; he is exceedingly proud.* Jb 21:[106] *Who is the Almighty, that we should serve Him?* ***but His eyes,*** that is, the complete gaze of the mind and solicitude, ***are upon his ways,*** namely, of the wicked one as he prospers. Jer 4:[107] *They are wise in doing evil, but they do not know how to act rightly.*

But he adds how unstable fortune, which he examines, is: **[24]** ***They have been lifted up for a short time,*** by worldly pride, of course, ***but they will not stand,*** supply: forever. 1 Mc 2:[108] *He is extolled today, but tomorrow will not be found.* Sir 10:[109] *All power is short-lived.* ***and,*** that is, because, ***they will be brought down,*** that is, so that the worthless will be cast down into the earth. Ps:[110] *You will cast them down into the fire; in miseries they will not stand.* ***as all,*** supply: worldly ***things.*** 1 Cor 7:[111] *The form of this world is passing away.* Gregory

102. That is, the oppressor of v. 22.
103. Gn 6.3.
104. Mt 4.17.
105. Is 16.6.
106. Jb 21.15.
107. Jer 4.22.
108. 1 Mc 2.63.
109. Sir 10.11.
110. Ps 139.11.
111. 1 Cor 7.31.

says: Whoever is supported by citizens of the world, it is unavoidable that he should fall when the citizens of the world fall.[112] ***and they will be taken away*** from the world and life. Ps:[113] *You will take away their spirit, and they will pass away.* ***and as the tops of the ears of grain,*** with seeds that have been shaken out, of course, ***they will be broken to pieces,*** namely, by the tribulations of punishments. Lk 3:[114] *Whose winnowing fan is in His hand, and He will purge His threshing floor and gather the wheat into His barn; but the chaff He will burn with unquenchable fire.*

Then Job apostrophizes,[115] and he turns toward his fellow-disputants, assigning to them the blame that they imposed on him: **[25]** ***And if it is not so,*** supply: just as I have said, ***who,*** namely, among you, who are at fault just like [the fault] you imposed on me, ***can prove that I have lied,*** and this is proper in rhetorical disputations, which take place in the presence of a judge, where the opponent is refuted on the grounds that he is similarly at fault.[116] Mt 7:[117] *You hypocrite, first cast the beam out of your own eye, and then you will see to remove the speck from your brother's eye.* Jn 8:[118] *Which of you will convict me of sin?* ***and place,*** namely, by finding fault, ***before God,*** the just judge, ***my words?*** since, of course, you share the blame that you impose on me. Jn 8:[119] *He who is without sin, let him cast a stone at her first.*

112. See Gregory, *Mor.* 17.9.11.

113. Ps 103.29.

114. Lk 3.17.

115. That is, he speaks by or in apostrophe, according to which a speaker turns away from his hearers and addresses some other person or thing rhetorically.

116. Albert understands the disputation between Job and his friends as a "rhetorical disputation" (*disputatio rhetorica*), as suggested also by his comments on Jb 10.1 and 11.3 (see *On Job,* vol. 1, 205 and 219). On the distinction between a "rhetorical disputation" and a "doctrinal disputation" (*disputatio doctrinalis*) or "demonstrative disputation" (*disputatio demonstrativa*), see Ruth Meyer, "A Passionate Dispute over Divine Providence: Albert the Great's Commentary on the Book of Job," in *A Companion to Job in the Middle Ages,* ed. Franklin T. Harkins and Aaron Canty (Leiden: Brill, 2016), 201–24, esp. 202–5.

117. Mt 7.5.

118. Jn 8.46.

119. Jn 8.7.

CHAPTER 25

BUT RESPONDING, ***Bildad the Shuhite said.***

This is the most extreme attack by which the opinion of blessed Job is assailed. Hence, in this response Bildad becomes soft and falters in his own opinion, and he reverts to agreeing with blessed Job. In this chapter, then, three things are asserted, namely: the excellence of those about whom he speaks, by means of which [excellence] he wishes to be excused if he has not brought forth evident truth; second, that through illumination effected from above, he reverted to agreement with blessed Job, in that place:[1] *Is there any numbering;* third, he makes clear the human weakness for grasping sublime realities, so that through this he might be justified again if he has said something less well, in that place:[2] *Can a human be justified?*

And that is: ***But responding, Bildad,*** who, on account of gray-haired wisdom, which he possessed, is understood as "old age alone," ***said,*** and he did not respond to the person, but only to his speech because even now he begins to agree with the opinion of blessed Job. Mt 5:[3] *Be in agreement with your adversary while you are with him on the journey.* **[2]** ***Power and terror are with Him,*** that is, terrible power, in such a way that one of the nouns becomes an adjective of the other, just as in that place: "arms and the man I sing,"[4] that is, the armed man. Ex 15:[5] *Terrible and praiseworthy and doing wonders.* And concerning [God's] power, he understands it to be as much in [His] wisdom as in [His] works, and even in the sublimity of nature. Ex 20:[6] *Being com-*

1. Jb 25.3.
2. Jb 25.4.
3. Mt 5.25.
4. Virgil, *Aen.* 1.1.
5. Ex 15.11.
6. Ex 20.18.

pletely terrified and struck with fear, they stood far off. ***who,*** supply: although exalted and immeasurable, nevertheless ***makes peace in His high places,*** that is, so that those examining His high realities—such as [His] wisdom, providence, governance, and things of this sort—may be in agreement. Ezek 1:[7] *I heard the sound of their wings like the sound of mighty waters, as it were the voice of God on high.* Dionysius says that the wings signify those soaring to divine contemplation, who are raised on high; and as long as individual animals fly, they fly in their own diverse ways.[8] Since, however, the voice came from above the firmament, as it is said in that very place, at the same time they stood and lowered their wings.[9] And, indeed, the voice signifies illumination descending from above, standing signifies agreement, and the lowering of their wings signifies the weakness of our intellect in relation to divine realities.

Moreover, he adds the manner of this agreement: **[3]** ***Is there any numbering of His soldiers?*** Those who serve by engaging in training exercises for the investigation of divine wisdom, of whom indeed there is no number from our perspective, are called "soldiers" of God. Dn 7:[10] *Thousands of thousands served Him, and ten thousand times a hundred thousand stood before Him.*

And since all serve, all are illuminated and exalted in the light, of course, and this is what follows: ***and on whom does His light not arise?*** Illumination according to truth is called "light." Ps:[11] *In your light we will see light.* 1 Cor 4:[12] *God, who commanded the light to shine out of darkness, has shined in our hearts.* And he says "arise" because those who inquire into God are exalted in the light continuously. Ps:[13] *Come near to Him and be illuminated.* And in that light they are turned back to agreement with the truth. Prv 4:[14] *The path of the just* [*is*] *as a light shining brightly*

7. Ezek 1.24.

8. See Dionysius, *CH* 15.3.

9. Ezek 1.25.

10. Dn 7.10.

11. Ps 35.10.

12. The text that follows is not 1 Cor 4.6, as the edition of Weiss indicates, but rather 2 Cor 4.6.

13. Ps 33.6.

14. Prv 4.18.

and growing into perfect day. Ps:[15] *They will walk in the light of your face, and in your name they will rejoice all the day,* that is, in perfect light, *and in your justice they will be exalted.* In such a way the face of Moses was illuminated from his conversation with the Lord, according to Ex 34;[16] and 2 Cor 3:[17] *We all, beholding the glory of God with unveiled faces, are being transformed into the same image from glory into glory.*

Then he adds how, if he said something having less [light] before he advanced in the light of God, it must be attributed to human weakness: **[4]** ***Can a human* (homo),** namely, one made from the soil (*ab humo*), ***be justified,*** that is, [can his] intellect and affect be regulated (*rectificari*), ***compared to God?*** that is, compared to divine realities. Wis 9:[18] *The thoughts of mortals are timid, and our foresight is uncertain.* And a little beyond this:[19] *We consider the things on earth with difficulty, and with effort do we find the things that are in our sight. But who will investigate the things that are in heaven? And who will know your thoughts, unless you give wisdom and send your Holy Spirit from on high?* ***or can one born of a woman appear clean?*** that is, of a pure intellect, as if he were saying: "One born of a woman possesses an intellect plunged both into flesh and into concupiscence, and therefore is hardly able to have a secure and clean intellect." For Avicenna says in *The Sixth Book on Natural Things* that the intellect that is free from phantasms and errors and is thoroughly turned away from the flesh is holy or clean.[20] Jb 14:[21] *Who is able to make clean one who was conceived from unclean seed? Is it not you [God] who are alone?*

15. Ps 88.16–17.
16. Ex 34.29.
17. 2 Cor 3.18.
18. Wis 9.14.
19. Wis 9.16–17.
20. Avicenna, *Sextus de naturalibus* 5.6 (Avicenna Latinus, *Liber de anima seu Sextus de naturalibus*, ed. S. Van Riet, 2 vols. [Louvain: Peeters, 1968 and 1972], 2.150–53). Cf. Albert, *ST* 2.5.25.2.2. See also Paul D. Hellmeier, OP, "Der *intellectus adeptus* und die Torheit der Philosophen. Philosophische Vollendung und christlicher Glaube in den Bibelkommentaren Alberts des Grossen," *Divus Thomas* 122 (2019): 144–84, esp. 162–63. I am grateful to Marco Vorcelli for locating this reference to *Sextus de naturalibus* and for bringing Hellmeier's article to my attention.
21. Jb 14.4.

And he proves this from the greater, adding: **[5]** ***Behold, even the moon,*** which was established principally for the purpose of illuminating the darkness, ***does not shine.*** Gn 1:[22] *He made the moon to rule the night,* and it does not shine by its own light. Sir 43:[23] *The moon* [*is*] *a light that diminishes in its perfection.* ***and the stars,*** which nevertheless seem pure, ***are not pure in His sight,*** that is, in comparison to Him. Wis 7:[24] *She*[25] *is more beautiful than the sun, and above the entire orderly arrangement of the stars; when compared to the light, she is found before it.* And it is added that, if what seems to belong more does not belong, then neither does what belongs less: that is, if what seems to shine more does not shine, then neither does what shines less.

And that is: **[6]** ***How much more a human being,*** supply: does not shine, **[*who is*]** ***rottenness,*** that is, who is rottenness. Mt 6:[26] *If the light that is in you is darkness, how great will the darkness itself be?* And note that the first human is rottenness in nature, but the second one, having been born from the first, is a worm born from rottenness.

And that is: ***and the son of a human being a worm.*** Ps:[27] *I am a worm, and not a human being.* Is 41:[28] *Do not fear, you worm Jacob.* And he intends [to say] that whoever is so bound to rottenness that he is not able to contemplate divine realities perfectly is a worm.

22. Gn 1.16.
23. Sir 43.7.
24. Wis 7.29.
25. Namely, divine wisdom.
26. Mt 6.23.
27. Ps 21.7.
28. Is 41.14.

CHAPTER 26

HEN JOB *responded and said.*

Since his opponents were faltering, Job here reinforces his own opinion. And his opinion consists of two points, namely: that the governance of God, by which He guides the world, is dissimilar to human rule, as that which is according to the excellence of the wisdom and the knowledge of God; and that it[1] is not according to the order of human justice. Therefore, this section, all the way up to the words of Elihu,[2] is divided into two parts. In the first of these, Job shows the excellence of God; in the second part, moreover, by setting himself forth as an example, he confirms that God does not govern human affairs according to the order of human justice. Below in that place:[3] *Job also added, taking up his parable.* The first part has three subdivisions, according to which the excellence of God is shown in three ways. In the first place, he shows it in the works of creation, of arrangement (*dispositionis*), and of adornment; second, in the repayment of merits, below in that place:[4] *Job also added;* third, in the search for the wisdom of God, according to which it shines forth through vestiges and images in creatures, below in that place:[5] *Silver has beginnings of its veins.*

The present chapter is divided into three parts. Indeed, first Job greatly confounds his opponent. Second, he shows from all[6] His works that God is excellent, in that place:[7] *He*

1. Namely, the mode of God's governance.
2. Elihu begins to speak in Ch. 32.
3. Jb 27.1.
4. Ibid.
5. Jb 28.1.
6. Here I read *omnibus* with MSS F and M rather than the *omnia* of Weiss's edition.
7. Jb 26.7.

has stretched out the north. Third, he sets forth an epilogue to his speech in that place:[8] *Behold, these things have been said partially.*

The first part has two paragraphs: in the first, Job confounds his opponent according to reason; in the second, he confounds him according to fear, in that place:[9] *Behold, the giants.* In the first paragraph there are two points by reason of which the opponent is confounded, namely, that he presumes to help the strong, and that he presumes to give counsel to the wise.

And that is: ***Then Job responded and said.*** "Responded," I say, to the person first and to his speech second. Rom 1:[10] *I am a debtor to the wise and to the foolish; therefore, insofar as is in me, I am ready.* Sir 5:[11] *If you have understanding, respond to your neighbor; but if not, let your hand be over your mouth lest you be caught in undisciplined speech and be confounded.*

And he adds that he has given help to the strong: [2] ***Whose helper are you?*** that is, carefully consider that the eminently strong one does not need your help. But he wanted to help when he wished to confirm the justice of God by means of human reasoning; and this is what he adds: ***can it be,*** supply: that you are the helper ***of the one who is weak?*** which is holy. Rom 15:[12] *We who are stronger ought to bear the infirmities of the weak.* And explaining this, he adds: ***and do you support the arm of him,*** that is, the arm of His rule, ***who is not strong?*** as if he were saying, "He has not done this, but you presume to comfort the strong when you strain to support His rule by means of human reason. Is 40:[13] *With His arm He will gather the lambs together.* Is 30:[14] *He shows the terror of His arm in the threatening of fury.*

Then Job adds, concerning the presumption of wisdom, that he has given counsel to the wise, and that is: [3] ***To whom have you given counsel?*** Is 40:[15] *Who has helped the spirit of the Lord? Or who has been His counselor?* And Job makes it clear to him, and by mock-

8. Jb 26.14.
9. Jb 26.5.
10. Rom 1.14–15.
11. Sir 5.14.
12. Rom 15.1.
13. Is 40.11.
14. Is 30.30.
15. Is 40.13.

ing [him] he adds ironically: ***perhaps to the one who has no wisdom?*** Rom 11:[16] *O the depth of the riches of the wisdom and the knowledge of God!* Jer 10:[17] *Yours is the glory: among all the wise men of the nations and in all their kingdoms there is none like you.* ***and,*** supply: because you have not been able to do this, ***you have shown your prudence,*** supply: to be ***very great.*** Indeed, wisdom is praiseworthy, but a very great amount is blameworthy. Rom 12:[18] *I say to all who are among you: do not be wiser than you ought to be wise, but be wise according to sobriety.* At the beginning of the *Almagest,* Ptolemy says: He who extends his knowledge beyond the purposefulness that is in him is like a feeble shepherd with many sheep.[19] Prv 25:[20] *Just as it is not good for someone to eat too much honey, so he who is a scrutinizer of majesty will be overwhelmed by glory.*

And he confirms this through reason, adding: [4] ***Whom have you wished to teach?*** supply: although you were not able to teach. Is 40:[21] *Who has instructed Him?* ***was it not He who made the breathing-passage?*** that is, the first receptacle of wisdom. Gn 2:[22] *He breathed into his face the breath of life.* Sir 17:[23] *He created in them the knowledge of the spirit, and He filled their hearts with understanding.*

Then Job adds the restraint of his opponents according to fear: [5] ***Behold, the giants,*** being presumptuous concerning their own strength, of course, and setting themselves up against God. Gn 6:[24] *Giants were on the earth in those days.* And after a few words:[25] *These are the powerful, renowned men of old.* ***groan under the waters,*** namely, of the surging of divine retribution. Lam 3:[26] *Waters have flowed over my head. I said: I have been destroyed.* ***and those who dwell with them,*** namely, imitators of them will groan similarly. Heb 2:[27] *Every disobedience has received a just recompense of reward.*

16. Rom 11.33.
17. Jer 10.7.
18. Rom 12.3.
19. See Alb. *Metaph.* 2.1.1 and *Phys.* 1.1.
20. Prv 25.27.
21. Is 40.14.
22. Gn 2.7.
23. Sir 17.6.
24. Gn 6.4.
25. Ibid.
26. Lam 3.54.
27. Heb 2.2.

And lest they believe they can escape notice, he adds: **[6] *Hell is naked before Him.*** Sir 23:[28] *The eyes of the Lord are far brighter than the sun, looking around and seeing all the ways of men, and the depths of the abyss.* Heb 4:[29] *There is not any creature invisible in His sight.* ***and there is no covering for destruction,*** that is, for those who ought to be destroyed. Jb 34:[30] *There is no darkness, and there is no shadow of death where those who work iniquity may be hidden.*

[7] ***He has stretched out the north.***

Now that the insolence of his opponents has been restrained, Job shows the excellence of God in three ways: namely, in the works of creation, of arrangement (*dispositionis*), and of adornment. And that is: ***He has stretched out the north,*** that is, heaven from the north. For Aristotle says in Book II of *On Heaven and Earth*[31] that the length of heaven is from the north to the south; and if we were to imagine a human being on the right-hand side of heaven traveling in a circuit from the east to the west, his head would be in the north and his feet in the south, just as the poets imagined Atlas to be. According to nature, therefore, the beginning of the extension of heaven is from the north. Ps:[32] *He stretched out heaven like a skin.* ***over the empty space.*** The capacity of the universe, with regard to which nothing had yet been made, is called "the empty space." For among creatures, the first created thing, according to nature, is heaven. Is 42:[33] *Thus says the Lord, who created the heavens and stretched them out.* ***and He has hung the earth upon nothing,*** so that heaven is at the limit in the highest place, and the earth is in the lowest place. Is 44:[34] *I am the Lord, who makes all things, who alone stretches out the heavens, who establishes the earth; and there is none with me.* Gn 1:[35] *In the beginning God created heaven and earth. And the earth was empty and void.*

And by the things at the limits (*per extrema*) Job understands the things in the middle as well, namely, fire, air, and water; and,

28. Sir 23.28.
29. Heb 4.13.
30. Jb 34.22.
31. See Aristotle, *Cael.* 2.2.8.
32. Ps 103.2.
33. Is 42.5.
34. Is 44.24.
35. Gn 1.1–2.

concerning the work of arrangement, he adds: **[8]** ***He binds up the waters in His clouds.*** "To bind up the waters in clouds" is to change the waters, by vaporization, into clouds and to hold them by the power of heaven, until the celestial powers pour out, by means of which, having been poured out onto the ground, they stir the earth to sprout forth. Jb 37:[36] *Can it be that you know the paths of the clouds, great and perfect knowledge?* ***so that they do not burst out and fall down together,*** supply: but so that, having been released drop-by-drop, the waters—which by bursting out together would upset the earth and destroy the power of things sprouting forth, just as in the deluge of Gn 7—may soak the earth proportionally. Is 55:[37] *As the rain and the snow come down from heaven and return there no more, but soak the earth and water it, and make it sprout forth.*

Indeed, the elemental qualities would not move toward the generation of species unless the celestial powers poured out [on them]. For fire would consume the hot [quality]; the cold would cut off and destroy the movement of the inferior elements—it would certainly cause the wet to disappear; and the dry would not extend to the quantity and form of bodies. Hence, they move toward the generation of species not *per se,* but by the powers of heaven. And Job indicates this, adding: **[9]** ***He withholds the face of His throne.*** The "throne" of God is heaven, in which He sits as on a throne, sustaining and ruling all things. Prv 20:[38] *The king, who sits on the throne of His judgment, scatters every evil with His gaze.* But the "face of the throne" of God is the surface [of heaven] that is turned toward what is below, and this is the surface set with stars. Indeed, through the form and power of the stars, God pours into the elements every power of generation and corruption; and He preserves this as long as He pours out the powers of generation and corruption, that is, as long as the world remains. Jb 23:[39] *Who will grant to me that I might know and find Him and come all the way to His throne?* Therefore, God, as the first cause, pours existence (*esse*) and movement (*motum*) into all things that exist. At the end of Isaiah:[40] *Heaven is my seat, and the earth my footstool.*

36. Jb 37.16.
37. Is 55.10.
38. Prv 20.8.
39. Jb 23.3.
40. Is 61.1.

and spreads His cloud over it. Vapor is called a "cloud" because, when the power of heaven is poured out onto lower things, it is necessary, in accordance with reason, that lower things be open to receiving it and be lifted up, and this is through evaporation. Sir 43:[41] *A remedy for all things is in the hastening of a cloud.*

[10] ***He has set a boundary around the waters,*** separating the wet from the dry, of course. Gn 1:[42] *Let the waters be gathered together into one place, and let the dry land appear.* Jb 38:[43] *Who shut up the sea with doors when it burst forth as if issuing from the womb.* And a little beyond this:[44] *I surrounded it with my boundaries, and I set bars and doors.* ***continuously until light and darkness,*** that is, the succession of light and darkness or of night and day, ***come to an end,*** that is, as long as the world will remain in accordance with the succession of generation and corruption. Gn 8:[45] *Night and day will not cease.*

Moreover, concerning the mode of reinforcing, Job adds: **[11]** ***The pillars of heaven tremble.*** The "pillars" are the orders (*praecepta*) reinforcing heaven, which "tremble" when they obey [God] with reverence. Bar 3:[46] *He who sends out light and it goes forth; and summons it, and it obeys Him with trembling.* ***and they are terrified at His command.*** The "command" (*nutus*) of God is a sign of His will, to which sign every creature is obedient. Mt 8:[47] *What sort of man is this, that the winds and the seas obey him?*

And it is the same with regard to the inferior elements. Hence, it follows: **[12]** ***In His strength,*** that is, in the strength of His order (*praecepti*), ***the seas are suddenly gathered together.*** Job says "seas" in the plural on account of Amphitrite and the Mediterranean.[48] Gn 1:[49] *The gathering together of the waters He called the seas.*

41. Sir 43.24.
42. Gn 1.9.
43. Jb 38.8.
44. Jb 38.10.
45. Gn 8.22.
46. Bar 3.33.
47. Mt 8.27.
48. In Greek mythology Amphitrite is the wife of Poseidon and the goddess of the sea, that is, the Mediterranean; and in Homeric poetry Amphitrite is simply another name of the sea.
49. Gn 1.10.

Ps:[50] *You have established a boundary, which they do not pass over; and neither will they return to cover the earth.*

And this is the case not only among corporeal things, but also among spiritual things. For God orders and arranges as well that which resists through the wickedness of the will. And this is what follows: ***and His wisdom has struck the proud one,*** that is, Satan in all his effects. Is 51:[51] *Have you not struck the proud one and wounded the dragon?* Wis 8:[52] *She reaches therefore from end to end with strength and orders all things sweetly.*

After [showing God's excellence in the work of] arrangement, Job adds concerning adornment, starting from the highest place: **[13]** ***His spirit,*** that is, of God, ***has adorned the heavens,*** by means of stars and likenesses of stars. Sir 43:[53] *The glory of the stars is the beauty of heaven; the Lord illuminates the world on high.* And suddenly Job transitions to the lowest: ***and the winding serpent.*** The "serpent" is the largest of the animals, by which is understood every adornment of the earth among the animals and also [every] adornment of the water and of the air. ***was brought forth,*** supply: from non-being (*non esse*) into being (*esse*) to adorn the earth, ***by His obstetric hand,*** that is, by the wisdom of His operation. Ps:[54] *This sea serpent, which you have formed to play therein.* Nevertheless, certain literal interpreters of this passage understand the serpent as a certain adornment of heaven, namely, the motion of the seven planets in their orbits carrying them away in the manner of a winding serpent and cutting across the zodiac. From this arises every motion of all the stars, which the philosophers[55] call planetary—that is, wandering—motion; and this orbit is called a serpent. Hence they[56] distinguish between the motion of the head and that of the tail of the serpent; but they call the head and the tail "nodes," according to which this orbit cuts across the zodiac. And they say that these nodes, in any particular year, are moved from the east to the west through

50. Ps 103.9.
51. Is 51.9.
52. Wis 8.1.
53. Sir 43.10.
54. Ps 103.26.
55. See Aristotle, *Metaph.* 12.8 and *Mund.* 2. Cf. Albert, *ST* 2.9.34.4.
56. That is, the philosophers.

eighteen positions, which the Arabs call "gauzahar."[57] In heaven, God has brought these [nodes] into being (*in esse*) as stars, which are, as it were, the life-giving beginning in heaven; [and] they are carried[58] everywhere by signs. So the Jewish philosophers—Abraham,[59] Isaac,[60] and Moses the Egyptian[61]—explain.

Having said these things, Job sets forth an epilogue, by means of which he returns to his intended conclusion; and that is: [14] ***Behold, these things,*** supply: that have been said, ***have been said partially,*** that is, imperfectly. 1 Cor 13:[62] *We know partially, and we prophesy partially.* ***of His ways* (viarum eius),** that is, concerning His ways, that is, concerning His works, because the Greeks do not have the ablative case, so they use the genitive

57. See Johan Ludwig Emil Dreyer, *History of the Planetary Systems from Thales to Kepler* (New York: Cosimo, 2007), who, in setting forth the views of the "Oriental Astronomers," explains: "The lunar system comprises an additional sphere outside the others, the centre of which coincides with the centre of the world, and which is called *al-ǵauzahar,* signifying the constellation Draco, as this sphere provides for the revolution of the lunar notes ('the head and tail of the dragon') round the zodiac" (260–61). See also Géza Fehérvári, "Masterpieces of an Unknown Iranian Metalworker," *The Journal of Dar al-Athar al-Islamiyyah* 25 (2008): 2–8, who describes a metal vessel produced at Herat in 1163 known as the Bobrinsky bucket, which displays an elaborate silver and copper inlaid decoration depicting the dragon-headed serpent. Fehérvári writes: "This dragon-headed serpent ... is actually *jawzahr,* the eighth unseen planet. According to pre-Islamic and early Islamic astronomy, it was held responsible for the eclipses of the sun and the moon. The importance of *jawzahr* was examined and discussed in great detail by Willy Hartner. He states that this eighth unseen planet 'appears to be a terrifying dragon's head whose serpentine neck and truncated body end in a knot.' The word is originally Persian *gùzchahar,* literally meaning a 'comet,' while its variation *gauzahar* means 'dragon's head and tail.' From this it became *jawzahr* in Arabic, but is also known as *al-tinnìn* 'the giant dragon'" (6–7).

58. Here I read *veherentur* with MSS F and M rather than the *inveherentur* of Weiss's edition.

59. See Abraham Ibn Daud, *Ha-Emunah ha-Ramah* (*The Exalted Faith*) 8. See also vol. 1, 105n82, of the present work.

60. This is likely a reference to the Jewish philosopher and physician Isaac Israeli (c. 855–955), whom Albert mentions in commenting on Jb 18.18 above (see vol. 1, 307).

61. See Moses Maimonides, *Dux* 2.10.

62. 1 Cor 13.9.

in place of the ablative.[63] And he finishes what he intends: ***and since we have heard,*** that is, we have perceived by hearing, ***barely a small drop,*** that is, the smallest something dripping from Him as a sign of His works, ***of His word,*** that is, from God Himself. Is 40:[64] *Behold, the nations are like a drop in a bucket, and they are counted like dust on the scales.* ***who will be able to behold the thunder of His majesty?*** "Thunder" is not heard without a disturbance of the head; and this signifies the excellence of the word concerning God in Himself (*in se ipso*), who is so excellent, [the word] which surpasses every thought and shakes and confuses understanding. Jb 37:[65] *He will thunder with the voice of His majesty; and He will not be investigated when His voice will be heard.* And in the same place:[66] *God will thunder marvelously with His voice.*

63. The Greek text here has the genitive construction ὁδοῦ αὐτοῦ, of which the Vulgate's *viarum eius* is the equivalent.

64. Is 40.15.

65. Jb 37.4.

66. Jb 37.5.

CHAPTER 27

J*OB ALSO* added.

Here begins the part in which Job makes known the excellence of God in the repayment of merits. This part, moreover, is subdivided into two. In the first subdivision, because speech concerning morals is believed by him who loves virtue and integrity, as the Philosopher says in Book IX of the *Ethics,*[1] Job shows the integrity of the one speaking. In the second subdivision, he sets forth his own speech, in that place:[2] *For what is the hope of the hypocrite?* In the first subdivision, there are two points, namely, the integrity of the one speaking and the injustice of the one contradicting [him], in that place:[3] [*Let my enemy be*] *as the impious.* Concerning the first of these points there are two things, namely, the purpose of the one aiming to persevere in the life of virtue; and the integrity of the original way of life, and indeed the dissatisfaction with evil in the other [purpose].

And that is: ***Job also added.*** Since he had demonstrated the ways of God in the creation of the world, Job "added" in order that he might demonstrate the same in the repayment of the good and the evil. ***taking up his parable,*** in which he mentions the manner of speaking: for he speaks by means of similitudes, proving what he intends. Ps:[4] *I will open my mouth in parables; I will utter propositions from the beginning.* Mt 13:[5] Without parables He did not speak to them. ***and said,*** by means of an oath, that is to say, confirming the truth concerning divine realities: **[2]** ***As***

1. See Aristotle, *EN* 9.3.3.
2. Jb 27.8.
3. Jb 27.7.
4. Ps 77.2.
5. Mt 13.34.

God lives* (Vivit Deus)**. "God lives" (*Vivit Deus*) is in place of an adverb, as also in 1 Kgs 17:[6] *As God lives* (Vivit Deus), *in whose sight I stand.* That is, "I swear by the life of God," and this is in place of an adverb of an oath, as "By Pollux and Castor," that is, "I swear by the temple of Apollo and by Castor." ***who has taken away my judgment, that is, He brings it about through punishments that no true judgment should obtain concerning me, but, in the same way, I should be declared guilty and liable to punishment. Is 53:[7] *In* [*his*] *humility, his judgment has been taken away.* Jb 16: *My wrinkles bear witness against me.* ***and the Almighty,*** supply: lives, who can use His creature for whatever He wishes, ***who has led my soul to bitterness,*** namely, [the bitterness] of loss and of bodily pain. Ru 1:[8] *Call me Mara, that is, bitter, because the Almighty has filled me exceedingly with bitterness.*

[3] ***As long as breath,*** that is, the life-giving spirit, ***remains in me.*** And explaining this, he adds: ***and,*** that is, ***the spirit of God,*** that is, given by God, ***in my nostrils.*** Job says this because natural breathing occurs through the nostrils, and defilement proceeds from the stomach through the mouth. Jn 6:[9] *It is the spirit that gives life.* Gn 2:[10] *He breathed into his face the spirit of life.* Wis 2:[11] *The breath in our nostrils is vapor, and speech a spark to move our heart.*

[4] ***my lips will not speak iniquity.*** The separation and articulation of words occurs by means of the lips; and Job intends [to say] that he has not brought forth iniquity by distinct and well-ordered speech. Mal 2:[12] *The law of truth was in his mouth, and iniquity was not found on his lips.* ***neither will my tongue,*** by means of which a concept of the heart is drawn out into a word, of course, ***contemplate lying.*** Is 53[13] and 1 Pt 2:[14] *He did not commit a sin, nor was deceit found in his mouth.* And note that Job says "contemplate": indeed, he has not brought forth falsehood from

6. 1 Kgs 17.1.
7. Is 53.8.
8. Ru 1.20.
9. Jn 6.64.
10. Gn 2.7.
11. Wis 2.2.
12. Mal 2.6.
13. Is 53.9.
14. 1 Pt 2.22.

contemplation, although perhaps he has spoken it at some time from deception. Ps:[15] *You will destroy all who speak a lie.*

And Job adds an execration of falsehood and depravity: [5] ***God forbid that I should judge you to be just,*** because indeed I have hated the iniquity in me, [and] I do not approve it in you. Prv 8:[16] *I detest arrogance and pride, and a perverse way, and a double-tongued mouth.* Hab 1:[17] *Your eyes are too pure to look upon evil, and you are not able to gaze at iniquity.* ***until I die,*** by death, of course, ***I will not depart from my innocence,*** namely, by which I have harmed no one through fault, nor has another's fault made me guilty by blame. Ps:[18] *I walked about in the innocence of my heart in the midst of my house. I did not set before my eyes any unjust thing: I hated the workers of iniquities.*

And therefore supply: **[6]** ***My justification,*** of my works, of course, ***which I have begun,*** namely, from the beginning of my life, ***I will not forsake.*** 2 Mc 6:[19] *Eleazar began to consider the eminent dignity of his period of life and his old age, and the natural nobility of his gray hair, and the actions of his honorable way of life from boyhood. And he answered quickly, according to the ordinances of the holy law made by God,* [*saying*] *that he wished rather to be sent ahead into hell,* namely, before he would do any unlawful things, for the love of life.[20] ***and indeed my heart has not condemned me during my whole life,*** supply: with regard to mortal sin, because that is true condemnation. 1 Jn 3:[21] *If our heart does not condemn us, we have confidence before God; and whatever we ask, we will receive from Him.* Ps:[22] *He will not deprive of good things those who walk in innocence.*

And Job adds how noxious is he who assails the opinion of truthfulness: [7] ***Let my enemy be as the impious.*** For he is void of dutiful conduct (*pietate*), which is benevolence toward good people, and he is an "enemy" of the good rather than of the

15. Ps 5.7.
16. Prv 8.13.
17. Hab 1.13.
18. Ps 100.2–3.
19. 2 Mc 6.23.
20. See 2 Mc 6.20.
21. 1 Jn 3.21–22.
22. Ps 83.13.

human. Ps:[23] *Instead of loving me, they detracted from me.* Est 7:[24] *A foe and our most wicked enemy is this Haman,* which means "wicked" and "impious." Explaining this, he adds: ***and,*** that is, ***my opponent as though the wicked one,*** that is, similar to the wicked one, for he attacks the truth and not the human. Ps:[25] *They have hated me with a wicked hatred.* Acts 13:[26] *O full of guile and of all deceit, child of the devil, enemy of all justice, you do not cease to subvert the right ways of the Lord.*

[8] ***For what is hope.***

After Job makes clear what he himself must believe concerning morals, he sets forth the judgment of God in the repayment of the wicked. And he does this in two ways, namely, in the expectation of the evil one and in the description of the evil one, which will happen by way of parts, in that place:[27] *If his sons are multiplied.* In the first way, there are two things, namely: the judgment of God, that the evil one expects nothing except evil; and that this judgment has been made manifest in the hearts of all, in that place:[28] *I will teach you.*

And that is: ***For what is the hope of the hypocrite,*** that is, the pretender, ***if he should pillage greedily,*** that is, take another's possessions through pretense. Prv 10:[29] *The hope of the wicked will perish.* Prv 11:[30] *With his mouth the pretender deceives his friend.* ***and God will not absolve his soul?*** The meaning is: What person, whose soul God wishes not to absolve, is able to hope? Jb 2:[31] *Skin for skin, and all that a human has he will give for his soul.*

And Job shows that he will not receive deliverance of [his] soul because God will not pay attention to him. And that is: [9] ***Can it be that God will hear,*** that is, pay attention to, ***his cry.*** At the end of Is:[32] *You will cry out because of anguish of heart, and you*

23. Ps 108.4.
24. Est 7.6.
25. Ps 24.19.
26. Acts 13.10.
27. Jb 27.14.
28. Jb 27.11.
29. Prv 10.28.
30. Prv 11.9.
31. Jb 2.4.
32. Is 65.14.

will howl because of grief of spirit. ***when distress will come upon him?*** namely, the hypocrite and the wicked one. Lam 3:[33] *But when I cry out and entreat, He has shut out my prayer.* Prv 1:[34] *Then they will call upon me, and I will not hear; they will rise early in the morning and will not find me.* **[10]** ***Or will he be able to delight in the Almighty?*** that is, in the help of the Almighty in returning [him] to delights, as if He were saying, "No." For the words of Lk 16[35] will be said to him: *You have received good things during your life, and Lazarus evil things; but now he is comforted, but you are tormented.* Prv 1:[36] *I will laugh at your destruction, and I will mock you when what you feared comes upon you.* ***and,*** supply: can it be that he can, ***call upon*** **(invocare)** ***God,*** that is, to call [God] to himself (*in se vocare*), as restorer and comforter, ***at all times?*** as if he were saying, "No." Is 1:[37] *When you stretch out your hands, I will turn my eyes away from you. When you offer many prayers, I will not listen.*

And concerning the manifestation of His judgment, Job adds: **[11]** ***I will teach you by the hand of God,*** that is, by means of the examples of the good and the evil, which [examples] God has provided, ***what the Almighty has,*** namely, as the pattern and standard of His judgment. Acts 20:[38] *I am innocent of the blood of all of you. For I have not avoided proclaiming to you every purpose of God.* And in the same place:[39] *How I have held back nothing useful to you, but I have proclaimed it to you, and I have taught you publicly.* And that is: ***and I will not conceal it.*** Wis 6:[40] *I will not conceal from you the mysteries of God, but I will search [after her, that is, wisdom] from the beginning of her birth, and I will bring [knowledge of her] into the light.*

And he adds that these things are known *per se:* **[12]** ***Behold, you all know it,*** for it has been written in the hearts of all. Jer 31:[41] *All people will know*[42] *me, from the greatest of them all the way down to*

33. Lam 3.8.
34. Prv 1.28.
35. Lk 16.25.
36. Prv 1.26.
37. Is 1.15.
38. Acts 20.26–27.
39. Acts 20.20.
40. Wis 6.24.
41. Jer 31.34.
42. Although Weiss's edition has *sicut* here, this appears to be a transcription

the least of them. ***and why,*** that is, for what reason, ***do you say vain things without cause?*** for falsehood, of course, under the pretense of debating the truth. Wis 13:[43] *All people in whom there is not the knowledge of God are vain.* Prv 12:[44] *He who is vain and foolish will lie open to contempt.*

Moreover, he adds what has been made clear to all, namely, that: **[13]** ***This is the portion of a wicked man.*** He says "portion" because the whole is infinite and it will never end, and therefore the whole cannot be explained. Ps:[45] *Fire, hail, snow, ice, and windstorms will be the portion of their cup.* ***in the presence of God,*** that is, in the presence of divine justice. Dt 32:[46] *When I accept a time, I will judge for justice.* ***and the inheritance,*** to which they will cling, of course, ***of the violent,*** that is, of those inflicting violence on others, ***which they will receive from the Almighty,*** whom no one is able to resist. Wis 6:[47] *The mighty will suffer torments mightily.*

And Job describes this by way of parts:

[14] ***If [his sons] are multiplied.***

And first he sets forth the punishments in the succession of [his] posterity, second in the expediency of wealth, [and] third in the multitude of infernal punishments. And that is: ***If his sons are multiplied.*** Successors according to nature and successors according to wickedness are called "sons." Wis 4:[48] *All children who are born of illicit unions are witnesses of wickedness against their parents in their trial.* And that is: ***they will be for the sword;*** punishment avenging iniquity is called "the sword." Jb 19:[49] *Flee, therefore, from the face of the sword, seeing that the sword is the avenger of iniquities.* Dt 32:[50] *If I sharpen my sword like lightning and my hand takes hold*

---

error on his part. In quoting Jer 31.34 earlier in *On Job,* Albert's text reads *scient* here; see *On Job* 21.29 (Weiss, col. 257; trans.: vol. 1, FOTC 19, p. 347); thus, I have rendered *scient* rather than *sicut* here.

43. Wis 13.1.

44. Prv 12.8.

45. Albert here conflates Ps 148.8 and Ps 10.7, as he does in commenting on Jb 6.16 and Jb 20.29 above (vol. 1).

46. The scriptural text here is not Dt 32.35–36, as Weiss indicates, but rather Ps 74.3.

47. Wis 6.7.

48. Wis 4.6.

49. Jb 19.29.

50. Dt 32.41.

of judgment, I will repay my enemies with vengeance. ***and his grandsons,*** the sons of his sons, of course, ***will not be filled with bread,*** that is, because of poverty, and they will have need of bread. Is 14:[51] *The seed of the most wicked* [*will not be named forever*]. *Prepare their children for slaughter for the iniquity of their fathers: they will not rise up.* Hos 9:[52] *He will lead his children away to the murderer.* **[15]** ***Those who have been left behind after him,*** that is to say, from all his progeny and every generation, ***will be buried in death.*** Is 14:[53] *I will destroy the name of Babylon, and the remnant, and the progeny, and the shoot.* ***and his widows,*** having been deprived of a most wicked husband, ***will not wail,*** but instead they will rejoice that they have been delivered from such evils.

And, concerning the loss of wealth, Job adds: **[16]** ***If he heaps up silver as if earth;*** this is hyperbole, that is, abundantly. And everything that is measured monetarily or in coins is called "silver," as Aristotle says in Book V of *Ethics.*[54] 1 Kgs 10:[55] *He made silver to be as abundant as stones.* ***and prepares garments,*** according to what is seemly, of course, ***like clay.*** Note that by "clay" [he means] that they are in abundance, as if to be trampled underfoot. Hab 2:[56] *Woe to him who heaps up what is not his own. And why does he load himself down with thick clay?* **[17]** ***he has prepared indeed,*** that is, he has collected them.[57] Lk 12:[58] *Whose will those things that you have prepared be?* ***but the just man,*** namely, the judge, condemning him and making his goods public property or gathering them into the public treasury, ***will be clothed with them,*** that is, he will distribute them to be used as clothing, ***and the innocent one,*** namely, the public judge, doing injury to no one through injustice, ***will divide,*** either for the public treasury or for the use of the state, ***the silver,*** supply: [that] he has collected. Jas 5:[59] *Go now, you rich people, weeping in your miseries, which will come upon you. Your gold*

51. Is 14.20–21.
52. Hos 9.13.
53. Is 14.22.
54. Aristotle, *EN* 5.5.10.
55. 1 Kgs 10.27.
56. Hab 2.6.
57. That is, garments.
58. Lk 12.20.
59. Jas 5.1, 3.

and silver have become corrupted. And their corruption will be a testimony against you, and it will eat your flesh like fire. Eccl 5:[60] *Riches accumulated to the detriment of their owner; indeed, they are lost in the midst of the worst affliction.* And Job adds a certain reason of all these things, and it is supplied: because **[18]** ***He has built his house as if a moth,*** which consumes whatever he builds; thus, that man has consumed through the defect of avarice whatever he has collected through resourcefulness. Is 14:[61] *The moth will be scattered beneath you, and worms will be your covering.* ***and like a guard,*** namely, of a vineyard or of a cucumber garden, ***he has made a shelter.*** And note the stupidity in this. For a guard is foolish if, for a brief period of time, he builds a large structure that he will abandon soon after; and in this way he who builds in the world is foolish. Is 1:[62] *It will be abandoned as a shelter in a vineyard, and as a cottage in a cucumber garden, and as a city that is ravaged.*

Moreover, Job explains how this happens, adding: **[19]** ***The rich man, when he sleeps,*** the sleep of death, of course, ***will take nothing*** from all his wealth ***away with him.*** 1 Tm, at the end:[63] *We brought nothing into this world, and without a doubt we cannot carry anything out.* ***he will open his eyes,*** which fault had shut, ***and find nothing.*** Ps:[64] *They have slept their sleep, and all the men of wealth have found nothing in their hands.*

Then he adds concerning the succession of punishments of hell, and that is: **[20]** ***Poverty, like water, will overtake him,*** that is, every defect of the good, which he clings to, [as] water covers him over outwardly and fills him inwardly to the point of overflowing, just as the inundations of hell envelop outwardly and torment inwardly by filling to the point of overflowing. Wis 5:[65] *The rivers will run together harshly.* ***and in the night*** **(nocte)**, which is so called from "going to be harmed" (*nocendo*) and signifies the darkness of hell, ***a tempest will overwhelm him,*** that is, the assault

60. Eccl 5.12–13. Although Weiss references only v. 12 here and includes only the first phrase as part of the biblical quotation, in fact Albert's quotation continues into v. 13, as the italics here indicate.

61. Is 14.11.

62. Is 1.8.

63. 1 Tm 6.7.

64. Ps 75.6.

65. Wis 5.23.

of divine anger attacking them. Zep 1:[66] *The Lord's ways are in a tempest.*

[21] ***A burning wind will lift him up.*** The succession of temptations of the devil[67] is "a burning wind," which causes him to be lifted up from the fellowship of every good. Wis 5:[68] *A mighty wind will stand up against them and, as if a whirlwind, it will divide them.* ***and,*** supply: the wind, ***will carry him away.*** Is 64:[69] *Our iniquities, like the wind, have carried us away.*

And this is what follows: ***and as a whirlwind will snatch him from his place,*** that is, from this life, where he lives among delights. A "whirlwind" is a rotating wind, and [here] it means that he will be completely enveloped by punishments. Is 30:[70] *In the flame of an engulfing fire; He will crush to pieces with a whirlwind and hailstones.* Is 28:[71] *As the assault of a hailstorm, a destroying whirlwind.*

[22] ***He will send forth upon him,*** punishments, of course, which at present He limits because of His mercy, ***and will be merciless.*** Prv 6:[72] *The jealousy and rage of a husband will be merciless on the day of vengeance; and he will neither acquiesce to the prayers of anyone nor accept the greatest number of gifts as a ransom.* Jb 20:[73] *So that God may send forth upon him the wrath of His fury and rain down His war upon him.* ***from His hand he will willingly flee,*** that is, from the hand of the one striking him unremittingly he seeks to flee on account of the bitterness of the punishments, and nevertheless he will not be able to escape. Is 16:[74] *He will be as a bird flying away.* **[23]** ***He,*** supply: the severe judge, ***will clasp His hands upon him,*** namely, the wicked one, so that he might not escape. 2 Mc 6:[75] *I will not escape the hand of the Almighty either alive or dead.* Dt 32:[76]

66. The text that follows is not from Zep 1, but rather is Na 1.3.

67. Here I read *successio temptationis diaboli* with MSS F and M rather than the *successio diaboli* of Weiss's edition.

68. Wis 5.24.

69. Is 64.6.

70. Is 30.30.

71. Is 28.2.

72. Prv 6.34–35.

73. Jb 20.23.

74. Is 16.2.

75. 2 Mc 6.26.

76. Dt 32.39.

There is no one who can deliver out of my hand. And he adds what he is like in the memory of the living: ***and will hiss at him,*** namely, in derision, ***looking at his place,*** from which he has fallen and into which he has fallen, of course. Lam 2:[77] *All who have passed by the way have clapped their hands at you; they have hissed at* [*you*] *and shaken their heads.* Is 14:[78] *How have you fallen from heaven, O Lucifer, who arose early in the morning? How have you fallen down to the earth,* [*you*] *who inflicted wounds on the nations?*

77. Lam 2.15.
78. Is 14.12.

CHAPTER 28

S**ILVER** ***has.***

In this chapter blessed Job shows the excellence of wisdom in the vestiges of creatures. And there are three other chapters [of Scripture] that come together in agreement on this, namely, Proverbs 8, Sirach 24, and especially Baruch 3.

And the present chapter is divided into three parts. In the first part, Job shows the depths of wisdom, according to which it shines forth among creatures. In the second part, an investigation into wisdom is set forth, in that place:[1] *But where is wisdom to be found?* In the third part, the acquisition and attainment of wisdom, in that place:[2] *But wisdom is drawn out of secret places.*

In the first part, there are two subdivisions. Indeed, in the first place Job shows the depth (*profundum*) of wisdom in the things that are generated in the deep [parts of the earth]; second, [he notes] wisdom's hiddenness, which results from the depth (*ex profunditate*), in that place:[3] *The bird has not known the path.*

In the first subdivision there are five sections: the first concerns the generation of things that are in the deep; the second concerns the place of generation; the third concerns the concealment of the place; the fourth concerns the transformation of the place; [and] the fifth concerns the change of the place into the place of another generation. And that is: ***Silver,*** produced in the deepest [parts of the earth], of course, ***has beginnings,*** namely, from which it arises through divine wisdom in the depths of the earth, ***of its veins,*** from which, one may know, it is generated.

1. Jb 28.12.
2. Jb 28.18.
3. Jb 28.7.

Dt 8:[4] *The land, whose stones are iron, and out of its mountains are dug mines of copper;* indeed, by "copper" [here] every metal is understood. ***and gold has a place in which it is refined.*** "It is refined" to this extent, that it is gold, not so much that it melts in the innermost parts of the earth, with nothing cooperating except divine wisdom, of course. Hence, God says in Hg 2:[5] *The gold is mine, and the silver is mine.* Indeed, that all these things exist in the first place from divine wisdom is proven both in the *Book of Causes*[6] and in Book II of the *Metaphysics*[7] through this kind of reasoning: Whatever is in many things through one cause (*per unam rationem*) in these things is in one first [principle], which is the cause of all of them; but what is formative according to species in many things exists through one cause in them; therefore, it is in one first [principle], which is the cause of all other things. Moreover, the first forming [principle], which is divine wisdom, stands unchangeable. For it [that is, divine wisdom] flows into understanding, and understanding flows into the soul, and the soul flows into nature, as it is said in the *Book of Causes.*[8] Hence, the highest and first [principle], which is investigated among the effects of nature, is divine wisdom, which is the first principle (*primum principium*) of life and of being (*esse*), and the first principle of light and virtue and peace, in which the entire mind rests, of course. Bar 3:[9] *Learn where wisdom is, where virtue is, where understanding is, so that you may know where length of days and of life are, where the light of the eyes and peace are.*

And Job adds concerning other metals generated in the deepest [parts of the earth]. He begins, in the first place, with silver, and second with gold. And that is: **[2]** ***Iron is taken out of the earth.*** For "iron" arises from fresh silver full of sediment and rough brimstone, from which—if the roughness and dregs are removed, and the mineral strength, causing what is moist to grow hard by means of the cold, remains—greatly purified silver

4. Dt 8.8–9.
5. Hg 2.9.
6. *Caus.* 8; cf. Alb., *Caus.et proc.* 1.4.6.
7. See Alb., *Metaph.* 2.1.6.
8. *Caus.* 8.
9. Bar 3.14.

is produced, as Avicenna says in *Alchemy*.[10] Hence, Dt 8:[11] *Whose stones are iron.*

And concerning what is accepted with regard to gold, he adds: ***and stone melted with heat is turned into brass.*** Everything that does not evaporate in fire is called "stone," as Hermes says, on account of the fact that it is generated by coagulation alone, which is the process of producing stone.[12] And it is generally true, as it is said in Book IV of *Meteorology*,[13] that everything that is coagulated from the moist cold is loosened by the hot dry, as are silver, gold, iron, brass, and all metals that are produced in the depths of the earth. For in the first action of generating, brass is mixed with stone, and when the fire loosens it, it becomes liquid and is purified. Dt 33:[14] *His shoe will be iron and brass;* that is, he will have them [that is, iron and brass] in such abundance that they exist for treading underfoot, for no one makes shoes out of brass. And Job intends [to show] that God does not form this in the most hidden and deepest parts of the earth except by divine wisdom. Blessed Gregory says[15] that the "silver" of eloquence takes its veins from Sacred Scripture, in order, of course, that eloquence sets forth no mode [of expression] that Sacred Scripture has not set forth. The very same Scripture is the place in which the gold of wisdom (*aurum sapientiae*) is refined. For we are not permitted to understand (*sapere*) unless Scripture has predetermined it. 1 Cor 2:[16] *We speak not in the learned words of human wisdom, but in the teaching of the Spirit, comparing spiritual things with spiritual things.* Moreover, by "iron," which vanquishes other metals,[17] is meant the knowledge of argumentation, which crushes heresies, which knowledge again one does not have except through divine wisdom. Wis 8:[18] *She knows the subtleties of speech and the solutions of arguments.* To be

10. See Alb., *De min.* 3.1.9 and 4.1.6, 8.
11. Dt 8.9.
12. See Alb., *De min.* 1.1.3, 4 and 2.1.3.
13. Alb., *Met.* 4.2.8.
14. Dt 33.25.
15. Gregory, *Mor.* 18.26.39.
16. 1 Cor 2.13.
17. Cf. Alb., *On Job* 20.24 (vol. 1, p. 331), and Gregory, *Mor.* 18.27.44.
18. Wis 8.8.

sure, by "brass," which is loud, as the Philosopher says,[19] since it is actually full of air, is meant Sacred Scripture itself, loud and full of the Spirit. Ezek 1:[20] *They sparkled like the appearance of shining brass.* But literally Job means that vestiges of the wisdom of God are revealed even in the deepest parts of the earth. In the letter to the Romans 1:[21] *The invisible things of God are clearly seen, being understood by the things that have been made; His eternal power also, and divinity.*

And concerning the place of the generation of these [metals], Job adds: **[3]** ***He has established a time for darkness,*** that is, He has established a time for the generation of these [metals] in darkness, that is, in the dark, innermost parts of the earth. Here the soil, set around on all sides, and a huge mass of rocks do not allow material to evaporate, and they return the heat to the deepest [parts] so that it may thicken. All things that are produced on the surface of the earth and arrive at the light, participate in life to some degree, such as plants, animals, and humans. ***and,*** that is, because, ***He Himself,*** namely, God, the highest wisdom, ***considers the end,*** to which it is able to be led through the generation, of course, ***of all things.*** Hence, since metals and stones have no life, the time of their generation is properly in darkness, for they have only[22] the form of coagulation. Jb 38:[23] *Show me where light dwells, and where the place of darkness is.*

Moreover, of the concealment that pertains to the works of wisdom, in the midst of these things, Job adds: ***even the stone of darkness,*** that is, [the stone] produced in darkness, ***and,*** that is, ***the shadow of death,*** that is, in the shadow, where there is no life.

[4] ***The torrent separates.*** A flow that has been released from the melted snow and descends from a mountain with the fury of the burning sun is called a "torrent"; and therefore it comes with fury, dragging with it rocks and trees and much soil, by means of which it buries and hides in the depths the things produced by

19. Aristotle, *De an.* 2.8.1.

20. Ezek 1.7.

21. Rom. 1.20.

22. Here I read *solam,* as an adjective modifying *formam,* with MSS EFMT rather than the *sola* of Weiss's edition.

23. Jb 38.18–19.

humans, and that is, that it separates such things from humans. And this is what is said in Is 45:[24] *I will give you hidden treasures and the concealed riches of secret places, so that you might know that I am the Lord.* And Job adds from whom the torrent separates: ***from the people on pilgrimage***. The "people on pilgrimage" are those living in lodgings for wanderers on the earth, as are those especially who are searching for metal mines, to whom it is said in Gn 4:[25] *A wanderer and a fugitive you will be on the earth* all the days of your life.

Job adds, moreover, how it [that is, the torrent] separates: ***those,*** namely, "stones of darkness," ***that the foot of the poor man,*** namely, of the one searching for treasures on account of his need, ***has forgotten;*** "has forgotten" is said because it [that is, the foot of the poor man] does not know [those stones]. ***and that are,*** that is, because [they are], ***impassable.*** Bar 3:[26] *They hoard silver and gold, in which humans put their confidence, and there is no end to their acquiring; they forge silver and are anxious, and their works are not found.* For such [metals], because they are produced in the deepest [parts of the earth], are found by few. Gregory explains this spiritually, saying that God established a time for darkness when, by means of shadows, He set up the time of the old law, so that they might return to the light of truth, or, for the unjust, when they might cease being unjust.[27] Is 9:[28] *The people who walked in darkness have seen a great light; for those who dwell in the region of the shadow of death, light has arisen.* Moreover, he[29] says that "the stone of darkness" is the heart that is dark with faithlessness, hard with an obduracy to piety, and ice cold with a frigidity toward charity. Ezek 36:[30] *I will take the heart of stone from you, and I will give you a heart of flesh.* He says[31] that a "torrent" is a fiery river, about which it is said in Dn 7:[32] *A rapid river of fire flowed*

24. Is 45.3.
25. Gn 4.12.
26. Bar 3.18.
27. See Gregory, *Mor.* 18.31.50.
28. Is 9.2.
29. That is, Gregory. See *Mor.* 18.30.47.
30. Ezek 36.26.
31. See Gregory, *Mor.* 18.30.47.
32. Dn 7.10.

forth from His presence. He says[33] that the "people on pilgrimage" are the number of the elect, who consider this life an exile for themselves and long for the life of heaven. Heb 11:[34] *Confessing that they are pilgrims and strangers on the earth.* He says[35] that "the foot of the poor man" signifies the steps of Christ, advancing in order to illuminate, convert, and sanctify the hearts of humans; his foot forgets such dark [stones].[36] 2 Cor 8:[37] *Although He was rich, He became poor on account of you, so that by His poverty you might be rich.* He calls the same ones "impassable"[38] because the words of holy preaching have not found a way to such people. In the Psalm:[39] *In a desert land that is impassable and where there is no water, so in a sacred place they have appeared to you.*

Having set forth the works of wisdom in the deepest [parts of the earth], Job mentions the works that it [that is, divine wisdom] fashions on the uppermost surface of the earth, and through the things that are in the deepest [parts]. And that is: [5] ***The land, out of which bread,*** that is, everything that pertains to the fruit of natural birth, ***arose in its own place, has been destroyed by fire,*** as is clear in the case of the Pentapolis according to Gn 19[40] and Wis 10:[41] *With fire descending upon the Pentapolis, a testimony to their wickedness is apparent: a smoking wasteland.*[42] Thus, Job even touches upon volcanoes and hot springs that are under the earth, by whose eruptions fruitful farms are frequently destroyed, with fire bursting forth from the deep and steam blow-

33. See Gregory, *Mor.* 18.30.48.

34. Heb 11.13.

35. See Gregory, *Mor.* 18.31.50.

36. That is, hearts that are dark with faithlessness, according to Gregory's interpretation of "the stone of darkness" that is cited by Albert immediately above.

37. 2 Cor 8.9.

38. See Gregory, *Mor.* 18.31.50.

39. Ps 62.3.

40. Gn 19.24–25.

41. Wis 10.6–7.

42. The term Pentapolis, as it occurs here in Wis 10.7, designates the league or confederacy of the "Five Cities" of the Plain—Sodom, Gomorrah, Admah, Zeboiim, and Segor (or Zoar)—that united to resist the invasion of Chedorlaomer (see Gn 14, esp. v. 2); all but one, however, were completely destroyed.

ing out immense quantities of ash, as it is said in Book III of *Meteorology*[43] and as is read in the *Life of Blessed Agatha.*[44]

And he also adds what advantage, by the order of divine wisdom,[45] comes forth from this: **[6]** ***The place of the sapphire,*** that is, the place of the generation of the sapphire, supply: is ***its stones,*** that is, [the stones] of that place. Indeed, provided that the moist mineral layer is refined by fire melting it, it is converted, as in the case of the purity of glass, into something that, when it penetrates the smoky gray of vapor, takes on the color of sapphire, for a smoky gray mixed with a penetrable clarity has the appearance of sapphire. And in such places, sapphires are often found. ***and [the place of] that clod [is] gold.*** For "gold" is generated often from the moist clarity of fresh silver and often from terrestrial sulfur that has been purified and separated, which appears especially in "clods" of such earth. To signify this, blessed Gregory says[46] that—because in the place where God's wrath is, someone is destroyed—the minds of the saints, for example, put on a heavenly way of life. Phil 3:[47] *Our way of life is in heaven.* And they convert the earthly substance that they bear into the splendor of gold as long as they conform themselves to the divine wisdom. Gn 2:[48] *There gold is found. And the gold of that land is very good.*

Moreover, Job adds how these works of wisdom are hidden from us: **[7]** ***The bird has not known the path,*** of these works of wisdom found in the deep [parts of the earth], of course. A subtle

43. See Alb., *Met.* 3.2.17.

44. See Jacobus de Voragine's *De sancta Agatha virgine,* in Appendix I of Andrew M. Beresford, *The Severed Breast: The Legends of Saints Agatha and Lucy in Medieval Castilian Literature* (Newark, DE: Juan de la Cuesta, 2010), 233–37. Toward the conclusion of his account, Jacobus writes: "Revoluto anno circa diem natalis eius mons quidam maximus circa civitatem ruptus eructavit incendium, quod quasi torrens de monte descendens et saxa terramque liquefaciens ad urbem cum magno impetu veniebat. Tunc paganorum multitudo descendit de monte et ad sepulchrum eius fugiens velum, unde coopertum erat sepulchrum, arripuit et ipsum statuit contra ignem statimque in die natalis ipsius virginis ignis stetit et ultra ullatenus non processit" (236–37).

45. Here I read *sapientia divina* with MSS F and M rather than simply the *sapientia* of Weiss's edition.

46. Gregory, *Mor.* 18.33.52.

47. Phil 3.20.

48. Gn 2.11–12.

and soaring intellect, which is not able to penetrate such profound things, is called a "bird." Bar 3:[49] *Who has found her place?* namely, wisdom's; *and who has entered into her treasures?* And after a few verses:[50] *The way of wisdom they have not known, nor have they remembered her paths,* because they have not understood the wisdom of God in such effects. ***nor has the eye of the vulture gazed upon it,*** namely, the path of divine wisdom. Avicenna relates in *The Sixth Book on Natural Things*[51] that, according to the opinion of some, the eye of the vulture can see carcasses up to 500 miles (*leucas*)[52] away; and it signifies those who examine the natures of things by means of the most subtle investigation but do not recognize the wisdom of God in them. Jb 39:[53] *She abides among the rocks,* namely, the eagle or vulture, *and dwells among steep stones and inaccessible cliffs. From there she looks for prey, and her eyes watch from far away.* Christ in the Ascension is understood mystically by the bird. Jb 5:[54] *The human is born to labor, and the bird is born to fly,* which bird has not known the path of the destroyed land, that is, the hearts of the reprobate. Mt 7,[55] according to the Greek translation, which Chrysostom[56] reads: *I will declare to them that I never knew you.* Gregory, however, reads "bird" (*avis*) in the genitive case because the reprobate have refused to know the paths of Christ.[57] Jb 21:[58] *They have said to the Lord God: Depart from us, we refuse to have knowledge of your ways.* The same Gregory says[59] that the vulture is Christ, who gazed upon the carcass of our mortality from heaven and submitted Himself by both descending and accepting it.[60]

49. Bar 3.15.

50. Bar 3.23.

51. I have been unable to find Weiss's reference in Avicenna's *Sextus de naturalibus;* cf. Alb., *AL* 23.1.114.

52. A *leuca* is a Gallic mile of 1500 Roman paces.

53. Jb 39.28–29.

54. Jb 5.7.

55. Mt 7.23.

56. See Chrysostom, *In Matth. op. imperf. hom.* 19 (PG 56:743).

57. Gregory, *Mor.* 18.34.54.

58. Jb 21.14.

59. Gregory, *Mor.* 18.34.54.

60. By accepting "the carcass of our mortality," Gregory is alluding to the doctrine of the Incarnation, according to which in the fullness of time the divine Son, existing from eternity, took up or assumed to Himself a complete

Jb 39:[61] *And wherever the carcass is, she*[62] *is there immediately.* Gregory also says[63] that the eyes of this vulture are holy preachers, whom the reprobate neither look at nor respect, on account of which he reads "eyes" (*oculos*) [in the accusative case], although the actual text (*vera littera*) has "eye" (*oculus*) [in the nominative case]. Acts 13:[64] *Paul and Barnabas shook the dust off against those who did not accept them, and they said resolutely: It was right for us to speak the word of God to you first; but because you reject it and judge yourselves unworthy of eternal life, behold we turn to the Gentiles.*

And Job adds how the way of wisdom has not been known even by those who search after it: [8] ***The children of the peddlers,*** that is, of the merchants, ***have not trodden it,*** that is, the path. And here those who search after the wisdom that is of the earth but do not find the wisdom of God are called "peddlers." Bar 3:[65] *The children of Hagar who search after the wisdom that is of the earth, the merchants of the land and of Teman, and the speakers and those who search after wisdom and understanding: the way of wisdom they have not known, nor have they remembered her paths.* ***neither has the lioness traveled by it,*** namely, the path of wisdom. A "lioness" is an animal eager for prey, and it signifies philosophers who seize all knowable things with the strength of their natural intelligence and a passion for study, but who nevertheless have not discovered the way of the wisdom of God as it ought to be discovered. Rom 1:[66] *Their foolish heart has been darkened. Declaring themselves to be wise, they were made fools.* 1 Cor 2:[67] *Which none of the princes of this world knew.*

Job adds, nevertheless, how this wisdom shines forth clearly among manifest works: [10] ***He has stretched out His hand to the flint,*** that is, [His] power to the mountains transformed into

---

human nature (constituted of a real human body and a rational soul), which enabled Him to suffer, die, and rise again for the sake of human salvation.

61. Jb 39.30.

62. That is, the eagle or vulture, whom Albert, following Gregory's interpretation, reads mystically as representing Christ.

63. Gregory, *Mor.* 18.34.54.

64. Acts 13.46 and 51.

65. Bar 3.23.

66. Rom 1.21–22.

67. 1 Cor 2.8.

flint. ***He has overturned mountains from their foundations,*** so that by the toppling of the mountains the precious things generated in the innermost parts of the earth might be revealed, which [toppling] Gregory says signifies the downfall of the proud and the cruel.[68] Is 40:[69] *Every valley will be filled in, and every mountain and hill will be made low, and the crooked will become straight.*

[10] ***He has cut out rivers in the midst of the rocks,*** according to the letter (*ad litteram*): He causes streams to flow forth from solid and hard stones. An example is found in Nm 20:[70] here, when Moses struck the rock twice with his rod, water came forth in great abundance. Gregory says[71] this signifies that the waters of doctrine, as from Augustine and certain other holy doctors, come out of cold and hard [hearts] that have been informed by the wisdom of God, ***and His eye has seen every precious thing,*** even what is hidden from human eyes. And it is said that He "has seen" when He makes to see. Sir 23:[72] *The eyes of the Lord are looking around and seeing the depths of the abyss and looking into the hidden places.*

[11] ***Likewise He has searched out,*** God, of course, through His wisdom, causes to be examined, ***the depths of rivers,*** that is, the "depths" from which by means of continual emanations flow rivers, either of water literally or of Scripture spiritually. Sir 24:[73] *I, wisdom, have poured out rivers. I, as though a brook out of a river of mighty water.* ***and He has brought forth hidden things into the light,*** that is, He has caused them to be brought forth. Mt 10:[74] *Nothing is concealed that will not be revealed, nor hidden that will not be known.*

[12] ***But wisdom.***

Here begins the investigation into wisdom, and Job speaks of two things, namely, the investigation and the approval of what ought to be investigated, in that place:[75] *Pure gold will not pay for it.* In the first subdivision, there are three things, namely, the

68. See Gregory, *Mor.* 18.36.57.
69. Is 40.4.
70. Nm 20.11.
71. Gregory, *Mor.* 18.37.58.
72. Sir 23.28.
73. Sir 24.40–41.
74. Mt 10.26.
75. Jb 28.15.

investigation of wisdom, the method of investigating, and where wisdom should not be sought.

And that is: ***But where is wisdom to be found?*** Job asks about two things, namely, wisdom and understanding, and concerning both he asks about the place of each; hence it must be noted in advance what wisdom is and what understanding is, and what the place of each is. "Wisdom" is said generally (*communiter*) and properly (*proprie*). Said properly, wisdom is, as Aristotle indicates in the first book of the *Metaphysics,*[76] the reception in the intellect of the first things, the highest things, the most difficult things for the human to know, on account of the fact that they are the most distant from the perception of the senses, because they are received neither by sense, nor together with anything sensible, nor mixed together with and blended among sensibles, nor separated from sensibles through abstraction. And they[77] are known through themselves (*propter se*) and not through any other thing; and these things are at the limit of what is to be known in them and are for the sake of what is to be known. Such things, however, are none other than God and divine realities insofar as they are divine. And of this wisdom it is said in Wis 13:[78] *All men in whom there is not the knowledge of God are vain.* For in no other knowable do all the designated differences [among things] come together except in this knowable, which is God. Wisdom spoken of generally is the excellence (*virtus*) of any particular science or art, which, in fact, attains to the reception of the highest and best in that [science or art], to which every other thing is ordered, and which is the principle (*ratio*) of the order and disposition of all other things [in that science or art].[79] On account of this, Aristotle says in the first book of the *Metaphysics*[80] that it pertains to the wise man to order, not to be ordered; and so excellent a reception of the highest thing, according to which is the principle of the order and disposi-

76. Aristotle, *Metaph.* 1.2.4.

77. That is, the first, highest, and most difficult truths.

78. Wis 13.1.

79. I do not translate the phrase that immediately follows here in Weiss's edition (*dicitur sapiens et ordinator et dispositor omnium aliorum*), as it is not attested in MSS F and M.

80. Aristotle, *Metaph.* 1.2.3.

tion of all other things, is called wisdom. And so Aristotle says in Book VI of the *Ethics*[81] that wisdom is the excellence (*virtus*) of a science or art; and it is assumed according to the definition of Cicero at the end of the *Rhetoric* that excellence (*virtus*) is the disposition of the perfect toward what is best.[82] The mediator of this excellence is, as Aristotle says,[83] right reason, by which all things are disposed and ordered to the single highest end of the science or art.

But here Job asks about wisdom properly understood and not [wisdom] generally accepted, namely, to know God in Himself (*in se*) and in all the distinctions of divine realities and of properties and of His effects. Understanding, however, is the reception of the principles of divine realities that can happen only through the authority that rests on and is supported by revelation. Hence, such a reception of principles through revelation and through Scripture is called understanding. Wis 9:[84] *Who will know your thoughts, unless you grant it to him and send your Holy Spirit from on high?* There cannot be a place of wisdom and a place of understanding, as al-Farabi says in the book *On the Intellect and Intelligibles,* except the intellect's attainment or possession [of each].[85] Attainment or possession, however, pertains to the unencumbered intellect: unencumbered, I say, on the part of the one who understands, and on the part of the intelligible.[86] On the part of the one who understands, so that the very one understanding, of course, is unencumbered by the passions. For the passions, as Aspasius said,[87] disturb the intellect, just as smoke and the blowing of the wind disturb the eye. Indeed, however clear the eye may be, when it is exposed to smoke and wind,

81. Aristotle, *EN* 6.7.1.
82. See Alb., *Eth.* 1.1.3.2.
83. See Aristotle, *EN* 6.13.4.
84. Wis 9.17.
85. See Alb., *Anim.* 3.3.6; and *Intellec. intellig.* 2.1.8.
86. That is, the object of understanding.
87. See Aspasius, *Comm. in Eth. Nic.* 2.2. For the Greek edition, see *Aspasii in Ethica Nicomachea quae supersunt Commentaria,* ed. Gustavus Heylbut (Berlin: Verlag Georg Reimar, 1889). See also the edited collection, *Aspasius: The Earliest Extant Commentary on Aristotle's* Ethics, ed. Antonina Alberti and Robert W. Sharples (Berlin: de Gruyter, 1999).

it does not see to the extent that it ought to see, and shifting and obscure visible forms arise in it. In the same way, the one who understands, having been overtaken by the passions—the passions, I say, of anger, concupiscence, illicit love, fear, sadness, and delight—does not receive [understanding] to the extent that he ought to receive it. Hence, Boethius says in the book *On the Consolation of Philosophy*:[88]

> You too, if you wish
> to discern the truth
> with an eye that is clear,
> drive out delights,
> drive out fear,
> chase away anticipation,
> and let not sorrow be near.
> The mind is cloudy
> and bound by a bridle
> wherever these [passions] reign.

Unencumbered on the part of the intelligible, on the other hand, means that it is unencumbered by what is successive and by time. Indeed, if what is simple is joined to the successive, the intelligible will return to likenesses of corporeal things; but if the simple is joined to sense, the intelligible will return to phantasms and the deceits of phantasms. And therefore neither of the ways spoken of is the proper place of wisdom or understanding, because by neither of the ways spoken of is there attainment and possession, as of the intellect. Indeed, of understanding that is driven out by the passions, it is said in Wis 1:[89] *Wisdom will not enter into a malicious soul, nor dwell in a body subject to sin.* Of understanding detained by phantasms it is said in Is 40:[90] *To whom have you likened God? Or what image will you set up for Him?*

Having noted these things in advance, the things that are said according to the letter (*in littera*) are easy [to understand]: ***But where is wisdom to be found?*** For wisdom is the reception of divine [truths] that have been impressed on the clearest and purest

88. Boethius, *CP* 3.90.
89. Wis 1.4.
90. Is 40.18.

intellect by God. 1 Cor 2:[91] *We have received not the spirit of this world, but the Spirit that is of God, so that we may know the things that have been given to us by God.* For in so excellent a place wisdom is always found. Prv 8:[92] *I, Wisdom, dwell in counsel, and I am present in learned thoughts.* ***and where is the place of understanding?*** namely, of the principles giving light to the investigation of wisdom. Wis 6:[93] *Love the light of wisdom, that you may reign forever.* Gregory says:[94] It allows comprehension as long as it illuminates the mind concerning things heard and read. And Job adds the reason why it should be sought, and it is supplied, because: **[13]** ***The human does not know its price;*** the reason is because it is priceless, and so it is not valued on account of its "price." For a price is always valued on account of something else (*propter aliud*), as Aristotle says in Book V of the *Ethics* that a price is valued because it is a guarantor against future need.[95] But wisdom is valued for itself (*propter se*). Prv 17:[96] *What does it profit a fool to have riches, seeing that he cannot buy wisdom?* Likewise, nothing is exchangeable for its price. It was said to Simon in Acts 8:[97] *May your money go with you into perdition, because you have thought that the gift of God may be purchased with money.*

And Job adds three places where it is not found. Concerning the first, he says: ***neither is it found in the land of those who live pleasantly,*** that is, of those directing their whole life to what is pleasing, as the Epicureans, of those choosing the life of beasts, as Aristotle says in the first book of the *Ethics.*[98] For these have a fat intellect, which cannot be the place of wisdom. Dt 32:[99] *The beloved grew fat, and he kicked his heels; having grown fat and thick and broad, he forsook God.*

Second, he adds concerning those who are clever and profound according to the wisdom of the world: **[14]** ***The abyss says:***

91. 1 Cor 2.12.
92. Prv 8.12.
93. Wis 6.23 and 22.
94. Like Weiss, I have been unable to find this reference.
95. See Aristotle, *EN* 5.2.13.
96. Prv 17.16.
97. Acts 8.20.
98. See Aristotle, *EN* 1.4.3; cf. Alb., *Eth.* 1.5.7.
99. Dt 32.15.

It is not in me. It is called the "abyss" (*abyssus*) because [it is] without foundation (*sine basi*) and without fine linen (*sine bysso*), that is, brightness, and it signifies a heart that is immovably established on nothing, dark, and profound in the cleverness of the world. Lk 16:[100] *The children of this world are wiser in their generation than the children of light.* Jer 17:[101] *The heart of man is perverse*—another translation has *profound*[102]—*and inscrutable: who can know it?* that is, the heart is filled with deceits, equivocations, and cunning, and therefore it cannot be the place of simple truth. Sir 1:[103] *The depth of the abyss, who will discover it?*

Third, he brings in [this]: ***and the sea says: It is not with me.*** The "sea," which follows the orbit of the moon, is constantly in motion and unstable and brackish; and it signifies the heart, which is restless and bitter with concerns. It says, by that very fact, that it is not the place of wisdom. Is 57:[104] *The heart of the wicked person is like the raging sea, which is unable to be at rest.* Sir 38:[105] *The wisdom of the scribe comes in his time of leisure; and he who reduces his activity will lay hold of wisdom, because wisdom will be restored to fullness.*

Moreover, Job demonstrates what ought to be investigated on account of its preciousness and beauty, first separately [and] secondly together.

Concerning its preciousness, Job says: **[15]** ***Pure gold will not pay for it.*** "Pure gold" is coarse gold, which, appearing in the purity of its own nature, is mixed with no other nature; and it is not forged for particular uses, which makes it most precious among metals. And the sense [of this text] is that the most precious things are nothing in comparison to it.[106] Jb 31:[107] *If I have thought gold my strength and have said to pure gold: My confidence.* Wis 7:[108] *All gold in comparison to her is but a little sand.* ***neither will silver be weighed out in exchange for it.*** By "silver," which is less pre-

100. Lk 16.8.
101. Jer 17.9.
102. See Origen, *Hexapla,* Jer 17.9 (PG 16:2054).
103. Sir 1.2–3.
104. Is 57.20.
105. Sir 38.25.
106. Namely, wisdom.
107. Jb 31.24.
108. Wis 7.9.

cious, is understood everything that is measured by silver or gold; and since an exchange takes place for something equal, as Aristotle says in Book V of the *Ethics,*[109] and [since] nothing is valuable enough to be equal to wisdom, nothing in the temporal world can be exchanged for it. Mt 13:[110] *He sold all that he had, and he bought it.* Song 8:[111] *If a man should give all the resources of his household to buy love, he will despise it as nothing.*

And concerning its beauty, Job adds: **[16]** ***It will not be compared to the dyed colors of India.*** The colors of things dyed are more beautiful where the land in which they are made is warmer and closer to the equator, where one finds the highest temperatures. And India is close to the equator, being equally distant from the poles, which are places of cold weather, and the tropics, which are places of the hottest weather; and India has summer weather on two occasions during the year, namely, in Aries and in Libra.[112] Therefore, in that place are found the most beautiful dyes, whose colors wisdom surpasses in beauty, because spiritual beauty surpasses all corporeal beauty. Wis 7:[113] *She is more beautiful than the sun, and above the entire orderly arrangement of the stars: compared to the light, she is found before it. For night follows the light, but wickedness cannot overcome wisdom.* Jdt 10:[114] *The Lord bestowed beauty on her, because all this dressing up did not proceed from desire, but from virtue. And therefore the Lord increased this beauty in her, so that she appeared incomparably beautiful to the eyes of all.* And Job adds that it [that is, the beauty of wisdom] surpasses all celestial beauty and terrestrial, corporeal beauty: ***nor with the most precious stone sardonyx.*** Sardonyx is similar to the reddest earth, and it seems to have the splendor of the purple with which royal purple was dyed; this purple gleams with a sparkling red in the eyes, according to which it is said in Song 5:[115] *My beloved is radiant and*

109. Aristotle, *EN* 5.5.12.

110. Mt 13.46.

111. Song 8.7.

112. Aries and Libra are the first and seventh astrological signs in the Zodiac, respectively. In the tropical zodiac, the sun passes through Aries on average between March 20 and April 21 each year, and through Libra between September 23 and October 22.

113. Wis 7.29–30.

114. Jdt 10.4.

115. Song 5.10.

ruddy. The beauty of wisdom surpasses this beauty, according to what Gregory says:[116] He who in the Psalm[117] says, *With me is the beauty of the field,* signifies the beauty of Christ, who is the wisdom of God. Song 1:[118] *Behold, you are beautiful, my love, and graceful.* And Job adds that it surpasses celestial beauty when he says: ***or the sapphire,*** whose color is that of the heavens, according to which in Lam 4[119] Jeremiah, praising wise men, describes them as *more beautiful than the sapphire.*

And, concerning both its beauty and its preciousness at the same time, Job adds: **[17]** ***Gold,*** which is precious, ***or crystal,*** which is light-permeable on account of its beauty and purity, ***will not be equal to it.*** And color, lying hidden under its very own impermeability, is extended so that it may appear more beautiful, because the beauty of wisdom surpasses all beauty, just as every idea of beauty appears in the first beauty, in which there is no mingling of impurity. Song 6:[120] *Who is she who comes forth like the rising dawn, beautiful as the moon, bright as the sun.* Song 7:[121] *How beautiful you are, and how graceful, my dearest, in delights.*

Moreover, he proves from wise people that wisdom is beautiful, adding: ***nor will any vessels of gold,*** that is, souls containing wisdom, ***be exchanged for it,*** according to equal economic value, of course. **[18]** **[*vessels*]** ***high*** among matter ***and eminent*** among the works of art.[122] For wise people shine forth because of wisdom, but wisdom shines forth through its very self (*per se ipsam*). Sir 50:[123] *As a solid vessel of gold, adorned with every precious stone.*

And because there is no comparison between wise people and wisdom, he adds: ***will not be mentioned in comparison to it,*** hence Wis 7:[124] *I loved her above health and beauty, and I chose to have her*

116. Gregory, *Mor.* 18.47.75.

117. Ps 49.11.

118. Song 1.15.

119. Lam 4.7.

120. Song 6.9.

121. Song 7.6.

122. With the glosses *in materia* and *in opere artis,* Albert here distinguishes between material things, which undergo production and corruption according to the order of nature, and those things that humans make according to an art, skill, or science.

123. Sir 50.10.

124. Wis 7.10–11.

instead of light, because her light is inextinguishable. Moreover, all good things came to me together with her, and immense honor through her hands.

But wisdom is drawn out.

Here begins the part that is on the acquisition of wisdom.[125] And here two things are spoken of, namely: the mode of acquiring [wisdom]; and through whom, as through a teacher, it is acquired, in that place:[126] *God understands.*

In the first [of these divisions], there are two things, namely: the mode of attaining wisdom; and a question concerning the teacher, in that place:[127] *Therefore, from where does wisdom come?*

In the first [of these subdivisions], there are two things besides, namely, from where it is acquired, and that it should be sought for its preciousness and beauty.

And that is: ***But wisdom is drawn out.*** For every science or intellectual wisdom, as Aristotle says at the beginning of the *Posterior Analytics*,[128] is from preexisting knowledge of principles, of course. Thus, even wisdom, which is the knowledge of divine realities, if it should be possessed by a human being, is necessarily drawn out from its own principles; for it is not possessed except through the mode of a conclusion. But knowledge of a conclusion is not had except from principles.

And this is what Job says: ***wisdom is drawn out of secret places,*** that is, from things most removed from sense perception, for these things are most hidden from the human person, although they are most manifest in themselves. Hence, the Philosopher says[129] that the disposition of our intellect toward the most manifest things of nature is like the disposition of the eyes of a bat toward the light of the sun. According to this, it is said in Acts 17, where Paul says to the Athenians:[130] *Men of Athens, I see that in all things you are, as it were, superstitious. For passing by and seeing your images, I also found an altar, on which it had been written, "To an*

125. That is, the third major part of this chapter. See above on Jb 28.1.
126. Jb 28.23.
127. Jb 28.20.
128. Aristotle, *APost.* 1.1.1.
129. Aristotle, *Metaph.* 1.1.2.
130. Acts 17.22–23.

unknown God," because our God has been hidden from your senses. Is 45:[131] *Truly you are a hidden God.* Is 53:[132] *His countenance was, as it were, hidden.* But the most prominent of these hidden things are inspiration and revelation. Hence, in Jb 4,[133] where Eliphaz testifies that he has received the knowledge of God, he speaks as follows: *Someone stood there whose countenance I did not know, an image before my eyes;* and in the same place:[134] *As if in secret my hearing has received the veins of its whisper.* In secret (*furtive*) is what is in the dark (*furvo*), that is, in the darkness or in concealment.

And Job demonstrates that it should be sought for its preciousness: **[19]** ***The topaz of Ethiopia will not be equal to it.*** Topaz (*topazius*), as Gregory says,[135] is so called as if "of everything" (*topandius*) on account of the fact that the colors of every precious stone shine brightly in it.[136] Ethiopia distributes it, and it signifies divine knowledge, in which the first light of every true and good thing shines brightly. Hence, in the Psalm[137] the Father, speaking to the Son, to whom wisdom is attributed, says: *From the womb before the morning star I begot you in the splendor of the saints;* and "of the saints" (*sanctorum*) is neuter in gender, that is, [indicating that] in the first place the splendors of all holiness and the elegance of the true and the good gleam. And Augustine says that wisdom is the complete art of all the reasoning of the living.[138] Ps:[139] *I have loved your commandments above gold and topaz.* And thus it [that is, wisdom] is precious and noble according to what follows: ***neither will it,*** supply: wisdom, ***be compared to the cleanest dyeing.*** For it is more beautiful than all dyes and colors, which colors are understood as its proofs and demonstrations, according to

131. Is 45.15.

132. Is 53.3.

133. Jb 4.16.

134. Jb 4.12.

135. Gregory, *Mor.* 18.52.84.

136. Although Albert has *topandius* here, Gregory makes clearer the verbal connection between *topazius/topazium* and *topantium,* a Latin term manufactured from the Greek *pan,* meaning "everything": "Topazium uero pretiosus lapis est; et quia graeca lingua *πav,* omne dicitur, pro eo quod omni colore resplendet topazium quasi topantium uocatur" (*Mor.* 18.52.84).

137. Ps 109.3.

138. See Augustine, *c. Acad.* 1.3.6.16; and *De Trin.* 14.1.3.

139. Ps 118.127.

which it is preferred to all the demonstrations of all the sciences because it is received from the divine Spirit Himself, who alone knows divine things. And demonstrations thoroughly purified of phantasms are designated "the cleanest dyeing." Wis 7:[140] *She is the radiance of eternal light, and the spotless mirror of God's majesty, and the image of His goodness.* And from this it is concluded that since, as Aristotle says,[141] every knowledge is of a portion of good and honorable things, but one more than another because it accords with a greater certitude of demonstration, or because it is of better and more wonderful things insofar as its subject [is concerned]; according to both [namely, its greater certitude and its nobler subject] this wisdom, which is knowledge of divine things, excels all others. For nothing is better or more honorable than God, neither is anything more certain than what is received through the inspiration of the Spirit. 1 Cor 2:[142] *No one knows the things that are of God except the Spirit of God. But we have received not the spirit of this world, but the Spirit that is of God, so that we may know the things that have been given to us by God.*

And Job adds a question concerning the teacher [of wisdom]: **[20]** ***Therefore, from where,*** that is, from what teacher, ***does wisdom come?*** Bar 3:[143] *Who has ascended into heaven, and taken her, and brought her down from the clouds? Who has passed over the sea, and found her, and carried her before choice gold? There is no one who is able to know her ways, nor who can search out her paths.*

and where is the place of understanding? The place of understanding, as has been said,[144] into which wisdom draws itself back, is rightly unencumbered and secure; to be sure, understanding is of hidden principles, from which it is drawn out. Wis 7:[145] *Although she is one, she can do all things; while remaining in herself, she renews all things, and throughout the nations she passes into holy souls; she makes of them friends of God and prophets.*

And Job shows its loftiness (*altitudinem*), adding: **[21]** ***It is hid-***

140. Wis 7.26.
141. See Aristotle, *APost.* 1.24.1.
142. 1 Cor 2.11–12.
143. Bar 3.29–31.
144. See above on Jb 28.12, vol. 2, p. 73.
145. Wis 7.27.

den from the eyes of all the living, in this mortal life, of course. Ex 33:[146] *The human shall not see me and live.* In this place Gregory says that one who lives a mortal life is not able to see God.[147] And here the Gloss says: As long as life is lived here, God cannot be seen by the appearance of His own nature.[148]

and it escapes the notice of the birds of the air, that is, the angels soaring to divine contemplation. In chapter 7 of *On the Celestial Hierarchy,* Dionysius says: "Indeed, I declare that only the contemplative origin of their going forth knows completely how many and what kinds of celestial essences there are above the world, and how the hierarchies are perfectly constituted by them. In addition, even they are ignorant of their own powers and illuminations, and their own holy and supermundane ordination."[149] The sense is that the angels do indeed completely, that is perfectly, know (*sciunt*) the divine worlds, but the divine power alone, the origin of their contemplation, completely recognizes (*agnoscit*) them. This is signified in Is 6,[150] where the seraphim *with two wings covered their faces,* indicating that they saw God among shadows and did not comprehend Him perfectly, as God Himself comprehends Himself.

[22] ***Destruction and death have said,*** that is, the demons, who are "destruction" according to fault, and "death" according to punishment, have said in actual fact: ***With our ears we have heard of its fame.*** Indeed, in the very proportion of punishments to fault, which, of course, is said in Wis 11:[151] *Because He disposes all things according to number and weight and measure.* Through another, as it were, they hear of His wisdom, which they do not see through contemplation; thus, indeed, into every land its sound has gone forth, as Basil says,[152] but its fame is small in comparison to what is seen in itself. 1 Kgs 10:[153] *I did not believe those who*

146. Ex 33.20.
147. Gregory, *Mor.* 18.54.89.
148. *GO* on Ex 33.20 (PL 113:290).
149. Dionysius, *CH* 6.1.
150. Is 6.2.
151. Wis 11.21.
152. See Basil, *In Isaiam* 5.161 (PG 30:383).
153. 1 Kgs 10.7.

told me, until I myself came and saw with my own eyes; and I found that not even half had been told to me.

And fifth, Job adds concerning the teacher [of wisdom]: **[23]** ***God understands its way***, that is, [the way] that leads to it. Bar 3:[154] *He who knows all things knows her; and He has discovered her by His providence.* ***and He knows*** through approval and love ***its place,*** hence to him whose face shone brightly with the clarity of wisdom,[155] [God says in] Ex 33:[156] *I know you by name, for you have found favor in my sight.* Wis 7:[157] *God loves no one except him who dwells with wisdom.*

Job adds, moreover, the reason for this: **[24]** ***For He,*** namely, God, ***considers the ends of the earth,*** that is, of all the things of the earth, toward whatever end they may be directed so that they may be perfect. Wis 8:[158] *She reaches from end to end with strength and disposes all things sweetly.* ***and,*** that is, ***He looks upon all things that are under heaven,*** that is, by providence He both determines the end in advance and orders how each thing will arrive at its end. Hence, after Wis 8[159] says, *She reaches from end to end with strength,* it immediately adds, *and has disposed all things sweetly.* But Job says "that are under heaven" because those things seem to be less ordered to an end. And since those things are ordered to an end, it is understood that all other things also are similarly ordered.

Job adds, moreover, things that are among more changeable things: **[25]** ***Who made a weight for the wind.*** Avicenna says:[160] The wind is vapor born of the earth, passing all the way over the air and driving it forcefully. A weight is granted to this when the boundary of its blowing and of its rising is established in advance. Hence, in the apocryphal book of Ezra,[161] the angel Uriel said to Ezra: "Weigh the wind for me!" Ps:[162] *He brings forth winds*

154. Bar 3.32.
155. Namely, to Moses: see Ex 34.29–35.
156. Ex 33.12.
157. Wis 7.28.
158. Wis 8.1.
159. Ibid.
160. See Alb., *Met.* 3.1.5.
161. 4 Esdras (2 Esdras) 4.5.
162. Ps 134.7.

out of His storehouses. ***and hung the waters according to capacity,*** that is, the aqueous vapors, insofar as they ascend, of course, and insofar as they expand through diffusion. Ps:[163] *You have established a boundary, which they will not pass over.* **[26]** ***When He set down a law for the rain,*** namely, concerning where it would rain and where it would not. Jb 38:[164] *Who gave a course to the most violent rainstorm, and a way for the reverberating thunder?* as if He[165] were saying, "No one, except God alone." ***and a way for the reverberating storms,*** of the winds, of course; as if he[166] were saying, "No one, except the wisdom of God, which preordains all things according to the reason of the end of each one."

And this is what follows: **[27]** ***Then He saw it,*** in its very self, of course, ***and explained it*** to the wise through inspiration, ***and prepared*** its place through refinement of the intellect ***and searched it out*** by moving hearts to study. Concerning the first of these, it is said in Jb 13:[167] *Behold, all these things my eyes have seen, and my ears have heard, and I have understood each one.* Concerning the second, Sir 24:[168] *I will pour out prophecy as if before the morning light, and I will expound it all the way into the distance.* Concerning the third, 1 Cor 2:[169] *That eye has not seen, nor ear heard, neither has it entered into the human heart what God has prepared for those who love Him.* Concerning the fourth, in the Psalm:[170] *Seek the Lord and be strengthened: seek His face.* Eccl 1:[171] *I have given my heart to know prudence, and doctrine, and errors, and folly.*

[28] ***And He said to the human*** in his heart: Ps:[172] *I will hear what the Lord God speaks to me.* ***Behold the fear of the Lord, that is, wisdom.*** This expression is by way of the cause (*per causam*). Indeed, "the fear of the Lord" flees sin, but to withdraw from one of [two] contraries is to draw near to the other; hence, to withdraw from

163. Ps 103.9.
164. Jb 38.25.
165. Namely, God, who speaks in ch. 38.
166. Namely, Job, who speaks in the present chapter.
167. Jb 13.1.
168. Sir 24.44, 46.
169. 1 Cor 2.9.
170. Ps 104.4.
171. Eccl 1.17.
172. Ps 84.9.

folly is to draw near to wisdom. Ps:[173] *The fear of the Lord is the beginning of wisdom.* Furthermore, fear, as the Damascene says,[174] concerns what is great, and so fear is wonder, which gives rise to the investigation into wisdom. Aristotle, in Book I of the *Metaphysics,* says that philosophizing, both then and now, has begun from wonder.[175] ***and to withdraw from evil is understanding.*** This expression is by way of the cause (*per causam*). For "to withdraw from evil" grants to wisdom the place of the passions and phantasms in the intellect. Wis 7[176] says that the soul of the just is the seat of wisdom. Speaking of Thrones in *On the Celestial Hierarchy,* Dionysius says that in the whole immateriality the Thrones are receptive to the divinely royal (*thearciti*)[177] arrival. But nothing at all is able to exist in immateriality as long as it is subject to the passions and phantasms. And these are the words of Dionysius in chapter 7 of *On the Celestial Hierarchy:*[178] "It is the characteristic property of the highest and most preeminent Thrones to be completely exalted above every dishonor of subjection; and to move upward to the highest supermundane [reality], ineffably from the extremity into the most sublime; and, with all of their powers, to be unchangingly and firmly established in order around the truly Highest; and to have a receptivity to the advent from above of the divine in all impassibility and immateriality, and to bear God; and to open themselves in friendship to the divine receptions." Such was the litter of King Solomon according to Song 3.[179] Ps:[180] *The Lord's throne is in heaven.* This is among the lofty realities of celestial elegance.

173. Ps 110.10.

174. See John Damascene, *F.o..* 2.15.

175. Aristotle, *Metaph.* 1.2.8.

176. See, e.g., Wis 7.27. See also Wis 7.7, 15.

177. The Latin text has *thearciti,* an apparent attempt to reproduce a Greek word. Weiss points out that this is a spelling error: the actual Greek word should be the adjective (fem. sing.) *thearchikēs.*

178. Dionysius, *CH* 7.6.

179. Song 3.9.

180. Ps 10.5.

CHAPTER 29

JOB ALSO *added.*

In the three preceding chapters blessed Job made clear, from the profundity of divine wisdom, part of his position, namely, that divine governance is dissimilar to every human governance. But because his own life is the subject matter of this disputation, in these three chapters that follow he reveals the second part of his position, namely, that he has suffered innocently and without the cause of evil deserved. For in this chapter Job shows how graced, renowned, and helpful he was—and how intent in persevering—in the state of dignity from which he fell. In the following chapter, namely, chapter 30, he shows how disgraceful, how wretched, and how debased he was in the state of misery into which he fell, in that place:[1] *But now they deride me.* In chapter 31, he shows how innocently he suffered all these things without the cause of evil deserved, in that place:[2] *I made a covenant with my eyes.*

This chapter, therefore, is divided into two parts. In the first, Job shows how renowned he was for deeds of excellence; in the second, he shows how firm he was in his intention, in that place:[3] *And I said: I will die in my little nest.*

In the first part there are four [divisions]. For [first] he describes how excellent he was in the grace of God; second, how excellent he was with regard to the respect of humans, in that place:[4] *When I went out to the gate;* third, how effectively helpful in liberating the oppressed, in that place:[5] *The ear that heard*

1. Jb 30.1.
2. Jb 31.1.
3. Jb 29.18.
4. Jb 29.7.
5. Jb 29.11.

blessed me; fourth, how honorable in virtue and faithful (*pius*) in coming to the aid of the wretched, in that place:[6] *I was clothed with justice.*

In the first [of these divisions] there are three things. First, he wishes for his former state; second, he describes it generally; third, [he describes it] specifically with regard to his family and goods.

And that is:

Job also added. The addition [here] indicates a confirmation of the other part of his opinion, on account of the fact that Job already developed one [part of his opinion] from the profundity of divine wisdom. And, therefore, it says "added" so that he might develop the other [part]. ***taking up his parable:*** this indicates that Job is speaking by way of likenesses. For such speech draws near to human understanding. Prv 1:[7] *Turn your mind to a parable and its interpretation, the words of the wise and their enigmas.* ***and said,*** that is, he proclaimed words of wisdom. Mt 13:[8] *He brings forth from his treasure things new and old.* And he speaks of the state of his past dignity, not in order to boast, but so that he might complete his discussion of wisdom. Sir 11:[9] *On the day of good things do not forget evil things, and on the day of evil things do not forget good things.*

[2] ***Who will grant me,*** that is: O if anyone would grant me! Ps:[10] *Restore to me the joy of your salvation, and strengthen me with a perfect spirit.* ***that I might be according to former months.*** A month is constituted from the gathering together of light on the moon, and it signifies the gathering together of the illuminations of [his] former dignity. Sir 43:[11] *The moon is the sign of a festal day, a light that diminishes in its perfection. "Month" is derived from the word "moon," increasing wonderfully in its perfection.* ***according to the days,*** that is, [according to] illuminations. Ps:[12] *This is the day that the*

6. Jb 29.14.
7. Prv 1.6.
8. Mt 13.52.
9. Sir 11.27.
10. Ps 50.14.
11. Sir 43.7–8.
12. Ps 117.24.

Lord has made. Prv 4:[13] *The path of the just* [*is*] *as a light shining brightly and growing into perfect day.* ***in which God kept me safe,*** that is, preserved me in the good. Wis 10:[14] *The Lord kept him safe from his enemies and defended him from seducers.*

[3] ***When His lamp shone.*** A light in a glass vessel is called a "lamp," and by way of a likeness divine wisdom shining in the human heart is called [a lamp]. Mt 6:[15] *The lamp of your body is your eye.* Is 62:[16] *Her savior is lit like a lamp.* ***over my head.*** "Head" is said on account of the fact that the head guides the whole body; hence when light was given to the head, light was given to the whole body. At the end of Prv:[17] *Her lamp will not be extinguished in the night.* These are the lamps that the wise virgins running to meet the bridegroom hold in their hands in Mt 25.[18] ***and by His light,*** that is, [by] the directing of His grace, ***I walked,*** that is, I made progress, ***in darkness,*** that is, in the midst of doubts. Jn 8:[19] *I am the light of the world: he who follows me does not walk in darkness.* Jn 1:[20] *The light shines in the darkness, and the darkness did not comprehend it,* that is, the light. The contrary is said concerning the wicked in a Psalm:[21] *They have not known nor understood: they walk in darkness.*

Explaining this, Job adds: [4] ***as I was in the days of my youth.*** He does not say "of infancy" or "of childhood" because that stage of life is not capable of divine illumination for the governing of life. Jer 2:[22] *I have remembered you, pitying your youth.* Prv 1:[23] *To give shrewdness to small children, and knowledge and understanding to the youth.*

And he explains this further still by way of parts: ***when secretly.*** What has come forth apart from the public use of the commu-

13. Prv 4.18.
14. Wis 10.12.
15. Mt 6.22.
16. Is 62.1.
17. Prv 31.18.
18. Mt 25.1–13, esp. vv. 1, 4, and 7.
19. Jn 8.12.
20. Jn 1.5.
21. Ps 81.5.
22. Jer 2.2.
23. Prv 1.4.

nity, and this is unusual, is here called a "secret." ***God was in my tabernacle,*** for the purpose, of course, of establishing and multiplying the good of the household, which is called the economic good, which was increased for blessed Job. Ps:[24] *The voice of exultation and of salvation is in the tabernacle of the just.* Similarly, Ps:[25] *You will protect them in your tabernacle from the contradiction of tongues.*

And this he explains by way of parts: **[5]** ***when the Almighty was with me,*** namely, in the progress of every grace. Jos 1:[26] *Take courage and be strong, for I will be with you.* And he adds, regarding the household of the tabernacle: ***and my servants,*** starting from the purity of speech and prepared for obedience to me. Ps:[27] *He who works pride shall not live in the midst of my house. He who says unjust things did not prosper before my eyes.* 1 Tm 3:[28] *If a person does not know how to rule his own household, how will he take care of the church of God?* ***surrounded me,*** certainly so that I could see and consider what all of them did. At the end of Prv:[29] *She has considered the paths of her household and has not eaten her bread at leisure.*

And Job adds concerning the abundance of his household, as much in animals as in resources arising from the earth. And that is: **[6]** ***when I washed my feet with butter,*** that is, I was abounding in every fatness of animals to such an extent that it was sufficient to wash my feet. Is 7:[30] *A person will nourish a young cow and two sheep, and in view of the abundance of milk he will eat butter.* ***and the rock poured out streams of oil for me,*** according to the letter: oil is pressed out of the watery fluid in concave rocks, and, purified in this way, it is poured out of the rock; by this every fatness of resources arising from the earth is understood. Gn 27:[31] *I have established him with grain, wine, and oil.* Is 55:[32] *Listen, you who hear me: eat what is good, and your soul will take pleasure in fatness.*

24. Ps 117.15.
25. Ps 30.21.
26. Jos 1.6, 5.
27. Ps 100.7.
28. 1 Tm 3.5.
29. Prv 31.27.
30. Is 7.21–22.
31. Gn 27.37.
32. Is 55.2.

[7] ***When did I go out.***

Job touches on how excellent he was with regard to the respect of humans, and he specifies five different kinds [of people], namely, judges, young men, old men, princes, and leaders. And that is: ***When did I go out to the gate of the city,*** so that, to be sure, I might preside over it in judgment, and where from antiquity[33] judges assembled, lest the tumult of lawsuits disturb the peace of the citizens. ***and,*** that is, even ***in the street,*** that is, in the wide area where judges came together, ***they prepared a chair for me?*** supply: in particular. The home of those skilled in speaking (*catheorantium aedes*), that is, of those teaching, is called a "chair" (*cathedra*). Ps:[34] *Let them exalt Him in the assembly of the people and praise Him in the chair of the elders.* Dn 13:[35] *Come and sit down in the midst of us, and reveal it to us, because God has given you the honor of old age.* At the end of Prv:[36] *Her husband is well known in the gates, when he sits among the senators of the land.*

And concerning young men, he adds: **[8]** ***The young men saw me,*** that is, youthful in their morals, they followed the strong impulse of their own passion. 2 Tm 2:[37] *Flee youthful desires.* And this is what follows: ***and hid themselves,*** feeling ashamed because of their unlikeness to Him. Gn 3:[38] *I heard your voice, Lord, in paradise, and I was afraid because I was naked, and I hid myself.* ***and the old men*** of hoary mind. Wis 4:[39] *The understanding of a man is his gray hair, and a blameless life is the attainment of old age.* ***rising to their feet, stood up,*** showing respect, of course. For respect ought to be shown to the wiser and more mature person. Lv 19:[40] *Stand up before the hoary head, and respect the person of old age.* **[9]** ***The princes ceased to speak.*** The "princes" hold the first place in wisdom and virtue. Is 32:[41] *He who is foolish will no longer be prince, neither will*

33. Here I follow MSS F and M, which read *antiquitus,* instead of Weiss's edition, which omits it.

34. Ps 106.32.

35. Dn 13.50.

36. Prv 31.23.

37. 2 Tm 2.22.

38. Gn 3.10.

39. Wis 4.8–9.

40. Lv 19.32.

41. Is 32.5.

the deceitful be called great. ***and they put their fingers over their mouths,*** which is the sign of the most attentive listening while maintaining silence; and the sense is that even the wise were listening to his words with such eagerness that they were pressing their mouths closed, so that they might not hinder the speech of the wise man by their own talkativeness. Sir 20:[42] *There is one who remains silent, he is found wise; and there is one who is odious, he is bold in speech.* And in that same place:[43] *There is one who remains silent, knowing the proper time. A wise person will remain silent until the right time.* At the end of Job:[44] *I will put my finger over my mouth.* Ps:[45] *I became as a man who does not hear, and who does not have any reproofs in his mouth.*

[10] ***The leaders,*** who became leaders of other people because of the excellence of their wisdom, ***restrained their voices.*** For Aristotle says in Book III of the *Topics*:[46] No one chooses young leaders, on account of the fact that it is not evident that they are wise. Sir 32:[47] *Listen in silence, and because of your reverence good grace will come to you.* And in that same place:[48] *In many things be as if you were ignorant, and listen in silence at the same time as you also inquire. When speaking in the company of important people, you should not be presumptuous; and where the aged are present, you should not speak much.* ***and their tongues,*** namely, of the leaders, ***cleaved,*** certainly so that they might meditate on the words of the wiser man, ***to their throats,*** which join their tongues to their hearts. Sir 6:[49] *Stand among the multitude of the prudent elders, and join yourself from your heart to their wisdom, so that you may be able to hear every account of God and so that the proverbs of praise may not escape you.*

[11] ***The ear that heard.***

Here Job touches on how excellent he was in his actions of

42. Sir 20.5.

43. Sir 20.6–7.

44. The words that follow are not from the end of Jb, but rather are similar to those of Jb 21.5. Albert seems to be working from memory and simply recalling the gist of this verse rather than its exact wording.

45. Ps 37.15.

46. Aristotle, *Top.* 3.3.5.

47. Sir 32.9.

48. Sir 32.12–13.

49. Sir 6.35.

leadership against the wicked: ***The ear that heard,*** supply: of my reputation, ***blessed me.*** Lk 1:[50] *For, behold, from this day forward all generations will call me blessed.* ***and the eye that saw,*** that his works were greater than his reputation, ***gave testimony to me,*** namely, [the testimony] of praise and virtue. 2 Chr 9:[51] *I did not believe those who told me, until I myself came and saw with my own eyes; and I showed that barely half of your wisdom had been told to me. You have exceeded your reputation with your virtues.*

Concerning the basis of his reputation, moreover, he adds: [12] ***because I had delivered the poor man,*** who did not have money for his own deliverance, ***who cried out,*** that is, complaining of his oppressor. Ps:[52] *He will save the children of the poor, and he will humble the oppressor.* ***and the orphan,*** who did not have the protection of a father, and that is: ***who had no helper.*** Ps:[53] *The poor man has been abandoned to you; you will be a helper to the orphan.*

[13] ***The blessing of the one who was about to die came upon me,*** that is, who would have been about to die at another time, if I had not come to help. Prv 24:[54] *Pluck up those who are being led to death, and do not hesitate to deliver those who are being dragged off to destruction.* ***and the heart of the widow,*** who did not have the protection of a husband, ***I comforted,*** namely, by coming to help in the manner of Elisha in 2 Kgs 4,[55] who, when the oil of his faithfulness (*pietatis*) had been multiplied, liberated the widow and her son from their creditor and supplied them with enough to live. 1 Tm 5:[56] *Honor widows who are truly widows.*

[14] ***I was clothed with justice.***

Here Job touches on his disposition toward justice and his work of faithfulness (*pietatis*) among the wretched.

And that is: ***I was clothed,*** that is, completely covered up, lest he appear to some extent stripped (*nudum*) of justice. ***with justice,*** in general, of course, which belongs to every virtue, according to which it corresponds to the law. For the law, as Aristotle

50. Lk 1.48.
51. 2 Chr 9.6.
52. Ps 71.4.
53. Ps 10.14 (according to the Hebrew).
54. Prv 24.11.
55. 2 Kgs 4.7.
56. 1 Tm 5.3.

says, instructs concerning every virtue.[57] Is 61:[58] *The Lord has clothed me with the garment of salvation, and with the robe of justice He has covered me.* Rv 3:[59] *So that you might be clothed in white garments, and that the shame of your nakedness might not appear.* Eccl 9:[60] *At all times let your garments be white, and let oil not depart from your head.* ***and I dressed myself with my judgment, as with a garment,*** as is usual for carrying out work. Ps:[61] *The queen stood at your right hand in a gilded garment, surrounded with variety.* Eph 4:[62] *Put on the new man, who is created according to God in justice and holiness of truth.* ***and with a crown,*** supply: you have clothed me. For a "crown" is a sign of right judgment according to reason. Ps:[63] *You have crowned him with glory and honor.* Sir 45:[64] *A crown of gold upon his mitre, engraved with a sign of sanctity, and the glory of honor, and the work of power.*

And concerning his faithfulness (*pietate*) among the wretched, Job adds: **[15]** ***I was an eye to the blind person,*** by giving light to him spiritually and bodily. Mt 11:[65] *The blind see and the deaf hear.* ***and a foot to the lame one,*** certainly by carrying him where he was not able to go by means of his own foot. At the end of Gal:[66] *Bear the burdens of one another; and in this way you will fulfill the law of Christ.* **[16]** ***I was the father of poor people.*** Sir 4:[67] *Do not turn your eyes away from the poor.* And in the same place:[68] *In judging be merciful to the fatherless as a father, and as a husband to their mother.* And this is what follows: ***and the cause that I did not know,*** according to justice, of course, with respect to both circumstances and allegations, ***I investigated most diligently,*** certainly so that I might omit nothing concerning the rule of law (*de ordine iuris*) and do

57. Aristotle, *EN* 5.1.14.
58. Is 61.10.
59. Rv 3.18.
60. Eccl 9.8.
61. Ps 44.10.
62. Eph 4.24.
63. Ps 8.6.
64. Sir 45.14.
65. Mt 11.5.
66. Gal 6.2.
67. Sir 4.5.
68. Sir 4.10.

injury to no one. Dt 16:[69] *You shall strive justly after what is just.* Tb 14:[70] *Seek to do the things that are pleasing to Him, in truth and with all your power.* Dt 13:[71] *Carefully examine the truth of the matter,* [*and*] *if you find that what is alleged is certain, and that this abomination has been committed, you shall strike the inhabitants of that city with the edge of the sword.*

[17] ***I crushed the jaws of the wicked one,*** with which he was devouring the poor, of course. 1 Sm 17:[72] *I grabbed their throats, and I strangled and killed them.* ***and I snatched the prey out of his teeth.*** Ps 57:[73] *The Lord breaks the grinders of the lions.* Prv 30:[74] *There is a generation that has swords for teeth, and grinds with their molars, to devour the needy from the earth.* 1 Sm 17:[75] *I pursued them, and struck them, and plucked the prey out of their mouth.* Am 3:[76] *Just as if a shepherd should pluck from the lion's mouth two legs or the tip of an ear, so shall the children of Israel be taken out.*

[18] ***And I said.***

Here Job mentions the firmness of his intention to persevere as much in good works in themselves as in good works of kindness toward his neighbor, in that place:[77] *Those who heard me.* [He treats his intention to persevere] in good works in themselves in a threefold way, namely, with regard to his intention, with regard to the cause of his intention, and with regard to its effect.

And that is: ***And I said,*** on account of my intention of persevering, of course. Ps:[78] *I speak my works to the king.* ***I will die in my little nest,*** that is, I will persevere all the way to death. He says[79] "little nest" according to humility. A nest is built by a bird from many things gathered together, so that it might rest there and nurture

69. Dt 16.20.
70. Tb 14.10–11.
71. Dt 13.14–15.
72. 1 Sm 17.35.
73. Ps 57.7.
74. Prv 30.14.
75. 1 Sm 17.35.
76. Am 3.12.
77. Jb 29.21.
78. Ps 44.2.
79. Here I read *dicit* with MSS F and M, rather than the *vocat* of Weiss's edition.

its chicks; and this signifies the tranquility of peace in conscience produced from many good works deserving of praise and from devotion to meditating, speaking, and working, in which [tranquility] the mind (*animus*) rests and nurtures its spiritual offspring. Ps:[80] *The sparrow has found a home for herself, and the turtledove a nest for herself where she may lay her chicks: your altars, O Lord of Hosts.* There are those, however,[81] who leave this nest behind, of whom it is said in Is 16:[82] *And it will come to pass: as a bird flying away and chicks flying out of the nest, so will the children of Moab be in the passage of Arnon.* Moab, a useless father, signifies the devil; the children of Moab signify souls enslaved to the devil; [and] Arnon signifies evil speech, for those who leave behind the peace of the heart tend toward evil speech. Prv 27:[83] *As a bird flying away from its nest, so is a man who leaves his place behind.* For the place of a good man is the quiet of the heart. Eccl 10:[84] *If the spirit of one who has power comes upon you, do not leave your place.* Moreover, to die signifies here[85] to die to the world, and to die to external things, and to be buried in the light of the Lord's face. Ps:[86] *Precious in the sight of the Lord is the death of His saints.* Explaining this, Maximus speaks thus:[87] The most precious passing over into the light of the Lord's sight, by which they are hidden from all external things and die to themselves and to the world. The death of the saints is worthy of the reward of beatitude.

On the dream of Scipio, Macrobius says:[88] A human is said to die when the soul, still established in the body, despises corporeal enticements, as philosophy teaches, and casts off the sweet snares of cupidity and all remaining passions.[89]

80. Ps 83.4.

81. Here I read the *autem* that MSS F and M add, rather than Weiss's edition.

82. Is 16.2.

83. Prv 27.8.

84. Eccl 10.4.

85. That is, in Jb 29.18, on which Albert is commenting.

86. Ps 115.15.

87. Cf. Maximus Confessor, *Loc. comm.* 36 (PG 91:899–902); and Alb., *ST* 2.4.14.

88. Macrobius, *CSS* 1.13.6.

89. This paragraph ("On the dream ... remaining passions") is an addition in MSS F and M.

Col 3:[90] *For you are dead, and your life is hidden with Christ in God.* ***and as a palm tree,*** which grows from something small into something great, and from something undeveloped into something beautiful and fruitful, ***I will multiply my days,*** that is, illuminations. Ps:[91] *The just one shall flourish like a palm tree in the house of the Lord.* Song 7:[92] *I said: I will climb up into the palm tree and will lay hold of its fruit.*

And lest such an excellent intention of making progress be thought to be presumption, Job adds the cause: **[19]** ***My root,*** that is, the intention of [my] devotion and desire, ***has been uncovered*** through desire ***beside the waters,*** that is, the downward course of the consolations and the gifts of the Holy Spirit. Jer 17:[93] *He will be like a green tree, which has been transplanted beside the waters, which sends out its roots toward moisture, and it will not fear when the heat comes. And its leaf will be green, and in the time of drought it will not be concerned, neither will it cease at any time to bring forth fruit.* Sir 24:[94] *I took root among an honorable people.* Eph 3:[95] *Rooted and established in charity.* And Job says this[96] with regard to prevenient grace. And, concerning subsequent grace, he adds: ***and dew will linger,*** which signifies grace descending from heaven, ***in the midst of my harvest,*** materially, that is, in the crops to be reaped and to be gathered into the storehouse of the Lord. That is, just as the dew increases, softens, and brings together [what is harvested] according to an orderly arrangement, so that the crops taste good, in this way heavenly grace will increase merits for me, soften them according to piety, moisten them, so that, ripened by the heat of charity, [the crop] might produce a good flavor. These two things[97] are similarly spoken of in Gn 27:[98] *In the abundance of the earth and in the dew of heaven from above shall your blessing be.* Is 26:[99] *Your dew is the dew of the light, and you shall*

90. Col 3.3.
91. Ps 91.13.
92. Song 7.8.
93. Jer 17.8.
94. Sir 24.16.
95. Eph 3.17.
96. Namely, the words of Jb 29.19a.
97. Namely, the dew and the harvest.
98. Gn 27.39–40.
99. Is 26.19.

drag the land of the giants down into destruction. Dt 33:[100] *The heavens shall be misty with dew.* By reason of such an excellent cause, therefore, Job took continuous progress for granted.

And this is what follows: [20] ***My glory,*** namely, of conscience, whose glory is in good merits, ***will always be renewed.*** 2 Cor 1:[101] *Our glory is this: the testimony of our conscience.* ***and my bow,*** that is, my purpose or intention of reaching the goal by means of all good meritorious works, just as a bow hits its mark by means of arrows, ***will always be established,*** so that it might always discharge more and more [good works], of course, ***in my hand,*** that is, in my working. Gn 48:[102] *I am giving you one portion beyond your brothers, which [portion] I took from the hand of the Amorites with my sword and my bow.* Ps:[103] *As arrows in the hand of the mighty, so the children of those who have been cast out.* The children of those who have been cast out are arrows hurled out from the bow to hit the mark.

Moreover, Job adds how excellent he was in his intention toward others, as much in teaching as in the example of his presence: [21] ***Those who heard me,*** teaching and making judgments, of course, ***waited for,*** stretching out toward me, to be sure, ***my opinion* (sententiam)**. An approved truth signified by words and having its strength from the authority of the one advancing it is called an "opinion" (*sententiam*). Wis 8:[104] *Through wisdom I shall be found keen in judgment, and I will be admired in the sight of the mighty.* ***and being attentive,*** to me, of course, ***they were silent at my counsel,*** that is to say, receiving my pronouncement with deference. "Counsel" is a pronouncement concerning things to be done, as Gregory says.[105] Prv 8:[106] *Counsel is mine, and equity; prudence is mine, fortitude is mine. By me kings reign and lawgivers decree just things.* The word in him (*in ipso*), therefore, was of such great authority.

And Job adds how excellent was the word according to itself

100. Dt 33.28.
101. 2 Cor 1.12.
102. Gn 48.22.
103. Ps 126.4.
104. Wis 8.11.
105. See Gregory, *Mor.* 20.2.2.
106. Prv 8.14–15.

(*secundum se*): **[22]** ***To my words they dared to add nothing,*** in which the full perfection of the word is signified, for that is fully perfect to which nothing can be added, as Aristotle maintains in Book I of *On Heaven and Earth.*[107] At the end of Rv:[108] *If anyone adds to these words, God will add to him the plagues that are written in this book.*

Then he mentions the order of words, in what way they were ordered, of course: ***and my speech fell in drops,*** my act of speaking having been ordered, ***upon them,*** namely, those listening. Dt 32:[109] *Let my speech fall gradually as the dew, as a shower upon the vegetation, and as drops upon the grass.*

And because his discourse was authentic, perfect, and ordered, for that reason it follows: **[23]** ***They,*** namely, the listeners, ***waited for me as for rain,*** which, to be sure, makes all things fruitful and makes them flourish and sprout forth. Ps:[110] *You shall set apart a gracious rain, O God, for your inheritance.* ***and they opened,*** in order to be receptive to instruction (*doctrinae*), ***their mouth,*** the desire of their heart, of course, ***as if for a belated shower,*** which certainly completes the orderly arrangement appropriate among the crops, lest, when that part of them that is in the ground has been burned up, they become bitter. Ps:[111] *Open your mouth, and I will fill it.* Hos 6:[112] *He will come to us as the early and the late shower* [*come*] *to the earth.*

And Job adds how excellent he was in the example [he gave] to his subjects: **[24]** ***If at any time I laughed at them,*** exhibiting lightheartedness, which should be done sometimes. Sir 4:[113] *Do not be as a lion in your house, destroying the members of your household,* ***they did not believe,*** that it was laughter that he had laughed, of course, but that it was the lightheartedness of benevolence with great, restrained maturity, possessing no foolishness. Eccl 2:[114] *Laughter I considered error; and to joy I said: Why are you deceived in vain?*

107. Aristotle, *Cael.* 1.2.9.
108. Rv 22.18.
109. Dt 32.2.
110. Ps 67.10.
111. Ps 80.11.
112. Hos 6.3.
113. Sir 4.35.
114. Eccl 2.2.

And he explains this, adding: ***and,*** that is, ***the light of my face,*** having been shown in lightheartedness, ***did not fall to the ground,*** that is, for trampling underfoot, as the light of those who possess a foolish and negligent joy, about whom it is said in Wis 14:[115] *When they are joyful, they are insane.*

Job adds, moreover, how this was: **[25]** ***If I wanted to go to them,*** by exhibiting a serene expression,[116] of course, ***I sat*** extending in front [of them] the peace and maturity of heart ***first,*** not freed from the responsibility of my office by foolish delight; on account of this, in fact, a seat is set in place for the judges, that by their sitting they may indicate peace and tranquility of the heart. Sir 21:[117] *A fool raises his voice in laughter; but a wise man will scarcely laugh in silence.* ***and when I sat as a king,*** he is called a "king" because he is the example for all by word and by deed, ***with an army standing around me,*** so that all would receive their form (*formam*) from me. Wis 18:[118] *On his priestly robe the whole world was depicted.* Prv 20:[119] *The king, who sits on the throne of His judgment, scatters every evil with His gaze.* ***I was nevertheless a comforter of those in mourning,*** for although he would be strict with respect to the wicked, nevertheless he was merciful toward the miserable. Prv 20:[120] *Mercy and truth preserve the king, and his throne is strengthened by clemency.* Is 16:[121] *His throne will be prepared in mercy, and He will sit upon it in truth.*

115. Wis 14.28.

116. Here I read *serenitatem vultus* with MSS T, F, and M, rather than the *securitatem vultus* of Weiss's edition.

117. Sir 21.23.

118. Wis 18.24.

119. Prv 20.8.

120. Prv 20.28.

121. Is 16.5.

CHAPTER 30

B*UT NOW they mock me.*

Here blessed Job describes in a threefold way the misery into which he fell; and accordingly this chapter is divided into three parts.

In the first part, in fact, he describes those who were inflicting misery [upon him]; in the second part, the magnitude of the misery that he sustained, in that place:[1] *And now within my very self* [*my soul withers*]; in the third part, that he seemed to be spurned even by God, in that place:[2] *I will cry out to you, and you will not hear me.*

In the first part there are two divisions: a description of those afflicting him; and the rationale of those deriding him, in that place:[3] *For He has opened His quiver.* In the first of these, those afflicting or deriding him are described in seven ways from [a consideration of] themselves *per se* and in one way from [a consideration of] their parents, which makes eight. And after these ways, a first conclusion is set forth.

And that is: ***But now they mock me,*** that is, they despise me by laughing. Jb 12:[4] *The simplicity of the just man is mocked.* Ps:[5] *All who have seen me have mocked me; they have spoken with their lips, and they have wagged their heads.* And he describes them, saying: ***the younger in time,*** not only in age but pursuing youthful things with respect to behavior, just as they derided Elisha in 2 Kgs 2; hence it is said:[6] *Boys, small not in malice but in age, came out of the city and mocked Elisha, saying: Go away, baldhead! Go away, baldhead!*

1. Jb 30.16.
2. Jb 30.20.
3. Jb 30.11.
4. Jb 12.4.
5. Ps 21.8.
6. 2 Kgs 2.23.

Second, Job also describes the baseness of these people, adding: ***whose fathers I did not deem worthy,*** for these are their children, and children not only according to nature but also according to baseness, ***to place with the dogs of my flock.*** This must be read with contempt, for shepherds are more worthy who have certain worthless [creatures] under them, who lead dogs with their flocks; and these people were not able to rise to the dignity of such worthless animals. 1 Sm 24:[7] *You seek a dead dog and a living flea.* Is 56:[8] *The most shameless dogs do not know satiety.* Ps:[9] *They will suffer hunger like dogs, and they will wander through the city.* And the sense is that they were reputed to be unworthy of the most worthless duties.

Third, Job describes them from the point of view of their forsaking of the mechanical craft (*artis mechanicae*): **[2]** ***The strength of whose hands,*** the "strength of the hands" indicates a craft that is cultivated with the hands, ***was to me as nothing;*** for these people were without skill, contributing nothing to city living, and therefore completely useless. In a letter Jerome says: Just as a broken vessel of a human is rendered useless, so are they; such ones are called idols because they have none of the action of a human. Wis 13:[10] *A piece thereof left over, which is good for no use, wood crooked and full of knots, he carefully carves in his leisure and shapes it by the knowledge of his craft.* Indeed, such have the figure of a human but not the action.

Fourth, he describes them from the point of view of the unworthiness of life because of the shameful acts they have committed. Ex 22:[11] *You shall not allow wizards to live.* And that is: ***and they were thought unworthy of life.***

Fifth, Job describes them as having the worst luck, and he expands on this; and that is: **[3]** ***Barren with poverty and hunger.*** The scarcity of the one who wanders around doorways is poverty, but failure from a lack of inner nourishment is hunger. Eccl 5:[12] *He has fathered a son who will be in extreme poverty.* And expanding

7. 1 Sm 24.15.
8. Is 56.11.
9. Ps 58.7.
10. Wis 13.13.
11. Ex 22.18.
12. Eccl 5.13.

on this, he adds: ***who gnawed in the wilderness.*** He says "in the wilderness" because, violating the community of human beings (*societatem hominum*), they were compelled to flee into the wilderness, in the manner of robbers. Lam 4:[13] *The daughter of my people is cruel, like the ostrich in the desert.* He says they "gnawed" because they did not have soft and palatable things to eat but were forced to gnaw hard things. There is a parallel in Lk 15:[14] *He longed to fill his stomach with the pods that the pigs were eating, but no one gave him anything.* And he adds the cause of this: ***filthy*** **(squalentes)**. One whose bodily complexion is made darker when loose skin has been burned is called "filthy." Lam 1:[15] *Her virgins are filthy, and she is oppressed with bitterness.* ***with calamity*** **(calamitate)**, that is, with the lack of produce from the stalk (*calami*), ***and with misery,*** that is, with the failure of inner strength. Lam 2:[16] *They said to their mothers: "Where are bread and wine?" as they fainted like the wounded in the streets of the city.*

And he expands on this more, adding: **[4]** ***and they ate grass,*** that is, they were compelled to eat raw vegetation, because food was insufficient, because Avicenna says that nature provides insufficient food for the human person apart from milk; other foods, however, should be boiled or baked. Jb 40:[17] *He will eat grass like an ox.* Dn 4:[18] *You will eat grass like an ox.* ***and the barks of trees,*** on account of the fact that they can be ground into powder, because it is not the wood [of the trees]. And he expands on this still more, adding: ***and the root of junipers,*** which were softer because of the moisture of the earth, ***was their food.*** Lam 4:[19] *Those who ate with pleasure have embraced the dung.* **[5]** ***who snatched these things up out of the valleys,*** for in "the valleys" things are more moist and edible, but in the mountains they are harder; and he says "snatched" in order to signify the vehement desire to take [edible things] to themselves on account of excessive hunger, ***and when they had found any of them,*** he says "any of them" (*sin-*

13. Lam 4.3.
14. Lk 15.16.
15. Lam 1.4.
16. Lam 2.12.
17. Jb 40.10.
18. Dn 4.22.
19. Lam 4.5.

gula) in order to signify a moderate number [of edible things], which did not satisfy their hunger, but drew out a miserable life. ***they ran toward them with a loud cry,*** in the manner of pigs, of course, who grunt when they see acorns. But in Greek such a craving is called *gastrimargia,* from *gastris,* which means "stomach," and *margino, marginas,* which means "I am mad, you are mad." Is 56:[20] *The most shameless dogs do not know satiety.*

Sixth, Job describes them from the point of view of their basest[21] dwelling place: **[6]** ***They dwelled in the deserted places of torrents,*** because "torrents," by flowing down and hollowing out the earth, produce hiding places. And he explains this, adding: ***and in caves of earth,*** for otherwise they would not safely have escaped notice. Is 2:[22] *Enter into the rock, and hide in the ditch in the earth from the face of the fear of the Lord.* ***or upon gravel,*** movable sand that is drawn out of the water is called "gravel," and here it signifies a firm place among the marshes where bandits live on account of its protection, because such places are inaccessible. There is a parallel in Heb 11:[23] *Wandering in wildernesses, in mountains, and in caves of the earth.* Jb 21:[24] *He was delightful to the gravel of Cocytus.*

Seventh, Job describes them from the point of view of their most miserable pleasures: [7] ***They rejoiced among things of this sort,*** if they were ever able to have them, due to excessive starvation, of course. Jb 6:[25] *The things that my soul previously was unwilling to touch, now because of anguish are my food.* Prv 27:[26] *A soul that is full will tread upon the honeycomb, but a soul that is hungry will take even something bitter for something sweet.* ***and they considered it delightful,*** that is, according to delights, ***to be under the briars,*** that is, to be under base things, provided that they were able to be [there]. Jer 48:[27] *He has rested on his dregs.* Is 36:[28] *They may eat their own dung and drink their own urine.*

20. Is 56.11.
21. Here I read *infima,* which is added in MSS F and M.
22. Is 2.10.
23. Heb 11.38.
24. Jb 21.33.
25. Jb 6.7.
26. Prv 27.7.
27. Jer 48.11.
28. Is 36.12.

Eighth, Job describes them from the point of view of their birth: [8] ***The children of foolish,*** that is, of those deprived of every good habit of the soul, ***and ignoble men,*** of those destitute of illustrious origins. Ex 34:[29] *Those who despise me will be ignoble.* ***And those not appearing at all on the earth,*** namely, through any dignity that they might have had. For they were destitute of any paternal or ancestral dignity, and they were respectable personalities among no one. Wis 4:[30] *All children who are born of the unjust are witnesses of wickedness against their parents.*

After all these things, Job sets forth a conclusion: **[9]** ***Now I have been turned into their,*** namely, such people's, ***song,*** so that they might compose derisive songs about me, of course. Lam 3:[31] *I have been made into a laughingstock to all people, their song all day long.* ***and I have been made into a proverb for them,*** namely, so that they might understand a proverb of cursing concerning me, saying: "May God curse you, just as He cursed Job." Ps:[32] *You have made us into a parable for the nations, a wagging of the head among the peoples.* Lam 1:[33] *Look, O Lord, and see, since I have become worthless.*

[10] ***They abhor me,*** that is, I am abominable to those who are abominable to all. The same is said in Jb 19:[34] *Even fools despised me; and when I had retreated from them, they spoke against me. Those who were formerly my counselors have hated me.* ***and flee far from me,*** lest they share anything in common with me, of course. Ps:[35] *Those who were close to me have stood far off.* ***and they are not afraid to spit in my face.*** According to the letter: just as they spat on the unclean, in fact, and the detestable.[36] Mt 26:[37] *Then they spat in his face and struck him with blows; and they slapped his face.*

Job adds, moreover, the reason they had for doing these inappropriate things. Supply: Because **[11]** ***For He,*** supply: God,

29. The following text is not from Ex 34, but rather is from 1 Sm 2.30.

30. Wis 4.6.

31. Lam 3.14.

32. Ps 43.15.

33. Lam 1.11.

34. Jb 19.18–19.

35. Ps 37.12.

36. Here I read *abominabilem* with MSS E, F, and M, rather than *abominatum* with Weiss's edition.

37. Mt 26.67.

has opened His quiver, in order to draw out projectiles (*missilia*), of course, ***and has afflicted me,*** by sending[38] His arrows (*sagittas*) into me. Jb 6:[39] *The arrows of the Lord are in me, the anger of which drinks up my spirit.* Lam 3:[40] *He has shot into my kidneys the daughters of His quiver.* He has wounded me severely ***and has put a bridle into my mouth,*** by which He might draw "my mouth" back tightly, of course, lest I be able to contradict Him.[41] And this "bridle" was a multitude of blows,[42] which was the reason of those disparaging [Job];[43] and it functioned to silence the one speaking against them.[44] Is 37:[45] *I will put a ring in your nostrils, and a bridle between your lips.* Ps:[46] *I became as a man who does not hear, and who does not have any reproofs in his mouth.* Similarly:[47] *I have established a defense for my mouth when the sinner made a stand against me.*

And therefore, supply: because in this way the Lord caused [me] to be silent, **[12]** ***At the right hand of my rising.*** In Book II of *On Heaven and Earth,* Aristotle says:[48] The right hand is the source of movement, that is, with perfect vigor and violence they rose and were lifted up. And that is: ***my calamities immediately,*** that is, without interruption, ***sprang up,*** that is, they lifted themselves up above me. Lam 1:[49] *Look, O Lord, and see, because my enemy has been lifted up.* And he adds what they have brought about: ***they have turned my feet upside down,*** by means of which I ought to have made progress in good deeds, of course. Gn 27:[50] *Behold, he has tripped me up a second time.* ***and have overwhelmed me,*** by bringing

38. Here I read *mittendo* with MSS E, F, and M, rather than *mittens* with Weiss's edition.

39. Jb 6.4.

40. Lam 3.13.

41. Here I read *ei,* which is added in MSS E, F, and M, but omitted from Weiss's edition.

42. Here I read *plagarum* with MSS E, F, and M, rather than *plagae* with Weiss's edition.

43. That is, it was the reason why those who disparaged Job did so.

44. Namely, Job.

45. Is 37.29.

46. Ps 37.15.

47. Ps 38.2.

48. Aristotle, *Cael.* 2.2.6.

49. Lam 1.9.

50. Gn 27.36.

in violence, of course, ***with their paths,*** coming over me certainly, ***as with waves,*** that is to say, coming upon [me] like waves. Ps:[51] *All of your waves have passed over me.* Jon 2:[52] *All of your billows and your waves have passed over me.* **[13]** ***They have scattered my paths,*** lest I have an unimpeded passage whereby to flee from them, of course. Ps:[53] *They have set up a stumbling block for me near the path.* ***they have lain in wait for me,*** like a birdcatcher or hunter. Lam 3:[54] *They have begun hunting my soul like a bird.* Ps:[55] *He lies in wait in secret like a lion in its den.* Hab 1:[56] *Judgment has occurred, but opposition is more powerful.* And a little beyond this:[57] *The wicked one prevails against the just man, perverse judgment therefore goes forth.* ***and there was no one who provided help.*** Sir 51:[58] *They surrounded me on every side, and there was no one who would help.* Is 63:[59] *I looked around and there was no helper; I sought, and there was none who would give aid.*

And therefore, supply: because no one was resisting: **[14]** ***As if when a wall has been broken,*** that is, when every impediment serving as defense has been removed. Lam 2:[60] *The wall has been destroyed altogether.*[61] ***and a gate has been opened,*** that is, a way has been made available. Is 51:[62] *You have laid your body as a way for those passing over.* Ps:[63] *My enemies have trampled me underfoot all day.* ***they have rushed in upon me,*** with a great assault of fierceness, of course, ***and have tumbled down,*** coming like a throng, to be sure, ***toward my miseries,*** supply: by augmenting and multiplying [them]. Above in [chapter] 16:[64] *He has cut me to pieces with wound after wound; He has rushed headlong against me like a giant.*

51. Ps 41.8.
52. Jon 2.4.
53. Ps 139.6.
54. Lam 3.52.
55. Ps 10.9.
56. Hab 1.3.
57. Hab 1.4.
58. Sir 51.10.
59. Is 63.5.
60. Lam 2.8.
61. Here I read *pariter,* which is added in MSS T, E, F, and M, but omitted from Weiss's edition.
62. Is 51.23.
63. Ps 55.3.
64. Jb 16.15.

And so, supply: by many tribulations **[15]** ***I have been reduced to nothing.*** Ps:[65] *I was reduced to nothing, and I did not know it.* Jb 7:[66] *I have given up hope. By no means will I live any longer now.* ***as the wind,*** blowing away, ***He,*** supply: God, ***has taken away my desire,*** that is, everything desirable to me. Lam 1:[67] *The enemy has stretched out his hand upon all her desirable things.* Ezek 24:[68] *I will take away from you what is desirable to your eyes.* Hos 9:[69] *Nettles shall inherit their desirable silver, burrs shall be in their tabernacles.* ***and my prosperity*** **(salus)**, namely, temporal, ***has passed away like a cloud.*** Hos 6:[70] *Your mercy is as a morning cloud, and as the dew that goes away early in the morning.*

[16] ***And now within my very self*** **[*my soul withers*].**

Here Job enumerates the sufferings that he sustained in his very self. First, in his soul; in his body; according to numerical magnitude; according to the extent of the trial, [and] according to the effect.

And that is: ***And now,*** namely, at the time of my affliction, ***within my very self,*** that is, according to sadness, which I have within my very self, and desertion, so that this expression is [uttered] by way of the cause [of this sadness]: ***my soul withers.*** 1 Mc 6:[71] *Into how much tribulation have I come, and into what great floods of sorrow, in which I now am, because I was pleasant and beloved in my power?* And this is what follows: ***and the days of affliction seize me.*** He says "seize" because, being destitute of his own power, he was in the power of the tribulation. Is 37:[72] *This is the day of tribulation and of the strait of correction, and the day of blasphemy.*

And Job adds concerning the body: **[17]** ***In the night,*** when the weak are afflicted more severely, ***my bone,*** for pain extends all the way to the depth of my bones, ***is pierced with pains,*** that is, with pricks of pain and with worms. Ps:[73] *My bones have dried up like firewood.*

65. Ps 72.22.
66. Jb 7.16.
67. Lam 1.10.
68. Ezek 24.16.
69. Hos 9.6.
70. Hos 6.4.
71. 1 Mc 6.11.
72. Is 37.3.
73. Ps 101.4.

And, concerning the continuous nature of his affliction, he adds: ***and those who eat away at me do not sleep,*** whether gnawing pains or even worms. For pains "eat away at" bodily strength, but worms gnaw the substance to pieces. Jer 51:[74] *The king of Babylon has eaten away at me, he has devoured me. He has made me as an empty vessel; he has swallowed me up like a dragon.*

And, concerning the multitude [of his sufferings], he adds: **[18]** ***With the multitude of them,*** namely, of pains and of worms, ***my garment is consumed,*** that is, the flesh is their nourishment, by which the internal body parts are clothed. There is a parallel in Is 14:[75] *The moth will be scattered beneath you, and worms will be your covering.* Jas 5:[76] *Your garments have been eaten by moths.*

And, concerning the extent of the pain, Job adds: ***and they have encircled me,*** that is, they have bound me tightly all the way to the point of cutting off my breathing, ***as if with the collar of my coat,*** which encircles my neck and suffocates me by binding tightly. Hence Jb 17:[77] *My spirit will be weakened; my days will be shortened.*

Concerning the effect, he adds: **[19]** ***I am compared to dirt,*** that is, to the rottenness of filth, ***and I have become,*** when mud has dried up by means of putrefying heat, ***like embers and ashes;*** "embers" as far as flying forth near a burning fire, "ashes" as far as dust remaining after putrefaction. Above in the tenth [chapter]:[78] *Remember, I beg you, that you have made me like clay, and you will turn me into dust again.*

[20] ***I will cry out to you.***

Here Job mentions that he does not find consolation in God hearing him. And he speaks of four things, namely: the severity (*duritiam*) of God; and that this severity is undeserved, in that place:[79] *I wept at one time;* and that the suffering that humans have inflicted [on him] is undeserved, in that place:[80] *I was walking around in mourning;* and that, because of this, his sorrow has

74. Jer 51.34.
75. Is 14.11.
76. Jas 5.2.
77. Jb 17.1.
78. Jb 10.9.
79. Jb 30.25.
80. Jb 30.28.

been made heavier, in that place:[81] [*My harp*] *has turned to mourning.*

And that is: ***I will cry out to you,*** namely, God, ***and you will not hear me,*** at present, of course. Lam 3:[82] *But when I cry out and entreat, He has shut out my prayer.* Prv 1:[83] *Then they will call upon me, and I will not hear; they will rise early in the morning and will not find me.* ***I stand up,*** persisting in the clamor of my prayer, of course, ***and you do not consider me,*** namely, with the eye of good will and of grace, because that was not a time of favorable answer to prayer. Is 1:[84] *When you stretch out your hands, I will turn my eyes away.* Hab 1:[85] *How long, O Lord, will I cry out, and will you not hear me? Will I, suffering violence, shout out to you, and will you not save?*

[21] ***You have turned cruel toward me,*** because there is no cruelty in the Lord, of course. Therefore, explaining this, he adds: ***and,*** that is, ***in the severity of your hand,*** striking, of course, ***you are opposed to me,*** and in this certainly you seem to be cruel. Hab 1:[86] *He is cruel and does not show mercy.* This cruelty is expressed in Prv 1:[87] *I will laugh at your destruction, and I will mock you when what you feared comes upon you.* Prv 17:[88] *A cruel angel will be sent against him.*

And Job reveals how bitter was the fall during the time of pristine happiness, from which he fell: **[22]** ***You have lifted me up,*** in health, wealth, and political power, of course, ***and set me as it were on the wind.*** For temporal things are the wind. Is 40:[89] *The grass has withered and the flower has fallen because the spirit of the Lord has blown upon it.* Jas 4:[90] *For what is our life? It is a vapor that appears for a little while and then will vanish.* Above:[91] *Remember me, O God, because my life is wind.* **[*and*]** ***you have crushed me mightily,***

81. Jb 30.31.
82. Lam 3.8.
83. Prv 1.28.
84. Is 1.15.
85. Hab 1.2.
86. Cf. Jer 6.23.
87. Prv 1.26.
88. Prv 17.11.
89. Is 40.7.
90. Jas 4.15.
91. Jb 7.7.

for the higher one's status, the more profound is his fall; indeed, falling in such a way as in this fall, he was crushed and battered. 2 Mc 9:[92] *It happened as he was advancing rapidly that he fell from his chariot, and his limbs were jolted by a painful battering of the body.*

By reason of these things Job says that the hopelessness of life makes a case for itself. And that is: **[23]** ***I know,*** that is to say, I presume, based on inferior causes, ***that you will hand me over to death.*** Above:[93] *I have given up hope; by no means will I live any longer now.* ***where,*** that is, in which death, ***a house,*** that is, a final dwelling place, ***has been established for everyone who lives*** this mortal life, of course. Eccl 12:[94] *The human will go into the house of his eternity.* Ps:[95] *Their graves will be their homes eternally.*

But, lest he seem[96] to despair of salvation, Job adds that he has hope in the Lord, and that is: **[24]** ***Nevertheless you do not send forth your*** striking and disciplining ***hand for the purpose of their consumption,*** namely, [the consumption] of eternal damnation. And he says "send forth" because this mercy of God is often held back in the hand, but it is sent forth when the hand strikes. Above:[97] *He wounds, but He cures; He strikes, but His hands will heal.* Dt 32:[98] *I will kill and I will make alive, I will strike and I will heal.* ***and if they fall down,*** when you do not sustain them, of course, ***you yourself will save them,*** namely, by raising them up. Ps:[99] *The Lord raises up the broken.* Prv 24:[100] *A just person falls seven times and will rise again, but the wicked fall down into evil.* Ps:[101] *When he falls, he will not be battered, because the Lord puts His hand under him.*

And Job adds how he suffers this undeservedly. And that is: **[25]** ***I wept at one time,*** supply: when I lived in favorable circumstances, ***for him who had been afflicted.*** Rom 12:[102] *Rejoice with those*

92. 2 Mc 9.7.
93. Jb 7.16.
94. Eccl 12.5.
95. Ps 48.12.
96. Here I read *videatur* with MSS E, F, and M, rather than the *credatur* of Weiss's edition.
97. Jb 5.18.
98. Dt 32.39.
99. Ps 145.8.
100. Prv 24.16.
101. Ps 36.24.
102. Rom 12.15–16.

who rejoice, weep with those who weep, being of a single mind with one another. Sir 7:[103] *Do not be lacking in consolation for those who weep.* Heb 10:[104] *You had compassion on those who were bound.*

And this is what follows: ***and my soul had compassion on the poor.*** 1 Pt 3:[105] *All of you be of one mind in your speech. Be compassionate, lovers of brotherhood.*

And Job adds what he expected for such excellent merits: **[26]** ***I expected good things; and evils,*** namely, [the evils] of penalty, ***have come to me.*** Is 5:[106] *I expected that it would yield grapes, and it yielded wild grapes.* ***I waited for light,*** that is, the illumination of consolation, ***and darkness has broken out.*** Prv 10:[107] *The expectation of the just is joy.* Is 57:[108] *The just person perishes, and there is no one who reflects on it in his heart.*

But Job adds in what [these] evils and darkness consist: **[27]** ***My inner parts,*** namely, vital organs, ***have begun to boil,*** with the heat of fever, of course. Hippocrates says:[109] A fever is in the generation of corrupted blood more than in corrupted blood already generated. ***without any rest,*** that is, without interruption.

And he adds the cause of this sort of thing: ***the days of affliction have preceded me,*** before I will come to rest. Jb 9:[110] *He does not allow my spirit to rest, and He fills me*[111] *with bitterness.*

He also adds how they were handling themselves with respect to evils: **[28]** ***I was walking around in mourning,*** for the evil things that were happening, of course. Ps:[112] *Zeal for your house has consumed me.* Bede says:[113] Zeal is anger and sadness concerning evil, which corrects whatever evils it sees if it is able; if it is not able,

103. Sir 7.38.
104. Heb 10.34.
105. 1 Pt 3.8.
106. Is 5.4.
107. Prv 10.28.
108. Is 57.1.
109. See Hippocrates, *Prog.* 24.
110. Jb 9.18.
111. Here I read *me* with MSS E, F, and M, rather than *spiritum meum* with Weiss's edition. Cf. the text of Jb 9.18 as set forth by Albert above (vol. 1.196–97).
112. Ps 68.10.
113. Like Weiss, I have been unable to find this reference.

it tolerates and bemoans them. Prv 14:[114] *The heart has known the bitterness of its own soul.* Lam 1:[115] *My sighs are many, and my heart laments.* Nevertheless, this sadness was not the cause of anger or fury. And therefore it follows: ***without fury I rose up,*** that is, out of zeal, of course, "I rose up" simultaneously in mind and body, [***and***] ***in the midst of the crowd,*** that is, against the crowd of sinners, ***I cried out,*** namely, by reproving and proclaiming and entreating. Ps:[116] *Crying out, I have been in distress; my throat has become hoarse while I have been crying out.* 2 Tm 4:[117] *Reprove, entreat, rebuke with the utmost patience and learning.*

Job adds, moreover, with what great charity he loved them: **[29]** ***I was the brother of dragons.*** Venomous people who poison others are called "dragons," of whom he was the "brother" because he loved them with fraternal affection, although he hated their sins. Jer 31:[118] *I have loved you with an everlasting love; therefore, I, showing mercy, have drawn you in.* ***and the companion of ostriches.*** "Ostriches" are similar to birds, but [are] flightless, and they signify feigning hypocrites and false brothers, whom he loved with the charity of a companion in order to convert him to the good.[119] Rom 12:[120] *Let love be without pretense; hate what is evil, cling to what is good. Love one another with the charity of brotherhood.*

He also adds the evils that happened to him after all these good things: **[30]** ***My skin has turned black upon me,*** as if it has been burned, of course. Lam:[121] *Our skin has burned up like an oven, from the scorching heat of famine.* Jb 7:[122] *My skin has become dry and has shriveled.* ***and my bones have dried up because of heat,*** as if devoid of their own strength and marrow. Lam 1:[123] *From on high He sent fire into my bones, and he instructed me.* To be sure, he calls the burning of a fever or an ulcer "heat."

114. Prv 14.10.

115. Lam 1.22.

116. Ps 68.4.

117. 2 Tm 4.2.

118. Jer 31.3.

119. Here I read *ad bonum,* which is added in MSS E, F, and M, but omitted from Weiss's edition.

120. Rom 12.9–10.

121. Lam 5.10.

122. Jb 7.5.

123. Lam 1.13.

And Job adds the effect of these things: [31] ***My harp has turned to mourning.*** The "harp" signifies the combining and arranging of the body coming together into one by means of all the combining and arranging of the members, which "has turned to mourning" when the combining is dispersed and the arranging is dissolved such that one member is not able to help another. Lam 5:[124] *The crown has fallen from our head.*

And this is what he adds: ***and my pipe,*** supply: has turned, ***into the voice of those who weep.*** He blows into a reed "pipe" and produces a melody, and it signifies the joy that he had in his household, that is to say, with all the excellent members of his household singing out for joy, namely, his wife and children, insignificant subordinates, and those who cultivate the land. Is 24:[125] *The joy of timbrels has ceased, the sound of those rejoicing has ended, the sweetness of the harp amid joy has become silent. They will not drink wine; the drink will be bitter to those who drink it.*

124. Lam 5.16.
125. Is 24.8–9.

CHAPTER 31

 **MADE A *covenant with my eyes.***

In this place blessed Job shows how innocently he suffered, and this by means of his doing good and abstaining from evil. And this chapter is divided into two parts. In the first of these, Job makes clear his innocence; in the second, he desires that this be written down and set forth in judgment, in that place:[1] *Who would grant to me a listener.*

The first part is divided into three. In the first [division], Job shows how excellent he was in cleanness of mind and in purity of body; in the second, how excellent he was in justice and responsibility (*pietate*), which is part of justice, and in the use of wealth, in that place:[2] *If I have despised administering justice;* in the third, how excellent he was toward others, namely, friends and enemies, in that place:[3] *If I have delighted in his downfall.*

In the first place, therefore, Job declares how excellent he was in cleanness of mind and in purity of body. And this is divided into two. In the first [subdivision], he shows how excellent he was toward unmarried women; second, how excellent toward those [women] joined in marriage, in that place:[4] *If my heart has been deceived.*

In the first of these [sections], Job shows how he refrained from sin; second, how he stayed away from those bound by sin, in that place:[5] *If I have walked in vanity.*

In the first [subsection], there are three points, namely: the care with which he avoided the sin of the flesh; the reason why

1. Jb 31.35.
2. Jb 31.13.
3. Jb 31.29.
4. Jb 31.9.
5. Jb 31.5.

he avoided it; and the fear of punishment, which he wished not to befall him as a result of sin, and that is: ***I made a covenant with my eyes,*** which bring word of some delightful sexual object, of course, ***that,*** supply: if my eye might bring word of the delightful thing, ***I would not even think,*** namely, in my heart, ***about a virgin.*** He says "a virgin" on account of the fact that a virgin moves one more toward concupiscence, for she is intact and therefore is desired to a greater extent with a view to wantonness, because she is more beautiful and for that reason she deceives more easily. Moreover, "think about a virgin" means to reflect with the mind on her beauty together with her shape and complexion, and the arrangement of her limbs and hair, and other pleasing features, which reflection often pollutes the mind even of him who is impotent according to the body. Sir 30:[6] *He sees with his eyes and moans, as a eunuch embracing a virgin and sighing.* Sir 20:[7] *The concupiscence of a eunuch will deflower a young woman,* supply: according to will, not according to act. Ps:[8] *Turn away my eyes, that they may not see vanity.* Mt 5:[9] *Whoever looks at a woman to lust after her has already committed adultery with her in his heart.* Sir 9:[10] *Do not gaze upon a virgin, lest you stumble on account of her beauty.* On account of this, therefore, he "made a covenant, that he would not think about a virgin," because such thinking draws him to lust [after her]. In the Gloss, Gregory says:[11] One should not look at what is not permitted to be desired. And he introduces that passage in Jer:[12] *Death has come in through our windows; it has entered our houses to destroy the children from outside, the youth in the streets.*

And Job sets forth the twofold reason for this care [with which he avoided the sin of the flesh]: one is that it [namely, this sin of the flesh] does away with God; the other is that it deprives the mind of reason. And that is: **[2]** ***For what part,*** supply: if I had been given up to the concupiscence of sexual activity, ***should God above have in me.*** God is said to be "above" among goods

6. Sir 30.21.
7. Sir 20.2.
8. Ps 118.37.
9. Mt 5.28.
10. Sir 9.5.
11. *GO* on Jb 30.1; cf. Gregory, *Mor.* 21.2.4.
12. Jer 9.21.

heavenly and most high, which pertain to the contemplation of wisdom, in which he who takes pleasure in the lowest things, and especially in the concupiscence of the flesh, cannot be delighted, for the one enticed by such things is dragged away from the highest things. Jas 1:[13] *Each one is tempted by his own concupiscence, being dragged away and enticed.* ***and***, that is, ***what inheritance,*** which is so called from "by clinging to" (*herendo*), supply: would He have, ***the Almighty,*** who, inasmuch as He exists in Himself (*in se*), contains all things, ***from on high?*** Indeed, "on high"—inasmuch as He exists in Himself, He contains all things—from which place the fornicator is cast out by reason of [his] concupiscence. This is signified in Nm 25, where it is said:[14] *Israel was initiated into [the cult of] Baal of Peor. And, being angry, the Lord said to Moses: Take all the leaders of the people, and hang them on gibbets toward the sun, so that my anger may be turned away from Israel.* Figuratively, "Baal of Peor" is the specter (*idolum*) of lechery in the groin of a man and in the groin of a woman, according to which Venus and Jupiter were worshiped in Cyprus. Having been initiated into [the cult of] such an idol and dedicated to it, none [of them] were freed from God's wrath except the leaders. This means that the superior parts of the mind are suspended toward the sun through contemplation, that is, toward the light of eternal truth.

Job also adds the reason from the perspective of an alienated mind: [3] ***Does not destruction,*** supply: of virtue, ***come to the wicked,*** that is, the fornicator, who is wicked, ***and alienation,*** of the mind, of course, ***to those who work iniquity?*** according to the concupiscence of the flesh, to be sure. Sir 19:[15] *Wine and women make even wise men fall, and they will rebuke the intelligent;* that is, they will prove them to be refutable, and the one who joins himself to prostitutes will be depraved. In such people God has no part. 1 Cor 6:[16] *Do you not know that your bodies are members of Christ? Shall I, then, remove the members of Christ and make them members of a prostitute? God forbid!* In Book VII of the *Ethics,* Aristotle sets forth a similar verse from Homer:[17] She who folds together deceits,

13. Jas 1.14.
14. Nm 25.3–4.
15. Sir 19.2.
16. 1 Cor 6.15.
17. Aristotle, *EN* 7.6.3; cf. Alb., *Eth.* 7.1.9; Homer, *Iliad* 14.217.

Venus, the daughter of Cyprus, has powerfully plundered the minds of the wise. Dn 13:[18] *O seed of Canaan and not of Judah, beauty has deceived you, and concupiscence has destroyed your heart.*

And he adds a reason from fear: [4] ***Does He,*** namely, God above, ***not consider my ways,*** both of my heart and of my work, of course. Sir 23:[19] *The eyes of the Lord are far brighter than the sun, looking around and seeing all the ways of men.* ***and***, that is, ***number***, that is, weigh according to judgment, ***all my steps?*** that is, my works. Jb 14:[20] *You certainly have numbered my steps, but spare my sin.* 2 Cor 5:[21] *Every one of us will stand before the judgment seat of Christ, so that each one might receive the proper things of the body, according to what he has done, whether good or evil.* 1 Cor 5:[22] *Fornicators and adulterers God will judge,* that is, He will condemn.

And Job adds how he refrained even from things related [to the sin of the flesh]. But there are two related things, namely, the game of vanity and the trickery of deceit; and [he treats] each one in a twofold way, namely, in [his] heart and in [his] works.

And that is: [5] ***If I have walked in vanity.*** Gregory says:[23] "Vanity pertains to levity," and it is an oath of imprecation. Tb 3:[24] *Never have I joined myself to those who play, nor have I made myself a participant with those who walk in levity.* Jer 31:[25] *How long will you be dissolute in delights, O wandering daughter?* Jerome says:[26] Touching and joking, laughing and whistling are customarily the beginnings of the imminent death of virginity. Jb 11:[27] *A vain man is roused toward pride, and, as if the colt of a wild ass, he thinks that he was born free.* The freedom of "the colt of a wild ass" inclines toward lasciviousness.

18. Dn 13.56.

19. Sir 23.28.

20. Jb 14.16.

21. 2 Cor 5.10.

22. Although fornicators are mentioned in 1 Cor 5 (see vv. 1, 9, 10), the text that follows here is not from 1 Cor 5, but rather is from Heb 13.4.

23. Gregory, *Mor.* 21.6.11.

24. Tb 3.17.

25. Jer 31.22.

26. Jerome, *Vita S. Hil.* 21 (PL 23:38).

27. Jb 11.12.

And Job adds concerning trickery: ***and my foot has hurried to deceit.*** He says "has hurried" because concupiscence spurs one on "to deceit," on account of the fact that lovers have become accustomed to beguiling themselves by means of deceits. Hence, Ovid says:[28] "If you make promises, fulfill them; for what harm is there in promising? Anyone can be rich in promises." Jer 9:[29] *Your dwelling is in the midst of deceit; through deceit they have refused to know me, says the Lord.* **[6]** ***let Him,*** supply God, ***weigh me in a just balance,*** that is, of equitable judgment, so that He may weigh [my] action according to intention. Jb 6:[30] *If only my sins, for which I have deserved wrath, and the calamity that I suffer were weighed in a balance.* Prv 11:[31] *A fair weight is the will of the Lord.* ***and let God know my simplicity,*** according to which, to be sure, I, being intent on one thing alone for myself, have turned aside neither toward vanity nor toward deceit. Prv 11:[32] *The simplicity of the upright will guide them; and the deceitfulness of the wicked will destroy them.*

And what Job spoke of as being in his heart according to the simplicity of intention, he shows that he also observed this in his works. Hence, he adds: **[7]** ***If my step has turned aside from the way,*** of virtue and of precept, of course, and [has advanced] among doubts concerning the way of counsel. Jb 23:[33] *His footprints my foot has followed.*[34] *I have kept His way.* Ps:[35] *Show your ways to me, O Lord.* Is 26:[36] *The way of the just is upright; the path of the just is right to walk in.*

And he adds concerning the intention of [his] reasoning: ***and if my eye,*** the intention of [my] reasoning, of course, ***has followed my heart,*** carnal, no doubt, and at times disturbed and tempted[37]

28. Ovid, *Ars amat.* 1.444.

29. Jer 9.6.

30. Jb 6.2.

31. Prv 11.1.

32. Prv 11.3.

33. Jb 23.11.

34. Here I read *secutus est* with MSS E, F, and M, rather than *custodivit* with Weiss's edition. Cf. on Jb 23.11 above (p. 19; Weiss ed., col. 274), where Albert's text reads *secutus est.*

35. Ps 24.4.

36. Is 26.7.

37. Here I read *turbatum et tentatum* with MSS E, F, and M, rather than simply *tentatum* with Weiss's edition.

by illicit things. For sometimes tares are sown in the heart, as is said in Mt 13:[38] *The enemy came and sowed tares.* ***and,*** supply: for that reason, according to the perversity of [my] intention, ***if a stain has clung to my hands,*** that is, to my works. Ps:[39] *The one with innocent hands and a pure heart, who has not received his soul in vain.* **[8]** ***then let me sow, and let another eat,*** that is, let another take away all my produce. Hos 7:[40] *Strangers have devoured his strength, and he did not know it.* Dt 28:[41] *You will cast much seed into the ground, but you will gather little, because the locusts will devour everything.* Is 17:[42] *Early in the morning your seed will flourish; the harvest is taken away on the day of inheritance, and it will cause you to grieve deeply.* ***and let my progeny,*** which has come forth from my seed as well, ***be rooted out,*** that is, torn out by the roots. Wis 4:[43] *Impure plantings will not set deep roots, nor establish a stable foundation.* Wis 3:[44] *Children of adulterers will not come to perfection, and offspring from an illicit bed will be driven away.*

And after he has declared his freedom from the sin of the flesh with regard to the unmarried, Job adds his innocence concerning adultery with the married, and that is: **[9]** ***If my heart has been deceived.*** For Venus destroyed by deceiving, on account of which she is called "she who folds together deceits" (*doli complicatrix*) by Homer.[45] ***by a woman,*** another's. Prv 5:[46] *Because you are seduced, my son, by a strange woman; you are caressed and seduced in the bosom of another.*

And Job mentions sins related to adulterers, from which he also has refrained, and that is: ***and if I have lain in wait at my neighbor's door,*** out of concupiscence for his wife, of course. Sir 21:[47] *The foot of a fool is soon in his neighbor's house;* and a little beyond this:[48] *A fool peeps through the window into the house; but a learned*

38. Mt 13.25.
39. Ps 23.4.
40. Hos 7.9.
41. Dt 28.38.
42. Is 17.11.
43. Wis 4.3.
44. Wis 3.16.
45. Homer, *Iliad* 14.217. See pp. 114–15 on Jb 31.3 (Weiss ed., col. 353).
46. Prv 5.20.
47. Sir 21.25.
48. Sir 21.26.

man will remain outside; and after this:[49] *It is the folly of a man to eavesdrop at the door.*

Then he adds the punishment: [10] ***let my wife be the harlot of another,*** so that I may be punished in him, of course, with regard to whom I have failed, and that is in effect: ***and let other men bend down over her,*** in the work of adultery, to be sure. In Hos 4 the Lord says to such people:[50] *I will not punish your daughters when they fornicate, and your wives when they commit adultery, seeing that the men themselves were associating with prostitutes.*

Then Job adds the offense of this sin: [11] ***For this is an abomination*** or crime ***and the greatest iniquity*** against one's neighbor, for to steal one's wife is a greater iniquity than to steal his possessions. Hence, in 2 Sm 12 the punishment for this sin is set forth through the prophet Nathan:[51] *Behold, I will stir up evil against you from within your own house, and I will take your wives before your eyes and give them to your neighbor, and he will lie with your wives in the sight of this very sun.*

And Job adds the harm this causes to the adulterer himself: [12] ***It is a fire*** through the raging of desire ***that devours all the way to consummation*** or destruction. Hos 7:[52] *They are all adulterers, like an oven that has been kindled by the cook.* Dt 32:[53] A fire has been kindled in my wrath, and it will burn all the way to the lowest regions of hell. And this is what follows: ***and roots out everything*** of the good and of virtue, of course, ***that springs up***. Prv 6:[54] *Can a human hide fire in his bosom, and his clothes not burn? Or can he walk on hot coals, and his feet not be scorched? So too he who sleeps with his neighbor's wife will not be clean when he has touched her.*

[13] ***If I have despised administering justice.***

Having made clear that he was free from the sin of lust, Job shows that he is free from the sin of injustice and of avarice, which always accompanies injustice, in that place:[55] *If I have thought gold.*

49. Sir 21.27.
50. Hos 4.14.
51. 2 Sm 12.11.
52. Hos 7.4.
53. Dt 32.22.
54. Prv 6.27–29.
55. Jb 31.24.

In the first [of these divisions] there are two points, namely: that he has refrained from injustice toward [the members of] his own [household]; and that he has refrained from injustice toward the poor, in that place:[56] *If I have denied to the poor what they desired.* In the first [subdivision] there are two points, namely: his refraining from sin, and the reason [for it]. And that is: ***If I have despised administering justice,*** [the justice] of the valuation of a good man, of course, ***with my servant*** **(servo)**, so called from *serviendo,* ***and my handmaiden*** **(ancilla),** which is so called from *an-*, that is "around," and *cillo, cillis,* which is "to be moved," because the handmaiden is moved in obedience to the mistress of the house. ***when they brought a complaint against me,*** sometimes about the oppression of work or about a reduction in wages. For sometimes there is a dispute about this [sort of issue], as Jacob disputed with Laban according to Gn 31:[57] *You have also changed my wages ten times.* Dt 24:[58] *You shall not withhold the wages of the needy and the poor, whether he is your brother or a stranger who lives with you in your land and is within your gates. But you shall pay him the price of his labor the same day, before the sun goes down, because he is poor, and with it he sustains his life.*

And Job adds the twofold reason: one on the part of divine judgment, the other on the part of the equality of nature. And that is: **[14]** ***indeed what will I do,*** that is, what just excuse can I have, ***when God rises up to judge?*** between him and me, of course. Dt 24:[59] *You shall not withhold the wages of the poor, lest he cry against you to the Lord, and it be imputed to you as a sin.*

and when He, supply: the Lord, ***inquires, how will I respond to Him?*** Jas 5:[60] *Behold, the wages of your laborers, who have reaped your fields, which have been embezzled by you, cry out; and their cry has entered the ears of the Lord of Hosts.* Sir 34:[61] *The bread of the needy is the life of the poor; whoever deprives them of it is a murderer.*

And Job adds the reason from the equality of nature: **[15]**

56. Jb 31.16.
57. Gn 31.41.
58. Dt 24.14–15.
59. Ibid.
60. Jas 5.4.
61. Sir 34.25.

Did not He who made me in the womb, supply: God, ***make that one also?*** and so we are equals by virtue of having the same Father. Mal 2:[62] *Has not the one God created us? Why then does every one of us despise his brother?* In this way, therefore, we are equals by virtue of the body. ***and did not one and the same,*** supply: who fashioned that one too, ***fashion me,*** supply: as far as to the soul, ***in the womb?*** that is, in the conception in the womb. Wis 6:[63] *He Himself made the small and the great, and He cares for all equally.* Eph 6:[64] *And you, masters, do the same to your servants. Stop threatening them, knowing that the Lord both of them and of you is in heaven, and there is no partiality with respect to persons in God's sight.*

And Job adds concerning his being innocent of injustice toward the poor, and this in a twofold way, namely: [he says] that he has not sinned by not sharing his property; and that he has not sinned by oppressing them either wrongfully or justifiably for the sake of judgment. Concerning the first, he says three things, namely: that he has shared his property; and that even concerning a small amount, he has divided it with the poor man; and that he has done this not only with regard to his food, but also with regard to his clothing. And that is: **[16]** ***If I have denied to the poor what they desired,*** that is, what they begged for. Sir 4:[65] *My son, do not defraud the poor of alms, nor divert your eyes from the needy.* Prv 3:[66] *Honor the Lord with your resources, and give to the poor from the first of all your produce.* Tb 4:[67] *Give alms out of your resources, and do not turn your face away from any poor person.* ***and have made the eyes of the widow,*** namely, of the needy one not having a protector, ***wait,*** supply: but I have come to help at once. Sir 4:[68] *Do not afflict the heart of the needy person, and do not delay in giving to the one who is in distress.* Prv 3:[69] *Do not say to your friend, "Go, and come back again; tomorrow I will give to you," when you are able to give at once.*

62. Mal 2.10.
63. Wis 6.8.
64. Eph 6.9.
65. Sir 4.1.
66. Prv 3.9.
67. Tb 4.7.
68. Sir 4.3.
69. Prv 3.28.

Then Job adds that even concerning a small amount, he has divided it, and that is: [17] ***If I have eaten my morsel alone;*** a "morsel" (*buccella*) is what is enclosed in the storehouse of the mouth (*in cella buccae*). ***and the orphan,*** not having anyone besides himself, of course, ***has not eaten of it,*** namely, of the morsel. Tb 4:[70] *If you have much, give abundantly; if you have a little, be eager to give a share of it.* Hence, in Mk 12[71] the Lord praises the widow, who with two small coins offered her whole livelihood.

And now Job adds the reason for this compassion: [18] ***because from my infancy,*** that is, from a consideration of my infancy, in which I was powerless and needy, ***compassion grew up with me.*** Gregory says:[72] In good people, as the age of the body increases, so too does the life of virtue; in others, as age increases, integrity decreases. ***and it came out with me from my***[73] ***mother's womb,*** and this through careful consideration; for carefully considering my[74] poor and needy birth, I had compassion on the poor. Hence, above in chapter 1[75] Job said: *Naked I came from my mother's womb, and naked I will return there.* Eccl 5:[76] *An utterly miserable weakness: just as he came, so will he return.* For in birth and in death both the rich and the poor are equally impoverished. 1 Tm 6:[77] *We brought nothing into this world, and without a doubt we cannot carry anything out.* Hence, carefully considering his own poverty and that he himself was helped by God through the things of this world, he comes to the aid of his poor brother and reflects upon the fact that he himself is a debtor to him. Sir 4:[78] *Incline your ear to the poor person without severity and repay your debt to him.* Prv 19:[79] *He who has compassion on the poor lends to the Lord, and He will repay him in full.*

70. Tb 4.9.
71. Mk 12.43.
72. Gregory, *Mor.* 21.18.28.
73. Here I read *meae,* which MSS F and M add but which Weiss's edition omits.
74. Here I read *meam,* which MSS T, E, F, and M add but which Weiss's edition omits.
75. Jb 1.21.
76. Eccl 5.15.
77. 1 Tm 6.7.
78. Sir 4.8.
79. Prv 19.17.

And concerning clothing, Job adds: [19] ***If I have despised the one who was perishing;*** he has perished completely who does not have a fixed abode that is his very own. Mt 8:[80] *Foxes have holes, and the birds of the air have nests; but the Son of Man has no place to lay His head.* And this is true of Christ in Himself and in His poor. ***because he did not have a garment;*** he who does not offer a garment "despises." Is 58:[81] *When you see someone who is naked, cover him.* And explaining this, Job adds: ***and,*** supply: if I have despised, ***the poor man without a covering,*** for God should be honored in the poor. Jas 2:[82] *God has chosen the poor in this world, rich in faith and heirs to the kingdom that God has promised to those who love Him. But you have dishonored the poor man.*

And these were indications of his humility. And concerning his responsibility (*pietate*), Job adds: [20] ***If his sides,*** that is, his vital organs having been restored by me and kept warm by means of clothing, ***have not blessed me.*** Jb 29:[83] *The blessing of the one who was about to die came upon me.* Sir 4:[84] *Do not turn your eyes away from the poor on account of anger, and do not leave those who ask of you free to curse you behind your back.*

Job also adds the reason for this blessing: ***and if,*** that is, because, ***he has not been made warm,*** that is, covered up and protected from the cold, ***with the fleece of my sheep.*** The opposite is said of the evil and impious in Jb 24:[85] *They send men away naked, taking away the garments of those who have no covering in the cold.*

And Job adds how even justifiably according to judgment he has not oppressed the poor with regard to their own case: [21] ***If I have raised my hand,*** that is, my power, ***against the orphan, even when I considered,*** that is, I knew, ***myself superior,*** that is, more powerful, ***in the gate,*** that is, in the cause of administering justice, which was being carried out in the gates. The sense is: Although I was more powerful in the cause of administering justice and I had a just complaint, I have not vigorously exacted from the

80. Mt 8.20.
81. Is 58.7.
82. Jas 2.5–6.
83. Jb 29.13.
84. Sir 4.5.
85. Jb 24.7.

orphan the debt that I, discharging this [duty of mine], could have justly exacted. And this is said in Mt 6:[86] *Forgive us our debts, as we also forgive our debtors.* Mt 18:[87] *You wicked servant, I forgave you all your debt because you asked me to. Therefore, should you not also have had mercy on your fellow servant, just as I have had mercy on you?*

Then Job adds the punishment if he has done this: **[22]** ***Let my shoulder,*** in which there is help for my life, ***fall,*** so that I cannot help myself, of course, ***from its joint,*** that is, from the structure of the body. Sir 36:[88] *Crush the head of the leaders and of the enemies who say: "There is no other beside us."* And this is what follows: ***and let my arm,*** that is, the power of my help, ***with its bones,*** that is, with its strength, ***be crushed.*** Ps:[89] *Crush the arm of the sinner and of the malicious one.* As a proof of this, in 1 Kgs 13[90] the arm of Jeroboam, which he extended against the man of God, withered, and he was not able to draw his hand back to himself.

And he adds the reason: **[23]** ***Indeed, as if waves were swelling over me,*** of divine justice overflowing, of course, which He has over against us, ***I have always feared God,*** because in comparison to His justice, our justice is injustice. Ps:[91] *Do not enter into judgment with your servant, because in your sight no living thing will be justified.* Is 64:[92] *All of our righteousness is, as it were, the rag of a menstruating woman.* ***and His weight,*** namely, of divine justice, ***I was not able to bear,*** supply: and therefore concerning the justice that I had over against others, I have remitted [their debts], lest, of course, He oppress me with the heavy burden of His justice. Jb 23:[93] *I wish that He would not contend with me with great strength, nor overwhelm me with the weight of His greatness.* Ps 35:[94] *Your justice is as the mountains of God.*

[24] ***If I have thought gold.***

Here Job touches on how excellent he was in the use of rich-

86. Mt 6.12.
87. Mt 18.32–33.
88. Sir 36.12.
89. Ps 10.15.
90. 1 Kgs 13.4.
91. Ps 142.2.
92. Is 64.6.
93. Jb 23.6.
94. Ps 35.7.

es: first, in the use of riches; second, in the veneration of fortune, in that place:[95] *If I have beheld the sun.* With regard to the use of riches he says two things, namely, that he does not trust in them, nor has he delighted in them with the delight of enjoyment (*laetitia fruitionis*).

And that is: ***If I have thought gold.*** He signifies all riches by the most precious metal, because, as Aristotle says in Book V of the *Ethics,*[96] all riches are measured in comparison to that metal. ***my strength,*** that is, the strength of my life, for this is consistent with gold, inasmuch as it is a guarantor against future need, as Aristotle says,[97] and money rescuing one from need, for in such a way it strengthens life. Sir 31:[98] *Blessed is the man who has not gone after gold, and has not trusted in money and treasures. Who is he, and we will praise him? For he has done wonderful things.*

And he explains this, adding: ***and have said,*** in my heart, mouth, and work, of course, ***to pure gold,*** that is, to coarse gold remaining in its natural purity: ***"My confidence."*** Prv 11:[99] *He who trusts in his riches will fall; but the just will sprout forth like a green leaf.* And ridiculing him, David says in a Psalm:[100] *They will laugh at him and say: "Behold, the man who has not made God his helper, but has trusted in the multitude of his riches."*

And concerning the joy of his profit, he adds: **[25]** ***If I have rejoiced over my many riches,*** in such a way, of course, that I valued them as an end in themselves, just as that [rich] man in Lk 12 who said [to his soul]:[101] *"Soul, you have many goods stored up over many years: eat, drink, and dine sumptuously." And God responded to him: "You fool, this very night they will demand your soul back from you. But the things you have obtained, whose will they be?"* Eccl 5:[102] *There is also another grievous ill that I have seen under the sun: riches accumulated to the detriment of their owner. For their loss brings the worst pain.* ***and because my hand,*** just as He [namely, God] who

95. Jb 31.26.
96. Aristotle *EN* 5.5.10.
97. Aristotle *EN* 5.5.14.
98. Sir 31.8–9.
99. Prv 11.28.
100. Ps 51.8–9.
101. Lk 12.19–20.
102. Eccl 5.12–13.

said in Is 10:[103] *My hand has found the strength of the people, as if a nest; and just as eggs that have been left behind are gathered, so have I gathered together the whole earth.* ***has obtained very many things*** in profits and revenue. Ps:[104] *If riches abound, refuse to set your heart upon them.* Therefore, he was not delighting in these, as Gregory says,[105] knowing that to whom more is committed, from him more is exacted.

And Job adds concerning fortune: **[26]** ***If I have beheld,*** with the eye of approval, of course, ***the sun,*** that is, the brightness of fortune, ***when it shined,*** that is, when it appeared by growing in brightness, ***and the moon,*** which signifies prosperity in earthly things, ***advancing,*** through the growth of prosperity, of course, ***brightly.*** Is 60:[106] *Your sun shall go down no more, and your moon shall not decrease.* **[27]** ***and my heart has rejoiced in secret,*** with the delight of enjoyment, of course, just as those do who put their hope in such things, like those who, according to Wis 2,[107] say: *Come, and let us enjoy the good things that exist, and let us make use of creation as we did hastily in youth.* ***and I have kissed my hand with my mouth,*** that is, if the work of my hands has been pleasing to me in such things and I have praised it. Gregory says:[108] The one who praises what he does "kisses his hand with his mouth." Prv 24:[109] *Do not deceive anyone with your lips.* For he who is praised is deceived. Prv 27:[110] *Let another person praise you, and not your own mouth; a stranger, and not your own lips.* ***which is the greatest iniquity,*** that is, the cause of the greatest iniquity. Prv 1:[111] *The prosperity of fools will kill them.* Concerning such people it is said in a Psalm:[112] *Their iniquity has sprung forth, as if from corpulence, and they have passed into the affection of the heart.* ***and a denial of the Most High God,*** because the one who trusts in riches does not trust in God, and in

103. Is 10.14.
104. Ps 61.11.
105. Gregory, *Mor.* 22.5.8.
106. Is 60.20.
107. Wis 2.6.
108. Gregory, *Mor.* 22.9.20.
109. Prv 24.28.
110. Prv 27.2.
111. Prv 1.32.
112. Ps 72.7.

this way he denies God. Hence, concerning such rich people it is said in Jb 21:[113] *They have said to the Lord God: Depart from us; we refuse to have knowledge of your ways.* Jer 17:[114] *Cursed is the human being who trusts in human beings, and who considers flesh his strength, and whose heart turns away from the Lord.* This last [part of the verse] can be explained with regard to idolatry. For certain people were worshiping the sun as the guide of fortune with regard to political power, glory, and fame, and the moon as the guide and illuminator [of fortune] with regard to the health and prosperity of those on earth, as it is said in Jer 7:[115] *They made cakes for the queen of heaven,* that is, for the moon. And when they worshiped, they extended their hands in the direction of the moon and the sun; and on account of their veneration of the light that fell upon their hands, they were kissing their hands, which was the greatest iniquity because it was idolatry and a denial of God, since [this iniquity] attributes to a creature what belongs to the Creator alone. Is 60:[116] *You will no longer have the sun to give light by day, neither will the brightness of the moon illuminate you; but you will have the Lord as an everlasting light, and your God for your glory.*

[29] *If I have delighted.*

Here Job touches on how excellent he was toward others, and he says three things: first, how he carried himself toward his enemies; second, he sets forth an anthypophora[117] of a tacit objection, in that place:[118] *If I have hidden;* third, how excellent he was toward his friends, in that place:[119] *If I have been frightened.*

And that is: ***If I have delighted in the downfall of him who hated me,*** fulfilling what the Lord says in Mt 5:[120] *Love your enemies;* for he who loves his enemy does not delight in his downfall. ***and have exulted that evil found him,*** just as joy belongs to the heart, in the same way exultation belongs to the body; and exultation

113. Jb 21.14.
114. Jer 17.5.
115. Jer 7.18.
116. Is 60.19.
117. Anthypophora is a rhetorical device according to which the speaker asks himself a question and then immediately provides an answer to it.
118. Jb 31.33.
119. Jb 31.34.
120. Mt 5.44.

happens when the joy of the heart is expressed in the movement of the body. Mi 7:[121] *Do not rejoice, my enemy, over me because I have fallen; I will arise.* Indeed, we ought to hate the faults of our enemies and to love their nature, and therefore not to love their downfall, but to raise them up, as much as we are able, toward the good. Hence, David mourned the downfall of Saul and Jonathan according to 2 Sm 1.[122] Rom 12:[123] *If your enemy is hungry, feed him; if he is thirsty, give him something to drink.*

And Job gives an account of his innocence: **[30]** ***I have not given my throat to sinning.*** The "throat" is the passage connecting the tongue to the heart, and it is said that "the throat sins" when sin proceeds from the heart into the mouth, ***so as to ask for a curse on his soul,*** or to hope for, that is, so as to ask for his misfortune (*malum*) by hoping for it, or so as to hope for it until a curse, which I could not impose immediately, should come upon him. For he loved his "soul," although he hated his iniquity. Sir 21:[124] *When the wicked man curses the devil,* that is, the adversary, *he curses his own soul.* Rom 12:[125] *Bless those who persecute you; bless and do not curse them.*

And Job adds how excellent he was toward the members of his household, and how he tolerated them: **[31]** ***If the men of my tabernacle,*** namely, tenants and those who dwell in my abodes, who seemed to be my friends, ***have not said: "Who will give us of his flesh, so that we may be satisfied?"*** for they so hated him that they demanded to be satisfied from his softer parts, but, pretending not to hear this, he nevertheless tolerated them. Of such people it is said in Jer 9:[126] *Let everyone protect himself from his neighbor, and let him not have faith in any brother of his.* Ps:[127] *With those who hated peace I was peaceable.* An example is that the Lord tolerated Judas in this way, according to Jn 13,[128] and thus He tolerated the Jews as well.

121. Mi 7.8.
122. 2 Sm 1.11–12.
123. Rom 12.20.
124. Sir 21.30.
125. Rom 12.14.
126. Jer 9.4.
127. Ps 119.7.
128. See especially Jn 13.21–27.

Then Job adds how excellent he was toward those outside his household—not his enemies, but those in need of hospitality. And that is: **[32]** ***The stranger has not remained outside,*** hospitality having been refused, of course, ***and,*** what is more, ***my door has stood open to the traveler,*** so that he found it wide open before he knocked, of course. Is 58:[129] *Bring the needy and the wandering into your house.* Heb 13:[130] *Do not neglect* [*to show*] *hospitality, for by this some have entertained angels, the recipients of their hospitality.* Examples are found in Abraham in Gn 18, in Lot in Gn 19, and in the disciples constraining the Lord in Lk 24; hence it is said there:[131] *They constrained Him, saying: Stay with us.*

Next Job excludes a tacit objection. For anyone could say that by means of all these good deeds he wished to hide his sins, although he is nevertheless a sinner. Hence, Job says: **[33]** ***If, as a human*** **(quasi homo),** ***I have hidden my sin.*** The Hebrew has "as Adam" (*quasi Adam*),[132] and it is an allusion to the one who says in Gn 3:[133] *I heard your voice and I hid myself,* that is, I twisted my fault into something else. Jb 20:[134] *Although evil is sweet in his mouth, he hides it under his tongue. He will keep it, and he will not abandon it, and he will hide it in his throat.* Here Gregory says:[135] He who conceals sin by excusing it "hides sin under his tongue." Prv 28:[136] *He who hides his evil deeds will not prosper, but he who confesses and forsakes them will obtain mercy.*

Hence, explaining this, he adds: ***and,*** supply: if, ***I have concealed my iniquity,*** as a hypocrite does or by excusing it, ***in my bosom,*** that is, in the secret place of my heart. Is 43:[137] *Declare your iniquities, so that you may be justified.* Ps:[138] *I said: "I will confess"; and you have forgiven.* Prv 18:[139] *The just person is the first accuser of himself.*

129. Is 58.7.
130. Heb 13.2.
131. Lk 24.29.
132. The transliteration of the Hebrew is *k*^{e}*'adam.*
133. Gn 3.10.
134. Jb 20.12–13.
135. Gregory, *Mor.* 15.11.13.
136. Prv 28.13.
137. Is 43.26.
138. Ps 31.5.
139. Prv 18.17.

And Job adds how excellent he was toward his relatives: [34] ***If I have been frightened by a very great multitude,*** supply: of needy relatives, for he received all of them with his bountiful bosom of charity. Lk 6:[140] *Give to everyone who asks of you.* And he explains this, adding: ***and,*** that is, ***the contempt of relatives,*** that is, relatives despised on account of their poverty, ***has terrified me.*** Is 58:[141] *Do not despise your own flesh.* An example is found in Tb 1:[142] *When Tobit saw Gabael in need among a great crowd of his kindred, by means of a handwritten document he gave him a sum of money.* ***and I have not rather remained silent***, lest, of course, by speaking I might terrify them, and so they might be afraid to come. Is 42:[143] *I have remained ever silent, I have not spoken, I have been patient.* ***and I have not gone away from the door,*** as certain people do who do not want to be found at home by visitors, so that the family may refuse [to show] hospitality to those who are not present before them. The opposite is said in Gn 18:[144] *The Lord appeared to Abraham in the valley of Mamre as he was sitting at the door of his tent in the very heat of the day.* For the heat of the day did not drive Abraham away from his door, with the result that he showed hospitality to those passing by.

[35] ***Who would grant to me a listener.***

Here Job asks that all his deeds be written down and that he be judged according to the writing of the truth, with a view either toward punishment or toward a crown.

And that is: ***Who would grant to me a listener,*** who may listen to the arguments of my defense, of course, just as Susanna [exclaimed] in Dn 13:[145] *O Lord, eternal God, you who are the knower of hidden things, you who know all things before they happen, you know that they have borne false witness against me.* And after a few words:[146] *And the Lord heard her voice.* ***that the Almighty may hear my desire.*** Ps:[147] *O Lord, hear my prayer, and let my cry come to you.* ***and that He Himself who judges,*** who will write nothing except true and

140. Lk 6.30.
141. Is 58.7.
142. Tb 1.17.
143. Is 42.14.
144. Gn 18.1.
145. Dn 13.42–43.
146. Dn 13.44.
147. Ps 101.2.

just things, ***would write a book,*** concerning my actions, of course. Jb 19:[148] *Who will grant me that my words be written down?* **[36]** ***so that I may carry it on my shoulder,*** before the judge, of course. Mal 3:[149] *A book of remembrance*[150] *was written in the Lord's presence;* but this is the book of conscience, which everyone carries before the Lord. Dn 7:[151] *The court sat in judgment, and the books were opened.* ***and place it,*** that is, what has been composed in a book, ***around me as a crown?*** For I know that I will be crowned as a result of things written in the book. Sir 45:[152] *A crown of gold upon his mitre, engraved with a sign of sanctity.* Ps:[153] *You have crowned him with glory and honor.* **[37]** ***With every step of mine,*** that is, of my virtues and works, ***I would proclaim it,*** that is, I would bring it forward in His presence. Jb 10:[154] *Show me why you judge me in this way.* ***and as if to a prince,*** to one judging rightly, of course, ***I would offer it,*** certainly so that he might judge me according to things written in the book. Zec:[155] *Every thief, as it has been written, will be judged, and everyone who swears will similarly be judged according to this.* Hab 2:[156] *Write down what you have seen, and make it plain on tablets, so that whoever reads it might run through it quickly.* And Job says "as if to a prince" because it is said in Is 32:[157] *The prince will reflect upon things that are worthy of a prince, and he will stand above the rulers.* And in the same place:[158] *Princes shall rule in judgment.* And in addition to this:[159] *He who is foolish will no longer be called prince.*

And to complement everything that has been said, Job adds concerning his justice for the one who is rich: **[38]** ***If my land cries out against me.*** By means of metonymy the "land cries out" when the laborers of the land cry out about wages taken away from

148. Jb 19.23.

149. Mal 3.16.

150. Here I read *monumenti* with MS E, rather than *in monumento* with Weiss's edition.

151. Dn 7.10.

152. Sir 45.14.

153. Ps 8.6.

154. Jb 10.2.

155. Zec 5.3.

156. Hab 2.2.

157. Is 32.8.

158. Is 32.1.

159. Is 32.5.

them. Jas 5:[160] *Behold, the wages of your laborers, who have reaped your fields, cry out.* ***and its furrows mourn with it.*** "Furrows mourn" when those plowing and cultivating the land mourn the loss not of the parcels supporting them, but of the crops that have been carried away. Jl 1:[161] *The farmers have been dismayed, the vineyard workers have howled over the wheat and the wine and the barley, because the harvest of the field has perished.* Is 17:[162] *The harvest is taken away on the day of inheritance, and it will cause you to grieve deeply.*

And explaining what he has said, Job adds: **[39]** ***if I have eaten,*** that is, have consumed, ***its crops,*** namely, of my land, ***without money,*** with which I might remunerate the laborers, of course, which is against the commandment of the Lord. Dt 24:[163] *Before the sun goes down, you shall pay him the price of his labor.* ***and have afflicted,*** supply: by not dividing its crops with them, ***the soul,*** that is, the animate life, ***of its farmers,*** that is, of the land. Sir 34:[164] *He who takes away the bread earned by sweat is like one who kills his neighbor. He who sheds blood and he who defrauds the hired worker are brothers.*

And he adds the punishment for this sin: **[40]** ***let thistles grow up for me instead of wheat,*** which is grain, of course, the food of human beings, and this is an allusion to the curse on human beings given by the Lord for the first sin. Gn 4:[165] *When you work the earth, it will not give its fruit. But it will bring forth thorns and thistles for you.*[166]

And because the earth brings forth not only food for human beings, but also fodder for beasts, Job adds: ***and thorns,*** supply: let them grow up for me, so that my beasts may not be without fodder, of course, ***instead of barley,*** which is the food of beasts. Is 30:[167] *Your oxen and the colts of donkeys, which work the land, will eat mixed grain, as it was winnowed on the threshing floor;* for mixed grain is barley blended with broken stalks, which is the food of beasts. Dt 25:[168] *You shall not muzzle the ox that threshes your grain on the floor.*

160. Jas 5.4.
161. Jl 1.11.
162. Is 17.11.
163. Dt 24.15.
164. Sir 34.26–27.
165. Gn 4.12.
166. This second sentence is not from Gn 4.12, but rather is from Gn 3.18.
167. Is 30.24.
168. Dt 25.4.

CHAPTER 32

SO THESE ***three men ceased.***

The opinion of Elihu is introduced in this portion [of the book], and it is divided into two parts. In the first of these, the order of the opinion introduced is determined; in the second, the opinion itself is delimited, below in that place:[1] *Listen, therefore, O Job.*

The first part is divided into three. In the first division, a preface to that opinion is presented in the mode of a narrative. In the second division, the concern of the preface is set forth in the words of Elihu, in that place:[2] *Elihu, the son of Barachel, responded.* In the third division, the mode of [his] speaking (*modus proponendi*) is set forth, in that place:[3] *And they were afraid.*

In the first division there are three things: for first it is shown how the three [friends] were in agreement about the opinion of Job; second, how Elihu, moved by zeal for the truth, prepared himself to respond, in that place:[4] *Then Elihu was angry and indignant;* third, how he began, in that place:[5] *Therefore, Elihu.*

But[6] it must be noted beforehand that the three opinions that have been set forth are called more ancient, because they are from common and general [principles], which have been present from the first discovery of the arts and sciences, as Aristotle says at the end of *On Sophistical Refutations.*[7] And those coming later have brought together and augmented these common

1. Jb 33.1.
2. Jb 32.6.
3. Jb 32.15.
4. Jb 32.2.
5. Jb 32.4.
6. Here I read *autem* with MSS E, F, and M, rather than the *tamen* of Weiss's edition.
7. Aristotle, *SE* 34.5.

[principles] and have delimited a proposition. And so it is with the three opinions, because they are merely taken from relevant common [principles] and from general first principles, just as from such [common principles] no one is condemned by a just judge except him who has sinned. "You have been condemned: therefore, you have sinned." For these are the first things that are presupposed in rhetoric, and all that the three friends said consisted of such things. And because this person [namely, Elihu] delimits and modifies such principles with a view to a proposition, and he argues more from particulars, which was the study of posterior things, as Aristotle says, therefore this opinion is called younger and posterior.[8] For it is not that he says things different from what the others had said; rather, because this one [namely, Elihu] has brought together and multiplied things relevant to the results of his study of first principles and has argued more plausibly from these things, therefore he says that he is younger and that he has received these things from the divine spirit. For in rhetorical disputations, which are obscured by peripheral issues, as Boethius says,[9] first principles and more general principles are often false; but particular and restricted things, which nevertheless are posterior according to the discovery of the art, are more effective at persuading.

And that is: ***So these three men,*** namely, Eliphaz the Temanite, Bildad the Shuhite, and Zophar the Naamathite, ***ceased to answer Job,*** [here "Job" is] in the dative case; and it adds the reason: ***because he seemed just to himself,*** that is, defending a just opinion. Wis 8:[10] *They will look to me when I speak; and if I discuss many things, they will put their hands over their mouths.* 3 Esdras 3:[11] *Above all things, truth is victorious.* For it is shameful to assail the truth having been recognized, and such a person is thought to be reckless. And therefore these [three men] abandoned responding [to Job] further. In the first book of the *Ethics*, Aristotle says:[12] With both friends, namely, philosophers, coming forth, and with the truth, they know to honor the truth highly. And therefore

8. See Aristotle, *APost.* 1.2.10.
9. See Boethius, *CP* 5.1.
10. Wis 8.12.
11. 3 Esdras (1 Esdras) 3.12.
12. Aristotle, *EN* 1.6.1.

these men, honoring the truth, ceased to answer. Jb 6:[13] *I would not contradict the words of the Holy One.* 2 Cor 13:[14] *For we cannot do anything against the truth, but all things for the truth.* Gal 3:[15] *O senseless Galatians! Who has bewitched you, that you should not obey the truth?*

[2] ***Then [Elihu was] angry.***

Here it mentions what moves Elihu to speak: namely, zeal for the truth and indignation at falsehood. And that is: ***Then Elihu,*** the text describes him from his name, from his birth, from the place of his enthusiasm, and from his family, so that his teaching might be more authentic. For Elihu means "this my God" or "the Lord God," and it signifies that his words are divine. 2 Sm 23:[16] *The Spirit of the Lord has spoken through me, and His word by my tongue.* ***the son of Barachel,*** which means "the blessing of the Lord," on account of the fact that Elihu says that he received knowledge by the blessing of the Lord through the inspiration of the Spirit. Jn 16:[17] *When he, the Spirit of truth, comes, he will teach you all truth.* Sir 39:[18] *His blessing will overflow like a river, and as a flood will saturate the earth.* And the text commends him from the place of his enthusiasm: ***the Buzite,*** which means "despicable" or "contemptible"; it says this, however, on account of his humility, because, on account of the fact that he was younger than the others, he seemed to be despised. Ptolemy says in the *Almagest:*[19] He who, among the wise, is humbler is wiser among the wise, just as deeper holes hold more water. Against this it is said in Sir 11:[20] *Do not despise a person for his appearance. The bee is small among flying creatures, but its fruit has the best sweetness.* Ps:[21] *I am very young and despised.*

Then the text adds [something] about his family. And that is: ***of the family of Ram.*** Abraham was first called "Ram," that is, "ex-

13. Jb 6.10.
14. 2 Cor 13.8.
15. Gal 3.1.
16. 2 Sm 23.2.
17. Jn 16.13.
18. Sir 39.27–28.
19. Like Weiss, I have been unable to find this reference.
20. Sir 11.2–3.
21. Ps 118.141.

alted" (*excelsus*). Afterwards "Ab-" was added and he was called Abram, which means "exalted father"; and "ham," which means "of many," was added at the end.[22] But when at first he lived in Chaldea, he was called only "Ram," from which family he is a descendant by nature; and it is understood [by this name] that he was excellent (*excelsus*) in eloquence and knowledge from his initial studies with his parents. Is 2:[23] *Turn away from man, whose spirit is in his nostrils.* Sir 47:[24] *He gave thanks to the Holy One and to the Most High with words of glory.*

was angry, with fury because of zeal, of course. Jn 2:[25] *Zeal for your house has consumed me.* ***and indignant*** against falsehood. Ps:[26] *Anger is in his indignation.*

Then the text adds why Elihu was angry and why zeal stirred him up. And that is: ***Now he was angry at Job,*** in the accusative case,[27] ***because he was saying that he was just before God.*** Especially in Jb 19, where he said:[28] *At least now understand that God has not afflicted me with an equitable judgment, and He has surrounded me with His scourges.* Indeed, this seems to me inappropriate (*inconveniens*) on account of the fact that it is said in Sir 7:[29] *Do not justify yourself before God, because He is the one who knows the heart.* **[3]** ***Moreover,*** instead of: but, ***he was indignant at [Job's] three friends,*** with indignation against falsehood, of course, ***because,*** supply: although they said that they were wise, ***they had not found a rational answer,*** to his speech certainly. Prv 8:[30] *I detest a perverse way and a double-tongued mouth.* ***but only had condemned Job,*** supply: not according to reason. Prv 10:[31] *Wisdom is found on the lips of the wise person; but there is a rod for the back of the one who lacks a heart.*

22. See Gn 17.5.
23. Is 2.22.
24. Sir 47.9.
25. Jn 2.17; Ps 68.10.
26. Ps 29.6.
27. Albert is simply noting that the name *Iob,* which is indeclinable in Latin, is to be understood here in the accusative case, that is, as the object of the preposition *adversus.*
28. Jb 19.6.
29. Sir 7.5.
30. Prv 8.13.
31. Prv 10.13.

And the text adds how he began: [4] ***Therefore,*** it has begun, but has not moved forward, ***Elihu waited while Job was speaking,*** as someone younger, of course. Jb 29:[32] *Those who heard me waited for my opinion, and being attentive they were silent at my counsel.* And this is what it adds: ***because those who were speaking,*** supply: with Job, ***were older than he.*** Sir 6:[33] *Stand in the multitude of wise elders, and join yourself from your heart to their wisdom, that you may be able to hear every discourse of God.* In this way, as Cicero says, Socrates at first remained silent for seven years before he said anything by responding.[34]

Then it adds the urgency with which Elihu began: [5] ***But when he saw,*** that is, when he had become aware through understanding, ***that they were not able to answer,*** supply: the three friends by means of a rational response, of course, ***Job,*** in the dative case,[35] ***he was exceedingly angry.*** For he saw that the truth had failed. Sir 5:[36] *If you have understanding, respond to your neighbor. But if not, put your hand over your mouth, so that you may not be caught in an undisciplined word and confounded.* [6] ***Then Elihu,*** supply: compelled by so great a necessity, ***the son of Barachel,*** inspired by the blessing of God, ***the Buzite,*** despised on account of his youth, ***answered.*** For wisdom is not believed to be among young people, although sometimes they are nevertheless wise. Dn 13:[37] *The Lord stirred up the spirit of a young boy.* So, because he rejected the wickedness of the old men, ***[and] said,*** supply: on behalf of the truth. Sir 4:[38] *For your soul do not be ashamed to speak the truth.* And after a few verses:[39] *Fight for justice for your soul, and struggle for justice even unto death.*

Then the text adds how Elihu began. And it says three things, namely, his demeanor in listening, his skill in responding, and his manner of disputing.

32. Jb 29.21.

33. Sir 6.35.

34. Like Weiss, I have been unable to find this reference.

35. Here again Albert clarifies the form, and thus the function, of the indeclinable name *Iob.*

36. Sir 5.14.

37. Dn 13.45.

38. Sir 4.24.

39. Sir 4.33.

And that is: ***I am younger in years,*** supply: and therefore my role is to listen, ***and you are older,*** supply: and therefore your role is to speak. Sir 32:[40] *Speak, you who are older, for it is fitting for you to speak the first word.* And in the same place after a few verses:[41] *Young man, scarcely speak with regard to your own case, even if it is essential. If you are asked twice, let your answer be short,* that is, a beginning. ***therefore, hanging my head down,*** in the manner of one listening respectfully, ***I was afraid to reveal my opinion to you.*** Sir 32:[42] *When speaking in the company of important people, you should not be presumptuous; and where the aged are present, you should not speak much.*

And it adds the reason: **[7]** ***For I was hoping that greater age would speak,*** but "I was hoping" because I was supposing that understanding also advanced with increasing age. Lk 2:[43] *The boy Jesus advanced in age and wisdom and grace before God and humans.* Jb 12:[44] *Among the ancients is wisdom, and in many years prudence.* Jn 9:[45] *He is of age; let him speak for himself.* ***and that a multitude of years*** through continuous experience ***would teach wisdom.*** Prv 20:[46] *The dignity of old men is their gray hair,* and this is understood as the gray hair of the mind. Wis 4:[47] *The understanding of a man is his gray hair, and a blameless life is the attainment of old age.* Sir 25:[48] *Three kinds [of people] my soul hates, and I am greatly grieved at their life: a poor man who is proud, a rich man who is deceitful, and an old man who is foolish and irrational.*

But because the knowledge of God comes not from humans, but from God, Elihu adds: **[8]** ***But, as I see,*** supply: from the weakness of the elderly, ***there is a spirit in humans,*** the gift of which is wisdom, of course. Dn 2:[49] *God gives wisdom to the wise, and knowledge to those who understand discipline.* 1 Cor 2:[50] *We have received*

40. Sir 32.4–5.
41. Sir 32.10–11.
42. Sir 32.13.
43. Lk 2.52.
44. Jb 12.12.
45. Jn 9.21.
46. Prv 20.29.
47. Wis 4.8–9.
48. Sir 25.3–4.
49. Dn 2.21.
50. 1 Cor 2.12.

not the spirit of this world, but the Spirit that is of God, so that we may know the things that have been given to us by God. ***and the inspiration*** **[*of the Almighty*],**[51] the secret suggestion of the Spirit teaching within, ***gives understanding,*** of divine things, of course. Jn 14:[52] *He* [*that is, the Holy Spirit*] *will teach you all things, and supply you with everything.*

And he introduces the logical consequence of that, and so it is supplied: **[9]** ***Those of great age are not wise,*** in divine things, of course, as a result of long life, because such great things are not learned by experience. Is 65:[53] *A child who is a hundred years old will die.* Indeed, "a child who is a hundred years old will die" when he has not been steeped in the wisdom of God. ***nor do the elderly understand judgment,*** namely, [the judgment] of God. There is an example in Dn 13, in the two elderly judges concerning whom the Lord said:[54] *Unfairness came forth from the older judges, who seemed to rule the people.*

And Elihu seeks to conduct himself according to the manner of disputants, and that is: **[10]** ***Therefore, I will speak,*** according to the truth, of course: ***Listen to me.*** Sir 24:[55] *He who hears me will not be confounded.* Is 55:[56] *Listen, you who hear me, and eat what is good.* ***and I will show you,*** by means of reasons and examples, of course, ***my wisdom*** materially, that is, what I actually know. Wis 7:[57] *Wisdom I have learned without pretense, and I communicate it without envy, and its honor I do not hide.*

And he adds the reason why he ought to have conducted himself in such a manner in disputing: **[11]** ***For I have waited for your words,*** supply: remaining silent and listening. Sir 32:[58] *Listen in silence, and because of your reverence, good grace will come to you.* ***I have listened to your wisdom,*** according to reason for those who are to be persuaded, of course, ***as long as you were debating,*** that is, dis-

51. Although, following most of the manuscripts, Weiss's edition does not read *Omnipotentis* here, MS F adds it in the margin.

52. Jn 14.26.

53. Is 65.20.

54. Dn 13.5.

55. Sir 24.30.

56. Is 55.2.

57. Wis 7.13.

58. Sir 32.9.

puting, ***with your words,*** for disputing, of course. Sir 32:[59] *Where there is no listening, do not pour out words, and refuse to be extolled inappropriately in your wisdom.* **[12]** ***and as long as I thought*** according to age ***that you were saying something,*** supply: contrary to Job, ***I considered it,*** supply: remaining silent. Ps:[60] *I became as a man who does not hear, and who does not have any reproofs in his mouth.* Ezek 3:[61] *I will make your tongue stick to the roof of your mouth, and you will be dumb, and not as a man who reproves.* ***but, as I see,*** through the actual experience of your words, of course, ***there is no one who can convict Job,*** in the accusative case.[62] Jb 6:[63] *Respond, I beg you, without contention; and, speaking that which is just, make your judgment. And you will not find iniquity on my tongue, nor in my throat will stupidity resound.*

And this is what follows: ***and answer his words among you.*** Jb 6:[64] *Why have you disparaged the words of truth, whereas there is none of you who can convict me?* Jb 9:[65] *If he wishes to contend with him, he will not be able to answer one [word] for a thousand.*

Then Elihu adds the necessity of his responding, namely, so that the truth would not appear to collapse. And that is: ***Lest perhaps you should say: We have found wisdom*** in his words, that is to say, in what follows from his words. ***God,*** supply: as if unjust according to his [namely, Job's] merits, ***has cast him down,*** by an unjust judgment, ***and not a human,*** supply: has been cast down according to his merits. Hence Jb 8:[66] *God will not reject the simple, nor stretch out His hand to evildoers.*

And he sets forth the mode according to which he, compelled by the need for the truth, will respond, and that is: **[14]** ***He has said nothing to me,*** by which, of course, he [namely, Job] might have provoked me to indignation, supply: as he has provoked

59. Sir 32.6.

60. Ps 37.15.

61. Ezek 3.26.

62. Here again Albert indicates the form and function of the indeclinable Latin name *Iob,* namely, that it is to be read in the accusative case and thus understood as the direct object of the verb.

63. Jb 6.29–30.

64. Jb 6.25.

65. Jb 9.3.

66. Jb 8.20.

you. Jb 18:[67] *Why have we been thought of as beasts and have been vile in your sight?* ***and I will not answer him according to your words,*** as one having been provoked, of course. For one who has been provoked is not able to answer sweetly and with love for the truth. Sir 4:[68] *Answer him with peaceable words in gentleness.*

[15] ***And they were afraid.***

Here the mode of [Elihu's] speaking (*modus proponendi*) is touched upon, and it is mentioned first that he spoke (*proposuit*) while the others remained silent; second, that he spoke with zeal for the truth constraining him; third, that he spoke without respect of persons.

And that is: ***And they,*** supply: the three friends, ***were afraid,*** and their fear was that of reverence for the truth, which is the fear of wonder, and this is what follows: ***and answered no more.*** Jb 40:[69] *Remember the battle, and speak no more.* ***and they withheld their speech,*** so neither Job nor Elihu answered further, of course. Lam 3:[70] *He will sit alone and remain silent, because he has taken it upon himself.* Sir 7:[71] *Refuse to be verbose in a crowd of elders, and do not repeat a word in your prayer.* [16] ***Since, therefore, I have waited,*** for others to speak on behalf of the truth certainly, ***and they have not spoken.*** Is 10:[72] *There was none that moved a wing or made the least noise.* ***they stood,*** not resisting falsehood, of course, ***and answered no more,*** by saying something as a testimony to the truth, although it is nevertheless written in Sir 4:[73] *And do not refrain from speaking at the time of salvation.*

And therefore, supply: for the sake of upholding the truth, [17] ***I will respond for my part.*** Acts 4:[74] *We cannot but speak the things that we have heard and seen.* ***and will show my knowledge,*** that is, the things that I truly know. 1 Jn 1:[75] *What we have heard, what we have seen with our own eyes, what we have observed, this we*

67. Jb 18.3.
68. Sir 4.8.
69. Jb 40.27.
70. Lam 3.28.
71. Sir 7.15.
72. Is 10.14.
73. Sir 4.28.
74. Acts 4.20.
75. 1 Jn 1.3.

announce to you. Rom 10:[76] *We believe with the heart according to justice; but confession with the mouth is made according to salvation.*

Then Elihu adds that he set forth the things that he said with zeal for the truth constraining him. And that is: **[18]** ***I am full of words,*** that is, with fruitfulness or knowledge of eloquence according to every rhetorical color and topic. Lk 21:[77] *I will give you a mouth and wisdom, which none of your enemies will be able to resist.* Wis 10:[78] *Wisdom opened the mouths of the mute and made the tongues of infants eloquent.* ***and the spirit of my belly constrains me,*** that is, the spirit of understanding in my inner parts urges me to speak. 2 Cor 5:[79] *The love of Christ urges us.* Something similar is said of Paul in Acts 17:[80] *The spirit of Paul was urged on within him when he saw that the city was given over to idolatry.*

Moreover, the text makes clear that Elihu spoke by means of a sign and a comparison: **[19]** ***Behold, my stomach,*** that is, my disposition (*affectus*) toward speaking on behalf of the truth, ***is as though new wine without vent,*** which, of course, pushes against its vessel so that it causes it to burst, ***which bursts new vessels,*** that is, it opens them so that it may breathe. There is a parallel in Acts 2, where certain people were saying to the apostles, who were speaking in various tongues as a result of the Spirit constraining them, *They are full of new wine.*[81] Mt 9:[82] *No one puts new wine into old wineskins. Otherwise, the wineskins burst, and the wine pours out.*

And he continues with a similitude: **[20]** ***I will speak and breathe a little,*** that is, I will bring forth a little something from the spirit, for not everything that is according to the spirit can be brought forth. Jb 26:[83] *Since we have heard barely a small drop of His word, who will be able to behold the thunder of His majesty?* ***I will open my lips,*** supply: about to say great things. Mt 5:[84] *And, opening His mouth,*

76. Rom 10.10.
77. Lk 21.15.
78. Wis 10.21.
79. 2 Cor 5.14.
80. Acts 17.16.
81. Acts 2.13.
82. Mt 9.17.
83. Jb 26.14.
84. Mt 5.2.

He taught them. The Gloss says:[85] as if He was about to say great things. Ps:[86] *O Lord, you will open my lips.* ***and I will answer,*** on behalf of the truth, of course. 1 Pt 3:[87] *Being prepared to respond to everyone who asks you with a reason for the hope that is in you.*

Moreover, Elihu adds how sincerely he is going to set forth his position and without respect of persons, and secretly he observes the three friends, noting that they are in agreement with Job, by taking each one's person into consideration.

And that is: **[21]** ***I will not take into consideration the person of a man,*** so as to stray from the truth, of course. Jas 2:[88] *Have faith in our Lord Jesus Christ of glory, but without respect of persons.* ***and I will not compare God to a human being,*** by taking the person of the human being into consideration, of course. Is 40:[89] *To whom have you likened God? Or what image will you set up for Him?* And a little beyond this:[90] *"And to whom have you likened me or compared me?" says the Holy One.*

And he adds the reason for this: **[22]** ***For I do not know how long I will persist,*** hence, according to the short span of corruptible life, of course, and I will not abandon the truth by means of doubt. Eccl 9:[91] *Man does not know his own end.*

And, explaining this, he adds: ***and,*** that is, ***whether after a short time my Maker may take me away,*** for it belongs to Him who made and gave the spirit to take it away. Eccl 12:[92] *The spirit will return to God, who gave it.* Ps:[93] *You will take away their spirit, and they will pass away, and they will return to their dust.*

85. Cf. *GO* on Mt 5.2.
86. Ps 50.17.
87. 1 Pt 3.15.
88. Jas 2.1.
89. Is 40.18.
90. Is 40.25.
91. Eccl 9.12.
92. Eccl 12.7.
93. Ps 103.29.

CHAPTER 33

HEAR, THEREFORE, *O Job, my speech.*

After touching upon the mode of his speaking lightly beforehand, Elihu follows the movement of the disputation according to the positions, and it [namely, Elihu's speech] is divided into four parts according to the four positions. The first is the position of Eliphaz, and Elihu argues against this in the present chapter. The second is the position of Bildad, and he disputes this in chapter 34, in that place:[1] *Proclaiming, therefore.* The third position is constructed from both, namely, from that of Eliphaz and Bildad, and Elihu pursues this onc in chapter 35, in that place:[2] *Therefore, Elihu.* In the fourth place he disputes the position of Zophar, and he pursues it in chapter 36 and chapter 37, in that place:[3] *Elihu also added.*

This chapter is divided into three parts. In the first part an entrance into the disputation is set forth on the part of the one disputing; in the second part the position in relation to which he disputes [is set forth], in that place:[4] *Now you have spoken in my hearing;* in the third part, the disputation [is set forth], in that place:[5] *I will answer you that God is greater than the human.*

In the first part Elihu calls [Job] to attention at first; second, he exhibits behavior customary for a fellow-disputant, in that place:[6] *If you are able, answer;* third, he excuses words that have been spoken imperfectly and grants boldness to his respondent,

1. Jb 34.1.
2. Jb 35.1.
3. Jb 36.1.
4. Jb 33.8.
5. Jb 33.12.
6. Jb 33.5.

in that place:[7] *Behold, God has created me also.* But Elihu rouses [Job] to pay attention, because he will speak plainly great things, and wisely things that have been contemplated, and with a simple intention things that have been proposed, and with certitude true and pure things, and prophetically things that have been inspired.

And that is: ***Hear, therefore, O Job,*** with the interior ear, of course. Mt 15:[8] *Hear and understand.* Jb 34:[9] *The ear examines words.* ***my speech,*** which I speak, that is, I speak outwardly, so that it may be clear for the purpose of understanding. Neh 9:[10] *They read in the book of the law [of God] distinctly and clearly, so that all were able to understand.* ***and pay attention to all my words,*** from the beginning, to be sure, all the way to the end, so that you may hear. Prv 1:[11] *A wise man who listens will be wiser.* Song 1:[12] *We will make for you golden [necklaces resembling] small eels* (murenulas), *inlaid with silver.* A small eel glides (*serpit*), and "speech" (*sermo*) is derived from *serpo, serpis;* speech inlaid with silver, however, is clothed with rhetorical colors so that it may glide into the ears of hearers more easily.

And Elihu adds that he will speak clearly and [say] great things: **[2]** ***Behold, I have opened my mouth,*** about to speak great things and clear things, of course. Ps:[13] *Open your mouth, and I will fill it.* And he adds: ***my tongue,*** which is connected to the heart, and therefore it brings forth things contemplated in advance and articulated, ***will speak*** things that have been contemplated and articulated, and learned things ***in my jaws,*** that is, movement near the jaws produces learned speech. At the end of Prv:[14] *She has opened her mouth to wisdom, and the law of clemency is on her tongue.* Sir 24:[15] *Wisdom will open her mouth in the churches*

7. Jb 33.6.
8. Mt 15.10.
9. Jb 34.3.
10. 2 Esdras (Neh) 8.8.
11. Prv 1.5.
12. Song 1.10.
13. Ps 80.11.
14. Prv 31.26.
15. Sir 24.2.

of the Most High, and will glory in the sight of His power. Ps:[16] *The mouth of the just person will contemplate wisdom, and his tongue will speak judgment.*

And he adds concerning his simple intention, [which is] both true and pure: [3] ***My words,*** supply: are going to be set forth, ***by a simple heart.*** Mt 6:[17] *If your eye is simple, your whole heart will be full of light.* And he says this, lest he seem to use the precautions of the sophists. ***and [my lips]***[18] ***will speak a pure,*** purified of the falsehood of perverseness, ***sentence,*** namely, of certain truth. Prv 8:[19] *All my words are just, and there is nothing wicked or perverse in them.* Sir 21:[20] *The words of the wise will be weighed in a balance.*

And Elihu adds that he will speak inspired things prophetically: [4] ***The spirit of God has created me,*** in the form of wisdom, of course. Wis 7:[21] *For in her,* namely, Wisdom, *is the holy spirit of understanding.* ***and the breath,*** that is, the inspiration, ***of the Almighty has given me life,*** certainly with a view to the life of wisdom. Sir 4:[22] *Wisdom breathes life into her children; she supports those who seek her and will go before them in the way of justice.*

Then Elihu adds how he exhibits behavior customary for a fellow-disputant: [5] ***If you are able, answer me.*** For this is the customary behavior of an opponent, that he receives and hears the answer of the respondent, because otherwise he is impudent, if he so overwhelms the respondent with his words that the respondent is not allowed to answer. Jb 11:[23] *Can it be that one who says many things will not also listen? Or will a verbose man be justified?* ***and stand up against my face,*** so that you can hear each word that flows from my mouth, of course. Jerome, in the Helmeted Prologue (*prooemio Galeato*), says: "I do not know what hidden energy the act of a living voice possesses; flowing from the mouth of

16. Ps 36.30.

17. Mt 6.22.

18. *Labia mea* is absent from Weiss's edition and from the MSS on which his edition is based, except MS F, where this phrase appears in the margin.

19. Prv 8.8.

20. Sir 21.28.

21. Wis 7.22.

22. Sir 4.12.

23. Jb 11.2.

the teacher, it resounds loudly in the student's ear."[24] Song 2:[25] *Show me your face. Let your voice sound in my ears.*

And Elihu sets forth an excuse for those who have spoken imperfectly. And that is: [6] ***Behold, God has created both me,*** the opponent, ***and you,*** the respondent, ***in the same way,*** namely, according to His own image with regard to the capacity of the intellect. Sir 17:[26] *God created him according to His own image.* And this [is said] as far as the soul is concerned. ***and from the same clay,*** as far as the body is concerned, ***I too was formed,*** supply: in the same way as you also. Jer 18:[27] *As clay is in the hand of the potter, so are you in my hand, O house of Israel.* And he says this in order to excuse the imperfect. Wis 9:[28] *The body, which is corruptible, weighs down the soul, and the earthly dwelling burdens the mind that ponders many things.*

Then Elihu adds by granting boldness to his respondent: [7] ***Nevertheless, let not my amazement,*** supply: that I glitter with such great brilliance, although I am from clay, ***frighten you,*** supply: from responding boldly. There is an example in Moses according to Ex 34:[29] *And when Aaron and the children of Israel saw the face of Moses horned or glittering, they were afraid to come near.* ***and let not my eloquence*** with regard to the force of argumentation and the order of holding forth and with regard to effectiveness ***be burdensome to you.*** For it is human for someone who is less skilled to be frightened and to become silent in the presence of one who is wiser and more eloquent. And Moses also suffered from this, according to Ex 4:[30] *I beseech you, O Lord, I have never been elo-*

24. Jerome, *Ep. 53 (alia 103) ad Paulinum* (PL 22:541). For a recent edition and French translation of the *Prologus in libro Regum,* see Jérôme, *Préfaces aux livres de la Bible,* textes latins des éditions de R. Weber et R. Gryson et de l'abbaye Saint-Jérôme (Rome), trans. Aline Canellis, Sources Chrétiennes no. 592 (Paris: Cerf, 2017), 322–37, esp. 332–33, where he describes this Prologue as "quasi galeatum principium omnibus libris, quos Hebraeo uertimus in Latinum."

25. Song 2.14.

26. Sir 17.1.

27. Jer 18.6.

28. Wis 9.15.

29. Ex 34.30.

30. Ex 4.10.

quent, neither yesterday nor the day before, on account of which you have spoken to your servant. I am encumbered in speech and slow of tongue.

[8] ***Now you have spoken.***

Here begins the part in which Elihu sets forth the position that he wants to pursue by means of disputing; and it is taken from the words of Job, which he spoke against Eliphaz. Moreover, its meaning is understood in that sentence that Job spoke in chapter 6:[31] *If only my sins, for which I have deserved wrath, and the calamity that I suffer were weighed in a balance.*

And that is: ***Now you have spoken in my hearing,*** in such a way that I understood what was heard, of course, ***and I have heard,*** that is, I have understood, ***the sound of your words.*** Jb 13:[32] *Behold, all these things my eyes have seen and my ears have heard, and I have understood each one.* [9] ***I am clean,*** from the root of sin, which is inordinate desire (*libido*) or concupiscence, ***and without fault,*** that is, without sins of omission; ***I am spotless,*** as much as a spot, which sin has caused in the soul, is concerned, ***and there is no iniquity in me,*** toward my neighbor. Job did not say these things with these [exact] words, but Elihu draws them out from what he did say in Jb 16:[33] *These things I have suffered with no iniquity of my hand, since I have offered to God pure prayers.* And he adds: [10] ***Because He has found complaints against me,*** namely, God; that is, He has provided the occasion for finding complaints; and Elihu has taken this from what Job said in chapter 13:[34] *How great are my iniquities and sins? My crimes and transgressions show to me. Why do you hide your face, and consider me your enemy?* And Elihu adds what is said in the same place after a few verses:[35] [11] ***He has put my feet in shackles,*** in order that He might hold me captive, as it were; ***and has watched over my paths,*** and if He wanted to number them, He would have taken the opportunity starting from some point. Jb 13:[36] *You have put my feet in shackles, and you have kept a close watch over all my paths, and you have inspected the steps of my feet.*

31. Jb 6.2.
32. Jb 13.1.
33. Jb 16.18.
34. Jb 13.23–24.
35. Cf. Jb 13.27, the words of which Albert sets down immediately below.
36. Jb 13.27.

[12] ***Therefore, is this the thing in which you are justified?*** because neither do you have a clean heart nor does God lie in wait for the human being so as to capture him.

I will answer you.

Here Elihu begins to dispute the position introduced. And he generally says the same thing that Eliphaz said, but he draws it out all the way to particulars, which Eliphaz did not do. For in rhetorical disputations the argument must be drawn out all the way to the farthest particulars, if the conclusion is bound to anticipate objections. Hence, concerning what Eliphaz said[37]—*Call to mind, I beg you, who that was innocent has ever perished? Or when were the upright destroyed?*—Elihu intends to show by means of such reasoning that, if God has scourged someone whom He warned earlier and the person has not set himself right, God has not condemned an innocent person; yet, if God has struck someone and has healed the one who has been reproved,[38] it is evident that God has struck the person for no reason except sin; and therefore, if Job was so struck, he was not struck as an innocent person, and so it is clear that this life is governed in such a way that each person is repaid according to merits. Hence, Elihu says:

I will answer you that God is greater than the human, and therefore He sees in the human what the human does not see in his very self. Ps:[39] *Darkness will not be concealed from you.* And again:[40] *My bone is not hidden from you.* And yet again:[41] *Your eyes have seen my imperfect being.* Jb 32:[42] *I will not compare God to a human being.*

And after this Elihu brings in a refutation: [13] ***Do you contend against Him,*** that is, God, concerning this, of course, ***because He has not answered all,*** supply: each one, ***of your words?*** that is to say, why He has done this and that particular thing to you. And Elihu takes this from what Job said in chapter 13:[43] *Call me, and I will*

37. Jb 4.7.

38. Here I read *correptum* with MSS EFM, rather than the *correctum* of Weiss's edition.

39. Ps 138.12.

40. Ps 138.15.

41. Ps 138.16.

42. Jb 32.21.

43. Jb 13.22–23.

answer you; or at least I will speak, and you answer me. How great are my iniquities and sins? My crimes and transgressions show to me.

And he sets forth a response to this point: [14] ***God speaks once,*** that is, in one manner He admonishes by scourging in general, ***and does not repeat the same thing a second time,*** so as to admonish a person for particular sins.

Then Elihu specifies three modes in which God speaks once in general to anyone whatsoever and does not repeat by admonishing a person for particular sins: the first of these is through hidden inspiration; the second is through tribulation hurled at the person; the third is through the admonition of an angel outwardly displayed. And if the person is corrected by means of any of these modes, he is liberated by God and is restored to his former state of health and prosperity. Nor is it necessary that the sinner be admonished for particular sins. And Gregory says[44] that admonition through Scripture is reduced to the admonition through inspiration. And this, therefore, is what he says, and this alone is what Elihu adds to the reasoning of Eliphaz, in order to make clear that an innocent person has never been destroyed.

And that is: [15] ***Through a dream in a nocturnal vision.*** He says "through a dream" because a dream is something that happens to one who is sleeping; but the act of sleeping or sleep is a tie that binds the senses, and when the noise of sensible things ceases, we perceive revelations, which happen during sleep, to a greater extent. Song 5:[45] *I sleep, but my heart remains awake.*

And he defines this mode of speaking still further: "in a nocturnal vision" on account of the fact that at night or in the dead of night noises cease to a greater extent, and through signs of revelation and through signs of celestial motion the soul more readily perceives the movements[46] of future things. Hence, Dn 7:[47] *I beheld in a vision of the night.* Nm 24:[48] *The human whose*

44. See Gregory, *Mor.* 23.19.34.

45. Song 5.2.

46. Here I read *motus* with MSS EFM, rather than the *eventus* of Weiss's edition.

47. Dn 7.7.

48. Nm 24.3–4.

eye was closed has spoken; the hearer of the words of God has spoken, he who beheld the vision of Almighty God, he who fell, and so his eyes are opened. And this text intends to say that during sleep Balaam received the revelation of future things.

And this is what Elihu adds: ***when deep sleep falls upon humans.*** "Deep sleep" is profound sleep that binds the sense perception of external things in such a way that no movement of external stimuli is able to come through to the soul. And he indicates this when he says it "falls upon," namely, the intensity of sleep [falls] upon the soul, so that it perfectly binds the soul lest anything external penetrate it; for then it more perfectly perceives the things that come about through revelation.

And this is what he also adds: ***and they are sleeping in their beds,*** in such a way that not even the hardness of the bed causes a certain restlessness, of course. Song 3:[49] *In my bed during the night I sought Him whom my soul loves;* for then I perceived His movement more readily, because at that time I rested from all motion. Jb 7:[50] *If I say, my bed will comfort me, and I will be refreshed speaking to myself on my couch, you will frighten me with dreams, and by means of visions you will shake me with horror.* **[16]** ***then He opens the ears,*** namely, the interior [ears], ***of men* (virorum),** that is, of those who are truly men, being vigorous (*virentes*) within and bold (*viriles*) with regard to the virtues. And therefore Aristotle says in the first book of the *Ethics* that the phantasms of the just are better than those of anyone else.[51] ***and educating them,*** supply: by means of revelation in a dream, ***He instructs,*** that is, He teaches and builds them within, ***with discipline,*** that is, with instruction pertaining to behavior. Indeed, in this way God instructed Jacob, according to Gn 28;[52] He instructed Pharaoh too in this way, according to Gn 41; in this way He instructed Nebuchadnezzar, according to Dn 2;[53] and in the same place[54] [He so instructed] Daniel himself, to whom the mystery concerning

49. Song 3.1.
50. Jb 7.13–14.
51. Aristotle, *EN* 1.13.13.
52. Gn 28.11–15.
53. Dn 2.1–49.
54. Dn 2.19.

the interpretation of Nebuchadnezzar's dream was also revealed in sleep through a vision in the night; in this way He instructed Joseph, the foster-father of the Lord, concerning all the things to be done, according to Mt 2.[55] All that instruction is reduced to this teaching, which through vigorous abstraction from the senses occurs for the human through an oracle or through a vision of revelation, or may occur through signs from heaven, or through angels, or even through unmediated divine inspiration. And there is scarcely a human who is not admonished concerning future things, as Cicero says in the book *On Divination and the Nature of the Gods.*[56]

And this is what Elihu adds: **[17]** ***that He may turn a human away from the things he has been doing,*** namely, from sins, for horrible dreams occur to sinners. Wis 17:[57] *But those who, during that truly powerless night*[58] *that came upon them from the lowest and deepest* [*hell*], *were sleeping the same sleep, that is, during a dream, were being harassed by the fear of monsters.* And he alludes to what Job had said in chapter 7:[59] *You will frighten me with dreams,* as if he had said: "If He frightened you with dreams, you should have withdrawn from wickedness." ***and,*** supply: by withdrawing him in such a way from these things that he has done, ***may deliver him from pride.*** Here arrogance of the heart, by which the sinner does not wish to be made subject to teaching (*praecepto*) and to God who teaches, is called "pride"; for in such a way the beginning of all sin is pride. Tb 4:[60] *Never permit pride to have dominion in your mind or in your words: for all perdition took its beginning from it.* Sir 10:[61] *The beginning of all sin is pride.* **[18]** ***rescuing his soul,*** namely, through this: that He frees him from such pride, ***from corruption,*** that is, from sin, which is the cause of corruption.

55. Mt 2.13.

56. See Cicero, *De div.* 1.6.12 and 1.19.37. It appears that Albert has conflated the titles of these two works.

57. Wis 17.13–14.

58. Here I read *impotentem vere noctem* with MS EFM, rather than *impotentes venere noctem* with Weiss's edition.

59. Jb 7.14.

60. Tb 4.14.

61. Sir 10.15.

Ps:[62] *They have been corrupted, and they have become abominable in their zeal.* ***and,*** supply: rescuing ***his life so that it may not pass to the sword,*** of eternal retribution, of course. Jb 19:[63] *Flee, therefore, from the face of the sword, seeing that the sword is the avenger of iniquities.* And notice that, because the words of Elihu are nothing but the conclusions and expressions of the words of the other three, and in the first place he expresses the words of Eliphaz, for that reason he begins speaking against Job, just as Eliphaz had done above in chapter 4:[64] *In the horror of a nocturnal vision, when deep sleep customarily overtakes humans,* etc.; here Eliphaz said that it was revealed to him that the human is not able to be clean.

[19] ***He rebukes also.***

Here Elihu mentions the second mode by which God speaks, admonishing the human being concerning sin, and does not repeat it a second time for particular sins: and this is through tribulations hurled at the person, which he expands upon in these three ways, namely, through their severity, through the cessation of the appetite, and through their effect.

And that is: ***He rebukes also,*** supply: not only through inspiration, but also ***by means of sorrow in the bed,*** that is [He rebukes] the one falling into the bed, as according to the Septuagint version of Jer 12:[65] *By every scourging you will be taught, O Jerusalem,* where we have: *If those who have been taught will have learned the ways of my people.* Heb 12:[66] *What son is there whom the father does not discipline?* The same [is said] in Prv 3:[67] *My son, do not reject the discipline of the Lord, and do not falter when you are reproved by*

62. Ps 13.1.

63. Jb 19.29.

64. Jb 4.13.

65. Jer 12.16. Like Weiss, I have been unable to find the text here quoted by Albert in the LXX. Rather, the LXX of Jer 12.16, as it has come down to us, reads: καὶ ἔσται ἐὰν μαθόντες μάθωσιν τὴν ὁδὸν τοῦ λαοῦ μου τοῦ ὀμνύειν τῷ ὀνόματί μου Ζῇ κύριος, καθὼς ἐδίδαξαν τὸν λαόν μου ὀμνύειν τῇ Βααλ, καὶ οἰκοδομηθήσονται ἐν μέσῳ τοῦ λαοῦ μου· (*And it shall be, if when learning they learn the way of my people, to swear by my name, "The Lord lives," as they taught my people to swear by the goddess Baal, and they shall be built up in the midst of my people* [NETS]). Albert may be working from memory here and recalling the text inaccurately.

66. Heb 12.7.

67. Prv 3.11.

Him. And Eliphaz said the same in Jb 5:[68] *Do not reject the rebuke of the Lord, because He wounds, but He cures; He strikes, but His hands will heal.*

But Elihu continues and expresses it [namely, the severity of the tribulations by means of which God admonishes concerning sin] in a rhetorical mode, as has been said among the things previously considered:[69] ***and He makes all his bones shrivel up***. By "bones," strength is understood; and Elihu intends [to say] that the stricken person is left destitute of strength by infirmity. Lam 1:[70] *From above He has sent fire into my bones, and He has instructed me.*

And he adds concerning the cessation of the appetite: **[20]** ***Bread,*** that is, any refreshment whatsoever, ***becomes abominable to him in his life*** on account of the disturbance of the appetite; and he alludes to what Job said in chapter 6:[71] *The things that my soul previously was unwilling to touch, now because of anguish are my food.*

And this is what follows: ***and to his soul,*** that is, to his animal life, ***the food that before was desirable,*** and this is the same as what is said in Jb 6:[72] *Or can something tasteless be consumed that is not seasoned with salt?* For sickness from inflamed bile (*per adustam choleram*) infects the palate and tongue, on account of which all these foods seem bitter to those who are sick.[73]

And Elihu expands on this through the effect [of these tribulations]: **[21]** ***His flesh will waste away,*** that is, it will be converted into corruption and putrefaction, ***and his bones, which had been covered,*** supply: by flesh, ***will be made bare***. And on account of words of this sort, as we have already said earlier,[74] Job appears to have been stricken with lupus, which is an ulcer that gnaws away at the flesh and bones and converts them into corruption. Jb 2:[75] *Satan went out from the face of the Lord, and struck Job with the*

68. Jb 5.17–18.

69. See Albert's brief explanation of the mode of rhetorical disputation in his comments on v. 12 above.

70. Lam 1.13.

71. Jb 6.7.

72. Jb 6.6.

73. Cf. Albert, *AL* 3.2.3.

74. See above on Jb 2.7 (*On Job,* vol. 1, 85–86), where, as here, Albert names Job's disease *herpes esthiomenus,* which is known today as lupus.

75. Jb 2.7–8.

worst type of ulcer, from the sole of his foot all the way to the top of his head. And he scraped the discharged pus with a potsherd while sitting on a dung heap. [22] ***His soul,*** that is, his animal life, ***will draw near to corruption,*** that is, to death. Here he alludes to what Job had said above when responding to Eliphaz in Jb 7:[76] *On account of which my soul has chosen suspension, and my bones death. I have given up hope; by no means will I live any longer now.*

And explaining this, Elihu adds: ***and,*** that is, ***his life,*** namely, animal [life], supply: will draw near, ***to death-dealers,*** that is, to signs of death. 1 Sm 2:[77] *The Lord kills and makes alive; He leads down to hell and brings back again.*

[23] ***If there should be an angel.***

Because Eliphaz had said in Jb 5,[78] *Call then, if there is anyone who will respond to you, and turn to any of the saints,* wishing by this to say that Job had offended the saints, and on account of this had no intercessor, therefore Elihu, here delimiting and expressing the words of Eliphaz, says that, thirdly, God admonishes through an intercessor, whom God hears favorably, in order that He might liberate the human. And here three things are said: first, of course, how the person is liberated through an intercessor; second, as if delivering an epilogue, Elihu concludes that God works this three times, in that place:[79] *Behold all these things;* third, he advises paying attention to these things that have been spoken, in that place:[80] *Pay attention, Job.* Regarding the first, there are three points, namely: the favorable answer to the prayer of the intercessor; the reason for the favorable answer, in that place:[81] *His flesh has been consumed;* and the restoration of the fallen person to his former state by means of the intercessor, in that place:[82] *And he will pray to God, and He will be gracious.*

And that is: ***If there should be an angel speaking on behalf of him.*** He calls whatever good being who is, by means of his own intercession, a messenger between God and the fallen person an "an-

76. Jb 7.15–16.
77. 1 Sm 2.6.
78. Jb 5.1.
79. Jb 33.29.
80. Jb 33.31.
81. Jb 33.25.
82. Jb 33.26.

gel." And he intends to say that if he keeps himself in relationship to the saints and to the angels in such a way that they grieve his plight and intercede on behalf of him, he will be restored by the intercession of the saints. Sir 24:[83] *She will be admired in the holy assembly, and in the multitude of the elect she will have praise, and among the blessed she will be blessed.* 2 Mc 3:[84] *Give thanks to Onias the priest, because on account of him the Lord has granted you life.* 2 Mc 15:[85] *This one is a lover of the brothers and of the people of Israel; this one is he who prays much for the people and for all the holy city.* ***one [person] with regard to similar things,*** supply: [similar] to those things that have been spoken, namely, that he has been corrected either by inspiration or by blows.

And this is what follows: ***to make known human justice,*** to which, of course, he has returned through penance. And this is what is said in the Psalm:[86] *I will praise you, O Lord, with my whole heart, in the council of the just and in the congregation.* For such is the council of the saints, and the congregation helps by interceding; in such a way Tobit was freed, even though he was ordered by the king to be killed, *because many loved him,* according to Tb 1.[87] *In this way Dorcas was raised up by the intercession of the widows,* according to Acts 9.

And this is what follows: **[24]** ***He will have mercy on him.*** Lam 3:[88] *The mercies of the Lord, that we have not been destroyed, because His compassion has not failed.* ***and will say,*** supply: to the intercessor,[89] or speaking to him through inspiration or through the effect. Ps:[90] *The Lord will speak peace in the midst of His people.* An example is found in Moses, according to Ex 32,[91] where, praying on behalf of the people, he was heard; and in Christ, according to Jn 17,[92]

83. Sir 24.3–4.
84. 2 Mc 3.33.
85. 2 Mc 15.14.
86. Ps 110.1.
87. Tb 1.23.
88. Lam 3.22.
89. Here I read *intercessori* with MSS TEFM, rather than the *intercessor* of Weiss's edition.
90. Ps 84.9.
91. Ex 32.31–35.
92. Jn 17.9.

who prayed on behalf of His disciples, and on behalf of Lazarus according to Jn 11;[93] and in Heb 5[94] it is said that in all things *He was heard on account of His reverence.* And that is: ***Free him, so that he may not descend into corruption,*** of death, of course. 1 Sm 2:[95] *He leads down to hell and brings back again.* And in that very place:[96] *He rouses the destitute man from the dust and raises the poor man from the dung heap.* Aaron was such an intercessor, according to Wis 18:[97] *A man without blame, hastening to pray for the people, bringing forth the shield of his ministry, prayer, and by incense making supplication, withstood the wrath and put an end to the calamity, showing that he is your servant.* And after a few verses it says that *he found that which is the way to life.*[98] Ps:[99] *You will not give your holy one to see corruption. You have made known to me the ways of life.*

And this is what he adds: ***I have found that in which,*** that is, according to which thing, ***I may propitiate him,*** supply: having been corrected already. 1 Kgs 21:[100] *Have you not seen how Ahab has humbled himself before me? Therefore, because he has humbled himself for my sake, I will not bring evil in his days.*

And this is what follows: **[25]** ***His flesh has been consumed by punishments,*** and supply: his sin has been consumed together with his consumed flesh. Is 40:[101] *She has received from the hand of the Lord double for all her sins, and He has declared: Because her wickedness has come to an end, her iniquity has been forgiven.* ***let him return to the days of his youth,*** that is, to the state of health and prosperity. Jb 29:[102] *Who will grant me that I might be according to former months, according to the days in which God kept me safe?* And a little beyond this:[103] *As I was in the days of my youth, when God was secretly in my tabernacle.*

93. Jn 11.41–44.
94. Heb 5.7.
95. 1 Sm 2.6.
96. 1 Sm 2.8.
97. Wis 18.21.
98. Cf. Wis 18.23.
99. Ps 15.10–11.
100. 1 Kgs 21.29.
101. Is 40.2.
102. Jb 29.2.
103. Jb 29.4.

And Elihu adds how, having been restored with regard to grace, he is preserved, first with respect to God and second with respect to human beings.

And that is: **[26]** ***He will pray to God,*** that is, he will pray for evils to be removed. Is 19:[104] *The Egyptians return to the Lord, and He will be gracious to them and heal them.* And that is: ***and He will be gracious to him.*** Dn 9:[105] *Listen, O Lord; be gracious, O Lord; do not delay for your own sake, O my God.* ***and he,*** having been restored in such a way with regard to grace, ***will see His face,*** that is, the effect of the grace of God, ***with joy.*** Ex 33:[106] *My face will go before you.* Ps:[107] *Show us your face, and we will be saved.* But "joy," as Gregory says,[108] is such great gladness of the heart that neither can the heart contain it nor can the mouth proclaim it. Is 35:[109] *They will return, and they will come into Zion with praise, and everlasting joy will be upon their heads. They will obtain gladness and joy, and sorrow and mourning will flee.* ***and,*** supply: in this way, ***He,*** supply: God, ***will give back to the human his own justice.*** Gregory says:[110] God's justice given is the human's justice received. But "to give back" is said because what the human had lost through sin has been restored now through penance. Is 63:[111] *I will remember the compassion of the Lord, the praise of the Lord for all the things that the Lord has given back to us, and for the multitude of His good things to the house of Israel, which He has bestowed upon them according to His kindness.*

And Elihu adds how God will turn to humans, calling them to mind again and not oppressing them. And that is: **[27]** ***He will look upon humans,*** that is, He will call them to mind again. Eliphaz said the same thing in Jb 5:[112] *Visiting your likeness, you will not sin.*[113]

And he adds how the one who has been justified will recog-

104. Is 19.22.
105. Dn 9.19.
106. Ex 33.14.
107. Ps 79.4, 8, 20.
108. Gregory, *Mor.* 24.6.10.
109. Is 35.10.
110. Gregory, *Mor.* 24.7.13.
111. Is 63.7.
112. Jb 5.24.
113. Here I read *peccabis* with the Vulgate text (see Albert's text of Jb 5.24

nize his sin in the presence of God and humans and he will confess it for the purpose of justification.

And that is: and ***he will say: I have sinned,*** namely, by transgressing, ***and truly I have fallen short*** by sins of omission. 2 Sm 24:[114] *I am he who has sinned, I have acted unjustly.* At the end of 2 Chr:[115] *I have sinned, O Lord, I have sinned and I acknowledge my iniquity; asking you, I beg you, O Lord, forgive me, forgive me!* ***and I have not received what I deserved,*** namely, eternal punishment; supply: but I have been punished temporally, so that I would not be condemned eternally, indeed in the same way that a good father instructs his son so that he might not be condemned by the Judge at death. Prv 3:[116] *He scourges every son whom He accepts.*

And this is what follows: **[28]** ***He has delivered his soul,*** supply: by scourging, ***lest it go into destruction,*** having relinquished it to its own desire by sinning. 2 Mc 6:[117] *Not as with other nations, [for whom] the Lord waits patiently so that, when the day of judgment arrives, He may punish them according to the fullness of their sins, does He deal with us also, so that, because we had fallen back into our sins in the end, He might finally take vengeance on us. And therefore, indeed, He never withdraws His mercy from us: although He certainly chastises His people with adversities, He does not abandon them.*

And this is what follows: ***but living,*** supply: and having been chastised by scourges, ***it may see the light,*** of truth and prosperity, of course. Is 28:[118] *Vexation alone will impart understanding of what you hear.*

[29] ***Behold, all these things.***

Here, as if delivering an epilogue, Elihu concludes that here God works three times.

And that is: ***Behold, all these things,*** for the correction of the human, of course, ***God works.*** Mi 6:[119] *What more is there that I ought to*

---

in Weiss ed., col. 94, which has *peccabis*), rather than the *precabis* here in Weiss's edition.

114. 2 Sm 24.17.

115. Cf. 1 Chr 21.8, 17.

116. Although Weiss's edition and all the MSS read *Prv III* here, the following words are actually from Heb 12.6.

117. 2 Mc 6.14–16.

118. Is 28.19.

119. Cf. Mi 6.3.

do for you that I have not done? Is 5:[120] *What more is there that I ought to do for my vineyard that I have not done for it?* ***three times within all individually,*** namely, [all] humans, of course, chastising them, namely, through inspiration, through tribulation inflicted, and through an intercessor. Is 40:[121] *Who has weighed out the huge mass of the earth with three fingers?* For with these three fingers, that is, with traces of His own hand, He hung the whole huge mass of the earth, lest it fall down. Prv 22:[122] *Behold, I have described it,* that is, wisdom, *to you in three ways, in thoughts and knowledge, so that I might show you the certainty and the words of truth out of which he might respond to those who sent you.*

And this is what follows: **[30]** ***so that He may call their souls back from corruption,*** that is, from sin, which is the cause of corruption. Is 38:[123] *You have delivered my soul so that it might not be destroyed.* ***and illuminate them,*** namely, their understanding of the truth and of grace, ***with the light of the living,*** that is, of the saints, who truly are alive. Ps:[124] *Because you have delivered my soul from death, and my feet from falling, so that I might be pleasing to God in the light of the living.*

[31] ***Pay attention, Job.***

Here Elihu reminds Job to pay attention to these things that have been said, yet he is also comporting himself with respect to blessed Job in this way: that if Job has a reason for his defense, Elihu will gladly listen to him.

And that is: ***Pay attention, Job,*** to these things that have been said, of course. ***and listen to me,*** by referring to the intellect the things that have been heard. Sir 32:[125] *Listen in silence.* And this is what follows: ***while I am speaking,*** that is, while I complete my speech. Prv 18:[126] *He who answers before he listens shows himself to be a fool and worthy of confusion.*

And Elihu adds that he is not refusing [to hear] the reason for [Job's] defense if he is able to defend himself. And that is: **[32]** ***But if you have anything to say,*** for yourself, of course, ***answer***

120. Is 5.4
121. Is 40.12.
122. Prv 22.20–21.
123. Is 38.17.
124. Ps 55.13.
125. Sir 32.9.
126. Prv 18.13.

me. Acts 26:[127] *You are permitted to provide a reason for yourself.* ***speak,*** by providing a reason for yourself, of course. Jb 13:[128] *Call me, and I will answer you; or at least I will speak, and you answer me.* ***for I want you to appear just,*** as a result of the reasoning of your defense, of course. Nm 11:[129] *Who will grant to me that all people might prophesy, and that the Lord would give them His spirit?* 1 Tm 2:[130] *Who wills that all humans should be saved and come to the knowledge of the truth.* **[33]** ***And if you do not have anything,*** that you can say for yourself, of course, ***listen to me.*** For as Aristotle says in the first book of the *Ethics,*[131] according to Homer, the best person is he who is good through his very own thinking; but he who is not good through his own thinking, but through another's, puts the other's thinking in his mind, and this one is good; but he who is neither good through his own thinking nor puts another's in his mind, this one is surely a useless man. And that is: ***remain silent, and I will teach you wisdom.*** At the end of Sir:[132] *Draw near to me, you ignorant ones, and gather yourselves together into the house of instruction.*

127. Cf. Acts 26.1.
128. Jb 13.22.
129. Nm 11.29.
130. 1 Tm 2.4.
131. See Aristotle, *EN* 1.4.7; and Albert, *Eth.* 1.5.6.
132. Sir 51.31.

CHAPTER 34

PROCLAIMING, ***therefore.***

Here Elihu argues on the side of Bildad by confirming, and by bringing together through delimiting particulars, and by expressing what Bildad said in general. Jb 8:[1] *Can it be that God trips up judgment? or that the Almighty overthrows what is just?* And for that reason, this chapter is divided into two parts.

In the first part, Elihu produces what has been said [by Bildad]; in the second, he warns that what has been said should be weighed out and received by the scales of reason, in that place:[2] *Because, therefore, I have spoken.* Furthermore, in the first part there are two divisions. For, first, Elihu delimits and expresses the speech of Bildad; second, he shows that he who contradicts this falls irremediably upon the judgment of God, in that place:[3] *Can it be that he who does not love judgment* [*is able to be healed*] ? Besides, in the first subdivision, there are three things, namely: an incitement to listen attentively; the position of blessed Job, with which he debates, in that place:[4] *For Job has said;* and the reason adduced against this position, in that place:[5] *May wickedness be far from God.*

With regard to the first [namely, an incitement to listen attentively], four things are said: for first Elihu makes use of a transition; second, he incites [them] to listen; third, he shows through a comparison how they are going to listen; fourth, he asks to be heard according to reason.

1. Jb 8.3.
2. Jb 34.31.
3. Jb 34.17.
4. Jb 34.5.
5. Jb 34.10.

And that is: ***Proclaiming, therefore.*** A word that the heart announces is called a "proclamation," which is called by Damascene an angel of understanding.[6] Ps:[7] *With my lips I proclaim all the judgments of your mouth.* ***Elihu also said these things,*** bringing forward divine truths, he transitioned. Indeed, this signifies that Elihu transitioned from the position of Eliphaz to the position of Bildad, for he wishes to provide a reason concerning particular things, paying close attention to that passage in Sir 24:[8] *Those who explain me* [*namely, Wisdom*] *will have life eternal.*

And Elihu arouses [their] attention: **[2]** ***Hear, wise men, my words,*** for such men know to ponder his words, whereas others neither hold them [in mind] nor ponder them. Sir 21:[9] *The heart of a fool is like a broken vessel, and it will not hold any wisdom at all.* ***and,*** that is, ***you learned ones*** or experts, ***listen to me.*** Boethius, in the book *On the Trinity,* says:[10] "It belongs to the learned man concerning anything whatsoever, as he considers the thing itself, to try to bring forth faith concerning it." Sir 21:[11] *A man possessing knowledge will praise every wise word he hears, and he will add to it; the immoderate man has heard it, and it will displease him, and he will throw it down behind him.*

But that it must be heard by such men Elihu proves by means of a comparison: **[3]** ***For the ear examines words,*** as if he were saying: Just as the ear, whose drum (*tympanum*) is well disposed by means of the auditory nerve, "examines words," ***and the throat,*** disposed by means of the gustatory nerve, ***discerns,*** supply: in the same way that a wise man is able to discern opinions, which a foolish man is not, hence Gregory says:[12] "Just as neither the ear recognizes food nor the throat words, neither therefore does any foolish man understand the judgment of the wise." ***foods,*** that is, the flavors of foods, ***by taste,*** according to which the sense of taste makes a judgment concerning flavors, as Aristotle says

6. See John Damascene, *In Ep. ad Cor.* 2.11.15 (PG 95:761–62); and *F.o.* 2.3 (PL 94:871–72).

7. Ps 118.13.

8. Sir 24.31.

9. Sir 21.17.

10. Boethius, *Trin.* 2 (PL 64:1250A).

11. Sir 21.18.

12. Gregory, *Mor.* 24.15.39.

in the book *On Sense and the Sensible.*[13] Jb 12:[14] *The ear discerns words, and the palate of the one eating* [*discerns*] *the taste.*

And Elihu asks that what has been said be weighed according to reason, and he turns himself toward those standing nearby: [4] ***Let us,*** supply: we who are wise, ***choose judgment for ourselves.*** Jb 6:[15] *Speaking that which is just, make your judgment. And you will not find iniquity on my tongue, nor in my throat will stupidity resound.* ***and among ourselves,*** supply: by conferring, ***let us see what is better,*** namely, whether the speech of Job or the speech of Bildad. Sir 17:[16] *He filled them with the knowledge of understanding, and He gave them a heart for thinking things through.*

And he sets forth the position that, according to the sequence of words, Job did not articulate, but that, according to Elihu's interpretation, follows from his words; and it is contrary to the position of Bildad.

And that is: [5] ***For Job has said*** in the manner of speaking whereby the consequence is said among what precedes: ***I am just.*** Jb 13:[17] *If I will be judged, I know that I will be found just.* ***and God has subverted my judgment,*** supply: by way of consequence, because He does not judge me according to merits. Jb 19:[18] *God has not afflicted me with an equitable judgment, and He has surrounded me with His scourges,* for an inequitable judgment has been subverted by the order of law.

And supply: as a consequence, he said, [6] ***Indeed, in judging me there is a lie.*** Here the corruption of the truth of judgment is called a "lie," which Job did not say by means of words, but Elihu says that this follows from his words—in this way "lie" is understood. Is 59:[19] *We have conceived and have spoken from our heart words of falsehood. Judgment has been turned backwards, and justice has stood far off.* ***my arrow is violent,*** supply: Job said, supply: since it is, ***without any sin.*** And that the "arrow is violent" Eliphaz understands

13. See Aristotle, *SS* 1.
14. Jb 12.11.
15. Jb 6.29–30.
16. Sir 17.5.
17. Jb 13.18.
18. Jb 19.6.
19. Is 59.13–14.

from this, [namely] that Job said in 19:[20] *Behold, I, suffering violence, will cry out, but no one will hear me.*

Moreover, "without [any] sin" is understood from what Job said in 17:[21] *I have not sinned, and my eye abides in bitterness,* and from what he said in Jb 16:[22] *These things I have suffered with no iniquity of my hand.* And before Elihu passes over to the contrary position of Bildad, he expands on Job's sin in such a position.

[7] ***What man is there like Job,*** incomparable among all sinners, of course, on account of the fact that in the teaching of the truth he both lies and blasphemes, as is said concerning Ahab in 1 Kgs 21:[23] *Therefore, there was no other like Ahab, who sold himself to do evil in the sight of the Lord.*

Who, that is, because he, ***drinks up,*** that is, takes in through concupiscence, ***scorn,*** that is, sins to be scorned, ***like water?*** that is, without the obstinacy of conscience resisting, just as water is drunk. Ps:[24] *He put on a curse like a garment, and it entered his entrails as if it were water and like oil in his bones.*

And he adds concerning work: [8] ***Who keeps company*** through the imitation of works ***with those who work iniquity***. Ps:[25] *If you saw a thief, you ran with him, and with adulterers you were a partaker.* ***and walks with wicked men?*** Against this it is said in Prv 1:[26] *My son, if sinners entice you, do not comply with them,* and a little beyond this:[27] *My son, do not walk with them; restrain your foot from their paths.* [9] ***For he has said*** by what he has done, of course: ***A man will not be pleasing to God,*** supply: in his work, ***even if he runs*** with the fleet feet of obedience, of course, ***with Him,*** that is, with God. Mal 3:[28] *You have said: He who serves God labors in vain. And what advantage is it that we have kept His commandments?* This, however, explains what Jb 21 declared on the contrary, where Job said: *Why do the wicked live, why are they placed in elevated positions, and*

20. Jb 19.7.
21. Jb 17.2.
22. Jb 16.18.
23. 1 Kgs 21.25.
24. Ps 108.18.
25. Ps 49.18.
26. Prv 1.10.
27. Prv 1.15.
28. Mal 3.14.

why are they strengthened with riches? For when he said this, [namely] that such people prosper, he seemed to assert that such ones are pleasing to God; and because, as Aristotle says, it belongs to the same customary practice that the wicked are pleasing to anyone and that the good are displeasing,[29] therefore it follows that he seemed to have said that a man will not be pleasing to God even if he runs with Him. Jer 12:[30] *Why does the way of the wicked prosper: why does it go well for all who transgress and act unjustly? You have planted them, and they have taken root; they prosper and bring forth fruit.*

And before Elihu transitions to the contrary position of Bildad, he begs to be heard. And that is: **[10] *Therefore, you prudent men* (viri cordati),** that is, wise men, for others are said not to have a heart (*cor*). [***hear me:***][31] Hos 7:[32] *Ephraim is like a dove that has been led astray, not having a heart.* Prv 11:[33] *He who deceives his friend is destitute of heart.*

And Elihu confirms the position of Bildad through assertion, reason, and effect. And that is: ***May wickedness be far from God,*** that is, this "wickedness" of infidelity, [namely, that says] that God trips up judgment, "may it be far from God." Hab 1:[34] *Your eyes are too pure to look upon,* that is, to approve *evil, and you will not be able to gaze at iniquity with your eye,* of good will, of course. ***and*** may ***iniquity,*** that is, perversity of judgment, be far ***from the Almighty,*** who, to be sure, has no superior. Ezek 18:[35] *Can it be that my way is not just, and rather are not your ways perverse?* Tb 3:[36] *All your judgments are just, and all your ways mercy and truth.*

And he shows this through reason. **[11] *For He will repay the human,*** with good or evil, of course, ***for his work,*** that is, according to the human's work. Rom 2:[37] *Who will render to each one*

29. See Aristotle, *Top.* 2.7.1.

30. Jer 12.1–2.

31. Although the Vulg. reads *audite me* here, this phrase is omitted from Albert's commentary.

32. Hos 7.11.

33. Prv 11.12.

34. Hab 1.13.

35. Ezek 18.25.

36. Tb 3.2.

37. Rom 2.6.

according to his works. ***and according to the ways of each one,*** these are plans (*cogitationes*), which are ways leading toward works, ***He will repay them,*** with good or bad things, of course. Prv 1:[38] *They will eat, therefore, the fruit of their own way, and they will be filled with their own schemes.*

And he confirms this reasoning to a greater extent by first asserting and strengthening the intended conclusion: ***For truly God will not condemn without cause,*** that is, without the cause of sin. Gn 18:[39] *Far be it from you to do this, and to slay the just with the wicked, so that what happens to the wicked should happen to the just.* ***nor does the Almighty subvert judgment,*** that is, He is not able to subvert it. Ps:[40] *You are just, O Lord, and your judgment is right.*

Then he adds a reason that cannot be contradicted: **[13]** ***What other has He appointed over the earth,*** to whom, of course, it may be permitted to accuse [God] with respect to the perversity of His own judgment. And explaining this further, he adds: ***or whom has He set over the world, which He has fashioned* (fabricatus est) *?*** according to ancient grammar, for here a deponent verb,[41] which sets aside its passive signification and retains its active meaning, is supplied; hence the sense is: He has fashioned (*fabricavit*). There is a parallel in a Psalm:[42] *Have you fashioned* (fabricatus es) *the morning light and the sun?* And it is as if Elihu were saying: "If there is no one superior, who may correct the error [of God], all the perversity of the inferior one will continue." And he will refute the consequence, namely, that not all things are able to be perverse; therefore, in the judgment of the superior there can be no error.

And Elihu shows this through effect, and therefore it is supplied: **[14]** ***If he,*** namely, the human, ***directs his heart,*** through conformity of the will, ***toward Him,*** God, of course. Sir 39:[43] *The just man surrenders his heart at dawn to watch for the Lord, who made him.* ***He will draw the spirit and the breath,*** that is, the spirit running

38. Prv 1.31.
39. Gn 18.25.
40. Ps 118.137.
41. Namely, *fabricor, fabricari, fabricatus sum.*
42. Ps 73.16.
43. Sir 39.6.

about through the body, which makes ready the members so that they may serve as instruments of virtue, ***of that person,*** who is a carrier of virtue toward works, ***to Himself,*** so that He may fashion all things according to the pattern (*formam*) of His justice. Prv 16:[44] *The Lord is the weigher of spirits. Reveal your works to the Lord, and your thoughts will be set in order.*

But apart from such power, which the inferior one draws to himself and controls, every human power fails (*deficit*) and is weak. Hence, nothing similar to that rectitude is found among humans. And that is: **[15]** ***All flesh will perish*** **(deficiet)** ***at once.*** Ps:[45] *My soul longs for and fails* (deficit) *in the courts of the Lord.*

He adds, moreover, that the human's bodily weight may fall (*deficiat*): ***and the human,*** that is, because the human, ***will return to ashes,*** and by the weight of ashes is dragged down to the failure (*defectum*) of such rectitude; and this is the same for him as what was said above in the words of Eliphaz in Jb 4: *Those who dwell in houses of clay, who have an earthly foundation, will be consumed as if by a moth.*

[16] ***If, therefore, you have understanding.***

After what he intended [to show] had been demonstrated, namely, that the rectitude of divine justice is so great that the human is not able [to arrive] at it, Elihu takes the opportunity afforded by this to teach [Job], namely, that he may praise the divine justice whereby he has been punished, and in this way he will be able to be healed by scourges. Hence, Elihu says two things here: first, of course, how he is able to be healed, namely, by confessing that he has been punished justly; and, secondly, he shows through effect how great the power of God's judgment is among the wicked and among the good, in that place:[46] *Who says to the king: You apostate!*

And that is: ***If, therefore, you have understanding,*** namely, to know to receive your instruction from these things. Ps:[47] *A good understanding for all who do it.*[48] ***hear what is said*** concerning the

44. Prv 16.2–3.
45. Ps 83.3.
46. Jb 34.18.
47. Ps 110.10.
48. Namely, fear the Lord.

rectitude of divine judgment. Ps:[49] *I will give you understanding, and I will instruct you.* ***and listen to the sound of my speech,*** namely, so that you may not detract from the divine judgment but may confess it. Eccl 5:[50] *Do not say anything rashly, and do not allow your heart to be quick to utter a word before God, for God is in heaven and you are on the earth. Therefore, let your words be few.*

And Elihu shows this through reason, adding: and it is supplied: **[17]** ***Can it be that he who does not love judgment,*** namely, [the judgment] of God, supply: but detracts from it, ***is able to be healed?*** as if he were saying: "No." For as long as he detracts from the [divine] judgment, he always provokes God against him. Eccl 5:[51] *Do not allow your mouth to cause your soul to sin, and do not say in the presence of the angel: There is no providence; lest perhaps the Lord, enraged over your words, destroy all the works of your hands.*

And when the general principle has been set forth, Elihu enters into it and adapts it, adding: ***and how do you condemn so much,*** that is, how do you dare to condemn so much, when you say that He subverts judgment, ***Him who is just?*** supply: by nature, and He is not able not to be just. Jb 40:[52] *Can it be that you will make void my judgment and condemn me, in order that you may be justified?*

And he shows that this cannot happen among the good and the wicked. First, among the wicked; second, in turn among the good and the wicked, in that place:[53] *For when He Himself grants peace.* In the first part, there are two points, namely: that He takes vengeance on the wicked; and that He does this justly according to the exigencies of their own merits, in that place:[54] *He has struck them, as though wicked.* Still further, concerning the first point there are two things: for, first, Elihu shows that God punishes the wicked; and, second, that they are not able to lie hidden, in that place:[55] *For His eyes.* Concerning the first [of these things], he makes two observations, namely, that in the

49. Ps 31.8.
50. Eccl 5.1.
51. Eccl 5.5.
52. Jb 40.3.
53. Jb 34.29.
54. Jb 34.26.
55. Jb 34.21.

judgment of [His] vengeance against the wicked, God shows no partiality; and that God extinguishes the wicked suddenly.

And that is: [18] ***Who says to the king,*** not showing deference to the person: ***You,*** supply: are an ***apostate!*** But He says[56] this when he pulls him down from his kingship as if an apostate. Dn 5:[57] *When [King] Belshazzar apostatized from right rule, the fingers of a hand appeared [to him], writing: [...] Mane, Thecel, Phares: that is, God has numbered your kingdom and has finished it; it has been weighed on the balance, and it has been found wanting; your kingdom has been separated from you and has been given to the Medes and the Persians.* ***who calls rulers,*** supply: those who, after the king, are greater, ***wicked.*** He calls them wicked when He reveals that they are wicked by deposing them. Sir 10:[58] *God has destroyed the thrones of proud princes and has made the meek to sit in their place.* In Est 7[59] there is the example of Haman, whom, though exalted, King Ahasuerus ordered to be hanged. [19] ***Who shows no partiality to princes*** according to predetermination, namely, of [His] just judgment. Acts 10:[60] *Truly I have realized that God shows no partiality.* An example appears in Nm 25:[61] *Take all the leaders of the people, and hang them on gibbets facing the sun, so that my fury may be turned away from Israel.* ***and does not recognize the tyrant,*** that is, the violent one, such that He may show partiality. ***when he arbitrates against the poor.*** Hab 1:[62] *Tyrants will be His buffoons.* There is an example in Sennacherib, who decided against Hezekiah, and an angel came and struck down in his camp one hundred eighty-five thousand, according to 2 Kgs 19.[63] There is also an example in Herod, who, after James had been killed, contended with Peter, and, having been consumed by worms, died, according to Acts 12.[64]

And Elihu adds the reason why God does not show partiality:

56. Here I read *dicit* with MSS EFM, rather than *dixit* with Weiss's edition.
57. Dn 5.5, 25–28.
58. Sir 10.17.
59. Est 7.9–10.
60. Acts 10.34.
61. Nm 25.4.
62. Hab 1.10.
63. 2 Kgs 19.35.
64. Acts 12.1–4, 21–23.

for all are the work of His hands. Wis 6:[65] *The mighty will suffer torments mightily.* And after a few words:[66] *Seeing that He Himself made the small and the great, and He cares for all equally.*

Moreover, he adds how God does this suddenly and beyond the expectation of the people themselves: **[20]** ***Suddenly they will die.***[67] Dionysius [says] to the monk Gaius:[68] "What is beyond expectation happens suddenly." For while they certainly expect to rule, they are struck down and taken away. ***and*** that is ***in the middle of the night,*** that is, when the time certainly has been obscured for them, ***the people,*** namely, the wicked, ***will be thrown into confusion***[69] through weakness ***and pass away,*** from life to death, of course. 1 Thes 5:[70] *When they will say, "Peace and security," then sudden destruction will come upon them.* ***and bear away the violent,*** namely, the power imposing the judgments of the Lord, of course, ***without the hand,*** that is, without the preparation of external power, for He does not send either armed soldiers or an infantry for this. Mt 24:[71] *The master of that slave will come on a day when he does not expect him, and at an hour that he does not know. And he will separate him and establish his portion with the hypocrites.* The same is said in Mt 13.[72]

Elihu adds, moreover, that they are not able to lie hidden: **[21]** ***His eyes,*** namely, God's, ***are upon the ways of men.*** Sir 23:[73] *Looking around and seeing all the ways of men.* ***and He inspects all their steps,*** that is, their works. Jb 13:[74] *You have kept a close watch over all my paths, and you have inspected the steps of my feet.* And supply: therefore **[22]** ***There is no darkness,*** of ignorance, of course, which may be associated with God, ***and there is no shadow of death,***

65. Wis 6.7.

66. Wis 6.8.

67. Here I read *morientur* with MSS EFM, rather than *moriuntur* with Weiss's edition.

68. Dionysius, *Ad Gaium* 3 (PG 3:1069).

69. Here I read *turbabuntur* with MSS FM, rather than *curvabuntur* with Weiss's edition.

70. 1 Thes 5.3.

71. Mt 24.50–51.

72. Mt 13.42.

73. Sir 23.28.

74. Jb 13.27.

that is, oblivion, whereby He may forget anyone. Gregory says:[75] Oblivion is called the shadow of death insofar as it imitates death, because it removes something from sense perception in the same way that death removes something from life. For any change whatsoever is an imitation of death, which is not in God. *With Him there is no change, nor shadow of alteration,* according to Jas 1.[76] And as God is immutable, so He sees in a penetrating way, and He does not forget, just as He is not changed. And this is what follows: ***where those who work iniquity may be concealed,*** that is, where they may be able to be concealed or to lie hidden. Wis 1:[77] *He who speaks unjust things is not able to hide, and chastising judgment will not pass him by.*

And he adds the reason for this: **[23]** ***For it is no longer,*** supply: after he has been caught in sin by the Judge, ***in the power,*** that is, the ability, ***of man to enter into judgment with God,*** namely, [the judgment] of debate, in order that he may say to God, "Why do you act in this way?" Ps:[78] *The sinner has been caught in the works of his own hands;* and just before this, it says: *The Lord will be recognized when He executes judgments.*

And Elihu shows that what he has said concerning certain people is [true] for all. And that is: **[24]** ***He will crush many,*** for He will not spare the multitude of the wicked. Wis 4:[79] *The multiplying multitude of the wicked will not be successful.* ***and innumerable,*** at least so [it seems] to us. Eccl 1:[80] *The number of fools is infinite.* Sir 10:[81] *God has made the roots of proud nations dry up and has planted the humble from these nations.* And this is what follows: ***and He will make others to stand instead of them.*** There is an example in the Egyptians, all of whom God killed, and an example in the [native] inhabitants of the promised land, in whose place He planted the children of Israel. Ex 15:[82] *Pharaoh went on horseback with his chariots and horsemen into the sea, and the Lord brought back*

75. Gregory, *Mor.* 25.6.22.
76. Jas 1.17.
77. Wis 1.8.
78. Ps 9.17.
79. Wis 4.3.
80. Eccl 1.15.
81. Sir 10.18.
82. Ex 15.19.

upon him the waters of the sea; but the children of Israel walked through the sea on dry ground.[83]

He adds, moreover, that God has executed this judgment justly: **[26]** ***He has struck them as though wicked;*** "as though" is expressive of the truth. Hab 3:[84] *You have struck the head of the house of the wicked; you have laid bare his foundation all the way to the neck.* ***in the presence of onlookers,*** so that, seeing the punishment of that [wicked] one, they might be corrected by his example, of course. Ezek 28:[85] *I have cast you down onto the ground; I have set you before the face of kings, so that they might behold you.* In the *Almagest,* Ptolemy says: Whoever is not corrected by others, others will be corrected by him.[86] Ezek 28:[87] *All who will see you among the nations will be astonished at you. You have become nothing* (nihili), *and you will be nothing forever.* There the word "nothing" (*nihil*) belongs to the second declension and is in the genitive case.

And Elihu adds the reason for this, [namely] so that condemnation may seem more just: **[27]** ***who,*** that is: because they, ***as it were, on purpose,*** as though it were expressive of the truth, as if he were saying, "not out of weakness, nor out of ignorance, but out of eagerness," ***have withdrawn from Him,*** that is, from God. Jer 2:[88] *They have departed from me, and they have walked after vanity, and they have become vain.* ***and have refused to understand all His ways.*** Materially, refusal pertains to apportionment, so that the sense is: "They have wished to understand none of His ways," that is, neither commandments nor counsels nor the works of exemplars. Jb 21:[89] *They have said to the Lord God: Depart from us, we refuse to have knowledge of your ways.* Ps:[90] *He has refused to under-*

83. Significantly v. 25 of Jb 34, which should appear at this point in Albert's commentary, is absent from all the MSS. The Vulgate text of v. 25, as it has come down to us, reads: ***Novit enim opera eorum, et idcirco inducet noctem, et conterentur (For He knows their works, and therefore He will bring night in [upon them], and they will be crushed).***

84. Hab 3.13.

85. Ezek 28.17.

86. Like Weiss, I have been unable to find this reference.

87. Ezek 28.19.

88. Jer 2.5.

89. Jb 21.14.

90. Ps 35.4.

stand that he might act rightly. **[28]** ***so that,*** supply [instead]: insofar as; it is consecutive, not causal, ***they caused the cry of the needy,*** supply: whom they oppressed, ***to come to Him.*** Gn 4:[91] *The voice of the blood of your brother Abel is crying out to me from the ground.* Jas 5:[92] *The wages of your laborers, who have reaped your fields, which have been embezzled by you, cry out; and their cry has entered the ears of the Lord of Hosts.* ***and He,*** namely, God, ***heard the voice of the poor.*** Ps:[93] *Because of the misery of the needy and the groans of the poor, now I will rise up, says the Lord.* Sir 35:[94] *Do not the widow's tears run down her cheek, and her cry against him who causes them to flow? For from her cheek they ascend all the way to heaven, and the Lord who hears them will not be pleased with them.*

[29] ***For when He himself grants peace.***

Here Elihu mentions, in turn, how God condemns certain people and illuminates others by His grace according to the diversity of merits, and that He does this not only with regard to each human being, but also with regard to each nation and the whole world. And Elihu answers a certain objection that could arise for him.

And that is: ***For when He Himself,*** namely, God, ***grants peace,*** through this, namely, that He grants the quiet of [external] conditions and the quiet of hearts. Jn 14:[95] *Peace I leave with you, my peace I give to you. I do not give to you as the world gives.* ***who is there who can condemn?*** that is, who is able to condemn, as if he were saying, "No one." Rom 8:[96] *It is God who justifies; who is it who will condemn?* In the same place:[97] *If God is for us, who is against us?* Ps:[98] *The Lord is my helper; I will not fear what man might do to me.* Prv 16:[99] *When the ways of man will be pleasing to the Lord, He will convert even His enemies to peace.* ***When He hides His face,*** by taking away the

91. Gn 4.10.
92. Jas 5.4.
93. Ps 11.6.
94. Sir 35.18–19.
95. Jn 14.27.
96. Rom 8.33–34.
97. Rom 8.31.
98. Ps 117.6. Weiss incorrectly identifies this reference as Ps 55.5.
99. Prv 16.7.

favorable conditions of His grace, of course. Jb 13:[100] *Why do you hide your face and consider me your enemy?* ***who is there who may behold,*** that is, may be able to behold, ***Him.*** For the furious face of the Lord cannot be withstood by man. Hence, those to be damned, as the Lord declares in Lk 23,[101] *will say to the mountains: Fall upon us; and to the hills: Bury us.* Elihu says that this happens ***whether concerning a nation or concerning all men?*** "concerning a nation" in the case of the Pentapolis, according to Gn 19;[102] "concerning all men" in the case of the flood, according to Gn 7.[103] From these words it is clear that the judgments of God are just, both in general and in particular, and so what Elihu intended [to show]—namely, that God does not trip up judgment, nor does the Almighty overthrow what is just[104]—has been built up in this way [by heaping things together].

But because one could object to him contrary to this—insofar as he said,[105] *Who says to the king: You apostate!*—that God sometimes permits evil kings to rule, Elihu answers by way of an anthypophora,[106] adding: **[30]** ***Who makes,*** that is, permits, ***a man who is a hypocrite,*** who is a figure and image of a king more than a king, ***to reign on account of the sins of the people,*** who deserved to have such a king, who crushes them. Hos 13:[107] *I will give you a king in my wrath, and I will take him away in my indignation.* And in this he indicates in a hidden way (*occulte*) blessed Job, whom God permitted to reign in the midst of hypocrisy, just as Nebuchadnezzar and many other evil kings.

[31] ***Because, therefore.***

Here Elihu touches on the commendation and correction of his own speech, if it can be corrected. And he says three things: namely, that his speech may be corrected; by whom it may be corrected, in that place:[108] *Indeed,* [*let*] *men of understanding;* and, if his speech is perfect, that the opponent may be compelled to

100. Jb 13.24.
101. Lk 23.30.
102. Gn 19.25.
103. Gn 7.12, 21–23.
104. See Bildad's words in Jb 8.3 and Albert's comments on 34.1 above.
105. Jb 34.18.
106. Anthypophora: see above, p. 126, n. 117, in chap. 31.
107. Hos 13.11.
108. Jb 34.34.

concede, in that place:[109] *My Father.* Concerning the first, there are three points: namely, an observation concerning the proper behavior for a fellow-disputant; the petition for correction; and the presenting of him who ought to correct according to reason, or the reprobation of the malicious corrector.

And that is: ***Because, therefore, I have spoken,*** that is, now I have delivered the final part of my speech and I have come to my intended conclusion, ***to God,*** the true[110] judge, who, of all [judges], must be defended, of course. Jb 9:[111] *Even if I have something just, I will not respond; but I will pray earnestly to my judge.* ***I will not hinder you also in speaking,*** for this is the proper behavior of those who are disputing, that one should listen to the other. 1 Cor 14:[112] *Let the prophets speak, two or three; and let the others judge. But if something is revealed to another person sitting [nearby], let the first person be silent. For all of you can prophesy one at a time, so that all may learn and all may be exhorted.* [32] ***If I have erred,*** by departing from reason in anything, ***teach me*** and supply: so that I may humbly recognize my error; for this belongs to fraternal love, to remove stumbling blocks that are in the presence of a blind person. Is 48:[113] *I am the Lord God who teaches you useful things and who guides you in the way that you walk.* ***if I have spoken iniquity,*** about the judgments of God, of course, ***I will add no more;*** for it is sufficient to have offended once. But he says this because his own words seem to him to contain a perfect account of the truth. Prv 8:[114] *All my words are just, and there is nothing wicked or perverse in them.* Jb 40:[115] *Remember the battle, and speak no more.*

And concerning the condemnation of the malicious corrector, Elihu adds: [33] ***Can it be that God demands it,*** namely, the iniquity that I have exposed by speaking, so that you may correct it, as if he were saying, "No." ***from you,*** who hear malevolently. Sir 1:[116] *You have come to the Lord wickedly, and your heart is full of*

109. Jb 34.36.
110. Here I read with MSS FM, which add *verum*.
111. Jb 9.15.
112. 1 Cor 14.29–31.
113. Is 48.17.
114. Prv 8.8.
115. Jb 40.27.
116. Sir 1.40.

cunning and deceit. ***because it,*** supply: my speech, ***has displeased you?*** Prv 18:[117] *A fool does not receive the words of prudence, unless you say those things that are pondered in his heart.*

He explains, moreover, why he had said things displeasing to himself: he did this because he was incited by real zeal for the truth. And that is: ***For you began to speak, and not I.*** Gregory says:[118] He says this because they are accustomed to being more culpable who begin to speak in the midst of the contention to which they respond. And he intends [to show] that Job began this speech in the third chapter, where he said:[119] *Let the day on which I was born perish.*

But if you know anything better, supply: than you have spoken thus far, ***speak.*** Eph 4:[120] *Let no evil speech proceed from your mouth; but whatever is good, so that it may give grace to those who hear.*

Then Elihu adds those whom he wishes to have as correctors: **[34]** ***Indeed, let men of understanding speak to me.*** Sir 5:[121] *If you have understanding, respond to your neighbor.* ***and let a wise man,*** who knows the order of words and the truth, of course, ***hear me.*** Ps:[122] *The mouth of the just person will contemplate wisdom, and his tongue will speak judgment.* And he condemns the fool: **[35]** ***But Job has spoken foolishly,*** that is, against the purpose of the Lord. Jb 1:[123] *In all this, Job did not sin with his lips, nor did he say anything foolish against God.* ***and his words do not express learning.*** Prv 15:[124] *The tongue of the wise furnishes knowledge; but the mouth of the foolish spouts out folly.* And because Job did not recognize the judgment of God, as Elihu says, Elihu turns to God and prays that Job may be restrained to such a degree that he recognizes that punishment may open the eyes that fault has closed. And that is: **[36]** ***My Father;*** Mt 6:[125] *Our Father who are in heaven.* ***let Job,*** who murmurs against the judgments of God, ***be tested,*** that is, let him,

117. Prv 18.2.
118. Gregory, *Mor.* 26.3.3.
119. Jb 3.3.
120. Eph 4.29.
121. Sir 5.14.
122. Ps 36.30.
123. Jb 1.22.
124. Prv 15.2.
125. Mt 6.9.

having been tried with blows, be revealed, ***all the way to the end,*** either of death or until he confesses that the judgments of God are just, and so comes to his senses. Ps:[126] *Prove me, O Lord, and try me; burn my reins and my heart, and see if the way of iniquity is in me.*[127] ***may you not desist,*** from beating, of course, ***from the man of iniquity,*** the emphasis is here, that is, from the most iniquitous man, until he ceases to be iniquitous, of course. Wis 12:[128] *You rebuke little by little those who wander off, and you remind and speak to them about the things through which they sin, so that, having left their wickedness behind, they may believe in you, O Lord.*

Elihu adds, moreover, why he asks for this: **[37]** ***He has added blasphemy,*** which is the imposition of a false accusation onto God, concerning this, of course: that he has found fault with the judgments of God as if they were unjust, ***to his sins,*** namely, general [sins], which he has committed with respect to himself and with respect to his neighbor. Lv 24:[129] *Lead the blasphemer outside the camp, and let all the people stone him.* ***let him be restrained,*** by scourges, of course, ***among us in the meantime,*** supply: as long as he lives. But "be restrained" is said lest he have the freedom of saying whatever he wishes, and Elihu says this on account of the fact that in chapter 15 above it was declared concerning him:[130] *Your iniquity has taught your mouth, and you imitate the speech of blasphemers.* Ps:[131] *The mouth of those who speak wicked things is stopped up.* ***and then,*** supply: finally in the end, ***let him provoke God to judgment,*** that is, to revenge or vengeance, ***with his words,*** namely, wicked and blasphemous [words]. Jb 12:[132] *Audaciously they provoke God.* Dt 32:[133] *They have provoked me with what is no god and have enraged me with their vanities.*

126. Ps 25.2.

127. This final phrase, *et vide si via iniquitatis in me est,* is not part of Ps 25.2, but rather Ps 138.24. Doubtless working from memory, Albert here conflates the two passages, which have a common theme, just as he does above in the commentary on Jb 23.10.

128. Wis 12.2.

129. Lv 24.14.

130. Jb 15.5.

131. Ps 62.12.

132. Jb 12.6.

133. Dt 32.21.

CHAPTER 35

THEREFORE, *Elihu.*

Here Elihu sets forth the third position, which is constructed from the position of Eliphaz and the position of Bildad. For Eliphaz said that a human will not be made righteous in comparison to God, nor will a man be purer than his Maker, according to Jb 4.[1] And Elihu says here in chapter 35 that Job, contrary to this, has declared:[2] *I am more just than God.* And for that reason, in the first part of the chapter Elihu, delimiting and explaining Eliphaz's position, disputes against the words of Job. Bildad, however, said in Jb 8:[3] *God does not trip up judgment, nor does the Almighty overthrow what is just.* Job seemed to have spoken against this in chapter 16:[4] *These things I have suffered for no reason, since I have offered to God pure prayers.* But pure prayers are heard favorably. And so, in the second part of the chapter, in that place:[5] *on account of the multitude of false accusers,* Elihu develops and explains the position of Bildad and disputes against the words of Job, showing that neither were his prayers pure nor should they have been heard favorably.

In the first part, there are three points, namely: a renunciation of Job's position; and a declaration of this same position, in that place:[6] *For you have said;* and an argument against this position, in that place in chapter 35:[7] *Therefore, I will respond.*

And that is: ***Therefore, Elihu;*** "Therefore" is introductory, not

1. Jb 4.17.
2. Jb 35.2.
3. Jb 8.3.
4. Jb 16.18.
5. Jb 35.9.
6. Jb 35.3.
7. Jb 35.4.

logical or causal. ***spoke these words,*** which follow, ***in turn.*** And that he says "in turn" indicates a transition from an argument in relation to one position that has been set forth to an argument to be mounted in relation to another [position], so that every falsehood may be destroyed. Ps:[8] *May the Lord destroy all deceitful lips and the boastful tongue.*

And Elihu sets forth a renunciation of falsehood: **[2]** ***Can it be that your thinking seems right to you.*** He says this in order to convince him also by the authority of proper reason, and he alludes to what was said above in chapter 15:[9] *Your own mouth will condemn you, and not I; and your own lips will respond to you.* Ps:[10] *I will convict you, and I will set* [*your evil deeds*] *before your face.* And he explains the position: ***that you should say: I am more just than God?*** Elihu understands that Job said this as a logical consequence of what he seems to have said previously when, above in chapter 23, he declared:[11] *I wish that He would not contend with me with great strength, nor overwhelm me with the weight of His greatness. Let Him show impartiality toward me, and let my judgment come to victory.* For if he prevails with regard to judgment in comparison to God, it follows that he is more just than God. And this is contrary to the position of Eliphaz, who said above in chapter 4:[12] *Can it be that a human* [*will be made righteous in comparison to God*], etc.

Then Elihu interprets and explains this position further: **[3]** ***For you have said:*** that is, from your words it follows that you intended this, as Aristotle says:[13] Whoever says one thing in a certain way says many things when many things are in one.

What is good or right is not pleasing to you. Jb 34:[14] *A man will not be pleasing to God, even if he runs with Him.* From this, however, it seems that God remains silent and pretends not to see whenever a good person is oppressed by someone wicked. Hab 1:[15] *Why do you look upon despisers, and remain silent when the wicked person*

8. Ps 11.4.
9. Jb 15.6.
10. Ps 49.21.
11. Jb 23.6–7.
12. Jb 4.17.
13. See Aristotle, *Metaph.* 9.6.4.
14. Jb 34.9.
15. Hab 1.13.

oppresses the one who is more just than he? ***or,*** supply: you have said what is more profane, ***what,*** that is, to what extent, ***will it profit you if I sin?*** and he mentions the error of some people who, according to what David said in the Psalm:[16] *Against you alone have I sinned, and I have done evil in your sight, so that you are justified in your sentence,* have said that the sin and falsehood of a human contribute something to God, although He alone seems truthful and just, of course. The Apostle argues against this error in Rom 3:[17] *If the truth of God has grown abundantly for his glory through my falsehood, why am I still judged as a sinner?* as if he were saying: "It is unjust that He punishes in me what contributes to His glory." And Elihu speaks in this way here. Moreover, he attributes this to blessed Job, not because he said this verbatim, but because it seemed to follow from the words that he spoke, understood in an evil sense. Jb 22:[18] *Can it be that you wish to keep the path of the ages, which wicked men have trod?* and a little beyond this:[19] *Who said to God: Go away from us; and judged the Almighty as if He could do nothing.* For such people thought that both evil and good things are subject to God. And from such thoughts the opinion follows that God Himself appears more truthful as a result of the falsehood of the human, and He appears more just as a result of [human] sin.

After he has explained this position, Elihu argues to the contrary. And in the first place, he makes this clear concerning the proposition; second, concerning the opposite. And that is: **[4]** ***Therefore, I will respond to your words,*** namely, by showing them to be false. Jb 13:[20] *Earlier I showed you fashioners of lies and cultivators of perverse teachings.* ***and,*** supply: I will respond, ***to your friends with you,*** who, remaining silent, seemed to assent to your error, of course. Jb 32:[21] *So these three men ceased to answer Job, because he seemed just to himself.*

And Elihu sets forth the reason for his disapproval: **[5]** ***Look up to heaven,*** that is, the height of heaven, ***and see,*** namely, by

16. Ps 50.6.
17. Rom 3.7.
18. Jb 22.15.
19. Jb 22.17.
20. Jb 13.4.
21. Jb 32.1.

directing your attention to the Mover and Governor of heaven. Gn 15:[22] *Look up to heaven and number the stars, if you can.* ***and contemplate the sky*** **(aethera)**, that is, the whole order of the fifth element, which is aether (*aether*).

Elihu adds, moreover, why this ought to be contemplated: ***because He is higher than you,*** that is, elevated beyond the entire sphere of active and passive powers, in which [heaven] none of our actions and passions occur. Jb 11:[23] *He is higher than heaven, and what will you do?*

And this is what he adds: **[6]** ***If you sin, what harm will you do to Him?*** that is, you will not be able to do harm, as if he were saying, "No harm,[24] but you do harm to yourself." ***and if your iniquities are multiplied,*** through dissimulation before God, ***what will you do,*** that is: what will you be able to do, ***against Him?*** that is, as a nuisance to Him. Jer 7:[25] *Can it be that they provoke me to anger? says the Lord. Is it not themselves, to the confusion of their own countenance?* Hence the sinner does harm to himself and not to God.

And Elihu also makes this clear concerning the opposite, adding: **[7]** ***On the other hand, if you act justly*** by virtuous works, ***what will you give to Him?***[26] to Him nothing can be added, of course, because He is the Highest Good. Acts 17:[27] *Nor is He served by human hands, as though He lacked anything, seeing that He Himself gives to all [humans] life and breath and all things.* Rom 11:[28] *Who has given to Him first, and it will be repaid to him?*

Then he makes this clear by setting one with a passible nature in opposition to the impassible God, according to this principle: When two things are opposed to one another, if one property is in one, the opposite property will be in the other.[29] And that is: **[8]** ***Your iniquity will do harm,*** that is, will be able to do harm by injuring either the person or the [person's] reputation. Con-

22. Gn 15.5.

23. Jb 11.8.

24. Here I read with MSS FM, which add *nihil sed.*

25. Jer 7.19.

26. The remainder of this verse, as it has come down to us in the Vulgate text—***aut quid de manu tua accipiet*** **(*or what will He receive from your hand*)?**—appears in none of the manuscripts used for Weiss's edition.

27. Acts 17.25.

28. Rom 11.35.

29. Albert's Latin here is: *Si oppositum de opposito et propositum de proposito.*

cerning these [modes of injury] it is said in a Psalm:[30] *The Lord will abhor a bloodthirsty and deceitful man.* ***to a man,*** who has a passible nature, ***who is like you,*** in this, of course: that something can be added to or subtracted from him. ***and your justice will help,*** that is, will be able to help, ***a son of man,*** who requires help. At the end of Gal:[31] *Bear the burdens of one another.* Through everything here Elihu intends [to show] that, because God does not inflict punishment when He is provoked, iniquity does not do harm to God, nor does justice profit Him; and if He inflicts punishment on anyone, He takes vengeance only on the iniquity that is in the person.

[9] *On account of the multitude.*

Here Elihu attends to the second part of the position.[32] Because, in fact, Eliphaz had said above in chapter 15:[33] *Inasmuch as it is in you, you have nullified fear, and you have carried away,* that is, you have removed, *prayers from the presence of God,* so that you might not be heard favorably, of course, on account of which even Job had declared in chapter 30:[34] *I will cry out to you, and you will not hear me; I stand up, and you do not consider me. You have turned cruel toward me,* and Bildad had asserted that God does not trip up judgment;[35] therefore, Elihu, delimiting the speech of Bildad, makes clear why God does not hear the sinner, and he speaks of three things, namely: sin against the neighbor, on account of which the prayer [of the sinner] is not heard favorably;[36] and sin against God, in that place in chapter 35:[37] *And he has not said: Where is God?* And thirdly he adds why the [sinner's] prayer is not heard, in that place in chapter 35:[38] *There they will cry out.*

30. Ps 5.7.

31. Gal 6.2.

32. As Albert explains in his comments on 35.1 above, the position that Elihu considers in this chapter is one constructed from the positions of Eliphaz and Bildad; so the second part of it is taken from Bildad's words.

33. Jb 15.4.

34. Jb 30.20–21.

35. See Jb 8.3.

36. Here I read *exauditur* with MSS TEFM, rather than the *auditur* of Weiss's edition.

37. Jb 35.10.

38. Jb 35.12.

And that is: ***On account of the multitude of false accusers,*** passively, that is, by whom they have introduced false accusations, ***they will cry out,*** namely, those introducing false accusations, ***and they will wail.*** Is 65:[39] *You will cry out because of anguish of heart, and you will howl because of grief of spirit.* ***because of the strength of the arm,*** that is, of oppression and violence, ***of tyrants.*** Boethius says:[40] A tyrant is one who establishes and does all things for his own advantage but in a manner that is harmful to the people. Sir 11:[41] *Many tyrants have sat on the throne, and one whom no one expected has worn the crown.* It is said of Jason in 2 Mc 4:[42] *Possessing nothing indeed worthy of the high priesthood, but having the mind of a cruel tyrant and the fury of a wild beast.*

And concerning sin against God, on account of which the [sinner's] prayer is not heard, Elihu adds: **[10]** ***And he,*** namely, the one seeking God, ***has not said: Where is God,*** Rom 1:[43] *As they did not approve of acknowledging God, God gave them up to a debased understanding.* ***who made me?*** that is, one knows at first about God that He is our Maker and Creator. Is 64:[44] [*You are*] *our Maker, and we all are the works of your hands.* ***who has given songs in the night,*** for "in the night" of this ignorance were the first songs about God. Ps:[45] *He put a new song in my mouth, a song to our God.* Cato says:[46] "If God is an intellect, as the songs declare to us, you should devote yourself chiefly to Him with a pure mind."

And Elihu adds how God has distinguished us from the animals with regard to the knowledge of good and evil: **[11]** ***who teaches us more than the beasts of the earth;*** he calls all things that face downward on the earth, which do not possess the knowledge of good and evil, "beasts." Gn 1:[47] *Let us make man according to our image and likeness.* ***and instructs us more than the birds of***

39. Is 65.14.

40. See Boethius, *CP* 2.6 and 3.5 (PL 63:703 and 740). Cf. Albert on Jb 15.20 (*On Job*, vol. 1, p. 271).

41. Sir 11.5.

42. 2 Mc 4.25.

43. Rom 1.28.

44. Is 64.8.

45. Ps 39.4.

46. Cato, *Dist.* 1.1.

47. Gn 1.26.

the air? which, although they are [made] of the lighter humors and they have heads raised more toward heaven than the beasts do, nevertheless have not received the knowledge of good and evil. Ps:[48] *You have subjected all things under his*[49] *feet, all sheep and oxen; in addition, the herds of the fields, the birds of the air, and the fishes of the sea.* Ovid says:[50] "He[51] has given man a face raised on high to survey heaven, and He has commanded elevated countenances to look upward to the stars."

Then Elihu adds that, on account of this, God does not hear sinners. **[12]** ***There,*** that is, in accordance with the guilt of those sinners, ***they will cry out,*** supply: in the course of their punishments, ***and He,*** namely, God, ***will not hear because of the pride of the wicked.*** Here the contempt for the commandment and for the one commanding, which is in every sin, is called "pride." Prv 1:[52] *Then they will call upon me, and I will not hear; they will rise early in the morning and will not find me: because they have hated instruction and have not received the fear of the Lord.*

And he adds the reason for this: **[13]** ***For God will not hear in vain,*** namely, the cry of those having been oppressed by them, which [cry] He would hear in vain if He heard the prayers of those who were oppressing them. Sir 34:[53] *When one builds and another destroys, what is the benefit to them except hard work? When one prays and another curses, whose voice will the Lord hear?* as if it were saying: "As long as those who have been oppressed by them pray, they curse them in the presence of the Lord, and they pray that they[54] will not be heard; and God does not overthrow what is just."[55] Therefore, God will not hear oppressors on account of the prior judgment of those who have been oppressed. ***and,*** that

48. Ps 8.8–9.

49. Namely, man's or the son of man's, specified earlier in Ps 8 (v. 5).

50. Ovid, *Metam.* 1.85–86.

51. Although Ovid's Latin here does not explicitly state the subject of the third-person singular verbs, the larger context in which Albert places this quotation suggests that, for his part at least, Albert assumes that the implied subject is *Deus.*

52. Prv 1.28–29.

53. Sir 34.28–29.

54. That is, their oppressors.

55. See Jb 8.3.

is, because ***the Almighty,*** [whom] it is not permitted to accuse, ***will consider,*** supply: and discern ***the causes of each one.*** Jer 11:[56] *But you, O Lord of Hosts, who judge justly and try minds and hearts: let me see your vengeance on them, for to you I have made my case known.* Lk 18:[57] *But will God not avenge His elect who cry out to Him day and night, and will He have patience in regard to them? I say to you: He will quickly avenge them.*

But because someone might be able to say that God sometimes dissembles for a long while, Elihu opposes and excludes this, adding: **[14]** ***Indeed, when you say,*** supply: in your heart, as the wicked say: ***He,*** supply: God, ***does not consider*** human deeds with a view toward vengeance. Ps:[58] *Why has the wicked man provoked God? For he has said in his heart: He will not seek to know it.* ***give judgment before Him,*** by comparing, of course, His wisdom and goodness, which they do, because He is not prone to vengeance; for it pertains to leaders to be slow to punish. Augustine says:[59] The more patiently one sees, the more wisely he does so. ***and wait for Him,*** until the time of vengeance arrives, of course; then He will wreak bitter vengeance. Dt 32:[60] *When I appoint the time, I will judge just conduct.* Ps:[61] *Wait for the Lord, do so manfully; and may your heart be strengthened, and wait for the Lord.* Ezek 21:[62] *But you, profane and wicked prince of Israel, whose day has come, in the time of preordained iniquity.*

[15] ***For now,*** that is, in an instant and immediately, ***He does not inflict His fury,*** supply: but He acts sparingly and provides a place for penance. Jb 24:[63] *The Lord has given him a place for penance.* Wis 11:[64] *Overlooking the sins of men for the sake of repentance.* ***nor does He punish wickedness exceedingly,*** that is, by final damnation now, but He overlooks it patiently. Sir 5:[65] *The Most High is a patient rewarder.*

56. Jer 11.20.
57. Lk 18.7–8.
58. Ps 10.13.
59. See Augustine, *pat.* 5.4 (PL 40:613).
60. The words that follow are not from Dt 32, but rather from Ps 74.3.
61. Ps 26.14.
62. Ezek 21.25.
63. Jb 24.23.
64. Wis 11.24.
65. Sir 5.4.

And after all these things Elihu returns to his intended conclusion: [16] ***Therefore, Job opens his mouth,*** contradicting the opinions of the elderly Eliphaz and Bildad, of course, ***in vain.*** Ps:[66] *The mouth of those who speak wicked things is stopped up.* For the opening of Job's mouth signifies that his contradiction has been opened up to view. ***and without wisdom,*** that is, without discretion, ***multiplies words,*** so that he appears to prevail by the multiplication of words, seeing that he cannot prevail by reason. Prv 10:[67] *In loquaciousness there will be no lack of sin; but he who controls his lips is most prudent.* Prv 14:[68] *Where there are many words, there is often poverty in works.*

66. Ps 62.12.
67. Prv 10.19.
68. Prv 14.23.

CHAPTER 36

E*LIHU ALSO added.*

In this part Elihu draws out the position of Zophar the Naamathite, which is found above in chapters 11 and 20. This, moreover, was Zophar's position: that God, by foreseeing (*providendo*) human affairs, rewards according to merits, and that He welcomes back those who are penitent as well and restores them to their former state; and that God does this according to a most profound plan, our knowledge of which is shallow (*brevis*).

And this part has three subdivisions. In the first of these, Elihu commends the sincerity of his own speech; in the second, he explains Zophar's position, proves it by reasons, and draws it out according to its particulars, in that place:[1] *God does not reject the mighty;* in the third [subdivision], Elihu advises that his words be listened to carefully and that it be understood that all of our knowledge that aims at investigating the judgments of God is shallow (*brevis*), in that place:[2] *Listen to this, Job: Stand and consider.*

In the first [subdivision], there are two things: for Elihu advises that his own words be listened to carefully, and he adds the reason.[3] At the beginning, however, he uses a transition because he passes over from one position to another. And that is:

Elihu also added, supply: to the position of Zophar, just as he had added to the positions of Eliphaz and Bildad, ***and said these things,*** which will follow, of course. Lk 10:[4] *But also if you spend*

1. Jb 36.5.

2. Jb 37.14.

3. Although Weiss's edition adds *et hoc est* ("and that is") here, I read with MSS FM, which omit this phrase.

4. Lk 10.35.

anything, when I return I will repay you. **[2]** ***Bear with me a little.*** He alludes to what he had said above, in Jb 32:[5] *I will speak and breathe a little.* For "a little" is what can be asserted by a human with respect to things to be spoken about the mighty deeds of God. Indeed, about the mighty deeds of God Zophar spoke, and this one [namely, Elihu] is speaking [now]. Sir 43:[6] *We say many things, and we fail in our words; the consummation of our speech is He Himself.* ***and I will show you,*** by means of reason, of course. Mi 6:[7] *I will show you, O human, what is good, and what God requires of you.* ***for I still have something,*** namely, in the position of Zophar, ***to say on God's behalf.*** He says "still" because, no matter how much anyone says about God, still he discovers what he might say, since God is infinite. Sir 43:[8] *Glorify the Lord to whatever degree you are able; He exceeds it still.* **[3]** ***I will recall my knowledge,*** that is, what I have known about God, ***from the beginning,*** namely, what Zophar set forth, drawing out that beginning and delimiting it through particulars, just as I did in the case of the positions of Eliphaz and Bildad. For as was said above,[9] the ancients set forth certain common principles, which future generations—the succession of which this one [namely, Elihu] represents—have drawn out and discussed according to particulars. Ps:[10] *What great things we have heard and known, and our fathers have told us. They have not been hidden from their children.* ***and,*** supply: from these things, ***I will prove my Maker,*** namely, God; Is 64:[11] *We all are the works of your hands.* ***just,*** in the governance and providence of human affairs, of course. Ps:[12] *The Lord is just and has loved justice.* Jer 23:[13] *This is the name that they will call Him: the Lord, our just one.*

Then Elihu adds the reason why he should be heard: **[4]** ***For truly my words are without falsehood.*** A word is compared to two

5. Jb 32.20.
6. Sir 43.29.
7. Mi 6.8.
8. Sir 43.32.
9. Cf. on Jb 32.1 above.
10. Ps 77.3–4.
11. Is 64.8.
12. Ps 10.8.
13. Jer 23.6.

things, namely, to the thing of which it is a sign, and to the notions (*species*) of things that are in the soul, of which it is a likeness (*species*) or messenger. From the first comparison, when it agrees with the thing, it is true; and Elihu notes this when he says "truly."[14] From the second comparison, when it agrees with the notions that are in the soul, it is "without falsehood." Eph 4:[15] *On account of this, putting aside falsehood, let each one of you speak the truth to his neighbor.*

But there is still a third thing,[16] which is required of the wise man, namely, that he might be proved by right reason. And concerning this, Elihu adds: ***and perfect knowledge,*** which is the condition of a conclusion that has been proved, as Aristotle maintains at the beginning of the *Posterior Analytics,*[17] ***will be proved to you.*** Elihu proves it through rhetorical reasons, just as rhetorical speeches are introduced throughout this whole book.

[5] ***God does not reject the mighty.***

Here Elihu begins to debate according to the position [of Zophar], and it has two parts. In the first, he proceeds on the basis of human judgments; and in the second, on the basis of the most profound and divine [judgments], in that place:[18] *Behold, indeed, God is exalted.* But Elihu takes this approach because Zophar's position also was constructed from two [views], namely, that God governs human affairs according to the order of human justice, and that He does this by a most profound plan (*altissimo consilio*), in relation to which all human knowledge is shallow (*brevis*).

The first part has two subdivisions. In the first, Elihu demonstrates his intention, namely, that God governs human affairs according to the order of human justice, and that He welcomes back those who are penitent when they go astray. In the second [subdivision], Elihu takes upon himself the instruction by means

14. Here I read with MSS TEFM, in which this final phrase—*et hoc notat cum dicit vere*—is added, rather than with Weiss's edition.

15. Eph 4.25.

16. This is the third thing in the first subdivision of this chapter, according to Albert, following (1) Elihu's advice that his words be listened to carefully and (2) his providing the reason why they should be heard.

17. See Aristotle, *APost.* 1.2.3.

18. Jb 36.22.

of which he teaches blessed Job, in that place:[19] *Your case has been judged as though* [*it were*] *that of a wicked man.* And he keeps to this order of proceeding because Zophar maintained the same order above, in chapter 11,[20] where first Zophar made clear that Job was condemned justly; second, that this was done by a most profound plan; and third, that if Job repented and removed the iniquity that was in his hand, he would return to his former prosperity.

In the first of these [subdivisions] there are two things, namely: demonstrative reasons; and a conclusion, in that place:[21] *Therefore, He will save you.* The first of these is divided yet again into two [sections]: for first Elihu makes clear his intention; second, he sets forth by way of anthypophora[22] a question that might arise, in that place:[23] *Dissemblers and crafty men.*

In the first [section] Elihu does four things: for first he shows that God sets up the mighty in the judgment seat; second, that He demands an account from those who have been set up in the [judgment] seat, in that place:[24] *And they are exalted there;* third, that they are warned about [their] pride, in that place:[25] *He will also open;* and fourth, if they hear the one who warns them, they are welcomed back—and if not, they are destroyed, in that place:[26] *If they will hear.*[27]

God does not reject the mighty. Rom 13:[28] *For there is no power except from God.* Dn 5:[29] *The Most High has power in the kingdom of men, and He sets over it whomever He wishes.* And he gives the reason: ***since He Himself also is mighty,*** as if he were saying: "If He detested power *per se,* He would cast His own power aside; but

19. Jb 36.17.

20. See especially Jb 11.12–19 (*On Job,* vol. 1, 223–27).

21. Jb 36.16.

22. Anthypophora: see above, p. 126, n. 117, in chap. 31.

23. Jb 36.13.

24. Jb 36.7.

25. Jb 36.10.

26. Jb 36.11.

27. Here I read with MS FM, which add *ibi (XXXVI, 11) si audierint,* rather than with Weiss's edition, which omits this final phrase.

28. Rom 13.1.

29. Dn 5.21.

because of the power that He Himself possesses, He does not detest it in others." Hence, He detests the abuse of power, but not power [itself]. Ex 15:[30] *Almighty is His name.* **[6]** ***but He does not save the wicked,*** namely, those who abuse their power. Jb 8:[31] *God will not reject the simple, nor stretch out His hand to evildoers.*

And Elihu adds the reason for this: ***and,*** that is, because ***He will grant judgment to the poor,*** that is, because the wicked have oppressed the poor, He renders judgment to the poor and abandons the wicked. Is 11:[32] *He will judge the poor with justice and decide with equity for the meek of the earth; and He will strike the earth with the rod of His mouth, and with the breath of His lips He will kill the wicked.*

He adds, by way of the opposite, how God strengthens the just one who is powerful: **[7]** ***He will not withdraw His eyes from the just one,*** that is, with respect to His grace. Ps:[33] *In this way, by which you will advance, I will fix my eyes upon you.* ***and He places kings,*** supply: such just ones ***on the throne forever,*** that is, so that they may reign forever. Prv 25:[34] *He removes wickedness from the face of the king, and his throne will be established in justice.* Prv 29:[35] *The king who judges the poor in truth, his throne will be established forever.* ***and there,*** that is, on the royal throne, ***they are exalted,*** finally in their pride, namely, those who were humble previously, just as Saul also showed too much pride when he had been exalted on the throne, according to 1 Sm 17.[36]

But because God detests pride, [as indicated in] Lk 1:[37] *He has pulled down the mighty from their thrones,* Elihu acknowledges how the deposed and the penitent are welcomed back according to penance. And that is: **[8]** ***And if they are in chains,*** namely, those who have been deposed from their royal thrones and bound by

30. Ex 15.3.
31. Jb 8.20.
32. Is 11.4.
33. Ps 31.8.
34. Prv 25.5.
35. Prv 29.14.
36. 1 Sm 17 does not refer or allude to Saul's excessive pride. Perhaps Albert, working from memory, intended instead to cite 1 Sm 13 (see especially vv. 13–14) or 1 Sm 15 (especially vv. 10–29).
37. Lk 1.52.

their enemies, ***and bound with the ropes of poverty,*** that is, they are bound to the greatest poverty by the things pulling them down. Prv 5:[38] *His own iniquities seize the wicked man, and he is bound with the ropes of his own sins.* [9] ***He will show them,*** by means of such captivity and tribulation certainly, ***their works,*** because they have ruled wickedly, of course. Ps:[39] *I will convict you, and I will set [your evil deeds] before your face.*

And Elihu adds[40] why God judges: ***because they,*** that is, oppressors of the innocent, ***have been violent.*** Wis 6:[41] *Power has been given to you by the Lord, and strength by the Most High, who will examine your works and search out your thoughts: because, although you have been ministers of His kingdom, you have not judged rightly, nor have you kept the law of justice, nor have you walked according to the will of God.* There is an example in Manasseh, according to 2 Chr 33,[42] whom the army of the king of the Assyrians and the leaders seized and led, bound with chains and fetters, to Babylon.

[10] ***He will also open their ears,*** through tribulations, of course, so that they may hear and recognize their very selves with the interior ear, and that is, ***so that He may rebuke them,*** namely, through tribulations, ***and He will speak,*** that is, with a scourge, ***so that they may return from iniquity.*** Wis 12:[43] *You rebuke little by little those who wander off, and you remind and speak to them about the things through which they sin, so that, when they have left their wickedness behind, they may believe in you, O Lord.*

[11] ***If they will hear,*** God, of course, speaking and rebuking in this way, ***and guard,*** supply: themselves from iniquity, ***they will complete their days in prosperity.*** There is an example in David, who listened attentively to Nathan rebuking him, according to 2 Sm 12,[44] and he completed his days in prosperity. Is 1:[45] *If you are willing and will listen to me, you will eat the good things of the earth.* ***and,*** supply: they will complete ***their years,*** supply: given to

38. Prv 5.22.
39. Ps 49.21.
40. I read *subdit* with MSS FM rather than *probat* in Weiss's edition.
41. Wis 6.4–5.
42. 2 Chr 33.11.
43. Wis 12.2.
44. 2 Sm 12.1–13.
45. Is 1.19.

them for reigning, ***in glory***. There is an example in Manasseh according to 2 Kgs 21[46] and 2 Chr 33,[47] of whom it is written as follows: Manasseh, *after he was in distress, prayed to the Lord his God, and did penance intensely before the God of his fathers. And he entreated Him and implored Him intently; and God heard his prayer and brought him back to Jerusalem into his kingdom.* [12] ***But if they will not hear, they will pass by the sword.*** Jb 19:[48] *The sword is the avenger of iniquities.* ***and they will be consumed,*** that is, they will be led down to final consumption, ***in folly,*** that is, for their own folly. Is 1:[49] *If you refuse to listen to me, and provoke me to wrath, my sword will devour you.* Bar 3:[50] *They did not find the way of knowledge; therefore, they perished. And because they did not have wisdom, they perished on account of their foolishness.*

Then Elihu adds an anthypophora. For someone could say that Job cries out but nevertheless is not restored. Elihu responds: [13] ***Dissemblers,*** those who pretend that they are good when they are evil, ***and crafty men,*** that is, those who are skilled in ambush like a serpent and are deceitful, ***provoke the wrath of God.*** Jer 4:[51] *They are wise in doing evil, but they do not know how to act rightly.* Jb 5:[52] *He catches the wise in their cunning and scatters the schemes of the corrupt.*

And he adds the reason: ***and they will not cry out,*** supply: from the heart to God, ***when they have been bound,*** by tribulation and misery, of course. And there is an example in Asa, according to 2 Chr 16,[53] of whom it is written as follows: *In his infirmity Asa did not seek God, but rather trusted in the skill of physicians. And he slept with his fathers, and he died.* And after a few words:[54] *And they laid him on his bed full of spices and the ointments of harlots.*

And this is what follows: [14] ***Their soul,*** that is, their animal life, ***will die in a tempest.*** And he calls the assault of God's wrath

46. 2 Kgs 21.9
47. 2 Chr 33.12–13.
48. Jb 19.29.
49. Is 1.20.
50. Bar 3.27–28.
51. Jer 4.22.
52. Jb 5.13.
53. 2 Chr 16.12–13.
54. 2 Chr 16.14.

a "tempest." Na 1:[55] *The Lord's ways are in a tempest and a whirlwind.* Ps:[56] *A fire will blaze in His sight, and a mighty tempest will surround Him.* ***and their,*** supply: animal ***life,*** supply: will end ***among the effeminate.*** Those who, having been reduced to the softness proper to a woman, resist no vice, but, as soft, submit to it are called "effeminate." On account of this, Aristotle, in Book VII of the *Ethics,* says that the soft man is more wicked than the intemperate one.[57] Is 3:[58] *The effeminate will rule over them.* Mt 11:[59] *Those who are clothed in soft garments are in the houses of kings.* These people are [called] *Sardanapalici,* because Sardanapalus[60] was always keeping company with women in vaulted rooms and with the ointments of harlots and amid sensual feasts, as the comment on the first book of the *Ethics* says.[61]

But Elihu adds what the consequence of the destruction of such people's advantage is: **[15]** ***He will rescue the poor man,*** when his oppressor has been destroyed, of course, ***from his distress,*** which his oppressor has caused certainly. Prv 11:[62] *The just man has been delivered from distress, and the wicked one will be handed over instead of him.* Ps:[63] *He will judge the poor of the people, and He will save the children of the poor, and He will humble the oppressor.* ***and,*** supply: like a merciful father, ***He will open his ears,*** of the oppressor, of course, which [ears] refused to listen to God in the midst of prosperity, ***in tribulation,*** that is, by means of tribulation. Is 35:[64] *Then the eyes of the blind will be opened, and the ears of the deaf unstopped.* Is 28:[65] *Vexation alone will impart understanding of what you hear.*

[16] ***Therefore.***

55. Na 1.3.
56. Ps 49.3.
57. Aristotle, *EN* 7.7.3.
58. Is 3.4.
59. Mt 11.8.
60. Sardanapalus was a celebrated effeminate king of Assyria who finally burned himself to death together with his treasures.
61. See Alb., *Eth.* 1.5.7.
62. Prv 11.8.
63. Ps 71.4.
64. Is 35.5.
65. Is 28.19.

From all these things [that have been said], Elihu concludes that if Job will repent, he will be welcomed back and restored to every good thing. And that is: ***Therefore, He will save you,*** supply: repenting and confessing your sin. Ps:[66] *For you have saved us from those afflicting us.* At the end of 2 Chr:[67] You will save me, [I who am] unworthy, according to your great mercy, and I will praise you all the days of my life. ***out of the narrow mouth,*** of tribulation, of course, which has chewed you up and swallowed you. Jer 51:[68] *He has swallowed me up like a dragon; he has filled his stomach with my tender meat.* ***most spaciously,*** that is, by leading you out into a most spacious freedom. Ps:[69] *He brought me out into a spacious place; He saved me because He wishes to have me.* ***and which,*** narrow mouth, of course, ***has no foundation,*** that is, base of support, ***under you.*** For the voracity with which the wicked devour the good lacks a foundation. Prv 13:[70] *The stomach of the wicked is incapable of being satisfied.* Ps:[71] *I am fixed in the mire of the depths, and there is no foothold.* Indeed, without a foundation, that into which the human is constantly plunged day by day is called "tribulation."[72]

Then, concerning the good, Elihu adds to what things he is restored: ***and the restfulness of your table,*** that is, the abundance of refreshment, ***will be full of richness.*** Gn 49:[73] *Asher's bread will be rich, and he will provide delicacies to kings.* Ps:[74] *You have prepared a table in my sight against those who afflict me.*

From these things [that have been said], moreover, Elihu takes the opportunity to instruct, teaching [Job] to recognize his sin and [telling him] from which things he should refrain. And that is: **[17]** ***Your case,*** which was between you and God, of course, ***has been judged as though,*** this is expressive of the truth, **[*it were*]** ***that of a wicked man;*** for by striking you, God shows that

66. Ps 43.8.

67. The following words are not from the end of 2 Chr; rather, they are thematically similar to those of Sir 51.15–17.

68. Jer 51.34.

69. Ps 17.20.

70. Prv 13.25.

71. Ps 68.3.

72. See v. 15 immediately above.

73. Gn 49.20.

74. Ps 22.5.

you are wicked. Jb 34:[75] *He has struck them as though wicked in the presence of onlookers.* Supply: and if you repent, ***your case,*** that is, the justice of your case, ***and judgment,*** which the just judge, God, owes the one who repents, ***you will recover,*** which is the restoration to all good things, for this judgment is determined. Ezek 18:[76] *But if the wicked person does penance for all the sins that he has committed, and keeps all my commandments, and brings forth judgment and justice, he will surely live and not die. I will not remember any of his iniquities that he has committed.*

Then Elihu adds five things from which he [Job] should refrain. The first is anger toward his subjects. **[18]** ***Therefore, do not let anger overcome you such that you oppress anyone,*** by the black and blue bruises of anger or vengeance, of course. Jas 1:[77] *Let every man be quick to listen, but slow to speak and slow to anger. For the anger of man does not produce the justice of God.*

and do not let the multitude of bribes turn you aside, namely, from justice, and this is the second. Dt 16:[78] *You shall not show partiality, nor shall you accept bribes: for bribes blind the eyes of the wise and change the words of the just.* Is 5:[79] *Woe to you who justify*[80] *the wicked man for bribes and snatch the justice of the just one away from him.*

And he adds the third: **[19]** ***Put down your greatness,*** that is, the achievement by which you seem great to yourself. Ex 33:[81] *So now put down your ornaments, so that I may know what to do with you.* ***without trouble,*** that you may choose humility voluntarily, of course. Mt 11:[82] *Learn from me, because I am meek and humble of heart.* Jas 4:[83] *God resists the proud, but gives grace to the humble.*

Then he adds the fourth, and that is: ***and,*** supply: put down ***all of the robust in strength.*** The "robust in strength" are the proud

75. Jb 34.26.
76. Ezek 18.21–22.
77. Jas 1.19–20.
78. Dt 16.19.
79. Is 5.23.
80. Here I read *iustificatis* and *aufertis* in the next phrase (both second-person plural) with MS E, rather than *iustificant* and *auferunt* (third-person plural) with Weiss's edition.
81. Ex 33.5.
82. Mt 11.29.
83. Jas 4.6.

who, presumptuous concerning their own strength, oppress others. Jb 40:[84] *Scatter the proud in your fury, and, beholding every arrogant man, humble him; look on all who are proud, and confound them.* **[20]** ***Do not prolong the night,*** that is, during the night, but that you may take vengeance on them promptly, of course. Do not prolong, I say,[85] this purposeful activity, ***that people may rise up for them,*** certainly who might, by means of intervention and attack, liberate them. Jl 3:[86] *Soon I will swiftly repay a recompense to you on your head.* Ps:[87] *In the morning I killed all the sinners of the land, that I might eliminate all the workers of iniquity from the city of the Lord.*

And he sets forth the fifth: **[21]** ***Avoid turning aside to iniquity.*** Here Elihu calls hypocrisy "iniquity," because Augustine says that feigned justice (*aequitas*) is not justice, but two-faced iniquity (*iniquitas*).[88] Mt 7:[89] *Beware of false prophets, who come to you in sheep's clothing but inwardly are ravenous wolves.* ***for this you have begun to follow after misery*** inflicted on you, that is to say, you make excuses for [your] iniquity even after [your] misery. Ps:[90] *Do not incline my heart to words of wickedness for the purpose of making excuses for sins.*

[22] ***Behold, God.***

Here Elihu begins to argue on the basis of divine [judgments] that make clear the profundity of God, and it is divided into two parts. In the first of these, he shows that God is incomprehensible in His very self; in the second, that God is wonderful in His effects and His government, in that place:[91] *He draws up the drops of rain.*

In the first [part], there are two [divisions]. For Elihu makes clear that God is incomprehensible in nature; and incomprehensible in eternity, in that place:[92] *The number of His years.* In this prior [division], there are again two points, namely: that God's nature is incomprehensible according to power and justice; and

84. Jb 40.6–7.
85. Here I read *dico* with MSS FM, rather than the *dicas* of Weiss's edition.
86. Jl 3.4.
87. Ps 100.8.
88. Augustine, *En. Ps.* 63.11.7 (PL 36:765).
89. Mt 7.15.
90. Ps 140.4.
91. Jb 36.27.
92. Jb 36.26.

second, Elihu limits our knowledge, in that place:[93] *Remember that you do not know.*

And that is: ***Behold, indeed, God is exalted,*** supply: in nature. Something high that is enclosed in or intermingled with nothing of inferior things is called "exalted," and God exists in such a way; on account of this, He alone is exalted. Ps 112:[94] *Who is like the Lord our God, who dwells on high?* Lk 2:[95] *Glory to God in the highest.* Is 57:[96] *Thus says the Lord, exalted and eminent, inhabiting eternity; and His name is holy who dwells in an exalted and holy place.* In the *Book of Causes,* Aristotle says:[97] "The First [Cause] rules all things, but it is not intermingled with them." ***in His strength,*** that is, in His power; for there is nothing that He is not able to do, and there is nothing that is able to oppose Him, and He is able to do more than can be conceived. Jb 9:[98] *If strength is sought, He is the strongest.* Nm 23:[99] *His strength is like that of a rhinoceros.* ***and none is like Him among the lawgivers.*** The reason for this is because, as Plato says,[100] all the laws of humans are for the sake of the wicked, for they were developed and enacted only on account of wicked people, and therefore they are imperfect for regulating life and often they are unjust. Nevertheless, they are just because they are for the purpose of [instilling] fear; and they are well established only on the basis of coerced virtue, because they bind [people] for punishments, [and] frequently they are actually [the laws] of tyrants more than of kings. Is 10:[101] *Woe to those who make wicked laws, and when they write, write injustice in order to oppress the poor in judgment and do violence to the humble among my people.* The law of the Lord, on the other hand, is the rule of life, reaching toward the end of beatitude, having been given to the good by the Good [Himself] not on the basis of coerced virtue, but on the basis of His own honor (*honestate*) drawing the desire

93. Jb 36.24.
94. Ps 112.5.
95. Lk 2.14.
96. Is 57.15.
97. *Caus.* 19.
98. Jb 9.19.
99. Nm 23.22.
100. See Plato, *Polit.* 294b.
101. Is 10.1–2.

of the human person. Sir 45:[102] *He gave him a heart for precepts, and the law of life and discipline.* Is 8:[103] *Bind up the testimony, seal the law among my instructions.* Ps:[104] *The law of the Lord is irreproachable, converting souls.* So, therefore, God is exalted in nature, power, and justice.

And because God is exalted in nature and power: **[23]** ***Who will be able to search out His ways?*** that is, His effects that lead to Him, so that from them one may know Him by means of science, [namely] what He is (*quid est*).[105] Ps:[106] *Your steps* (vestigia) *shall not be known.* In Jb 11 it is said ironically:[107] *Will you perhaps comprehend the steps of God, and can you get to know the Almighty perfectly?* Supply: and because God is exalted in justice: ***or who dares to say to Him,*** as if reproving His works: ***You have worked iniquity?*** Jb 9:[108] *Who is able to say: Why do you act in this way?* Rom 9:[109] *O man, who are you to argue with God? Does not the potter have power over the clay?* Jb 34:[110] *May wickedness be far from God, and iniquity from the Almighty.*

From these things [that have been said] Elihu concludes that God is incomprehensible, and that is: **[24]** ***Remember,*** supply: therefore, ***that you do not know His work,*** because, [even] if we know [His] work according to substance, we still do not know how great His work is, such that from His work itself we are able to know what God is (*quid est*); and this is so because an effect of His is not interchangeable with Him, as a *per se* cause is interchangeable with a *per se* effect. And Elihu wishes [to show]

102. Sir 45.6.

103. Is 8.16.

104. Ps 18.8.

105. Like Thomas Aquinas after him, Albert holds that we humans cannot properly know *what* God is (*quid est*)—that is, God's essence or nature—from observing His created effects, though we can know from them *that* God is (*quod est*)—that is, God's existence. See, e.g., Albert, *ST* 1.3.13.3, where he teaches that God's triune nature is not naturally knowable; and *ST* 1.3.14.1. For Aquinas, see, e.g., his *ST* I.2.2, 3; I.3; and I.32.1, where he also affirms the impossibility of attaining to the knowledge of the Trinity by natural reason.

106. Ps 76.20.

107. Jb 11.7.

108. Jb 9.12.

109. Rom 9.20–21.

110. Jb 34.10.

from this that Job wickedly reproved the work of God, for which reason God punished Job, because Job was not able to recognize God's justice. Gregory says:[111] "It is as if he were saying: In what way can He, whose activity cannot be searched out, be reproved? For no one judges rightly what he does not know."

Then he adds the reason why the work [of God] is not known: ***about which***, that is, about whose work and power, ***men have sung.*** He calls prophets who from the beginning poetically sang of certain divine [works] through verse compositions, "men." For Aristotle says[112] that the *Hesiodistae,* the first to philosophize, were those who, theologizing poetically, sang certain [songs] about God, and all of them directed themselves toward the splendor of their subject matter, composing certain wonderful things in tales and referring them back to philosophy. In the first book of the *Metaphysics* Aristotle says:[113] A tale is composed from wonderful things, and from the perspective of philosophy those who sing invent many things.

And Elihu adds the general reason for these things, and it is added: because **[25]** ***All men see Him,*** that is, in His effects they know that He exists. Wis 13:[114] *From the greatness of the beauty of the creature, the Creator of them will be able to be seen recognizably.* Rom 1:[115] *The invisible things of God are clearly seen, being understood through the things that have been made.* ***everyone looks from far away,*** for He is not known from creatures, except that He exists (*quia est*), and what He is not (*quid non est*), and what He is infinitely (*quid est infinite*). Gregory says:[116] "Every man, from the very fact that he has been created rational, ought to infer on the basis of reason that He who created him is God." But "to look" at Him "from far away" is not to perceive Him already by means of sight (*per speciem*), but as yet to ponder Him on the basis of the admiration of His works alone.

And Elihu brings in the conclusion: **[26]** ***Behold, God is great,***

111. Gregory, *Mor.* 27.3.5.

112. Weiss's citation is Aristotle, *Metaph.* 2.4.12; see also Albert, *Metaph.* 1.3.4.

113. Aristotle, *Metaph.* 1.2.8.

114. Wis 13.5.

115. Rom 1.20.

116. Gregory, *Mor.* 27.5.8.

namely, in essence, power, and justice, ***surpassing our knowledge,*** namely, of comprehension. Ps:[117] *Your knowledge has become astonishing to me; it has grown very high, and I cannot reach up to it.* And he adds concerning eternity: ***the number of His years,*** that is, of His unfailing eternity in relation to the years of all times and of [an eternity] surpassing them, ***is beyond reckoning,*** because it surpasses them infinitely. Ps:[118] *But you are always the same, and your years will not come to an end.*

Then Elihu adds how wonderful God is according to His effects, and it is divided into two parts. For first he points out certain effects by reason of which He is shown to be wonderful; second, he specifies the agony of the one admiring [the divine effects], and he adds still more terrifying effects, below in that place:[119] *At this my heart trembled.* In the first part, Elihu sets forth three conjunctions of opposite effects, namely, of drought and humidity, of darkness and illumination, and of happiness and unhappiness. And that is: **[27]** ***He draws up,*** supply: at times, ***the drops*** **(stillas)** ***of rain,*** and supply: and introduces insufferable drought. Gregory[120] reads "stars" (*stellas*), although in Hebrew it is "drops" (*stillas*), and then the sense is that God draws up the stars, which are the sources of moisture, like Pleiades and Hyades, until they are not able to cause moisture. Jer 3:[121] *There was no rain late in coming.* Jer 14:[122] *The word of the Lord that came concerning the drought.* ***and,*** supply: by means of the opposite, at other times, ***pours out showers,*** abundantly, of course, ***like floods.*** Gn 7:[123] *All the fountains of the great deep burst forth, and the flood gates of heaven were opened; and rain fell on the earth.* **[28]** ***which,*** floods, of course, ***flow from the clouds,*** to be sure, when they release [precipitation] as water. Jb 38:[124] *Will you lift your voice up to the clouds, so that a flood of waters will cover you?* ***which,*** clouds, of course, ***have covered all things above,*** so that, to be sure, they

117. Ps 138.6.
118. Ps 101.28.
119. Jb 37.1.
120. Gregory, *Mor.* 27.8.12.
121. Jer 3.3.
122. Jer 14.1.
123. Gn 7.11–12.
124. Jb 38.34.

may be able to rain down everywhere. Plato discusses these two floods, namely, of fire or drought and of water, in the *Timaeus;*[125] and Ovid describes the flood of fire in the myth of Phaethon, and the flood of water in the myth of Pyrrha and Deucalion.[126]

And concerning the effects of darkness and of illumination, Elihu adds: **[29]** ***If He wishes to spread out the clouds,***[127] so they may conceal the luminaries of heaven, of course, lest they illuminate the earth. Is 13:[128] *The stars of heaven and their brilliance will not distribute their light; the sun has been made dark in its rising, and the moon will not shine with its light.* **[30]** ***and,*** supply: by the opposite, ***to illuminate with His light from above,*** and to dry all things up and to set fire to them by means of lightning. Ps:[129] *You illuminate wonderfully from the eternal mountains.* ***He will cover even the ends of the sea.*** The shores, within which the sea encloses the land, to which the falling rains are led down so that the entire earth may be made fertile and bring forth fruit everywhere, are called "the ends of the sea." Ps:[130] *You have visited the earth, and you have drenched it; you have enriched it in many ways.* And after a few words:[131] *Fill up its streams, multiply its fruits.* Concerning brightness, moreover, [it says] in another Psalm:[132] *Flash forth lightning, and it will scatter them.* Likewise, in another Psalm:[133] *Because of the brilliance in His sight, the clouds passed away, hail and coals of fire.* **[31]** ***For by these He judges the peoples,*** by means of the judgment of discretion, of course, because it rains upon one person and not upon another. Am 4:[134] *I withheld the rain from you when there were still three months until the harvest. And I caused it to rain upon one city, and I caused it not to rain upon another: one region was rained upon, and the other region, upon which I did not cause it to rain, dried*

125. See Plato, *Ti.* 22C; cf. Alb., *On Job* 14.11 (vol. 1, p. 256).

126. See Ovid, *Metam.* 2.31–328, 1.313–347.

127. The phrase that follows here in the Vulgate text as it has come down to us, ***quasi tentatorium suum*** **("as His tent"),** is not found in any of Weiss's MSS.

128. Is 13.10.

129. Ps 75.5.

130. Ps 64.10.

131. Ps 64.11.

132. Ps 143.6.

133. Ps 17.13.

134. Am 4.7.

up. ***and gives food to many mortals.*** Is 55:[135] *The rain and the snow come down from heaven and return there no more, but soak the earth and water it, and make it sprout forth, and give seed to the one who sows and bread to the one who eats.*

Then Elihu adds concerning the effects of happiness and unhappiness—they are called happiness and unhappiness according to good fortune and misfortune—and that is: **[32]** ***By means of the monstrous***[136] ***He hides the light.*** Those are called "monstrous" who transgress the boundaries of nature, reason, and positive justice by their own tyranny, whereby the light of grace and prosperity is hidden on account of their sins. Bar 3:[137] *There were giants there, those renowned men who were present from the beginning, great in stature, skilled in war. The Lord did not choose them, neither did they find the way of knowledge; therefore, they perished.* Secretly, however, Elihu brands blessed Job [as monstrous] because, on account of [his] barbarity, he lost the light of grace and good fortune (*prosperitatem*).[138] ***and He commands it,*** namely, the light, ***to come again,*** supply: to the one who is penitent and has been freed from faults. Is 58:[139] *Your light will arise in darkness, and your darkness will be as midday.* Mi 7:[140] *He will bring me forth into the light. I will see His justice.* And lest there be doubt about this, Elihu adds: **[33]** ***Concerning it,*** namely, the light, ***He makes known to His friend,*** devoted and holy, of course, ***that it is his possession.*** Wis 18:[141] *Your saints had a very great light.* Ps:[142] *They will walk in the light of your face.* ***and that he is able to rise,*** from darkness, of course, ***to it,*** namely, the light to be possessed. 1 Pt 2:[143] *Who called you out of darkness into His marvelous light.*

135. Is 55.10.

136. Here Albert's text has ***Immanibus,*** whereas the Vulgate as it has come down to us reads ***In manibus*** (**"In His hands"**). Cf. Gregory, *Mor.* 27.13.24, who also has ***Immanibus.***

137. Bar 3.26–27.

138. Here I read with MSS FM, which add *et prosperitatem.*

139. Is 58.10.

140. Mi 7.9.

141. Wis 18.1.

142. Ps 88.16.

143. 1 Pt 2.9.

CHAPTER 37

A*T THIS MY heart trembled.*

After enumerating the effects proceeding from the wonderful power and wisdom [of God], Elihu touches on the movement of the heart by way of astonishment regarding these effects, and especially insofar as these are led back (*reducuntur*) to God, who as mighty creates this [universe], as wise orders it, and as the supreme ruler (*dux optimus*) of all creatures draws each one together toward the good of the universe and toward perfection. For Aristotle says that the good of the universe is in the Prime Mover or the First Cause, just as the good of an army is in its commander (*duce*).[1] And that is: ***At this,*** that is, at these effects [of God] that have been considered, ***my heart trembled,*** with the terror of astonishment, of course. For the heart trembles and is moved according to its beating (*secundum systolem*)[2] when it examines what is lofty. Jb 21:[3] *When I remember, I become very afraid, and trembling seizes my flesh.* ***and was moved out of its place.*** For it is natural that, when the heart recoils into its very self from beholding greatness, it returns little by little to consider that great thing (*illud magnum*): and this Elihu calls being "moved out of its place," when little by little the heart recovers its strength and inquires concerning the lofty thing that it beheld. And this is what the Psalm says:[4] *He has arranged steps of ascent in his heart, in the vale of tears, in the place that He has specified.* And again:[5] *The human will come to a lofty heart, and God will be exalted.*

1. See Aristotle, *Metaph.* 11.10.1, as cited by Weiss.
2. Cf. Alb., *AL* 20.2.3.
3. Jb 21.6.
4. Ps 83.6–7.
5. Ps 63.7–8.

And Elihu adds other effects [of God] still more wonderful (*mirabiliores*) than the first ones,[6] and this part is divided into three: first, he specifies effects in things generated on high; second, he shows how, among these things, He has distinguished the works of men and of beasts; third, he makes clear how incomprehensible God is in all these effects, the Maker of all of them. The second division begins in that place:[7] *He [inscribes] in the hand of all men;* and the third in that place:[8] *Listen to these things, Job.*

In the first [of these divisions], Elihu speaks of two things, namely: the wonderful act (*miraculum*) of God in things generated on high from dry vapor; and the wonderful act of God in things generated on high from moist vapor, in that place:[9] *He commands the snow.* In the first [of these subdivisions], there are two things, namely, preliminary remarks and a conclusion. And that is: [2] ***It,*** supply: my heart, ***will hear His news,*** which is His, as the First Efficient Cause, ***in the terror of His voice.*** Indeed, "voice" is said because all these effects are produced by His order; and this is what follows: ***and the sound,*** supply: of thunder, ***proceeding from His mouth,*** for from His command it proceeds and is produced, because everything that happens in an army proceeds from the mouth of its commander. Ps:[10] *The voice of your thunder in a wheel.* Sir 43:[11] *The voice of His thunder struck the earth.* Indeed, all these things are ordained by God. Jb 38:[12] *Who gave a course to the most severe rain showers, and a way for the reverberating thunder?* Ps:[13] *The Lord thundered from heaven, and the Most High sent forth His voice.*

Elihu adds, moreover, how these things in heaven and on earth are from God: [3] ***Above all the heavens He considers [all things],*** namely, by ordering the motion of the heavens to their proper effects and the impressions that they stamp onto the

6. Namely, those he enumerated in chapter 36.
7. Jb 37.7.
8. Jb 37.14.
9. Jb 37.6.
10. Ps 76.19.
11. Sir 43.18.
12. Jb 38.25.
13. Ps 17.14.

whole sphere of active and passive realities. Sir 24:[14] *I alone have encircled the course of heaven.* ***and His,*** namely, God's, because He governs by means of the stars, ***light,*** supply: is ***to the ends of the earth.*** He calls the differences in climates, which are distinguished by the amount of light [they receive] according to their accepted latitudes from the equatorial plane, on account of which a day is longer or shorter, "the ends." Is 24:[15] *From the ends of the earth we have heard praises, the glory of the Just One.* And, supply: among all these things, **[4]** ***After Him,*** as after the ruler of the universe, ***a noise,*** either of obedient creatures or of thunder, ***will roar.*** Ps:[16] *Their sound has gone forth into all the earth.* And, supply: because, ***He will thunder with the voice of His majesty,*** over the universe, of course, just as the commander of an army [thunders] over the army. Mt 8:[17] *What sort of man is this, that he commands the winds and the sea, and they obey him?* The seraphim express this loud cry according to Is 6:[18] *Holy, holy, holy, Lord God of Hosts, all the earth is full of your glory.* For a host is an army, because God's command extends to all creatures in the universe, just as that of the commander of an army extends over the [entire] army. ***and He will not be investigated,*** according to the first and highest causes of God's wisdom, although [His creatures] have been investigated according to proximate causes by the foolishness of the philosophers, ***when,*** that is, although, ***His voice will be heard.*** Jn 3:[19] *You hear His voice, but you do not know where He comes from or where He goes.* Supply: because **[5]** ***God will thunder marvelously,*** that is, from the wondrous height of His wisdom, ***with His*** great ***voice,*** penetrating all creatures, of course. Ex 19:[20] *Behold, thunder began to be heard, and lightning to flash.* And after a few words:[21] *The blast of the trumpet resounded exceedingly.* And below this:[22] *The sound of the trumpet gradually grew and was drawn out longer.*

14. Sir 24.8.
15. Is 24.16.
16. Ps 18.5.
17. Mt 8.27.
18. Is 6.3.
19. Jn 3.8.
20. Ex 19.16.
21. Ibid.
22. Ex 19.18.

From all these things [that have been said], Elihu draws a conclusion, and it is [to be] supplied: Therefore, God Himself is ***He who does great and inscrutable things;*** "great [things]" in Himself, "inscrutable things" according to the highest causes of wisdom.

Then Elihu adds concerning things generated on high from moist vapor, first concerning things that have been transformed and frozen: **[6]** ***He commands the snow,*** supply: to be generated on high and thus ***to fall down.*** Sir 43:[23] *By His command He caused the snow to fall more quickly.* Ps:[24] *He scatters the snow like wool,* for snow rarely falls like carded wool, and this is a sign that from warm vapor it is simultaneously both transformed and frozen. ***upon the earth,*** to water the earth so that it might sprout forth, of course. Is 55:[25] *As the rain and the snow come down from heaven and return there no more, but soak the earth and water it, and make it sprout forth.* ***and,*** supply: He commands ***the winter rains.*** And they are called the "winter rains" because in the winter, when the sun has become less intense and is sufficient to elevate vapors but not to consume them, they descend more. ***and the showers of His strength.*** Rains coming down with violent motion and making [the ground] very wet are called "showers," and "of His strength" indicates this, hence Song 2:[26] *Winter has now passed; the rain is over and gone.*

And Elihu adds how, through this, God has distinguished the activities (*operationes*) of men and of beasts, and that is: **[7]** ***He inscribes in the hand of all men,*** that is, so that they may inquire beyond the signs of heaven,[27] ***that every individual may come to know His works,*** that is, what must have been made at what time. For some things must have been made in the spring, others in the summer, some others in autumn, and still others in winter. Hence the Lord, reproaching certain people, says in Lk 12:[28] *When you see a cloud rising from the west, immediately you say: A rain-*

23. Sir 43.14.
24. Ps 147.5, although Weiss wrongly gives this citation as Ps 147.16.
25. Is 55.10.
26. Song 2.11.
27. That is, beyond the constellations.
28. Lk 12.54–56.

storm is coming; and so it happens. And when you see the south wind blowing, you say: It will be hot; and it happens. You hypocrites, you know how to discern the appearance of heaven and earth: but how is it that you do not discern this time?

And not only among men, but also among beasts. And that is: **[8]** ***The beast will go,*** supply: during its cold season, of course, when phlegm[29] is produced, ***into its den,*** that is to say, whatever beast has a cold physical constitution, eats cold and viscous food, has a thick skin, [and] possesses little digestive heat, such as the snake, frog, stork, swallow, dormouse, quail, and certain others; for these animals draw many viscous humors together around the site of digestion, and unless they lie down and sleep during this time, namely, during the time of phlegm production, as during the winter, the heat of digestion in them is strangled, and they die. For during sleep, heat grows very strong, and viscous moisture is diminished, so that it can nourish the [bodily] members.

And this is what follows: ***and will stay in its cave.*** Jer 8:[30] *The kite in the sky knows its time; the turtledove and the swallow have observed the time of their arrival: but my people do not know the judgment of the Lord.* And so it is with regard to any animal whatsoever, because it is led to its cave around the time of sleep and digestion.[31] Ps:[32] *The sun has risen, and they have gathered together; and they will lie down in their lairs.*

Then Elihu adds how God separates these things[33] from the regions of heaven, giving the latter their distinction and usefulness. And that is: **[9]** ***From the inner parts a tempest will emerge.*** He calls the parts that are around the South Pole "the inner parts" because that pole remains removed from us,[34] and clouds rising from that pole are stormy and blow [the wind] in a circular

29. See Alb., *AL* 3.2.3.

30. Jer 8.7.

31. Here I read *tempore dormitionis et digestionis* with MSS TEFM, rather than simply *tempore digestionis* with Weiss's edition.

32. Ps 103.22.

33. Here I read *ista* with MSS TEFM, rather than *ita* with Weiss's edition.

34. See Alb., *On Job* 9.9 (vol. 1, 193), where he explains that the areas around the South or Antarctic Pole "are kept out of sight from us who live in the northern quarter of the earth."

motion. Is 21:[35] *As whirlwinds come from the south, it comes from the desert.* Jb 1:[36] *A violent wind blew from the region of the desert and shook the four corners of the house.* The region of the desert is toward the south. ***and cold weather from Arcturus,*** that is, from the North Pole. Sir 43:[37] *Cold wind blows from the north, and the water has frozen into crystal.* Jb 9:[38] *He who makes Arcturus and Orion, and Hyades and the inner parts of the south.*

And because God brings this about by means of winds and vapors, Elihu adds: **[10]** ***When God breathes out,*** supply: from Arcturus, ***the frost collects*** in ice and snow. Sir 43:[39] *He will pour frost like salt on the earth.* Ps:[40] *He sends His rock crystals like morsels: who will stand before the face of His cold weather?* ***and again,*** supply: when the south wind blows from the inner parts, ***the waters are poured out abundantly,*** for the south wind draws the waters together and reveals the land, and it calls the land forth and causes it to sprout forth. Ps:[41] *His spirit will breathe out, and the waters will flow.* Song 4:[42] *Arise, O north wind, and come; O south wind, blow through my garden, and let its aromatic spices flow.*

And, concerning the uses of these things, Elihu adds: **[11]** ***Produce desires the clouds.*** Everything ordered toward the enjoyment (*fructum*) of men is here called "produce" (*frumentum*), having been designated from "I enjoy," "you enjoy" (*fruor, frueris*); that is, it desires the clouds, in order that by the shadow of the clouds it may be protected from the heat of the sun, and that from the moisture of the clouds it may be irrigated by means of the early rain and the late rain. Hos 6:[43] *He will come to us as the early and the late shower [come] to the earth.* ***and the clouds scatter their light,*** that is, the benefit received from the light of the stars in accordance with their elevation. For when clouds rise, the powers of the stars flow through the clouds into the produce, and by the benefit of

35. Is 21.1.
36. Jb 1.19.
37. Sir 43.22.
38. Jb 9.9.
39. Sir 43.21.
40. Ps 147.6, although Weiss wrongly gives this citation as Ps 147.17.
41. Ps 147.7, although Weiss wrongly gives this citation as Ps 147.18.
42. Song 4.16.
43. Hos 6.3.

those powers the produce is made capable of germinating; and on that account the clouds are moved around the earth. For water, since it is cold and wet, does not of itself have the power of germination, but it takes it from the stars. Sir 43:[44] *A remedy for all is in the speedy arrival of a cloud.*

And this is what follows: **[12]** ***which*** all ***circle about,*** so that they may make [the earth] fruitful on all sides, of course. Is 45:[45] *Drop dew, O heavens, from above, and let the clouds rain down on the just; let the earth be opened and bud forth a savior.* ***wherever the will of Him who governs,*** namely, of God, who orders all things, ***them,*** namely, the clouds, ***guides them;*** hence, concerning certain ones, it is said in Is 5:[46] *I will command my clouds not to rain on it.* Jb 11:[47] *If He should overturn all things or compress them into one, who will speak against Him?*

And explaining this, item by item, Elihu adds: ***to every place that He commands them,*** namely, the clouds. Ps:[48] *He spoke, and they were made; He commanded, and they were created. He has established them everlastingly, and forever and ever: He has made a decree, and it will not pass away.* ***upon the face of the earth,*** supply: in general the clouds effect His decree. **[13]** ***whether among one tribe,*** that is, one people of a distinct land, ***or in His own land,*** that is, in one climate, ***or in whatever place of His mercy,*** that is, in whatever place by His mercy He wishes to overhang the benefit of clouds, ***He orders them,*** namely, the clouds, ***to be found,*** this is indicated in a Psalm:[49] *You shall set apart a voluntary rain, O God, for your inheritance,* that is, you will give a particular [benefit of clouds]. Am 4:[50] *I caused it to rain upon one city, and I caused it not to rain upon another.*

[14] ***Listen to these things, Job.***

Here Elihu admonishes [Job] to pay attention to the words he has spoken, and he says three things. First, indeed, he declares in general that he should pay attention to his words. Second, [he mentions] those that he should heed principally, in

44. Sir 43.24.
45. Is 45.8.
46. Is 5.6.
47. Jb 11.10.
48. Ps 148.5–6.
49. Ps 67.10.
50. Am 4.7.

that place:[51] *Can it be that you know?* Third, he concludes that the author of these things is incomprehensible and indescribable, in that place:[52] *Show us.*

And that is: ***Listen to these things, Job,*** with an attentive ear, of course. Ps:[53] *Incline your ear and forget your people and your father's house.* Song 8:[54] *You who dwell in the gardens, friends are listening.* ***stand,*** with the heart meditating on the same thing, of course, so that you may examine them more carefully and not pass over them in a perfunctory way. Jer 6:[55] *Stand firm in our ways and see which one is the good way.* ***and consider,*** things antecedent, of course, and things consequent, things attendant, things contradictory, and things signifying. Mt 24:[56] *Look and lift up your heads.* Bar 4:[57] *Look around, O Jerusalem, toward the east, and see the joy that comes to you from God.* ***the wondrous works of God,*** for all of these are lofty and marvelous. Ps:[58] *Marvelous is the Lord on high. Your testimonies have become exceedingly trustworthy.*

Then Elihu mentions the things [namely, the wondrous divine works] that Job should consider principally, and there are four in order. First, [wondrous divine works] in things generated from moist vapor; second, in the motion of those things; third, in things generated from dry vapor; fourth, in the instrumental cause of these three. And that is: **[15]** ***Can it be that you know,*** that is, that you are able to know. Wis 9:[59] *Who will know your thoughts, unless you grant wisdom and send your Holy Spirit from on high?* ***when,*** in eternity, of course, ***God commands the rains,*** that is, the production of the rains, so that they might come about at a suitable time. Ps:[60] *He spoke, and they were made: He commanded, and they were created.* ***to show*** by means of effect ***the light of His clouds?*** that is, the benefit of the light of the stars received in

51. Jb 37.15.
52. Jb 37.19.
53. Ps 44.11.
54. Song 8.13.
55. Jer 6.16.
56. The following words are not from Mt 24, but rather are from Lk 21.28.
57. Bar 4.36.
58. Ps 92.4–5.
59. Wis 9.17.
60. Ps 32.9.

the clouds, for in this way the order of heaven is established on earth, in the place of generation. Jb 38:[61] *Can it be that you know the order of heaven, and will you establish its plan on earth?*

And concerning the motion [of these], Elihu adds: **[16]** ***Can it be that you know the paths of the clouds,*** namely, the ways by which the benefit received may pour forth onto things generated, ***great and perfect knowledge?*** "great" in what is known, "perfect" in the reason of knowing, as if he were saying, "You are not able to know, because this knowledge is referred to the highest causes of the wisdom of God." Ps:[62] *Your eyes have seen my imperfect being.* Indeed, from all these [effects] we know only that God exists; but we cannot fully investigate by what skill and with how much wisdom He has disposed these things.

And third, he adds concerning things generated from dry vapor: **[17]** ***Are your clothes not hot,*** feeling hot in accordance with external things, ***when the south wind blows upon the earth?*** as if he were saying, "yes," although supply: nevertheless, the southern part of the sky is regulated by neither hot nor cold [wind]; for the blowing of the south wind is hot and moist, opening and warming[63] the earth, and causing bodies to breathe, and bringing rain. Hab 3:[64] *God will come from the south.* And it is said concerning divine power in Song 4:[65] *Arise, O north wind, and come, O south wind.*

And fourth, concerning this, Elihu specifies the instrumental cause of all three, and there is ironic derision [in his words]: **[18]** ***You perhaps with Him,*** that is, with God, ***have fashioned,*** that is, have made, ***the heavens,*** by means of which, of course, as by means of an instrument He makes all these things, ***which,*** namely, the heavens, ***are most solid*** by way of incorruptibility ***as if cast***[66] for the purpose of continuing, of course, in perpetual motion, as if he were saying, "You have not made [the heavens]," ***of brass,***

61. Jb 38.33.

62. Ps 138.16.

63. Here I read *evaporantes* with MSS FM, rather than *evocantes* with Weiss's edition.

64. Hab 3.3.

65. Song 4.16.

66. Here I read *fusi sunt* with MS M, rather than *fundati sunt* with Weiss's edition.

that is, as if from brass. And he says "of brass" because brass is ductile and able to be stretched out, like heaven. Ps:[67] *He stretched out heaven like a skin.* Moreover, that the heavens are moved perpetually and cause these things is said in a Psalm:[68] *Forever, O Lord, your word endures in heaven.* He says "of brass" also because, by a miracle, things resounding tell of the glory of God, just as it is said in a Psalm:[69] *The heavens tell of the glory of God.*

From these things Elihu shows that God is incomprehensible, and he adds ironically: **[19]** ***Show us what we may say,*** about God, of course, about whom nothing can be spoken. In the *Book of Causes,* the Philosopher [says] in proposition 21:[70] "The First Cause is above every name by which it is named, because no diminishment pertains to it." Gn 32:[71] *Why do you ask my name, which is wonderful?* Expounding this, Dionysius declares that this—what it says, [namely,] "which is wonderful"—is a rebuke of the one asking the name of Him who is intrinsically (*secundum se*) unnamable.[72] ***We indeed are covered in darkness,*** because by reason of the reverberation of incomprehensible light, the eye of our intellect is enveloped in darkness, just as the eye of the body that gazes directly at the light is enveloped in the wheel of the sun. This is signified in Ex 20[73] and Ex 34,[74] where it is said that Moses advanced toward the Lord in the darkness—and this darkness was nothing other than the recoil of Moses's intellect from the incomprehensible light of the presence of God. And this is what Dionysius says concerning mystical the-

67. Ps 103.2.

68. Ps 118.89.

69. Ps 18.2.

70. *Caus.* 21.

71. Although both Gn 32.29 and Jgs 13.18 have the words *Cur quaeris nomen meum,* only Jgs 13.18 adds *quod est mirabile?* to this initial phrase. It is clear from his comments that Albert understands *quod est mirabile?* as part of the biblical verse he is quoting (namely, Jgs 13.18), but in providing Gn 32 as the reference he appears to misremember the source. Weiss obviously understands Albert to be setting forth the words of Gn 32.29 here, and so his edition has *Quod est mirabile* as a separate sentence following *Cur quaeris nomen meum?,* which question Weiss places in quotation marks.

72. Dionysius, *DN* 1.6 (PG 3:595).

73. Ex 20.21.

74. Ex 34.33.

ology in a letter that he writes to Gaius the monk:[75] "Darkness is concealed by the light, and to a greater extent by much light; thoughts conceal ignorance, and to a greater extent many thoughts." That is, the hiddenness of darkness signifies light beyond great light, that is, disproportionate light; and ignorance signifies thought beyond great thought, that is, disproportionate thought, concerning Him, of course, whose ability to be known is not proportionate to our intellect. Ps:[76] *He has made darkness His hiding place.*

Then Elihu directs his speech to those standing nearby: **[20]** ***Who will tell him,*** that is, who is able to tell him, namely, Job, ***the things I speak?*** and this should be read with disdain and derision, and as if he were saying: "Who is that foolish and presumptuous man who would have insinuated himself concerning this?" Wis 17:[77] *For your judgments are great, O Lord, and your words are inexpressible.* Hence, he adds: ***Even if a man will have spoken,*** that is, if he will have presumed or begun to say something, ***he will be devoured,*** that is, he will be swallowed up by the abyss of darkness and immensity. This was signified in Gn 15,[78] where, when the Lord appeared immediately after the sacrifice of Abraham, He appeared to him when the sun was setting, and at that time fear fell upon Abraham, and a very great and gloomy dread seized him. The Philosopher, in Book I, proposition 5, of *Of Causes,* says:[79] "The First Cause is above description, and tongues fail to describe it only because they are unable to describe its being (*esse*)."

And therefore, because of this, Elihu adds that no one will be able to describe God, neither a human nor an angel: **[21]** ***Yet,*** that is, but ***now,*** supply: in this life, ***they,*** namely, humans, ***do not see the light,*** by means of sight (*per speciem*), of course, and therefore God can in no way be described now. Ex 33:[80] *The human shall not see me and live.* Dn 10:[81] *At the sight of you, my joints were loosened, and no strength remained in me.*

75. Dionysius, *Ad Gaium* 3 (PG 3:1065–66).
76. Ps 17.12.
77. Wis 17.1.
78. Gn 15.12.
79. *Caus.* 5.
80. Ex 33.20.
81. Dn 10.16.

Nevertheless, through His effects and through vestiges something about God is known, and therefore Elihu says: ***suddenly the air will be condensed into clouds,*** that is, vapor in the form of air is bound together into the form of thick clouds, and, in this, God's wisdom and power are known. Ps:[82] *His magnificence and His power are in the clouds.* ***and the wind passing by,*** blowing among the clouds, of course, ***will drive them away,*** so that they may produce the benefit of irrigation in suitable places, of course. Ps:[83] *He brings forth winds out of His storehouses.*

From these things Elihu moves forward, as it were, and it is supplied in this way: **[22]** ***From the north gold will come.*** "Gold" has a more orderly arrangement and a better composition than other metals.[84] With regard to this, however, it is estimated that the external cold that besets the innermost parts of the earth may hold the mineral-heat in check, so that it is strong enough to separate the substance of metal; and, therefore, in the north, where there is cold weather, better gold is produced. And this is also the reason why gold is more often produced among the fine sand of frigid rivers: for cold water drives heat into the depths, so that it better separates the substance and makes it purer. In Gn 2[85] it is said that Pishon, which is a turbid river, encircles the whole region of Havilah, which is to the north, where gold is formed, and the gold of that land is the best. ***and,*** supply: just as gold from the north, so too ***from God fearful praise,*** supply: will come; for by fearing we name and praise God, because we name and praise Him from these things that are beneath Him[86] and not from His very self. Is 6:[87] *The things that were under Him filled the Temple.*

And Elihu adds the conclusion of this: **[23]** ***We are not able to find Him properly.*** Something that is found through its proper characteristics, and what it is definitively (*quid est definite*) is found through science, is "found properly"; but God is not

82. Ps 67.35.

83. Ps 134.7.

84. That is to say, the element gold is a pure substance, not a mixture or compound.

85. Gn 2.11–12.

86. That is, from God's created effects.

87. Is 6.1.

found in this way. Is 45:[88] *Truly you are a hidden God.* And he adds the reason for this: ***He is great in strength,*** in creating, of course, ***and in judgment,*** that is to say, great in discerning each one by its own appearance certainly, ***and in justice,*** namely, in determining the proper end for each one. Wis 11:[89] *You have disposed all things according to number and measure and weight.* And that God is called "great" [here] means [that He is] immeasurable with regard to these things, because He exceeds every heart. Is 53:[90] *Who will describe His generation?* Ambrose says:[91] "It is impossible for me to know the secret of generation. The voice remains silent—not only mine, but even that of the angels." And not only is the generation of the Son from the Father not understood; so too the generative power, by which every created thing is produced by Him. At the end of Isaiah: *Shall I, who grant generation to others, be barren? says the Lord.* On account of this, Dionysius says that every generation, whether in heaven or on earth, is from a patriarch.[92]

And this is what Elihu adds: ***and He cannot be described.*** Sir 43:[93] *We say many things, and we fail in our words; the consummation of our speech is He Himself.* 2 Cor 3:[94] *Not that we are sufficient to think anything of ourselves, as if coming from ourselves; but our sufficiency is from God.*

And this is what follows: **[24]** ***And therefore men will fear Him,*** that is, they will praise Him with fear; and Elihu calls those "men" whom earlier he designated "prudent men,"[95] namely, the vigorous in intellect and mature in virtue. Jer 17:[96] *Blessed is the man who trusts in the Lord, and the Lord will be his confidence. For he will be like a vigorous tree.* But Elihu says, "they will praise Him with fear,"[97] because, since all praise is given on account of

88. Is 45.15.
89. Wis 11.21.
90. Is 53.8.
91. See Ambrose, *De fide* 1.10.64.
92. See Dionysius, *CH* 1.1 (PG 2:122, 130). Cf. Is 66.9.
93. Sir 43.29.
94. 2 Cor 3.5.
95. See Jb 34.10 above.
96. Jer 17.7–8.
97. These are not Elihu's exact words according to the scriptural text (v.

[some] power, as Aristotle says,[98] He whose power is not known perfectly by reason of His own excellence is praised with fear. ***and all who seem to themselves,*** according to the truth, of course, ***to be wise will not dare to contemplate Him,*** namely, by means of perfect contemplation, which is by means of sight and what He is (*per speciem et quid est*). This is signified in Is 6,[99] where seraphim standing upon the throne covered their faces with two wings, signifying by this that they did not see God except among shadows and that they did not perfectly comprehend the one whom they saw.[100] And therefore, Jb 36:[101] *And all men see Him, everyone looks from far away.*

In this way, therefore, Elihu draws out all the positions of the other disputants all the way to particulars. For in rhetorical disputations that are taken from peripheral issues, confidence [in the conclusions drawn] from general principles does not arise unless they are drawn out all the way to the furthest particulars by means of circumstances and proofs. This, then, is the conclusion of the disputation. And all the disputants suppose that God's governance of human life is based on His consideration of lower and temporal merits, although in general Eliphaz says that good things are repaid to good people and bad things to the wicked. Bildad, however, adds that, if at any time it should happen otherwise, namely, that bad things happen to good people and good things happen to the wicked, God compensates both for this in the reward of final retribution. Moreover, Zophar, although he says the same, adds this: that, if at any time, and rarely, it should happen otherwise, this happens according to the profundity of the divine plan and will, the cause of which must not be sought. And Elihu joins together these general principles that these three disputants suppose, and he draws them out to particulars by means of circumstances and things peripheral. But Job alone denies this, namely, that God provides for

---

24a), but rather what Alb. takes Elihu's words here to mean, as is evident from his gloss immediately above.

98. See Aristotle, *EN* 2.6.12.

99. Is 6.1–2.

100. Cf. on Jb 28.21 above.

101. Jb 36.25.

and governs human life by considering the merits of humans, but [he maintains that] God's governance is dissimilar to every [mode of] human rule, and that God, in governing human life, considers nothing temporal. But God alone is able to determine this disputation, and therefore He is introduced as determining it.

CHAPTER 38

THEN THE LORD *responded to Job.*

Here the judge who determines the question concerning the governance of human life [namely, God] is introduced.[1] He determines the question, moreover, in favor of blessed Job and against the friends, namely, [concluding] that God provides for humans and rules human life with no consideration of human works, but that His [mode of] governance is dissimilar to every [mode of] human rule. And this is established on a certain proposition presupposed by all the saints, which is this: that nothing temporal can be the cause of the eternal; and this [presupposition] is taken from Rom 9, where the Apostle says:[2] *For before they had been born or had done anything good or evil, so that the purpose of God according to election might remain, not by works but by Him who calls, it was said to her* [*Rebecca*]*: The elder will serve the younger.* And a little beyond this:[3] *Therefore, it is not of him who wills nor of him who runs, but of God who shows mercy.* According to this, it is accepted that divine governance and providence are admitted and have no consideration for human merits, whether good or bad, according to which the four interlocutors who were introduced—namely, Eliphaz, Bildad, Zophar, and Elihu—did not speak correctly; rather, they supposed that divine rule operates according to human merits. But it was Job alone who said that there is something dissimilar in this divine rule to every [mode of] human governance, on account of which this determination is divided into two parts.

The first of these parts demonstrates that in none of the

1. Here I read *inducitur* with MSS TFM rather than the *inducit* of Weiss's edition.

2. Rom 9.11–13.

3. Rom 9.16.

works of providence does God have consideration for anything temporal; in the second part, with this having been proven, God determines that Job spoke correctly, but the others did not, below in chapter 42 in that place:[4] *Then Job responded to the Lord and said.*

The first part is divided further into two. Indeed, in the first subdivision God shows that He looks to nothing temporal in the governing of the creation, disposition, adornment, and propagation of nature; in the second subdivision, that He looks to nothing temporal in governing the works of Satan, below in chapter 40 in that place:[5] *Then the Lord responded to Job out of the whirlwind.*

The first of these subdivisions is divided further into two. For in the first, God proves what was said; in the second, He inclines to agree with blessed Job, before the end of chapter 39 in that place:[6] *And the Lord went on and said to Job.*

The first of these subdivisions is divided further into two. For in the first, God proves what was said in the case of the works of creation, disposition, and adornment; in the second, He demonstrates the same in the case of the works of propagation, in that place:[7] *Who has put wisdom in the heart of man?*

The first of these subdivisions is divided further still into three. For in the first, God introduces the work of disposing the earth, which is the place of generation; in the second, He introduces the work of disposing the water, in that place:[8] *Who shut up the sea with doors;* in the third, He introduces the work of disposing things generated on earth and things generated in the water and of things causing this [generation] in heaven, in that place:[9] *Can it be that since your birth you have commanded the break of day?*

In the first of these subdivisions, there are two things: the determination with regard to man, and the determination with

4. Jb 42.1.
5. Jb 40.1.
6. Jb 39.31.
7. Jb 38.36.
8. Jb 38.8.
9. Jb 38.12.

regard to prayer, in that place:[10] *Where were you.* For it is the obligation of the judge first to rebuke the one who argues badly, and afterwards to prove and point out the truth. But He who rebukes the one who argues employs a transition to a rhetorical mode at the beginning. Indeed, God crosses over from hearing the arguments to the determination [of the question].

And that is: ***Then the Lord responded to Job,*** that is, to those things that had been argued and to those [interlocutors] arguing on behalf of Job, ***speaking out of the whirlwind,*** that is, out of the conflict of this disputation, lest they remain in error, of course. Concerning this whirlwind, it is said in Is 19:[11] *The Lord has mingled a spirit of confusion among them, and they have caused Egypt to wander in all its works.* Ps:[12] *Contempt was poured out upon their princes, and He made them wander through an impassable place and not on a road.*

In order that He may banish that error, God accuses the one arguing unjustly, and He responds for Job. Is 38:[13] *Lord, I suffer violence; respond for me!* [2] ***Who is this,*** namely, Elihu; this should be read with disdain, as is the case in that place in Jer 49:[14] *Who is that shepherd and rustic?* And God accuses Elihu before all the others because he followed the others in sequence and drew out their positions. ***who obscures sentences.*** A "sentence" is a confirmed and determined and certain truth drawn out of many arguments. And that such sentences can be brought forward concerning the governing of providence is clear from the things said above. Moreover, "to obscure" these sentences is to show them on the basis of peripheral issues, by which they are obscured, for a rhetorical question is obscured by peripheral issues, as has been said many times.[15] ***by means of unskilled words?*** Peripheral "unskilled words" are common words that relate to the subject as more general than the subject, on the basis of which one cannot argue except according to a secondary image

10. Jb 38.4.
11. Is 19.14.
12. Ps 106.40.
13. Is 38.14.
14. Jer 49.19.
15. See, e.g., on Jb 32.1, on Jb 33.12, and on Jb 36.24 above.

in this way: "A thief is one who wanders around at night; and this man is one who wanders around at night; therefore, this man is a thief." This manner of speaking, although it contains an image, nevertheless—because it cannot be reduced to any rule—is a useless conjoining [of words]. And this kind of argumentation is characteristic of all four [of Job's interlocutors] as follows: "God does not punish anyone except the wicked; He has punished you; therefore, you are wicked." On account of this, because this is a useless conjoining [of words], the words are called unskilled. Is 32:[16] *The fool will speak foolish things, and his heart will work iniquity.*

Moreover, because God is about to speak the truth by means of determination [of the disputed question] and concerning morals, He incites Job to pay close attention, and that is: **[3]** ***Gird up your loins like a man.*** A "man" is one who is vigorous on the inside and virile, and one who has strength and virtue. Jer 17:[17] *Blessed is the man who trusts in the Lord, and the Lord will be his confidence, and* [*he will be like*] *a vigorous tree.* And the "loins" are the seat of pleasures and concupiscence, which—unless they are girded up and restricted—send forth the fumes[18] of concupiscence, which prevent the intellect from choosing the good as concerns morals because it does not see the optimal as it ought to see it, so that it may choose what is true and good and detest what is not good, of course. Prv 31:[19] *She has girded up her loins with strength.* Eph 6:[20] *Stand, therefore, with your loins girded up in truth.* Lk 12:[21] *Let your loins be girded.* ***I will interrogate you,*** concerning the consensus of truth, of course, ***and you answer me.*** Jb 13:[22] *Call me, and I will answer you; or at least I will speak, and you answer me.*

[4] ***Where were you.***

Here God touches on the arrangement of the earth, and He speaks of three things, namely: its position according to place, its

16. Is 32.6.
17. Jer 17.7–8.
18. Here I read *fumos* with MSS TEFM, rather than *fluvios* with Weiss's edition.
19. Prv 31.17.
20. Eph 6.14.
21. Lk 12.35.
22. Jb 13.22.

proportion to the other elements, and the measure of its diameter and its foundation. And after these three things, He brings in the praise of wisdom.

And that is: ***Where were you,*** so that I might have asked for you or your actions, of course, ***when I laid the foundations of the earth?*** there is an intransitive construction here, that is: "the earth before the foundation of all the elements." For those elements that are not restricted by their own boundaries, such as water and air, are established and restricted according to the earth itself. Nor is this contrary to what is said in a Psalm:[23] *Who established the earth above the waters.* For it is established above the waters, which are the seed of generation, according to which it is the place of generation; but in itself, according to which it is the center with boundaries marked out by its own ends, it establishes all the other elements and is established with respect to no other. Prv 8:[24] *When I hung the foundations of the earth.*

And concerning the proportion of its magnitude, God adds: ***Show me,*** that is, speak within and speak by means of inward causes, ***if you have understanding,*** that is, of my works. [5] ***Who determined,*** that is, disposed according to proportion, ***its measurements,*** its proportion, of course, to the other elements, according to which from one handful of water there are made ten [handfuls] of air, and from one handful of earth [there are made] ten of water, for in such a way the place of water is ten times greater than the place of earth, ***if you know.***[25] Wis 11:[26] *You have disposed all things according to measure and number and weight.*

And God adds concerning the measure of its diameter, and that is: ***or who stretched the line upon it?*** [the line] of the three diameters, [namely] of the length, of the breadth, and of the depth, to which every corporeal reality attains; for according to this measure, the earth is the smallest of simple bodies besides Mercury and the moon. Indeed, in this way all things were made

23. Ps 135.6.

24. Prv 8.29.

25. Here I read with MSS FM, which add ***si nosti*** to the Vulgate text on which Albert is commenting.

26. Wis 11.21.

in proportion. Prv 8:[27] *With a certain law and compass He enclosed the depths.* For all bodies have a certain magnitude. In the second book of *On the Soul* Aristotle says:[28] By nature all existing things have an end and a ratio of magnitude and increase.

Then God adds concerning its foundation with respect to place: **[6]** ***Upon what are its bases,*** that is, its most stable parts with respect to place, ***grounded?*** so that they might not be moved, of course. Ps:[29] *He has founded the earth upon its bases; it will not be moved forever and ever.*

And He expresses this by means of a metaphor: ***or who set down,*** from the height of power, of course, ***its cornerstone?*** A "cornerstone," both in itself and in relation to the other walls, establishes and strengthens[30] and supports the building, and it is understood that in itself, of course, it is immovable and secures the other parts [of the building] immovably, so that they cannot fall. Metaphorically this is called the cornerstone, that is, what is said in Is 40:[31] *Who has weighed out the huge mass of the earth with three fingers?* namely, by the measure of proportion, by the measure of the diameter, and by its foundation upon the center.

After this God adds the praise of wisdom, because in all these things God required no human works, and that is: [7] ***when the morning stars,*** which were made at the dawn of the universe, at the first appearance of light, of course, before the human, ***together praised me,*** with none faltering, of course. Ps:[32] *Praise Him, O sun and moon; praise Him, all you stars and light.* ***and all the sons of God,*** that is, all the angels, ***sang joyfully***. For at that time God did these things without looking to anything pertaining to humans because no human existed nor did any human works. And so it was spoken concerning the disposition of the earth and of heaven.

And God transitions to the disposition of the water, and that is what is said in Bar 3:[33] *The stars have given light during their*

27. Prv 8.27.

28. Aristotle, *De an.* 2.4.8.

29. Ps 103.5.

30. Here I read with MSS FM, which add *et firmat,* rather than with Weiss's edition.

31. Is 40.12.

32. Ps 148.3.

33. Bar 3.34–35.

watches, and they have rejoiced. They were summoned and they said, "Here we are." And with delight they have shown forth for Him who made them. [8] ***Who shut up the sea with doors.*** He calls the shores of the ocean "doors"; these are called "doors," just as what blocks up an opening for entry is called a door, on account of the fact that the sea is shut up within the shores. ***when it burst forth,*** what remained behind, of course, from the first commingling of vapors, ***as if issuing from the womb,*** that is, from the place in which a fetus is first conceived in a shapeless way and grows according to shape and a distinct place. Gn 1:[34] *Let the waters be gathered together into one place, and let the dry land appear.* Ps:[35] *He contained the waters as if in a vessel.*

And He mentions the mode: [9] ***when I made a cloud its garment.*** In fact, when at first the water was brought together in its place, foggy air remained in the circle of the water as if a garment; because the air close to the water was dark and higher [and] more tranquil, therefore God adds: ***and wrapped it,*** namely, the sea, ***in darkness as if in the swaddling cloths of an infant?*** that is, of the first formation. Ps:[36] *Dark water in the clouds of the air.*

And God adds how He bound fast the ebb and flow of the sea, and that is: [10] ***I surrounded it with my boundaries,*** until it flows out and recedes, of course, and that is: ***and I set bars,*** namely, a restraining power, ***and doors,*** through which the inland streams and rivers flow, of course. [11] ***And I said,*** by my command, to be sure: ***Up to this point you shall come,*** namely, by flowing forth and spreading yourself out widely through the inland streams and rivers, ***and you shall advance no further,*** to occupy the land, of course, ***and,*** that is, ***here,*** that is, at this boundary, ***you shall break your swelling waves,*** so that you may return to your shores, of course. He says "swelling waves" because waves begin to swell from vapor that has been lifted up from the bottom, and they are flung upon the shores, from which they fall back by evaporating and return within their shores. Ps:[37] *You have established a boundary, which they will not pass over; and neither will they return to*

34. Gn 1.9.
35. Ps 77.13.
36. Ps 17.12.
37. Ps 103.9.

cover the earth. Mt 8:[38] *He commanded the winds and the sea, and there came a great calm.*

[12] ***Can it be that since your birth.***

God mentions things generated from the earth and the sea, and He previews the cycle of generation. And God speaks of these three things here.

And that is: ***Can it be that since your birth,*** indeed you were able to do nothing before your birth by which you help me, ***you have commanded the break of day,*** so that the sun would arise in its place, of course, ***and,*** that is, ***have shown the dawn its place?*** so that, to be sure, by its own path around the sloping sphere [of the earth] it would produce constant generation, as if God were saying: "You have not helped me in this; on the contrary, I alone have done it." Eccl 1:[39] *The sun rises and goes down, and returns to its place; and rising again, it goes back around through the south and turns again to the north.*

And God adds concerning the governing of the human who has been placed on earth: [13] ***Can it be that you have held,*** by securing, of course, ***the extremities of the earth,*** that is, humans from one end of the earth all the way to the other. Ps:[40] *The earth is the Lord's and the fullness thereof.* ***shaking it violently*** through their attacks on one another; for the wicked always shake one another violently. Is 24:[41] *By breaking, the earth will be broken into pieces; by a commotion, the earth will be moved; by shaking, the earth will be jostled as a drunk man.* ***have you flung the wicked from it?*** supply: thus shaking the earth violently, of course, just as I did in the flood according to Gn 7, and in submerging the Egyptians [in the waters of the Red Sea] according to Ex 14, and with regard to the Pentapolis,[42] and in the case of Sennacherib and his army according to Is 36.[43]

Moreover, God adds how He did these things: [14] ***The seal will be restored,*** by such a shaking out, of course, ***as clay,*** that is,

38. Mt 8.26.
39. Eccl 1.5–6.
40. Ps 23.1.
41. Is 24.19–20.
42. See Gn 19.24–25 and Wis 10.6–7; and above on Jb 28.5.
43. See Is 36.1.

the human will be restored to the earth as the seal and image of God, according to which he was made, "as clay," that is, as a vessel of clay. Ps:[44] *His breath will pass away, and he will return into his earth.* 1 Mc 2:[45] *He is extolled today, but tomorrow will not be found, because he has returned into his earth.* ***and it will stand like a garment,*** which, as long as it is being worn, holds the shape of the person wearing it, of course, but, when it is taken off, falls down onto its very self; so too the body, when it is taken off by the soul, falls down, dies, and withers away, as Aristotle says at the end of the first book of *On the Soul.*[46]

And so supply: **[15]** ***Their light,*** namely, which they see here in the present life, ***will be taken away from the wicked.*** Lam 3:[47] *He has driven me, and He has led me into darkness, and not into light.* ***and [their] exalted arm,*** certainly because it has oppressed others, ***will be broken,*** through eternal damnation, of course. Is 14:[48] *The Lord has broken the staff of the wicked, the rod of the rulers that struck the people in anger.*

[16] ***Can it be that you have entered?***

He mentions the arrangement of the places of the earth and of the sea, which no one except God, looking to nothing temporal, has disposed. And that is: ***Can it be that you have entered the depths of the sea?*** of the ocean, of course, such that you disposed all things that exist in the depths of the sea, as if He were saying: "Not you, but I." Sir 43:[49] *Let those who sail on the sea describe the dangers thereof; and when we hear with our ears, we will marvel. There are splendid and wonderful works in that place: various kinds of animals, and all kinds of living things and beastly creatures. By Him [namely, God] the end of their journey has been established, and by His word all things have been ordered.* ***and have you gone for a walk in the lowest parts of the abyss?*** as if He were saying, "Not you, but I alone, looking to nothing temporal." And He calls the lower hemisphere, in which the spheres of the earth and the water

44. Ps 145.4.
45. 1 Mc 2.63.
46. Aristotle, *De an.* 1.5.24.
47. Lam 3.2.
48. Is 14.5–6.
49. Sir 43.26–28.

have been suspended, the "abyss." Sir 24:[50] *I have entered the depths of the abyss, and I have walked among the waves of the sea.*

And concerning the effects of these things, God adds: **[17] *Can it be that the gates of death have been opened to you,*** so that you may see all the most secret realities of death, and, explaining this, He adds: ***and,*** that is, ***you have seen the dark doors?*** The "dark doors" are the most secret realities of the earth and of the sea, which, on account of the privation of light, are called the "gates of death," because light is the beginning of life, and where there is a privation of light, there is a privation of life; and these realities are accessible to God alone. Ps:[51] *He has established me in darkness, just as* [*He has established*] *the dead of old.* Because of this, the saints actually propose that this is Hell, to which Christ descended. Sir 24:[52] *I will penetrate the lower parts of the earth; I will examine all who sleep.*

[18] *Can it be that you have considered the breadth* (latitudinem) *of the earth?* that is, of each region, whose breadth (*latitudo*) is a measure [of north-south distance] from the equator to the highest point where people live in that region; for according to that [latitudinal measure] the length of days and nights vary and alterations in hot and cold weather occur. Sir 1:[53] *Who has measured the height of heaven, and the breadth* (latitudinem) *of the earth, and the depth of the abyss?*

Show me, if you know all things, supply: as God, **[19] *where is the way where light dwells?*** For its dwelling is the relation of the sun to the earth. Gn 1:[54] *God said: Let there be light! And there was light.* ***and where is the place of darkness,*** which is the relation of the darkness of the earth to heaven, whose cone of shade extends all the way to Mercury exclusively. Gn 1:[55] *He divided the light from the darkness. And He called the light day and the darkness night.* **[20] *that you may lead each one,*** namely, both light and darkness, ***to its own boundaries.*** The boundaries of light are what [parts] of the earth

50. Sir 24.8.
51. Ps 142.3.
52. Sir 24.45.
53. Sir 1.2.
54. Gn 1.3.
55. Gn 1.4–5.

the sun illuminates according to the entire range of its own motion. The boundaries of darkness, however, are what [parts] of the hemisphere the earth obscures with its own shadow. Ps:[56] *You put darkness in place, and the night was made.* ***and,*** supply: so ***understand the paths of its house,*** namely, of light and of darkness. And the Lord says this because each one [that is, light and darkness] is diffused in a pyramidal pattern, as in the shape of tents, but the base of the shadow of the earth is the earth's diameter, and the cone rises upward. But the cone of light is the center of the sun, and the base descends downward to less than the diameter of the earth. Indeed, it was proven by Euclid that rays going out from the same point toward a spherical body or toward a circle enclose less than half of it, because, whenever it appears spherical, the ray seems [to cut] less [of the sphere] than at the midpoint.[57] And He says "paths" because, as the sun is moved, in this way its pyramidal houses, both of light and of darkness,[58] change. Hab 3:[59] *The sun and the moon stood still in their dwelling place; in the light of your arrows they will go.*

He adds, moreover, that human work added nothing to God in the arrangement of these things: **[21]** ***Did you know then,*** when I arranged these things in such a way, of course, ***when you were going to be born,*** which you were not able to know since you did not exist, ***and did you know the number of your days?*** which, that is, you were destined to live, as if He were saying: "No, but I alone know." Ps:[60] *I spoke with my tongue: Enable me to know my end, Lord, and what the number of my days is.* For in [the disposition of] such things I [namely, God] was able to look to no human works.

[22] ***Can it be that you have entered?***

Here He touches on things generated from moisture high up in three ways, namely, as far as the place of generation and the substance, and as far as the Prime Fashioner (*primum formantem*),

56. Ps 103.20.

57. See Euclid, *Elements* 3.8. See *The First Latin Translation of Euclid's* Elements *Commonly Ascribed to Adelard of Bath, Books I–VIII and Books X.36–XV.2*, ed. H. L. L. Busard (Toronto: PIMS, 1983), 94–96, esp. the diagram on 96.

58. Here I read *tenebrae* with MSS FM rather than *umbrae* with Weiss's edition.

59. Hab 3.11.

60. Ps 38.5.

in that place:[61] *Who is the father of rain,* and as far as the one moving instrumentally, in that place:[62] *Can you join together?*

And that is: ***Can it be that you have entered,*** through understanding, of course, so that you may know all things definitively, ***the storehouses of the snow.*** The "storehouses of the snow" are the unfailing lifting up of warm and moist vapor, and the unfailing cold weather of the interstitial middle, which, when the vapor has been raised up to it, freezes before it condenses. ***or have you looked upon the treasures of hail?*** The "treasures of hail" are the unfailing lifting up of the warmest moist vapor, which, when it has been raised up to the middle of the interstices, cold weather enters by stealth from every direction and seizes and condenses and freezes. Sir 43:[63] *The treasures have been opened, and the clouds have come out like birds. In His greatness He stations the clouds, and the hailstones are broken.* And a little beyond this:[64] *He scatters the snow, and its falling is like locusts descending. The eye will admire the beauty of its whiteness.*

Then He touches on the use of those things:[65] **[23]** ***Which I have prepared for the time of the enemy,*** for by means of this He assails the inhabitants of the earth on account of their sins. Wis 5:[66] *Large hail will be cast down from His rocky anger.* There is an example in the case of Pharaoh according to Ex 9.[67] ***for the day of battle,*** that is, of taking sinners by storm, ***and war?*** which I set in motion against sinners, of course. Wis 5:[68] *The entire earth will fight with Him against those who are senseless.* Ps:[69] *Fire, hail, snow, ice, and windstorms will be the portion of their cup.*

And, supply: show me **[24]** ***Through what way is light scattered and is heat distributed over the earth?*** God connects these two be-

61. Jb 38.28.
62. Jb 38.31.
63. Sir 43.15–16.
64. Sir 43.19–20.
65. That is, the snow and hail that are generated high up on account of moisture.
66. Wis 5.23.
67. Ex 9.23.
68. Wis 5.21.
69. Albert here conflates Ps 148.8 and Ps 10.7, as he does in commenting on Jb 6.16 and Jb 20.29 (vol. 1) and on Jb 27.13.

cause heat follows light, and the measure of heat follows the mode of light; for where light is scattered toward a right angle, there its rays are reflected on themselves, and where [it is scattered] toward an acute angle there is less heat, and where [it is scattered] toward an obtuse or expanded angle there is the least heat. And so the measure of heat always corresponds to the size of the angle against which light is reflected. Sir 43:[70] *At noon He burns the earth, and who can withstand His burning heat? One attending to a furnace regards the works of heat; the sun burns the mountains three times as much, blowing out fiery rays, and, shining brightly, it blinds the eyes.*

And He adds concerning things generated from moist vapor in the form of the moist, and that is: **[25]** ***Who,*** supply: unless I did, having been helped by no one, ***gave a course to the most violent rainstorm,*** that which has been driven out vigorously and impelled by the wind is most violent in its fall from its high position. And because, when it is enclosed in an aqueous dry cloud, it thunders, He adds: ***and a way for the reverberating thunder,*** supply: unless I alone did, since I disposed all things. Dn 3:[71] *All you waters that are above the heavens, bless the Lord,* and again:[72] *All rain storms and dew, bless the Lord; all spirits of God, bless the Lord,* for these things, by their substance, must bless the Lord on account of the fact that He made and arranged them.

And He touches on their use: **[26]** ***that it should rain on the earth,*** soaking it and making it fruitful, of course. Is 55:[73] *It soaks the earth and waters it.* And lest it be believed that God looks to the work of humans, He adds: ***away from the human in the desert,*** where there is no dwelling place for the human, of course. And this is what He adds by elaborating: ***where no mortal dwells.*** Dt 32:[74] *He found him in a deserted land, in a place of horror and of vast wilderness.* **[27]** ***that it should satisfy,*** certainly by means of generative moisture, ***the impassable,*** which is not traveled by humans, ***and desolate land,*** away from human civilization, ***and should bring***

70. Sir 43.3–4.
71. Dn 3.60.
72. Dn 3.64–65.
73. Is 55.10.
74. Dt 32.10.

forth, by the good work of the rain, ***green grass?*** not ordained for human use. Is 35:[75] *The deserted and impassable land shall be glad, and the wilderness shall rejoice, and it shall flourish like the lily. It shall sprout forth and blossom, and it shall rejoice with great joy and be glad.*

[28] ***Who is the father of rain?***

Here God refers this to the Prime Fashioner (*primum formans*), that is, to His very self; for the prime fashioner in every act of generation is the father. Eph 3:[76] *I genuflect before God the Father, from whom every paternity in heaven and on earth is named.*

And the sense is: ***Who is the father,*** that is, the fashioner, ***of rain?*** unless I am, as if He were saying: "No one." Is 44:[77] *There is no maker God* (formator Deus) *before me.* ***or who has begotten the drops of dew?*** by forming drops in dew, of course. Is 26:[78] *Your dew is the dew of the light.*

And He mentions frozen things: **[29]** ***From whose womb has the ice come forth?*** The place of formation in the middle interstice of the atmosphere is called the "womb," but no one except God has given the "womb" formative power such that ice might be formed within the thin, warm, and moist element.[79] Dn 3:[80] *You frost and cold, bless the Lord; you ice and snow, bless the Lord.* For it pertains to these things, by their substance, to bless the Lord on account of the fact that He made and arranged them. ***and from heaven,*** which is an ethereal body and so is on fire, as Aristotle says in *Meteorology*,[81] ***who has given birth to the frost?*** as if contrary from contrary. For the light of Saturn is the cause of frost. Sir 43:[82] *He will pour frost like salt on the earth; and when it blows away, it will become like the shoots of thistles.*

And He elaborates on this further: **[30]** ***The waters are hardened like stone.*** In the second book of the *Posterior Analytics*, Aristotle says:[83] When warmth has been altogether removed from

75. Is 35.1–2.
76. Eph 3:14–15.
77. Is 44.8.
78. Is 26.19.
79. Namely, air.
80. Dn 3.69–70.
81. See Aristotle, *Mete.* 1.3.4; and *Mund.* 2. See also Alb., *Met.* 1.1.2.
82. Sir 43.21.
83. See Aristotle, *APost.* 2.11.1.

water, an ice crystal is produced. Sir 43:[84] *Cold wind blows from the north, and the water has frozen into crystal.* ***and the face of the deep,*** that is, the surface of the water, under which is the deep, ***is frozen,*** namely, by means of frost. God did this, according to Ex 14,[85] when He held back the partitions of water so that they would be for the children of Israel like a wall both on their right and on their left.

[31] ***Can you join together.***

Here God reduces the things that have been said to the prime instrumental mover (*primum movens instrumentaliter*), which nevertheless does not have motive power except from God. And that is: ***the shining stars of Pleiades.*** "Pleiades," as if they are called "rain-bringing" (*pluviales*) because these stars have the power of moving and elevating what is moist and those things that are generated from moist vapor, about which we have already spoken.[86] And this is the constellation at the boundary of Aries. ***or can you stop the circular course of Arcturus?*** It is called a "circular course" (*gyrus*) because those stars always circle (*gyrant*) around the pole and never fall. And there are seven stars in Arcturus or in Ursa Major and Minor, but more light in Major and less light in Minor: four stars in the body and three in the tail. And He mentions these stars by name because they are the beginning of the cold weather, which causes the things that arise from moist vapor to freeze. Of these it was said in Jb 9:[87] *He who makes Arcturus, and Orion, and Hyades, and the inner parts of the south.*

And God mentions in particular the stars of which He has been speaking, the stars that reveal light and darkness. And that is: [32] ***Can it be that you will bring forth the day star,*** which is always either Venus or Mercury, ***in its own time?*** Each has "its own time" for revealing light in the morning, when, according to the order of signs, it is twelve grades or more behind the sun, for then it rises before the sun in the morning. ***and make the evening star,*** that is, the star of the evening, which is always either Venus or Mercury, because those two stars do not have a perfect distance

84. Sir 43.22.
85. Ex 14.22.
86. See on Jb 37.11, pp. 209–10 above.
87. Jb 9.9.

from the sun, ***to rise upon the children of the earth,*** that is, born of the earth; as if He were saying, "Not you, but I." And God does this when Mercury or Venus, according to the order of the signs, is in front of the sun, for then, when the sun is going down, it rises from the rays under the sun and reveals that the sun has set; but no one has caused this order except God alone. Sir 24:[88] *I caused in the heavens an unfailing light to arise.*

And to what God spoke of particularly He adds generally, both according to itself (*in se*) and according to a twofold effect. And that is: **[33]** ***Can it be that you know the order of heaven?*** according to every power of the constellations, of course. Ps:[89] *He counts the multitude of the stars, and He gives names to all of them.* ***and will you establish its plan*** **(rationem)** ***on earth?*** namely, through its effect, as I can. Jgs 5:[90] *The stars, remaining in their order and courses, fought against Sisera.* And in that very place:[91] *From heaven war was made against them.*

And God sets forth the general effect [of heaven] among moist things: **[34]** ***Will you lift your voice,*** namely, of command, so that it may ascend, ***up to the clouds,*** that is, to moist vapor, ***and,*** supply: immediately ***will a flood of waters,*** supply: of rains, ***cover you?*** that is, you do not do this, but I alone do. 1 Kgs 18,[92] at the prayers of Elijah: *Behold, the heavens grew dark, and there were storms and wind, and there fell a great rain.* **[35]** ***Can it be that you will send forth flashes of lightning.*** Flashes of lightning are produced from dry vapor, for lightning flashes are coruscations that accompany thunder. ***and they will go,*** obediently and respectfully, ***and returning,*** after the effect has been completed, ***they will say to you: Here we are?*** for the sake of thanksgiving and repeated obedience. And this signifies those who obey as swiftly as lightning and return according to the mandates of obedience. Ezek 1:[93] *The animals were going and returning like flashes of lightning.*

[36] ***Who has put.***

88. Sir 24.6.
89. Ps 146.4.
90. Jgs 5.20.
91. Ibid.
92. 1 Kgs 18.45.
93. Ezek 1.14.

Here God touches on the arrangement of animals according to a particular nature, and it has two parts. In the first part, He defines (*determinat*) the animals according to habit of the soul; in the second,[94] the same according to the mode of generation and of nature, in that place:[95] *Can it be that you know the time of birth?*

The first part is divided into two, namely: the determination of the animals according to the habit of apprehension; and secondly, according to the habit of the motive part, in that place:[96] *Can it be that you will capture [the prey] for the lioness?*

The first of these is further subdivided into two, namely: the habit of the intellect and the habit according to the sensible; and according to the cause of sensible apprehension, in that place:[97] *Who will explain?*

And that is: ***Who has put,*** through natural apprehension, of course, ***wisdom,*** that is, the power of apprehending wisdom, ***in the heart of man?*** that is, in the inmost part of man. Sir 17:[98] *He gave them a heart for thinking things through, and He filled them with the knowledge of understanding. He created in them the knowledge of the spirit, He filled their hearts with understanding, and He showed them both good and evil.* According to Gn 1[99] and Gn 2,[100] *Let us make man according to our image and likeness.* Augustine:[101] "According to the image" is in the power of knowing, and "according to the likeness" is in the power of loving.

And God adds concerning the power of estimation and of apprehending the sensible. And that is: ***or who has given understanding to the cock?*** He calls the ability that the cock has to estimate the distinct hours "understanding." For the cock crows according to changes in the sun's angle in the sky in the morning, at midday, in the evening, and at midnight, and even according to changes in daylight produced by patterns of weather. Other ani-

94. Here I read *in secunda* with MSS FM, rather than the *secundo* of Weiss's edition.

95. Jb 39.1.

96. Jb 38.39.

97. Jb 38.37.

98. Sir 17.5–6.

99. Gn 1.26.

100. See Gn 2.7.

101. See Augustine, *c. Faustum* 24.2; and *De Gen. litt. imp.* 16.57.

mals too, because they are not worried about the direction (*regimen*) of their lives, easily detect impressions made in their bodies or by the movement of the sky or from weather patterns, and according to these they are moved to cry out or to remain silent. Hence Tb 8:[102] *About the time of cockcrow, Raguel sent* [*his servants*] *to see how things were concerning Tobias and Sarah, his daughter.* And Mt 26:[103] *Before the cock crows, you will deny me three times.*

Hence, concerning the cause of all these things, God adds: **[37]** ***Who will explain the order*** **(rationem)** ***of the heavens,*** He who perfects these things by His own motion, of course. Ps:[104] *Praise Him, you heavens of heavens.* ***and who can cause the concord of heaven,*** that is, the harmony of heaven and of the celestial motions that perfect all these things, ***to sleep?*** that is, to rest, supply: unless I alone can, when the number of the elements was perfected, on account of the generation of which the concord of heaven was produced. Jb 14:[105] *Until heaven is worn away, he will not rise up, nor will he awake from his sleep.*

And returning to the disposition of the earth, which is the place of generation, God adds: **[38]** ***When was the dust poured on the earth,*** here He speaks of the disposition of the first mixture, in which, by way of dust, the earth was brought forth like a vapor among what is moist. And this is what follows: ***and the clods bound together?*** when the dust settles at the bottom, of course. Gn 1:[106] *Let the waters be gathered together into one place, and let the dry land appear.* Indeed, God alone did this, looking to nothing among temporal things. And it must be noted that clods are bound together in two ways, namely: according to place, and in this way earth is distinguished from the other elements; and according to composition, and in this way [earth's] composition more nearly approaches equality with heaven, [namely] it receives a soul for apprehending and desiring what is better, as Avicenna says in *The Sixth Book on Natural Things.*[107] And for that reason God

102. Tb 8.11.
103. Mt 26.34.
104. Ps 148.4.
105. Jb 14.12.
106. Gn 1.9.
107. I have been unable to find this reference in Avicenna's *Sextus de naturalibus;* cf. Alb., *Anim.* 2.3.9.

introduces this here, after both of those things, for He spoke previously both about the distinctions among the elements and about the distinctions among the compositions of animals.

And God adds concerning the disposition of the motive part in animals, according to the irascible and according to the concupiscible. And that is: **[39]** ***Can it be that you will capture the prey for the lioness.*** The irascible is the cause of the concupiscible in the lioness; and God names the lioness and not the lion because, on account of the care and nurture of the young, she is more eager for prey. ***and satisfy,*** namely, by giving all that is required by their desire, ***the soul*** **(animam),** that is, the animal nature that requires food, ***of her cubs,*** the lioness's, of course.

And expanding on this, He adds: **[40]** ***when they rest in their dens,*** that is, when they need food both for nourishment and for growth, and therefore they need and desire it more then. And because their desire moves them to hunt, God adds: ***and lie in wait in their holes?*** on account of which, in Jb 4, Eliphaz compared Job to a lion, his wife to a lioness, and his children to lion cubs, saying:[108] *The roaring of the lion, and the voice of the lioness, and the teeth of the lion cubs are broken.* Ps:[109] *He lies in wait in secret like a lion in its den.* Prv 28:[110] *As a roaring lion and a ravenous bear, so is a wicked prince*[111] *over his poor people.*

And God adds concerning the disposition of the appetible and providence concerning the appetible: **[41]** ***Who prepares food for the raven,*** supply: unless I do, who provide for all things, of course. Ps:[112] *All creatures look to you to give them food at the proper time.* And He expands on this: ***when her chicks cry out to God,*** as to the Prime Provider (*primum provisorem*), ***wandering about,*** that is, distracted from their hunger by wandering here and there, ***because they have no food?*** Ps:[113] *Who gives the beasts their food, and to the young ravens that cry out to Him.* And God names the raven more than other animals because it is more ravenous and more

108. Jb 4.10. See *On Job,* vol. 1, 121.

109. Ps 10.9.

110. Prv 28.15.

111. I have corrected Weiss's edition here against the Vulgate: whereas Weiss has *princeps ipsius,* the Vulgate reads *princeps impius.*

112. Ps 103.27.

113. Ps 146.9.

desirous of food. Proof of this is that, according to Gn 8, the raven sent out from the ark came to rest on a carcass.[114]

114. Gn 8.6–7. Although the text of Genesis does not indicate why the raven did not return to the ark, Albert, like other readers, provides an explanation based on the bird's nature as a scavenger; such explanations offer a rationale for why Noah sends out a dove after the raven (v. 8). See also Augustine, *c. Faustum* 12.20, who indicates that the raven did not return because it was "either prevented by the water or attracted by some floating carcass." I am grateful to Brian Dunkle, SJ, for bringing this text of Augustine to my attention.

CHAPTER 39

C**AN IT BE *that you know the time of birth.***

Here God touches on the principles (*leges*) introduced for animals regarding generation, customary practice, and habitation, and it is divided into two parts.

Indeed, in the first part, He mentions [these principles] among animals; and in the second, among birds, in that place:[1] *Can it be that by your wisdom the hawk grows feathers?*

The first of these is divided again into two: In the first subdivision, God touches on [these principles] among wild animals; in the second, among more noble domesticated animals, in that place:[2] *Can it be that you will give to the horse?*

The first of these subdivisions is divided again into two sections: in the first, God speaks of the perfect wild animals, which are simply animals and can walk; in the second, He speaks of the ostrich, which is constituted by the ability to walk and the ability to fly, in that place:[3] *The wing of the ostrich.* The first of these sections is divided again into two: in the first, God speaks of the principles of generation; in the second, of the principles of customary practice and of freedom, in that place:[4] *Who has let the wild ass go free?*

In the first of these subsections, God specifies the principles of conception, pregnancy, birthing, and caring for offspring. And that is: ***Can it be that you know the time,*** and this is understood as an active knowledge, which causes whatever it knows to exist, just as divine providence does. But "the time" is understood as that period from first conception all the way until complete

1. Jb 39.26.
2. Jb 39.19.
3. Jb 39.13.
4. Jb 39.5.

birth, which Aristotle calls the time of pregnancy.[5] And that is: ***of the birth of the ibexes.*** An ibex is a horned goat, a climbing animal that tends to abide among the rocks and in the mountains, having horns so huge that they extend from its head all the way back to its hindquarters; sometimes when it falls, it catches its entire body between its horns, lest it be crushed in the fall. ***among the rocks,*** abiding, of course; and the sense is that God has set forth the principles of conception and pregnancy without looking to anything pertaining to humans or anything temporal,[6] so that the human and the human's work contributed nothing to this. ***or have you observed the deer when they are in labor?*** namely, by such active observing, which regulates their pregnancy and birthing. These two animals[7] are identified by name among the perfect wild animals because they are more well known; but through these He understands all others. There is a parallel in the Psalm:[8] *The highest of them is the home of the heron.*

And God elaborates, adding: **[2]** ***Have you counted*** **(Dinumerasti),** supply: *-ne* [to form the interrogative verb *Dinumerastine*], that is, have you made them countable (*dinumerabilesne fecisti*)? ***the months of their,*** namely, the deer's, ***conception,*** that is, of their pregnancy. With respect to which [question] it is said: You have not done this, but I alone have.

And in addition to this, God says: ***and have you known*** **(scisti),** supply: *-ne* [to form the interrogative verb *scistine*], ***the time of their bringing forth?*** That is, within what span of time the offspring is formed for being sent forth, as if He were saying, "By active knowledge you have not caused this, but I, who grant to all things the principle of generation (*legem generationis*), have." Gn 1:[9] *God made the beasts of the earth according to their kinds, the cattle, and everything that creeps on the earth according to its kind.* And after a few verses:[10] *Increase and multiply and fill the earth.* In all these things, however, God looked to nothing temporal.

5. See Aristotle, *De historia animalium* 7.4.1, 3.

6. Here I read with MSS FM, which have *ad nihil humanorum vel ad aliquid temporale,* rather than simply *ad aliquid temporale,* according to Weiss's edition.

7. Namely, the ibex and the deer.

8. Ps 103.17.

9. Gn 1.25.

10. Gn 1.28.

And He adds concerning the mode of generation, which God, without looking to anything temporal, distributes to them. [3] ***They crouch to bring forth young.*** For crouching widens the birth canal for the purpose of sending forth, ***and they give birth*** by sending the young forth, ***and they emit roars,*** from the pain of being in labor, of course, on account of the narrowness of the birth canal.

And God adds concerning the manner of guiding [the young]: [4] ***Their young are weaned,*** supply: not receiving the care of domesticated animals, ***and go out to pasture,*** provided for them by nature, of course, ***they go out,*** namely, beyond the care of their parents after they have developed fully and grown strong in their members, ***and do not return to them,*** namely, the deer, as the children of humans return to their parents.[11] Bar 3:[12] *He who has prepared the earth for all time and has filled it with cattle and four-footed beasts.* For beasts conceive, give birth, and nourish their young by means of such principles, which are not appropriate to rational humans; and indeed no one could have introduced these principles [among the beasts] except God.

Then God adds concerning the principles of customary practices in the behavior of animals, and it has two parts. For in the first part, He speaks of those animals that are not domesticated on account of their love of freedom alone; in the second, of those animals that cannot be domesticated on account of their audacity regarding their own strength and their anger regarding servitude, in that place:[13] *Can it be that [the rhinoceros] will be willing?*

And that is: [5] ***Who has let the wild ass,*** namely, the ass that inhabits the countryside, ***go free,*** lest it be made subject to the rule of domestication. And this is what follows: ***and who has loosened its fetters,*** not those by which it had been harnessed, but those by which it was able to be subdued. Ps:[14] *You have broken my fetters.*

And, explaining the manner of freedom, God adds: **[6]** ***to***

11. Albert is distinguishing here between how deer and other beasts rear their young and how humans do: in contrast to human children, who customarily live with their parents for many years after birth, young animals detach from their parents relatively quickly and do not return.

12. Bar 3.32.

13. Jb 39.9.

14. Ps 115.16.

whom, that is, because to that one[15] ***I have given a home,*** that is, a habitation, ***in the wilderness.*** Aristotle says that one is free that is its own cause and, lest it serve the human, inhabits the wilderness.[16] And God explains this, adding: ***and,*** that is, ***its dwelling,*** that is, the shelter in which it generates [offspring], ***in the barren land?*** that is, which bears no fruit as a result of human action. Jer 2:[17] *A wild ass, accustomed to being alone in the wilderness, in the desire of its soul drew in the wind of the love of itself,* that is, it possesses freedom, wishing[18] to do nothing except what it pleases.

And this is what follows: **[7]** ***It despises the multitude of the city,*** that is, it is not domesticated, lest it be forced to carry loads. And explaining this, God adds: ***it does not hear,*** that is, it does not heed, ***the shouting of the driver,*** that is, its owner, who would drive it forth from him so that it might carry his loads if it were domesticated. And He says "shouting" because domesticated animals are summoned, urged on toward their tasks and loads, and instructed by shouting. But the opposite of these things[19] is [seen] among domesticated animals, according to Is 1:[20] *The ox knows its owner, and the ass its master's trough.* On the contrary, the wild ass is not concerned about a trough. **[8]** ***It looks around the mountains for its pasture,*** that is, it grazes in whatever place is more pleasing. ***and searches everywhere for any green thing,*** tender and delectable, of course, according to its freedom. Ezek 34:[21] *On the green grasses I will feed them; their pastures will be in the high mountains* [*of Israel*].

Then God adds concerning an animal that, because of its audacity regarding its own strength, is angry at the prospect of being in servitude and being domesticated; and that is: **[9]** ***Can it be that the rhinoceros will be willing,*** *rhinos* in Greek means "of the nose," and *ceros* means "horn," on account of the fact that it bears a horn on its nose, as do certain fish of the sea, which

15. Namely, the wild ass.

16. Cf. Aristotle, *Metaph.* 1.3, as cited by Weiss.

17. Jer 2.24.

18. Here I read *volens* with MSS EFM, rather than *volet* with Weiss's edition.

19. Namely, the description of the wild ass provided here in v. 7, that it despises city crowds and does not heed an owner.

20. Is 1.3.

21. Ezek 34.14.

have a horn coming out from the nose in the shape of a sword (*ad figuram gladii*).[22] But the horn of a rhinoceros is remarkable in length, twelve feet or longer, and with a very sharp point. It is solid, not hollow, like the horn of a deer; and at its base, where it is joined to the head, its diameter is greater than a palm width.[23] Of the rhinoceros, Gregory says:[24] The rhinoceros has an untamable nature; if it is held captive, it will die immediately. And therefore God says: ***to serve you,*** for it is angry at the prospect of being in servitude, ***or will it stay at your trough?*** as if He were saying: "No, it will not stay, because it is not domesticated."

And God expands on this still further, adding: **[10]** ***Can it be that you will bind,*** that is, will you be able to bind by means of a yoke or halter, ***the rhinoceros*** **(rhinoceronta)**, this is the Greek accusative, which is *rhinocerontem* in Latin, ***with your thong,*** namely, of the yoke or halter, as if He were saying: "You will not be able"; hence, this signifies the powerful of this age, who cannot be bound. ***for plowing.*** Jer 2:[25] *A long time ago you broke the yoke, you destroyed my bonds, and you said: I will not serve.* ***or will it break up the clods of the valleys behind you?*** supply: by plowing, as if He were saying: "No." Hence, this signifies those who wish to live in freedom. Ps:[26] *They do not experience the hardship of men, and they will not be scourged like other men.*

And expanding on this further, God adds: **[11]** ***Will you have***

22. The swordfish (*gladius*) and the narwhal (*monoceros*) are two such fish that Albert describes in his treatment of aquatic animals in *AL* Book 24. Of the latter, Albert says: "The *monoceros* [narwhal] is a sea fish bearing one horn on its forehead with which it is able to pierce fish and some ships. But it is a slow animal and, as a result, those it attacks are able to escape" (*AL* 24.44; *On Animals: A Medieval Summa Zoologica,* rev. ed., trans. and annot. Kenneth F. Kitchell, Jr. and Irven Michael Resnick, vol. 2 [Columbus: The Ohio State University Press, 2018], p. 1693). Albert describes the swordfish thus: "It is called the *gladius* because its nose is long, more than a cubit and a half in length, and it has both the point and shape of a sword.... But it is with its sword that it kills fish and, so they say, punctures ships. I have seen one of these fish dead and whole and have examined it with my own hands" (*AL* 24.35, trans. Kitchell and Resnick, vol. 2, p. 1685).

23. Cf. Alb., *AL* 12.224 (Kitchell and Resnick, vol. 2, pp. 981–82).

24. Gregory, *Mor.* 31.2.2.

25. Jer 2.20.

26. Ps 72.5.

confidence in its great strength, with respect to which it may carry your loads, of course, and help you in your work. And this is what follows: ***and,*** supply: in accordance with such confidence, ***leave your labors to it?*** supply: by taking pains, as if He were saying: "You will not do it, because it will refuse to work or to carry your load."

And God explains this further still: **[12]** ***Will you trust,*** that is, will you rely on, ***it to bring the grain back to you,*** supply: by threshing it and shaking it off its feet, as the ox does, ***and gather,*** namely, by carrying or hauling or bearing, ***it on your threshing floor?*** that is, the produce of your threshing floor. In all these things, God wills to say nothing else except that to the animals mentioned He distributes principles (*leges*) for guiding such kinds of life without looking to anything temporal.

[13] ***The wing of the ostrich.***

Here God mentions an animal constituted by the ability to walk and the ability to fly,[27] which, according to Gregory, signifies the hypocrite;[28] and He makes clear the principles (*leges*) that direct it in life and generation.

And that is: ***The wing of the ostrich.*** The ostrich is a bird of Libya that always lives in deserted places. It has fleshy shins like those of some quadrupeds, and three clawed toes on each foot, just as a quadruped does. But it has: a beak, a head, and a neck like that of a swan; broad haunches like those of a quadruped; and during its first year, ash-colored wings like those of a goose, which in old age change to a black down like the fleece of a black sheep. Apart from [the flapping of] its wings, it does not fly, but it dances by leaping about, benefiting from the movement of its wings, like a locust. ***is like the wings of the heron,*** not with regard to vital heat or the power to fly,[29] but simply by vir-

27. Cf. Albert's description of the ostrich immediately below with that of *AL* 23.139 (Kitchell and Resnick, vol. 2, pp. 1648–49). Albert concludes his observations on the ostrich in *AL* 23.139 in much the same way as he begins here, namely, by describing it as "a creature which seems to me to be not so much a bird as midway between a bird and a walker [*gressibilis*]" (Kitchell and Resnick, vol. 2, p. 1649).

28. Gregory, *Mor.* 31.2.2.

29. Here I read *non in calore vel potentia ad volandum* with MS FM, rather than simply *non in calore* with Weiss's edition.

tue of the fact that it has a wing. The heron (*herodius*) is an eagle that is called the hero of the birds (*heros avium*).[30] ***and of the hawk.*** Any bird that is greedy after taking prey for itself is called a hawk.[31] And God wishes to say that although the ostrich may have wings, it nevertheless uses its wings differently.

And God adds concerning the directing of the ostrich's generation: **[14]** ***When she leaves her eggs on the ground,*** by not keeping them warm, of course, because if she were to sit on them, she should crush them, so she does not sit on them, as neither does the snake, the lizard, nor the turtle. ***will you perhaps,*** this should be read mockingly and ironically, ***warm them in the sand?*** supply: having been placed there, for she covers them completely with sand. It is as if God were saying: "No." But by the warmth of the sun the egg's inner heat, which is inside the shell and forms the chick and leads it out of its shell, is awakened. And what is [sometimes] said, that the mother keeps the egg warm by sight, is false; but to the ignorant this seems to be the case because the mother is often near her eggs, and she watches them as a means of protection. Hence, the harshness of those who abandon their children is compared to the ostrich. Lam 4:[32] *The daughter of my people is cruel, like the ostrich in the desert.*

And this is what follows: **[15]** ***She forgets,*** that is, she behaves in the manner of one who is not taking care of [her eggs], ***that the foot,*** of a human passing by, of course, ***may trample them,*** that is, may break them into pieces, ***or that the beast of the field may crush them.*** "Beast" (*bestia*), as if it is called a ravager (*vastia*), which, as it happens, makes a treacherous attack on the nest. Hence, it is said of the forsaken land in Is 34:[33] *It will be a den for snakes and a pasture for ostriches.*

And God adds the cause of this on the part of the ostrich, and it is supplied: because **[16]** ***She is hardened against her own young,*** by not providing for them, of course, ***as though they were not her own,*** for she does not keep them warm, nor does she attend to their nourishment, as other birds do. Hence, of the land that

30. Cf. Albert, *AL* 23.7 (Kitchell and Resnick, vol. 2, p. 1547).
31. Cf. Albert, *AL* 23.16–18 (Kitchell and Resnick, vol. 2, pp. 1153–54).
32. Lam 4.3.
33. Is 34.13.

human concern has abandoned, it is said in Is 13:[34] *Their houses will be filled with snakes, and ostriches will dwell there.*

Then He assigns the cause on the part of understanding: ***she has labored in vain,*** because she abandoned those that she conceived and carried in her womb and brought forth, as if they were ones not cared for, since she neither kept them warm nor attended to their nourishment, and in this she seems to be similar to the partridge. Jer 17:[35] *As the partridge warms eggs that she did not lay, so is he who has gathered riches but not according to justice: in the midst of his days they will abandon them* [*the wealthy*], *and at his end he will be a fool.*

And this is what follows: ***with no fear constraining her.*** For she is not chased away from the nest, but in fact by her own neglect she abandons her chicks and casts them aside, that is, away from the guidance of her own life. Hence, she is compared to those who actually do not take care of their own children, but in fact cast them aside. Is 10:[36] *Just as eggs that have been left behind are gathered, so have I gathered together the whole earth; and there was none that opened the mouth, or moved the wing, or made a sound.*

And what follows provides the reason for this: **[17]** ***For God has deprived her of wisdom,*** namely, natural wisdom, which consists in the care of future generations and of offspring, the wisdom that nevertheless God distributes to almost all animals. For all animals, with very few exceptions, take care of their offspring. And so the ostrich is compared to foolish people who are not concerned about the health of their posterity. Dt 32:[37] *Is this the return that you make to the Lord, O foolish and senseless people?* that is, people having no concern for their posterity. ***and He has not given her understanding.*** God calls the practical "understanding," that is, the valuation of caring for the nest and for offspring, which many animals possess, just as the Lord says, in fact, in Mt 8:[38] *Foxes have holes, and the birds of the air have nests.*

God adds, however, how the chick that parents had not cared

34. Is 13.21.
35. Jer 17.11.
36. Is 10.14.
37. Dt 32.6.
38. Mt 8.20.

for grows strong: [18] ***When the time comes,*** namely, the time of the growth of feathers, after the chick emerges from the egg, ***she raises her wings on high,*** so that she may be stirred by both her feathers and her wings to dance, of course, and so that she may take care of herself without any supervision by her parents. Eccl 3:[39] *For everything there is a season, and all things happen in their own times.* And then, having already been perfected according to movement, ***she scorns the horse,*** whose speed is not able to catch her, ***and its rider,*** whose ambushes she does not worry about. Prv 1:[40] *A net is cast in vain before the eyes of those who have wings.* For the ostrich chick flees more quickly than it[41] can follow because both its feet and its wings help it to escape. But God does not intend another meaning of this passage according to the letter, except that His own eternal providence, which looks to nothing temporal, distributes such principles (*leges*) for guiding life even to wild animals, and therefore in governing the lives of humans He looks[42] to nothing temporal.

[19] ***Can it be that you will give to the horse.***

Here God transitions to the governance of domestic animals, the strongest and most perfect of which is the horse; and because of this He sets forth an example concerning that animal, and He indicates its power and a proof of its power as well as its courage and proofs of its courage.

And that is: ***Can it be that you will give,*** your cooperation, of course, ***to the horse.*** A "horse," as Isidore says,[43] is called a horse (*equus*) for this reason: because, whenever two march along, they have become habituated to march along together equally (*ex aequo*). And this is understood of horses that have not been castrated. ***its strength.*** He calls boldness and power "strength" because strength is, as it were, near courage. Hence, in the Psalm:[44] *Deceptive is the horse for salvation,* because, although it is strong, it

39. Eccl 3.1.

40. Prv 1.17.

41. Namely, the horse with its rider.

42. Here I read *respicit* with MSS FM, rather than *respexit* with Weiss's edition.

43. See Isidore, *Etymol.* 12.41; cf. Albert, *AL* 22.52 (Kitchell and Resnick, vol. 2, p. 1477): "Horses are so called from equalness [*equalitas*] or pairedness, since they were yoked in pairs in chariots in antiquity."

44. Ps 32.17.

does not save in war; rather, God does. ***or surround its neck with neighing?*** It is described as a neck surrounded with neighing because according to the roundness of its neck or windpipe, the movement of the horse's tongue produces sounds that are not distinct like [those of] a learned [person's] voice, nor does it form different words as an articulate voice does. It is a neighing animal, however, on account of its libido and boldness. But it is libidinous, as Aristotle says,[45] because of an excess of food, and it is bold from its confidence in its strength and in the weapons that are its kicking feet; hence libidinous people are compared to horses. Jer 5:[46] *Each one was neighing for his neighbor's wife.* Sir 33:[47] *A friend who is a mocker is like a stallion horse: he will neigh under every person who sits upon him.* And so both the bold person and the libidinous one are compared to the horse.

[20] ***Can it be that you will stir it up like the locusts?*** Indeed, by whistling the horse is aroused and stirred up toward courage and running and especially toward leaping, and then by means of its back feet it begins to leap like the locusts. Sir 23:[48] *He will be chased away as if a colt.*

And God explains the proofs of the horse's boldness: ***The glory of its nostrils is terror***, for when the warhorse is running or leaping, it blows air (*spiritum*) through its dilated nostrils, which is a proof of its great boldness, hence Aristotle says in the third book of the *Ethics,* according to Homer, that the mighty were breathing the spirit (*spiritum*) out through their nostrils and their blood boiled up; and therefore bold and furious men are compared to the horse. Is 2:[49] *Turn away from a man whose spirit is in his nostrils, and know that he himself is thought to be exalted,* that is, courageous and bold. And God adds another proof of the horse's boldness: **[21]** ***It digs up the ground with its hoof,*** as if sharpening its hoof while treading down, just as a wild boar cuts its teeth when it wants to fight. For there is a greater nuisance that the horse introduces, that is, it tramples and thrusts

45. See Aristotle, *De historia animalium* 6.17.1, 4, 6–7.
46. Jer 5.8.
47. Sir 33.6.
48. Sir 23.30.
49. Is 2.22.

its forefeet when treading down, but it strikes and pushes away with its back feet. 2 Mc 3:[50] *There appeared to them a certain horse having a terrible rider, equipped with the best coverings; and it furiously struck Heliodorus, leading with its forefeet,* that is, it assaulted them by striking out.

And because the horse is a wild animal, for this reason God says that ***it leaps about,*** that is, it bestirs itself proudly and in an exalted way, and if it provokes other animals against it, on account of this it is an animal of war, with respect to which the most excellent Solomon, as the commander of wars, gathered many horses in Jerusalem. 1 Kgs 10:[51] *Horses were brought to Solomon from Egypt and from Kue.* And God adds a further proof: ***it proceeds boldly into battle with armed men,*** according to which it is an instrument of war, hence it is said in a Psalm:[52] *Some trust in chariots, and some in horses.* For it has been proven that when an uncastrated horse sees a lion, even if its rider is reluctant, it moves toward the lion. And even if the horse has been castrated, the lion withdraws and flees regardless of how much it is pursued; thus, on account of fear it seems to urinate blood.

And, elaborating on this characteristic, God adds: **[22]** ***It does not submit to the sword,*** gleaming and glittering and striking nearby, of course, and therefore He adds that ***it disregards fear,*** that is, the cause of fear, which is being in danger of death; and as far as this [is concerned], the prelate, who fears no danger in the face of his obligation to defend the faith, is compared to the horse. Mt 10:[53] *Do not fear those who kill the body but cannot kill the soul.*

Then God adds further signs of danger, which the horse does not fear: **[23]** ***Above it the quiver will rattle,*** that is, the rushing arrow taken from the quiver. Jb 41:[54] *The archer will not put him to flight.* ***The spear will glitter,*** that is, the horse does not flee the glittering spear, which signifies threatening words, because those who bear Christ do not submit on account of the threats of the

50. 2 Mc 3.25.
51. 1 Kgs 10.28.
52. Ps 19.8.
53. Mt 10.28.
54. Jb 41.19.

powerful. ***And the shield also,*** which signifies secular power. Ps:[55] *He will crush the bow and break the weapons, and the shield he will consume with fire.* [24] ***Seething*** on the inside with the heat of courage ***and raging*** by the roar of the voice grating because of anger, ***it drinks in the ground,*** He calls it drinking because the horse makes the sound loudly with its nostrils set down on the ground. Na 3:[56] *The noise of the rattling of the wheels, and of the raging horse, and of the seething chariot, and of the approaching horsemen, and of the gleaming sword, and of the glittering spear.* Hence the person who rages in anger is compared to a horse. Ps:[57] *Why have the nations raged?*

and it does not reflect upon the blast of the trumpet when it sounds, for by this the horse is inspired and not frightened, because men have become accustomed to blast their trumpets during battles. Hab 3:[58] *In your rage you will trample the earth underfoot, and in your fury you will stupefy the nations.* Jer 8:[59] *The raging of His horses was heard from Dan; the whole land was disturbed at the sound of the neighing of His warriors.* [25] ***When it hears the trumpet,*** supply: urging it on toward war, of course, by every motion and sign; ***it says: Ha!*** which is the interjection of one exalting, and accordingly the horse is compared to those who fight the Lord's battles with joy and courage. 2 Mc 11:[60] *And when they were going forth together with a willing mind, there appeared in Jerusalem a horseman going before them in a white garment, with golden armor, brandishing a spear. Then all together they blessed the merciful Lord and grew strong in spirit, being prepared to break through among not only men, but also the fiercest beasts and even walls of iron.*

From afar it smells* (odoratur) *the battle. Here God uses a passive verb so that the expression may correspond to what it signifies; for "to smell" (*odorare*) in the active voice has a passive signification. And He touches on this, namely, that a horse, when it senses other horses by their scent, immediately flares its nostrils and is made ready to fight. ***the exhortation of the commanders,*** supply: when it hears it, ***and the shouting of the army,*** supply: then it is

55. Ps 45.10.
56. Na 3.2–3.
57. Ps 2.1.
58. Hab 3.12.
59. Jer 8.16.
60. 2 Mc 11.8–9.

roused and made ready for war, and it is prepared. Ex 32:[61] *The noise of battle is heard in the camp.* Hence, those who everywhere oppose the enemy in the battles of the Lord are compared to horses.[62] 2 Mc 11:[63] *They were advancing eagerly, having a helper from heaven and with the Lord's compassion on them. And rushing headlong upon the enemy, like lions, and they slew from among them 11,000 foot-soldiers and 1,600 horsemen; and they put all the rest to flight.*

[26] ***Can it be?***

Here God transitions to birds and the guiding of their life, showing that He orders such guidance by His own wisdom without looking to anything temporal. And He mentions the guiding of the hawk and the eagle on account of the fact that these two kinds of birds are more perfect than all other birds.

And that is: ***Can it be that by your wisdom,*** supply: uniting something to this, ***the hawk grows feathers,*** strong feathers, by means of which it may swiftly pursue other birds and overtake them. And God adds how it uses those [feathers]: ***spreading its wings to the south,***[64] that is, to the heat of the south, so that they may become robust, lest, when their wings have been agitated vigorously, they be bent by the wind pushing against them. And therefore holy men are compared to hawks, as it is said in Is 40:[65] *They will fly and not grow weak.* ***and to the south?*** That is, to the light and heat of the Holy Spirit they spread the wings of intellect and affect together with the feathers of the virtues, by means of which they pursue wild souls in order to capture them for God. Lam 3:[66] *By chasing they have captured my soul like a bird.*

And concerning the eagle, God adds: **[27]** ***Can it be that the eagle will lift off at your command,*** so that she may fly high, of course, and, from on high, see far in the distance, as if God were saying:

61. Ex 32.17.

62. And other animals such as lions, as attested in the following scriptural text.

63. 2 Mc 11.10–12.

64. Although MS B omits the phrase *ad austrum* here in order to avoid the repetition of the phrase that occurs in the scriptural text immediately below, Weiss adds it here based on its attestation in all the other MSS, viz. TEFM. I follow MSS TEFM and Weiss in retaining and translating this repetition.

65. Is 40.31.

66. Lam 3.52.

"Not at your command, but at mine. For I have introduced this principle (*legem*) of the guiding of her life." And "eagle" (*aquila*) is derived from acuteness (*acumine*), because she sees acutely (*acute*); hence she is said to test her young also to see if each one can gaze at[67] the disk of the sun after the rays of the eyes have been repelled; and she cares for those who can, but she abandons those who cannot. For it is said by certain people that she travels to carcasses that she has seen up to 500 miles away.[68] But others say that she does so by her sense of smell, according to which she signifies the person who is soaring into divine contemplation. Ezek 1:[69] *And the face of an eagle extended above all four.* Rv 4:[70] *And the fourth living creature was like an eagle flying.* ***and build her nest in high places?*** Ob:[71] *You have been exalted like an eagle and have built your nest among the stars.* For she teaches her young to aim at things lofty and beyond the clouds, and to abide among things that are pure and highest and heavenly.

And God explains what kind those things are: **[28]** ***She abides among the rocks,*** so that she may sharpen both her talons and her beak on the rock, of course, and thus always be renewed and armed for her prey. Hence, the eagle is compared to the man who always renews his appetite's desire and his comprehension's understanding, and his wings in the revival of his powers for the most perfect truth, so that he may always learn new things from the First Truth. Ezek 17:[72] *A large eagle with great wings, long limbs, and full of feathers and variety came to Lebanon and took away the marrow of the cedar,* that is, the sweetness of the incorruptible truth.

and dwells among steep stones. "Stones" are untamable by the sword and [are so by] their natural character. For the eagle does not want any climbing thing to approach her nest, and therefore she builds her nest "among steep stones," where there are no boulders by means of which something could climb up. ***and inaccessible cliffs,*** and this is an explanation of what comes before;

67. Here I read *aspicere* with MSS FM rather than *videre* with Weiss's edition.

68. See the commentary on Jb 28.7 above.

69. Ezek 1.10.

70. Rv 4.7.

71. Ob 4.

72. Ezek 17.3.

for there[73] she sees far in the distance through the clear sky. Nm 23:[74] *I will see him from the highest stones, and I will consider him from the hills.*

And this is what follows: **[29]** ***From there she looks for prey,*** that is, animals that she may seize, or carcasses. Hence in Prv 30[75] Solomon says of the one who should be given over to eagles for food: *The eye that mocks his father and despises his own mother's giving birth* [*to him*], *may the ravens of the rushing streams pluck it out and may the young eagles devour it!* ***and her eyes watch from far away.*** Nm 24:[76] *I will look at him, but not close by.* Hence this signifies the person who will see the most remote things, that is, divine things, in which he may be restored. Jb 36:[77] *All men see Him, everyone looks from far away.* **[30]** ***Her young lick up the blood,*** on account of the fact that with their delicate talons and beak they are not able to cut dense flesh, and "blood" here is understood to mean flesh made soft from coagulated blood, like that of the brain and liver of young animals. And therefore the young licking up the blood is compared to the man who is restored by the blood of Christ, who was not hardened by sin. Jn 6:[78] *Unless you eat the flesh of the Son of Man and drink His blood, you will not have life in you.* ***and wherever the carcass is,*** supply: by smelling the strong odor of the carcass, ***she is there immediately.*** And on account of this she is compared to the man who, having perceived the aroma of the body of Christ, is moved quickly toward it. Mt 24:[79] *Wherever the body is, there the eagles also will be gathered.*

[31] ***And the Lord went on.***

Here God mentions Job's consent to the words of the Lord, and He speaks of two things, namely: surprise at Job's quick consent; and Job's confession of his imperfection in comparison to the Lord's wisdom, in that place:[80] *Then Job responded to the Lord and said.*

73. That is, from the height of inaccessible cliffs.
74. Nm 23.9.
75. Prv 30.17.
76. Nm 24.17.
77. Jb 36.25.
78. Jn 6.54.
79. Mt 24.28.
80. Jb 39.33.

And that is: ***And the Lord went on,*** after exhibiting His own wisdom, ***and said to Job,*** concerning his consent to the [Lord's] words of wisdom, of course: **[32]** ***Can it be that he who contends with God,*** concerning the governing of his own life, of course, doubting whether he has been stricken justly or unjustly, ***is so easily silenced?*** certainly so that he may not doubt concerning the words of the one disputing against him. Jb 13:[81] *But nevertheless I will speak to the Almighty, and I want to debate* (disputare) *with God.* ***Surely he who accuses God,*** and seems to argue according to reason, ***ought to answer Him.*** Is 1:[82] *Come and accuse me, says the Lord.* Mi 6:[83] *O my people, what have I done to you, or how have I been burdensome to you? Answer me!* Jeremiah did so in Jer 12:[84] *You, indeed, are just, O Lord, if I should debate with you; nevertheless, I will say just things to you.* **[33]** ***Then Job responded to the Lord and said,*** by confessing his own foolishness, of course, in comparison to eternal wisdom. Jb 13:[85] *Call me, and I will answer you; or at least I will speak, and you answer me.* **[34]** ***I, who have spoken thoughtlessly.*** A person who asserts that what is true in one sense (*uno modo*) is true absolutely (*simpliciter*) "speaks thoughtlessly," just as Job has done, who, because he was stricken unjustly according to the order of human justice, asserted that he had been stricken unjustly absolutely (*simpliciter*). Jb 19:[86] *At least now understand that God has not afflicted me with an equitable judgment, and He has surrounded me with His scourges.*

how can I answer? Jb 9:[87] *If he wishes to contend with Him, he will not be able to answer one word for a thousand.* Rom 9:[88] *O man, who are you, that you should respond to God?* ***I will put my hand over my mouth,*** for holding back, of course, lest he say something against God. Ps:[89] *Do not speak iniquity against God.* Ezek 1:[90] *When a voice came from above the firmament, which was overhanging the heads of the*

81. Jb 13.3.
82. Is 1.18.
83. Mi 6.3.
84. Jer 12.1.
85. Jb 13.22.
86. Jb 19.6.
87. Jb 9.3.
88. Rom 9.20.
89. Ps 74.6.
90. Ezek 1.25.

animals, they stood still and let down their wings. Zep 3:[91] *I will remove from your midst your proud boasters.*

And Job confesses his sin: **[35]** ***One thing I have spoken,*** namely, that *God has not afflicted me with an equitable judgment,* Jb 19.[92] And he adds his repentance: ***which I wish I had not said.*** For His judgment is just, which is for His own glory or the exercise of virtue.[93] Concerning the first, it is said in Jn 9:[94] *Neither has this man sinned, nor his parents; but [this man was born blind] so that the works of God may be made manifest in him.* Concerning the second, Tb 12:[95] *And because you were pleasing to God, it was necessary that temptation should prove you.* ***and another,*** supply: [thing] I have spoken, namely, I spoke about my scourge with murmuring. Above in chapter 6:[96] *If only my sins, for which I have deserved wrath, and the calamity that I suffer were weighed in a balance.* For I said this without carefully considering that, according to strict justice, no one is just in God's sight, and no one receives the things that he deserves; rather, each one always[97] deserves more scourges than he receives. Jb 11:[98] *And you would understand that He exacts much less of you than your iniquity deserves.* ***to which I will add no more.*** Gn 4 according to another translation:[99] *Have you sinned? Keep quiet.* Sir 7:[100] *Refuse to do evil, and evil will not lay hold of you.*

91. Zep 3.11.
92. Jb 19.6.
93. Cf. Gregory, *Mor.* Pref. 5.12, who offers a very similar explanation of why God allowed Job to suffer.
94. Jn 9.3.
95. Tob 12.13.
96. Jb 6.2.
97. Here I read with MSS FM, which add *semper.*
98. Jb 11.6.
99. Gn 4.7 according to the LXX.
100. Sir 7.1.

CHAPTER 40

T*HEN THE LORD responded to Job.*

Up to this point, God has determined in general what He intended by this: namely, that He has looked to nothing temporal in any [instance of the] governing of animal life, seeing that He introduced to each animal the principles (*leges*) of the directing of its own life, and so neither in the governing of human life has God looked to anything temporal. From here He passes over to universal nature, and He shows—through the perversity of a certain universal nature—that the perversity in man concerning his ways of working according to nature is so great that man cannot be immune from sin and from fault. And, therefore, he murmurs in vain about his scourges, because he ought to be scourged and he ought to be purified through scourges.

And it is divided into two parts. For in the first part, God makes this clear from the perversity of the animal or beastly nature that is in man, which, by the multiplicity of its temptations, subverts everything that is right in man's reason. Because of this, Avicenna says in the last part of his *Metaphysics,* which treats morals, that everything that is right in reason is corrupted because of the joining of the intellect to imagination and sense perception by reason of the din of delightful things in sense perception.[1] In the second part, however, God proves this from the blending of a serpentine and a venomous nature into a nature that the serpent in the beginning launched against Eve's nature accord-

1. See Avicenna, *Metaph.* 10.1.2 and 10.3.5 (Avicenna, *The Metaphysics of The Healing,* trans. Michael E. Marmura [Provo, UT: Brigham Young University Press, 2005], 358–59 and 369). Cf. Alb., commentary on Jb 28.12 above and Alb., *Anim.* 3.1.6.

ing to Gn 3.[2] And this part begins in that place:[3] *Can it be that you will drag out Leviathan with a hook?*

The first part is subdivided into two. In the **first subdivision,** God, while speaking to man, makes clear that he will not be able to be innocent (*purus*). In the second, He shows the cause—[namely] on account of a beastly or animal nature—of man's impurity or perversity, in that place:[4] *Behold Behemoth, whom I made with you.* And the first subdivision is, as it were, a response to the man; but the second is a speech.

In the first subdivision there are three elements. In the first place, God makes use of a transition. Second, He sets forth a question that He intends to debate (*disputare*), in that place:[5] *Can it be that you will make void?* Third, He provides the reason for determining the question, in that place:[6] *And do you have an arm like God's?*

And that is: *Then the Lord responded to Job.* Here "Job" is in the dative case, and, in responding to Job, God responded to his other friends also. Mk 13:[7] *What I say to one, I say to all.* ***out of the whirlwind,*** that is, out of the conflict of the disputation and of the trial of Job, who has been under consideration. Jb 9:[8] *For He crushes me as if in a whirlwind and multiplies my wounds without cause.*

But God makes clear the cause of man's perversity, saying: **[2]** ***Gird up your loins like a man.*** For unless the loins are girded by means of the evaporation of concupiscence, you will not be able to hear words concerning morals with the clear eye of reason, as has been said in the things considered above. Hence, 2 Kgs 1[9] says of Elijah that he was *a hairy man well girded with a leather belt about his loins;* "hairy" [meaning] "of intense meditation," of course, having girded his loins with a leather belt, such that the recollection of death restrained his pleasures, so that he might

2. Gn 3.1.
3. Jb 40.20.
4. Jb 40.10.
5. Jb 40.3.
6. Jb 40.4.
7. Mk 13.37.
8. Jb 9.17.
9. 2 Kgs 1.8.

not be able to go astray in his choices. ***I will question you,*** concerning your conclusion, of course, and your choice regarding the truth, ***and you show me,*** by your response, namely, what is true or what should be chosen.

And God sets forth the question: **[3]** ***Can it be that you will make void my judgment,*** that is, right judgment concerning me—I who am unable to be unjust—while you argue about your merits against my scourges, ***and,*** that is, ***condemn me,*** as if I struck you unjustly, ***in order that you may be justified?*** that is, you may seem to be just and stricken unjustly, as if He were saying: "You will not." Ps:[10] *You are justified in your sentence, and you may prevail when you are judged.* For God is always found to be just, and through this prevails; and man is unjust when the judgment of man is brought before God. Ezek 18:[11] *Can it be that my way is not just, and rather are not your ways perverse?*

And God sets forth the reason why this cannot be, deducing to the impossible, if this is considered. And that is: **[4]** ***And do you have an arm like God's?*** that is, operative power, which can be nothing but upright, as is said in Hab 1:[12] *Your eyes are too pure to look upon evil, and you are not able to gaze at iniquity.* ***and can you thunder,*** so that there can be nothing false in your words, contrary to what is said in Rom 3:[13] *God is truthful, but every man is a liar.* Ps:[14] *I said in my excess: Every man is a liar.* ***with a voice like His?*** supply: like God's. Supply: then, I say, if it is so, **[5]** ***Clothe yourself with beauty,*** that is, a manner of life that, in every word and in every action, is beautiful—this belongs to God alone. Ps:[15] *The Lord has reigned; He has been clothed with beauty.*

But concerning the manner of man's life, it is said in Jb 9:[16] *If I were washed as if with water from snow, and my hands were to shine as if most pure, nevertheless you will immerse me in filth, and my own clothes will abhor me.* And God continues further with the impossible; supply: if you are beautiful, ***and raise yourself up on high,*** and

10. Ps 50.6.
11. Ezek 18.25.
12. Hab 1.13.
13. Rom 3.4.
14. Ps 115.11.
15. Ps 92.1.
16. Jb 9.30–31.

this is not fitting for you, seeing that you have been created from the lowest element. Gn 18:[17] *I will speak to my Lord, although I am dust and ashes.* ***and be glorious,*** that is, dignify yourself with glorious and great things, which in no way is fitting for you. 1 Tm 1:[18] *To God alone be honor and glory.* ***and put on beautiful garments,*** namely, by a manner of life in no way dirty, which is not fitting for man on account of the frailty of the human condition. Zec 3:[19] *Joshua was clothed in filthy garments.*

And this is in comparison to the good, in regard to which you are not able to be innocent (*purus*); even by withdrawing from evil, you are not able to be perfect. And that is: **[6]** ***Scatter the proud in your fury.*** He who consents to no proud person and is indignant at every proud person "scatters the proud in fury." Tb 4:[20] *Never permit pride to have dominion in your mind or in your words: for all perdition took its beginning from it.* And He says "in your fury" because pride should be driven away with indignation. And pride here is understood generally as all arrogance and loftiness of heart, by which the heart does not want to make itself subject to a command and to a commanding God. Ps:[21] *Let not the foot of pride come to me, and let not the hand of the sinner move me. All of them have fallen.* ***and beholding,*** supply: with the eye of indignation, ***every arrogant man,*** namely, the one who, among great things, attributes to himself what is not fitting for him, ***humble him,*** namely, so that he may not think great things about himself, but rather lowly things. Jas 4:[22] *God resists the proud but gives grace to the humble.* Salustius says:[23] God crushes all the proud.

And God expands on this still further: **[7]** ***Look,*** indignantly, of course, ***on all who are proud,*** so that you may detest their pride, of course. Am 6:[24] *The Lord God has sworn by His own soul, says the*

17. Gn 18.27.
18. 1 Tm 1.17.
19. Zec 3.3.
20. Tb 4.14.
21. Ps 35.12–13.
22. Jas 4.6.
23. Latin: *Frangit Deus omnem superbum.* Cf. Prudentius, *Psychomachia,* line 285: *Frangit Deus omne superbum.* Weiss informs his reader that he has been unable to find this quotation in the works of Sallust the Roman historian.
24. Am 6.8.

Lord God of hosts: I detest the pride of Jacob. ***and confound them,*** by penance, of course. Jer 31:[25] *I am confounded and ashamed because I have borne the reproach of my youth.* ***and crush the wicked,*** that is, every movement of impiety, ***in their place,*** that is, in their first beginning, so that they may be reduced to nothing, of course. Is 33:[26] *The sinners in Zion have been crushed; fear has seized the hypocrites.* God expands on this: **[8]** ***Hide them in the dust together,*** supply: as though they are to be buried immediately; and this happens especially when we are mindful that we are going to return to dust. Sir 7:[27] *In all your works remember your last day, and you will never sin.* Sir 10:[28] *Why is earth-and-ashes proud?* ***and plunge their faces,*** that is, immediately at their first appearance, provided that they are visible, ***into the pit,*** by the threat of the pit of hell, of course. Is 14:[29] *Your pride has been dragged down to hell; your dead body has fallen down.* And in the very same place:[30] *You will be dragged down into hell, to the bottom of the pit.* **[9]** ***And,*** supply: if you are thus perfect in the good and in withdrawing from evil, ***I will confess,*** I will give witness to you, ***that your right hand,*** that is, operative power, for that is the right hand of God, ***is able to save you,*** because then divine power—rather than human weakness—belongs to you. Ps:[31] *The right hand of the Lord has wrought power; the right hand of the Lord has exalted me.* But this is not fitting for man, who has within himself nothing but the cause of destruction (*causam perditionis*); and his salvation is from the Lord. Hos 13:[32] *Destruction is your own, O Israel; your help is only from me.*

[10] ***Behold Behemoth.***

Having made clear that man is not able to be clean, and therefore that he murmurs unjustly about the beating [he receives] as a result of the beastly nature that is in man, God explains the cause of his uncleanness. For the cause of perversity is, as Avicenna says, that, whereas the intellect is upright in itself, it is joined

25. Jer 31.19.
26. Is 33.14.
27. Sir 7.40.
28. Sir 10.9.
29. Is 14.11.
30. Is 14.15.
31. Ps 117.16.
32. Hos 13.9.

to the imaginative and the sensible, which, by the din and the multiplicity of delightful sensibles, turn the intellect's choosing upside down.[33] But the imaginative and the sensitive powers are natural to animals (*animalia*), as the Apostle says in 1 Cor 2:[34] *The natural man* (animalis homo) *does not perceive the things that are of the Spirit of God;* here the Gloss says:[35] "The natural animal life (*animalis vita*) is one in which dissolute wantonness is produced according to the delights of the five senses, a wantonness that the helmsman of the spirit does not contain within its own limits." And here God calls that nature thus corrupted and infected, which is the cause of perversity, Behemoth, because "Behemoth" means "animal." Jude, in his own epistle, says:[36] *In the last times there come mockers, walking according to their own desires, not in piety. These are ones who separate themselves, animals, not having the Spirit.*

Therefore, describing the cause of such corruption, God articulates two things, namely: the power of that corruption of nature in us; and the way in which it can be conquered and brought back to virtue, in that place:[37] *In his eyes, as with a hook.* In the first of these parts, there are three sections. In the first section, God describes the strength [of Behemoth], which he has because of the delightful and because of the arrangement of bodily members, with respect to which he has dominion. In the second section, his strength because of the multiplicity of delightful things, in that place:[38] *For him the mountains.* In the third section, because of the inclination of reason, in that place:[39] *Behold, he will swallow up.*

And that is: ***Behold,*** as if He were saying, "The cause of your destruction is apparent," ***Behemoth,*** which means "animal," that is, the animal and beastly nature that is in you, ***whom I made with***

33. Cf. Alb., commentary on Jb 28.12 above, pp. 69–73; see also the *divisio textus* at the beginning of the commentary on ch. 40 above, pp. 256–57; see also Alb., *Anim.* 3.1.6.

34. 1 Cor 2.14.

35. *GO* on 1 Cor 2.14 (PL 114:522).

36. Jude 18–19.

37. Jb 40.19.

38. Jb 40.15.

39. Jb 40.18.

you, so that you might not be a pure intellect alone, but that you might have the understanding of an animal, even as if that of an ox. And this is what follows: ***he eats grass like an ox,*** that is, he will thoroughly enjoy carnal delights, which appear green. This was signified in Dn 4:[40] *Your dwelling shall be with beasts and wild animals; and you shall eat grass like an ox.* And in the same place it is said:[41] *Let his heart be changed from a human heart and let the heart of a wild animal be given to him.* For a man's heart is changed from a human heart when he does not follow his upright intellect, but rather a wild and beastly nature.

And God adds [a description of] the arrangement of bodily members, with respect to which Behemoth has dominion to a greater extent, first in the male and second in the female. And that is: **[11]** ***His strength is in his loins,*** as far as the male is concerned. For "in the loins" there are sensitive nerves, through which semen, when it descends from the head and from the body and touches by titillation the innermost parts of the nerves, inflames desire and, by the power of delight, turns the mind away from wisdom and subverts it. And this is what Aristotle says, according to Homer, in Book VII of the *Ethics*:[42] That multiplier of deceits was Venus or Cypris; and the belt of Venus powerfully plundered the minds of wise men. Sir 19:[43] *Wine and women make even wise men fall, and they will rebuke the intelligent. And he who joins himself to prostitutes will be wicked.* ***and his power,*** that is, of his potential ultimately, ***in the navel of his belly,*** as far as the female is concerned. For a female breeder, whose nerves the semen, received in sexual intercourse, touches, has a cone toward her navel; and as long as those nerves are touched, the female experiences intense pleasure. Ezek 16:[44] *On the day of your birth, your navel was not cut.*

Moreover, God adds how semen is pressed toward the genital organs: **[12]** ***He draws his tail tight like a cedar.*** He calls the genital organ the "tail" because it is the end of all the nerves and it is

40. Dn 4.29.
41. Dn 4.13.
42. Aristotle, *EN* 7.6.3.
43. Sir 19.2–3.
44. Ezek 16.4.

constituted from the extremities of all the nerves. With respect to the genital organ, by the force of pleasures he draws tight all the nerves, by whose constriction semen is pressed out from the whole body through nerve cavities and through the porousness of the flesh; and the semen is drawn down to the place of generation, as Avicenna says, just as whey is strained out from cheese.[45] But God compares this to the structure of a "cedar" because cedar is a strong wood and when it is pressed hard it discharges a blood-red sap. Hence, by reason of its strength the cedar is compared to the strength of desire, and by reason of its blood-red sap it is compared to the seed of generation. Because, as Avicenna says, superfluous semen pertains to the fourth digestion, the liquid (*humor*) of the fourth digestion is squeezed out of the blood and is purified.[46]

As far as how semen may be drawn down to the place of generation, God adds further: ***the sinews of his testicles are wrapped together***. The "testicles," as Aristotle says,[47] draw the semen to themselves, as by the windy choler, that is, by the heat of choler, from which they were made, by the windy heat of the fire [of passion] introduced into them. The testicles are suspended, moreover, at the tails of the nerves; and the nerves bordering on their tails are part of a network that runs through the entire body, so that they may draw semen and squeeze it out from every part of the body. Amid such power, they have cultivated the idol of desire, concerning which it is said in a Psalm:[48] *They were initiated into* [*the cult of*] *Baal of Peor*. Nm 25:[49] *Israel was initiated into* [*the cult of*] *Baal of Peor. And the Lord became angry*. For "Baal of Peor" (*Beelphegor*) is said as though *bel phogor*, that is, god of lecherousness, who was shaped by shamefulness and disgrace drawn tight and stretched [around him]; his whole body, wrapped up in disgrace, was being drawn by a snare.

God explains Behemoth's bodily strength still further, adding: [13] ***His bones,*** speaking metaphorically, by "bones" God means

45. See Avicenna, *Liber Canonis* 3.20.1.1.
46. See Avicenna, *Liber Canonis* 3.20.1.3.
47. Cf. Aristotle, *GA* 1.12; and Alb., *AL* 1.2.24.
48. Ps 105.28.
49. Nm 25.3.

the vigor and strength of animalian pleasure, hence He adds: ***are like pipes of brass.*** For brass is sonorous, and a pipe whistles sweetly; and God understands "pipe" as deceit, which animalian pleasure induces, according to what is said in poetry also: "The pipe sings sweetly while the fowler deceives the bird."[50] And this accords with what is declared in Ovid:[51] that, although Argus had a head encircled with a hundred eyes, nevertheless his eyes were closed by the whistling of pipes, and the act of adultery was carried out; and so the force of carnal pleasure weakens the power of the mind, and pleasure prevails.

his cartilage like plates of iron. Cartilage is a mean between the hardness of bone and the softness of flesh, and it is introduced by nature into the spaces of wide joints where two bones come together, lest, when a hard bone rubs against a hard bone, they break one another and shatter. And concupiscence acts in the same way. Everything that is hard depends on something soft to come next to it, so as not to feel anything harsh. Such softness, because it is extended everywhere throughout the body, is here called a "plate." And because it subdues and softens the severity of reason, it is called "iron," for iron subdues other metals, as is said in Dn 2.[52] This is said under a different metaphor in Ezek 13:[53] *Woe to the one who destroys little pillows under every elbow.* Mt 11:[54] *Those who are clothed in soft garments are in the houses of kings,* that is, of delicate ones. For kings especially, like Sardanopolus, are associated with carnal desires (*concupiscentiis*).[55]

God makes clear, moreover, how many cling to this softness of sensuality, adding: **[14]** ***He is the beginning of the ways of God.*** The first traces (*prima vestigia*) of divine power in the generation of man, in which at the beginning it is apparent that he is an animal before the manifestation of reason, are called "the ways of God." 1 Cor 15:[56] *What is spiritual is not first, but what is natural* (animale); *then what is spiritual.* Aristotle also says in Book 16 of

50. Cato, *Dist.* 1.27.
51. Ovid, *Metam.* 1.677–721.
52. Dn 2.40.
53. Ezek 13.18.
54. Mt 11.8.
55. See Alb., *Eth.* 1.5.7; and the commentary on Jb 36.14, pp. 193–94.
56. 1 Cor 15.46.

On Animals that something is not a living thing and an animal at the same time, neither is one a man and an animal at the same time.[57] Hence, because this pleasure has been planted together with nature, on account of this it binds tight to a greater extent and holds to a greater extent and it is more invincible, as Aristotle says in the second book of the *Ethics*.[58]

Yet, lest there be complete despair, but that it not be reducible to the mean of the virtue of temperance, God adds: ***who made him,*** namely, Behemoth, supply: by divine power. ***he will apply his sword,*** by which he fights against reason, of course, lest he be able to run through it completely.[59] For he is able to be obedient to reason, as Aristotle says,[60] and then what is said in Is 2 is fulfilled:[61] *They shall turn their swords into plowshares, and their spears into pruning hooks.* For at that time by means of the plowshare of discipline, the concupiscible will be cultivated so that it may bear the fruit of justice and virtue.

[15] ***For him, the mountains.***

Here God makes clear the aggressiveness of Behemoth's animal nature because of the multiplicity of the delightful, and in this place three things are mentioned: namely, the multiplicity of the delightful, the place of delight, and the adherence of the delight. And that is: ***For him,*** namely, Behemoth, ***the mountains,*** that is, projections of delightful things in the concupiscence of the flesh according to touch and according to taste, according to which there is a certain effect. For in these things, there is the greatest pleasure, as Aristotle says in the second book of the *Ethics*.[62] ***bring forth grass,*** that is, a verdant and beautiful pasture. Dn 4:[63] *Among the grass that is outside, and let it be wet with the dew of heaven, and let its portion be with the wild beasts in the grass of the earth.* And this is said about the person who has exchanged his

57. Aristotle, *GA* 2.3; cf. Alb., *AL* 15.1.10.

58. Cf. Aristotle, *EN* 3.1.24 and 3.12.7.

59. Here "he" refers to Behemoth, which, as Albert notes in the commentary on v. 10 above, signifies "the animal and beastly nature" that is in man, and "it" refers to reason.

60. See Aristotle, *EN* 1.13.17.

61. Is 2.4.

62. Cf. Aristotle, *EN* 3.10.11.

63. Dn 4.12.

human nature for a bovine nature. ***all the beasts of the field,*** that is, all movements like a beast passing through a field, ***will play there,*** that is, on that grass. Ps:[64] *They changed their glory into the likeness of a calf that eats grass.* And this is said of those who transform the glory of reason into the ruin of concupiscence.

And, concerning the place of greatest delight, where they rest, God adds: **[16]** ***He sleeps in the shade,*** that is, in the deepest shady place, with his belly bound beneath, he sleeps, that is, he rests. Hence, in his book on the politics of Plato, Apuleius introduces Plato, who says that he has buried concupiscence in the deepest places, as if in hell, where there is shade because of the darkness of reason. Jb 24:[65] *The eye of the adulterer watches for darkness, saying: No eye will see me.* ***in the covert of the reed,*** that is, according to whom it is a secret place, because it is shameful. "Of the reed," that is, the cavities of nerves, veins, and the porous places of the body [that] descend, just like certain reeds, ***in moist places.*** For moisture that flows down through reeds is furnished for the mitigation of desire; indeed, in the place where desire is aroused and moved by something hot, it possesses the potential (*habet materiam*) for something moist. By means of what is changeable (*ventoso*) the male genital member grows rigid with a view to a shameful act; hence, that is the proper place of Behemoth. These are the reeds shaken by the wind (*vento*), among which John did not live. Mt 11:[66] *What did you go out into the desert to see—a reed shaken by the wind?* as if he were saying, "No."

And God adds concerning the adherence [of the delight]: **[17]** ***The shades cover his shadow.*** He calls the appearances of delightful things (*species delectabilium*) "shades," just as a form in a mirror is called a shade. These appearances, having been multiplied in the senses, cover his shadow, that is, the appearance of the delightful thing received in concupiscence, on account of which Aristotle says in the second book of the *Ethics*[67] that in the case of such concupiscence it is necessary to strive for the opposite and to flee, and because the elderly among the com-

64. Ps 105.20.
65. Jb 24.15.
66. Mt 11.7.
67. Aristotle, *EN* 2.9.6.

mon people were suffering in relation to Helen, it is necessary that we suffer in relation to delight. For the elderly among the common people, when they saw Helen, said: "Let us flee, let us flee!" Among the tales of Ovid,[68] this is also said of the Gorgon [Medusa], who, when she was looked at, caused men to stand immovable and insensible, as if they had been bound fast. Having been protected by a reflective shield and with his face turned away from her, Perseus, who signifies reason, killed Medusa by cutting off her head with the sword of severity. Jb 31:[69] *I made a covenant with my eyes, that I would not even think about a virgin.* Ps:[70] *Turn away my eyes, that they may not see vanity.*

And concerning the adherence, God adds further still: ***the willows of the brook will enclose him.*** Instead of a flower, the "willow" causes viscous and frothy moisture to foam, which is driven out by the wind into a fresh woolliness. But his shadow is cold and it is raised and expanded near the brooks, by which God wills to say poetically that near the brooks of food and drink Venus grows strong and begins to froth with desire; on account of this, in the tales of Ovid[71] she is said to have been born from the foam of the sea, and having been cooled externally, she did not dry up at all internally. Gregory says:[72] A stomach churning from pure wine easily froths down with desire. Jerome says to Marcella:[73] Neither the mountains of Etna nor the fires of Vulcan seethe as much as youthful marrow inflamed by wine and sumptuous food.

[18] ***He will swallow up a river [and not be amazed].***[74] Here God mentions with what great power Behemoth turns reason; and He calls the things that flow into concupiscence, which brutishness swallows up, a "river," and this is not amazing. It is said

68. Ovid, *Metam.* 4.698–752, 775–87.
69. Jb 31.1.
70. Ps 118.37.
71. Ovid, *Metam.* 4.532–39.
72. Cf. Gregory, *Mor.* 31.45.89.
73. Jerome, *Letter 54 to Furia*, 9 (PL 22:554).
74. The manuscripts of *Super Iob* omit the words that follow *Absorbebit fluvium* in the Vulgate as it has come down to us, namely, *et non mirabitur,* although Albert's comments below presuppose this phrase.

of the libidinous person in Gn 49:[75] *You have been poured out like water, you shall not increase; because you have climbed into your father's bed, and you have defiled his couch.* 2 Sm 14:[76] *We all die, and like water we fall down into the earth.* ***and he has confidence*** from the ferocity of the temptation and of the adherence [of the delights] ***that the Jordan,*** which is understood as the descent of judgment, and which signifies the judgment of reason descending into sensuality, ***may flow into his mouth,*** so that reason may be swallowed up, of course, and the whole man may be delivered over to concupiscence, just as it flowed into the mouth of Reuben, the oldest son of Jacob, in Gn 49,[77] so too of Samson in Jgs 16,[78] of David in 2 Sm 11, and of Solomon in 1 Kgs 11.[79] Sir 47:[80] *You have turned your thighs to women, and you have been subjugated to the rule of your body. You have put a stain on your glory, you have profaned your seed.* In this way the Israelite people was initiated into [the cult of] Baal of Peor, according to Nm 25.[81] So it is said in 3 Esdras 4 that women are stronger.[82]

Lest there be despair, however, God adds how Behemoth can be conquered, and that is: **[19]** ***In his eyes.*** "His eyes"—because the irrational is, by its nature, capable of obeying reason, obediently—are, with their concupiscible and irascible gaze (*respectus*), [directed] toward reason. Aristotle says at the end of the first book of the *Ethics*[83] that the possession of reason is twofold: indeed, in this way principally, by possessing reason in oneself; but in another way as something audible from one's father. For he accepts reason just as a son hears his father; and in those eyes with which he looks to reason, as to his father, reason itself ***as with a hook will capture him,*** namely, Behemoth, and draw him. Eccl 9:[84] *Just as fish are caught with a hook and birds with a snare, so*

75. Gn 49.4.
76. 2 Sm 14.14.
77. Gn 49.4.
78. Jgs 16.16.
79. 1 Kgs 11.1.
80. Sir 47.21–22.
81. Nm 25.3.
82. 3 Esdras (1 Esdras) 4.14–35.
83. Aristotle, *EN* 1.13.18.
84. Eccl 9.12.

too men are taken in an evil time. Regarding this it is clearly said in Song 1:[85] *Draw me after you.* Sir 26:[86] *On a daughter who does not turn herself away,* supply: from delightful things, *set a strict watch, lest, when she finds an opportunity, she squander herself.* ***and with stakes,*** that is, with severe precepts and with the practice of difficult works, ***it***[87] ***will bore through his nostrils,*** through which he draws in the aroma of delightful things, of course. But "it will bore through" [his nostrils] so that he cannot draw in [the aroma]. And God continues the metaphor of an ox because, when it runs wild, it is brought back to the yoke by means of a ring in its nose. Is 37:[88] *I will put a ring in your nostrils, and I will bring you back by the way by which you came.* Sir 33:[89] *The yoke and the thong bend a stiff neck, and incessant labors bow a slave.*

Through all these things, God has aimed to determine that question with which the greatest part of the disputation has been concerned, namely, whether anyone born of a woman can be so clean (*mundus*) that he should in no way be punished, and whether nothing can be found in him to be corrected by blows. And God determines this question negatively, namely, that there is not [any such person] because of the excessive power and manifold nature of sensual delights; and this has already been considered.[90]

And God transitions to the second reason of the same [determination], hence He adds:

[20] ***Can it be that you will drag out.***

Just as Behemoth is understood as sensuality, which is the natural animal life (*animalis vita*) in man, who is carried off in the midst of the delights of the five senses by a dissolute wantonness that the helmsman of the spirit does not contain within its own limits, so too Leviathan is understood as the infection of the

85. Song 1.3.

86. Sir 26.13.

87. Namely, reason itself (*ipsa ratio*), which, as he makes clear immediately above, Albert takes to be the subject of both *will capture* (*capiet*) and *will bore through* (*perforabit*) in this verse.

88. Is 37.29.

89. Sir 33.27.

90. See the commentary on Jb 40.1, pp. 256–57 above.

first serpent, which, having been poured like poison into Eve, our first mother, overflowed into the whole human race as into a certain sea, on account of which, as it is said in Eph 2,[91] *We are all born children of wrath.* And in a Psalm:[92] *I was conceived in iniquities, and in sins my mother conceived me.* And that place in Jn 9:[93] *You were born entirely in sins.* Because of this infection, it is proven, as if by a second way, that no one born of a woman is able to be perfectly pure (*perfecte mundus*), but something is always found in him that must be purged and punished. And on this point even Job himself agrees with those who were disputing against him. Hence, above in chapter 9 he said:[94] *Indeed, I know that this is so, and that man cannot be justified in relation to God.* For these things that are said here concerning Job have been described poetically and in verse, as Jerome says in the Helmeted Prologue (*proëmio Galeato*).[95] What begins in prose declines in verse and ends with prosaic speech; for it is exceedingly fabulous and fabricated from Jewish lies that Behemoth is an ox whose body weighs seven thousand pounds and, with one neck and one head, contains nine parts in all, and whose tail is like cedar wood. Leviathan, however, is a serpent or a fish with the ring of its body encircling the entire sphere of the earth; it strives to lay hold of and devour the sun's rays and the sun, and so it always drives the sun, fleeing [from it], out of its place. Because of this we understand Leviathan as the first serpent's infection poured into human nature, which does not allow man to be entirely clean and pure, as it is said in Is 64:[96] *You are angry, and we have sinned; and in our sins we have always existed. All of us have become as someone unclean, and all our righteousness is, as it were, the rag of a menstruating woman. We have all fallen as a leaf, and our iniquities, like the wind, have taken us away.*

And this makes the name "Leviathan" clear; for it is inter-

91. Eph 2.3.

92. Ps 50.7.

93. Jn 9.34.

94. Jb 9.2.

95. See Jerome's *Prologus in libro Regum* in Jerome, *Préfaces aux livres de la Bible,* ed. Weber, Gryson, et al., 322–37, esp. 332–33.

96. Is 64.5–6.

preted as their addition, because so great an infection, having been added above human nature, is the cause of all perversity. With respect to this, again it is said that Leviathan is the wickedness of privation, which has been poured into all matter. As the Jewish philosophers—namely, Moses the Egyptian,[97] Abraham of Spain,[98] and Isaac,[99] and Jacob Alkindi,[100] and certain others—have declared, nothing is according to plan.[101] For from this [original divine plan], as from a proper principle, it cannot be concluded that man is not able to be pure, which the Lord certainly intends to show here. Hence, we understand "Leviathan" here as the infection of the first serpent, and accordingly this discussion is divided into two parts. In the first of these, God shows that this infection cannot be atoned for perfectly by human nature. In the second, He shows that it is both rooted and

97. That is, Moses Maimonides. On this notion that Albert here attributes to the Jewish philosophers, namely, that "nothing is according to plan," see, e.g., Maimonides, *Dux* 1.2, 24.

98. As Weiss indicates, Albert seems to be referencing Abraham ibn Daud (d. 1180) and his work *Ha-Emunah ha-Ramah* (*The Exalted Faith*). See also the commentary on Jb 3.8 in *On Job*, vol. 1, 104–5, esp. n. 82.

99. Isaac ben Solomon Israeli (c. 855–955), a Jewish philosopher and physician who wrote several philosophical and medical treatises in Arabic, including the *Book of Definitions* and the *Book of the Elements,* that were subsequently translated into and widely read in Latin and Hebrew. Albert cites Isaac (often as "Isaac Israelita" or "Isaac Iudaeus") throughout his corpus: see, e.g., *Veg.* 1.1.2 and 6.2.15; *Somn.* 3.1. 7; *AL* 11.1.6; *NOA* 2.11; and *Metaph.* 11.2.24. I am grateful to Irven Resnick for his kind assistance in identifying this "Isaac" and these references. For more on Isaac Israeli, see Leonard Levin, R. David Walker, and Shalom Sadik, "Isaac Israeli," *The Stanford Encyclopedia of Philosophy* (Fall 2022 edition), ed. Edward N. Zalta and Uri Nodelman (URL: https://plato.stanford.edu/archives/fall2022/entries/israeli/).

100. The ninth-century Arabic philosopher Abu Yusuf Ya'qub ibn Ishaq al-Kindi (c. 800–870), who was the first philosopher in the Arabic tradition. His Arabic name "Ya'qub" may have been read as "Iacob" in Latin, hence "Jacob Alkindi," as here and, e.g., in *Super IV libros Sententiarum,* Bk II d. 13 art. 2. Al-Kindi was not Jewish, but it may be that Albert here so identifies him by association, specifically because of his influence on Isaac Israeli and other Jewish philosophers. Once again, I am grateful to Irven Resnick for his kind assistance here. For more on al-Kindi, see Peter Adamson, *Al-Kindi* (New York: Oxford University Press, 2007).

101. That is, according to God's original purpose or intention for humankind at creation.

established in human nature, and that it cannot be removed by any pure human (*puro homine*),[102] in that place:[103] *I will not stir him up, like one who is cruel.*

The first part is divided further into two sections. For in the first section, God makes clear what has been said; in the second section, He corrects an error concerning this, in that place:[104] *Remember the battle.*

In the first section, there are two subsections. For in the first, God says generally that Leviathan cannot be atoned for by human nature. In the second, He makes this clear as if inductively through particular methods, in that place:[105] *Can it be that you will put a ring?*

And that is: ***Can it be that you will drag out the Leviathan with a hook,*** as if He were saying: "You will not be able." And by "hook" is understood reason's drawing out (*abstractio*) [Leviathan] according to the uprightness of virtue. For the sins of concupiscence are drawn out with the hook of reason. But the infection that has been poured into nature cannot be dragged out, which is signified in Mt 17,[106] where the Lord told Peter that he should cast a hook into the sea and take the fish that comes up. This is also signified in Tb 6,[107] where Tobias dragged out one fish, but could not draw out all of them. Therefore, total corruption cannot be drawn out, ***and,*** supply: can it be that ***with a cord,*** that is, the band of grace or of virtue. Eccl 4:[108] *A threefold cord is broken with difficulty,* which is, of course, a seizing [of Leviathan] by prevenient grace and subsequent grace and moral virtue, ***you will tie his tongue?*** The "tongue" of a serpent, as Aristotle says,[109] is forked and divided, through which it pours out venom; it cannot

102. For Albert and other scholastic theologians, a "pure human" (*purus homo*) is an ordinary person who is only or merely human, as opposed to Jesus Christ, who is a divine person possessing a fully human nature and thus not a *purus homo.*

103. Jb 41.1.

104. Jb 40.27.

105. Jb 40.21.

106. Mt 17.26.

107. Tb 6.4.

108. Eccl 4.12.

109. Aristotle, *De part. animal.* 2.17.

be tied, but rather the venom poured out through the serpent's tongue always comes forth gradually by nature. For that verse in Jas 3,[110] *The tongue, a restless evil, full of death-dealing venom,* is principally understood as being about this.

And God sets forth specific methods by which the Leviathan is not able to be dragged out: **[21]** ***Can it be that you will put a ring in his nostrils.*** God calls those through which Leviathan sends out his death-dealing spirit "nostrils." Jb 41:[111] *Out of his nostrils proceeds smoke, like that of a pot heated and boiling.* Rv 9:[112] *The smoke of the pit ascended, as the smoke of a great furnace; and the sun and the air were darkened with the smoke of the pit.* Because of his profound wickedness, Leviathan is compared to a pit.

or bore through his jaw with a buckle? as if He were saying: "You will not do it." The "jaw" is used, as Galen says, to confine the teeth, which chew, lest they escape [from the mouth]. And this signifies the power of Leviathan, by which he confines human nature between his teeth. A "buckle," however, is an ornament of someone skillful performing great works of heroic virtue. And the sense is that no work of virtue can bore through Leviathan's jaw, but that he always confines human nature for the purpose of eating. For that verse in Prv 30,[113] *There is a generation that has swords for teeth, and grinds with their molars, to devour the needy from the earth and the poor from among men,* is principally understood as being about this.

And because someone could say that, if Leviathan is not able to be dragged out, he is nevertheless able to be compelled and subjugated, God responds to this and says that he cannot be. And that is: **[22]** ***Can it be that he will multiply his prayers to you,*** supply: as one trampled upon and subjugated, as if He were saying: "No." For he is obstinate and shameless in wickedness. Ps:[114] *The pride of those who hate you rises up continually.* Is 48:[115] *You are stubborn, and your neck is as an iron sinew, and your forehead as bronze.* ***or speak soft***

110. Jas 3.8.
111. Jb 41.11.
112. Rv 9.2.
113. Prv 30.14.
114. Ps 73.23.
115. Is 48.4.

words to you? namely, by showing consideration for and humbly beseeching you; as if He were saying: "He will not do it." Wis 12:[116] *Their natural wickedness could not be changed.* Jb 41:[117] *His heart will be hard as a stone, and it will be firm as a smith's anvil.*

Again, because someone could say that one who has been compelled will enter into a covenant not to injure [anyone] further, God responds that he will not. And this is: **[23]** ***Can it be that he will make a covenant with you,*** as if He were saying: "He will not do it, but he always seeks an occasion to injure." 1 Pt 5:[118] *Your adversary the devil goes around as a roaring lion, seeking whom he may devour.* ***and,*** supply: can it be ***that you will take him as a servant forever?*** namely, so that, having been made subject, he may be a slave, and not so that, being very powerful, he may be a master. Jer 3:[119] *Behold, you have spoken, and you have done evil things, and you have been able.* And instead of words of penance, you have blasphemed with words of pride; you have fulfilled your evil intention, and you have made clear, contrary to your power as a man, that you are able to do what you have discussed by your word.

And because, again, someone could say that if Leviathan is not able to be compelled, he is able to be trapped and therefore to be hindered, God excludes this, adding: **[24]** ***Can it be that you will play with him as with a bird,*** supply: so that you may trap him; as if He were saying: "No." Jer 4:[120] *They are wise in doing evil, but they do not know how to act rightly.*

And because, again, it could be said that many things could be tied up by a strong family, so that Leviathan might not harm them or rage violently, God excludes this, adding: ***or tie him up for your handmaids?*** that is, for the power and strength that serve you as handmaids. Concerning these "handmaids" it is said in Prv 9:[121] *Wisdom has sent her handmaids, so that she might invite to the tower and to the walls of the city.*

And because, again, someone might say that by a multitude of friends helping him he could be cut to pieces and killed,

116. Wis 12.10.
117. Jb 41.15.
118. 1 Pt 5.8.
119. Jer 3.5.
120. Jer 4.22.
121. Prv 9.3.

God excludes this, adding, and it is supplied: Can it be that **[25]** ***friends will cut him to pieces?*** as if He were saying: "No," but he, more savage, cuts every human to pieces. Jb 16:[122] *He has cut me to pieces with wound after wound; He has rushed headlong against me as a giant would do.*

Again, however, it could be said that he could be vanquished by many hired men, and God excludes this, adding, and it is supplied: Can it be that ***merchants*** **(negotiatores)** ***will divide him?*** as if He were saying: "No." And He calls those who, on account of a negotiated price (*propter pretium negotiandum*), had fought against Leviathan by dividing him into parts "merchants" (*negotiatores*). Jb 15:[123] *May he not believe in vain, having been misled by error, that he is going to be redeemed with any price.*

And God adds another method of dragging out: **[26]** ***Can it be that you will fill nets with his skin?*** He calls the many methods and studies (*artes et studia*) aimed at dragging out [Leviathan] "nets," just as the Stoics engaged in many studies in order to master the vices. To be sure, He calls the external surface of Leviathan "skin." And they were not ever able to remove the skin forcibly, so that the skin of the Leviathan did not appear in their conversations; thus, they seemed to be clothed with vices. Rather, on the contrary, Leviathan drew them into his net. Hab 1:[124] *He drew all of them with his dragnet, and he gathered them into his net.* ***and,*** supply: can it be that you will fill ***the cabin*** **(gurgustium)** ***for fish with his head?*** as if He were saying: "You will not do it." A "cabin" (*gurgustium*) is a piece of equipment used by fishermen, interwoven with twigs, [and] plunged into the depths; and the name is artificial, because water moving through the gaps makes a gurgling sound, and hence the piece of equipment is called a *gurgustium.* Big fish put their heads into it, and afterwards, when they have been speared, they are not able to go back out. And this signifies the profound study of the moral sciences. The "head," however, signifies the beginning of the infection of Leviathan, which cannot be prevented by profound studies. Hab 1:[125] *He spreads out his net, and he will never spare the nations from destruction.*

122. Jb 16.15.
123. Jb 15.31.
124. Hab 1.15.
125. Hab 1.17.

After enumerating [these] many methods by which it seemed that Leviathan could be dragged out, God adds generally: **[27]** ***Lay your hand upon him,*** supply: if you will be able, so that what cannot happen in this life may be within your power, of course. Hab 1:[126] *He will triumph over kings, and tyrants will be his buffoons; and he will laugh at every fortification.*

Remember the battle.

Here God removes the error that can arise from the things that have been said. For someone could believe that Leviathan might be able to be dragged out by a certain method mentioned, and thus that the human is clean from sin.

But excluding this, God says: ***Remember the battle,*** that is, of the disputation introduced concerning Behemoth and Leviathan, by which, waging war against you, I have refuted you, and this is what follows:[127] ***and speak no more,*** asserting, of course, that in my judgment you are clean and have been stricken without fault. 1 Kgs 8:[128] *There is no man who does not sin.*

Again, it could be believed that Leviathan should never be purged from human nature. God excludes this, adding: **[28]** ***Behold, his hope,*** namely, by which he hopes that the human race itself will always be held in his power, ***will fail him.***

For in the end, by the last judgment, he will be sent away in the midst of the saints, and this is what follows: ***and,*** that is, because, ***in the sight of all he will be cast down,*** at the last judgment, and his power will be taken away. 1 Cor 15:[129] *Death has been swallowed up in victory. Where, O death, is your victory? Where, O death, is your sting?* Is 30:[130] *At the voice of the Lord the Assyrian will fear being struck by the rod. And His rod's passing over will be firmly established,* that is, determined, *which the Lord will make to rest upon him.* Is 25:[131] *He will cast death down forever; and the Lord God will wipe away every tear from every face, and He will take away the reproach of His people from the whole earth.*

126. Hab 1.10.
127. Here I read with MSS TEFM, which add *et hoc est, quod sequitur.*
128. 1 Kgs 8.46.
129. 1 Cor 15.54–55.
130. Is 30.31–32.
131. Is 25.8.

CHAPTER 41

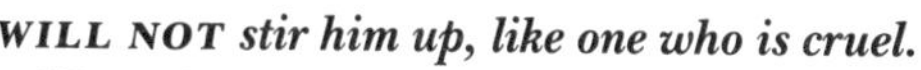

I ***WILL NOT stir him up, like one who is cruel.***

Here God shows that the infection of the serpent has been established and rooted in human nature in such a way that it cannot be cleansed by the power of a pure human (*virtute hominis puri*). And the chapter has two parts: in the first of these God shows what has been said; in the second He shows how in [His] terrible judgment he [that is, Leviathan] will be swept away, in that place:[1] *When he will be destroyed.*

In the first part, there are two things: for first He resolves a certain question that could arise; second, he shows the dreadfulness of the serpent from the taking root and establishment of wickedness, in that place:[2] *Around the circuit of his teeth there is terror.*

In the first of these divisions, there are two things: namely, the solution, and the proof (*ratio*) of the solution, in that place:[3] *Who will reveal the face of his garment?* But the question that can arise is this: Because it is so cruel and so harmful, why does God permit him to be stirred up by the temptation and vexation of the saints? For in doing this, God seems to be cruel toward the saints. And the Lord responds that He permits this as one who is good and wise, although that one [namely, Satan], as cruel, intends only to harm and kill those whom he tempts.

And that is: ***I will not stir him up, like one who is cruel,*** that is, I permit him to be stirred up, and this is a response to what was said [by Job] above in chapter 30:[4] *I will cry out to you, and you will not hear me; I stand up, and you do not consider me. You have*

1. Jb 41.16. For "pure human" (above), see p. 272, n. 102.
2. Jb 41.5.
3. Jb 41.4.
4. Jb 30.20–21.

turned cruel toward me, and in the severity of your hand you are opposed to me. And the Lord responds that, not as one who is cruel, but rather as a devoted father, He stirs him by His permissive power: indeed, He stirs him toward the purification of sin, the practice of virtue, and the preservation of humility. Is 10:[5] *Woe to the Assyrian; he is the rod and staff of my anger; my indignation is in his hand. I will send him to a deceitful nation, and I will deliver him over to the people of my wrath.* And a little beyond this:[6] *But he will not think in this way, and his heart will not consider it so; but his heart will be for fighting, and for the slaughtering of not a few nations.* Prv 13 and Heb 12:[7] *What son is there whom the father does not discipline?* that is, does not permit to be disciplined, because if you are outside of the discipline of which all have been made partakers, then you are illicit offspring and not sons.

And as if someone asked by what power God did this, He adds: ***For who is able to resist my countenance?*** that is, my grimacing, because my facial expression grows angrier; and therefore supply: I am able to snatch away whomever I wish and whenever I wish. Jb 9:[8] *God, whose wrath no one is able to resist.* Rom 9:[9] *Who resists His will?*

And just as someone might ask how, according to justice, God could permit this, since simple and good people, as Job was, do not deserve this, God responds to this, adding that He owes nothing to anyone. And that is: [2] ***And who has given to me previously so that I should repay him?*** Rom 11:[10] *Who has given to Him first, and it will be repaid to him?* And He adds the reason for this: ***All things that are under heaven are mine.*** And therefore supply: No one precedes me with regard to the giving of gifts. Jn 17:[11] *All things that are mine are yours, and yours are mine, and I have been glorified in them.* Mt 28:[12] *All power in heaven and on earth has been*

5. Is 10.5–6.

6. Is 10.7.

7. The following words are from Heb 12.7. Similarly, Prv 13.24 reads: *He who spares the rod hates his son, but he who loves him trains him vehemently.*

8. Jb 9.13.

9. Rom 9.19.

10. Rom 11.35.

11. Jn 17.10.

12. Mt 28.18.

given to me. 1 Chr 29:[13] *All things are yours, and we have given to you what we received from your hand.*

Moreover, God adds how according to such power He restrains him and his wickedness: [3] ***I will not spare him, nor his mighty words,*** that is, because of the words with which he tosses power to and fro, namely, how he is able to make the human race subject to himself, which words are set forth in Is 10:[14] *Are not my princes at the same time kings also?* And a little beyond this:[15] *By the strength of my hand I have done it, and by my wisdom I have understood; I have removed the boundaries of the nations, and I have plundered their princes, and as a strong man I have pulled down those who sat on high.* For God evacuates this power quickly. ***and framed to make supplication;*** for at length, he cleverly turns back to supplication, lest he be hindered by sustaining an injury. According to Lk 8,[16] the demoniac, in whom an evil spirit had been firmly established, *when he saw Jesus, fell down before him; and crying out with a loud voice, he said: What do I have to do with you, Jesus, Son of the Most High God? I beseech you, do not torment me.* For he meant that he would be tormented if the spirit ceased from harming him. Hence, in that very place:[17] *For He commanded the unclean spirit to go out of the man;* on account of such words, therefore, Jesus does not dismiss the spirit, but rather restricts his power. Gregory says:[18] He brings forth power in this, that He says *framed to make supplication,* because many believe that they are heard favorably because of framed words, but this is not to pray rightly. Hence, Gregory [also] says:[19] "In fact, to pray truly is to lament bitterly with compunction, not to sound out framed words."

Because someone might say, moreover, that he [Satan] is so cunning that his ways cannot be comprehended, God adds: [4] ***Who will reveal,*** that is, who will be able to reveal, ***the face,*** that is, the outward appearance, according to which he rules himself,

13. 1 Chr 29.14.
14. Is 10.9.
15. Is 10.13.
16. Lk 8.28.
17. Lk 8.29.
18. See Gregory, *Mor.* 33.23.43.
19. Gregory, *Mor.* 33.23.43.

of his garment? so that he might deceive under the appearance of the good. 2 Cor 11:[20] *Satan himself transforms himself into an angel of light. It is not surprising, therefore, if his ministers are transformed as ministers of justice.* But no one can remove his cunning except God alone, who examines the intentions of the heart.

And, expanding on this further, God adds: ***and who,*** supply: except me, ***will go into the middle of his mouth,*** namely, by which he speaks deceptively to the human, either flattering him by persuasion or deceiving him with promises. Moreover, he "goes into" when he reveals the intrinsic wickedness to which he intends to persuade [the human]. Ps:[21] *His words are smoother than oil, and they are darts.* Jer 9:[22] *Their tongue, a piercing arrow, has spoken deceit.* But because he does this by flattery, he tempts frequently and through the enticements of the flesh, just as he tempted blessed Job through the tongue of his wife; therefore, it is said in Prv 7:[23] *Say to wisdom: You are my sister; and call prudence your friend, that she may keep you from the woman who is not yours and from the stranger who makes her words sweet.*

And, expanding on this further, He adds: [5] ***Who,*** supply: except me, ***will open the doors of his face,*** that is, openings through which one enters to get to know him inside his face. For he presents a flattering (*blandum*) face and pours out poison on the inside. Prv 23:[24] *It goes in pleasantly* (blande), *but in the end it will bite like a snake.* Thus, with a flattering face Ishmael son of Nethaniah came to Gedaliah son of Ahikam and killed him, according to Jer 41;[25] in the same way, according to 2 Sm 3,[26] Joab came to Abner and, when Abner had been led off the road peacefully, killed him. And this is the sense: that in all these cases God, not as one who is cruel, but as one who is devoted and prudent, stirs him; and as one who is powerful, He is able to restrict him when He wishes; and as one who is wise, He knows how to meet his cunning.

20. 2 Cor 11.14–15.
21. Ps 54.22.
22. Jer 9.8.
23. Prv 7.4–5.
24. Prv 23.31–32.
25. Jer 41.2.
26. 2 Sm 3.27.

Around the circuit.

Here God shows the frightful wickedness of the serpent from his taking root and establishment, and He describes it in five ways, namely: from the composition of his body; from his frightful appearance, in that place:[27] *His sneezing;* from his harmful effect, in that place:[28] *In his neck;* from the joining together of his members, in that place:[29] *The members of his flesh;* and from the hardening of his heart, in that place:[30] *His heart.*

And that is: ***Around the circuit of his teeth,*** namely, the upper and lower ones, ***there is terror;*** that is, so big, so strong, and so sharp are his teeth that they strike fear in those who see him. Moreover, the methods of harming humans by which he chews them up are called "teeth," which blessed Gregory designates when he says:[31] Everything that he seizes by oppression, everything on which he makes a treacherous attack by hovering around,[32] everything that he terrifies by threatening, everything that he flatters by persuading, everything that he crushes by despairing of, everything that he deceives by promising, and as long as he does each one of these openly or secretly or falsely or truly, they become[33] many teeth; and if such actions are multiplied by [various] methods, then his teeth become innumerable. Dn 7:[34] *The beast, terrible and extraordinary and exceedingly strong, had iron teeth, chewing up and breaking* [*some*] *into pieces, and trampling upon the rest with its feet.*

And concerning the external composition [of the serpent], God adds further: **[6]** ***His body,*** that is, the entire mass of vices regarding external things, ***is like molten shields,*** that is, bronze shields or shields cast from bronze. These shields signify the protection by which he defends himself in his wickedness; for Leviathan, just as he has been widely diffused among humans with

27. Jb 41.9.
28. Jb 41.13.
29. Jb 41.14.
30. Jb 41.15.
31. See Gregory, *Mor.* 33.27.48.
32. Here I read *circumvolando insidiatur* with MSS EFM rather than *insidiando circumvolat* with Weiss's edition.
33. Here I read *fiunt* with MSS ETFM rather than *sunt* with Weiss's edition.
34. Dn 7.7.

the mighty sound of assaulting those who are good and defending his own malice, makes use of these defenses. Hence, under another metaphor it is said of him in 1 Sm 17:[35] *A round shield of bronze protected his shoulders.* What is here under the figure of Leviathan is described there under the figure of a giant.[36] And because the serpent is scaly, it explains what has been said: ***and,*** that is, ***joined together*** with regard to the external ***by scales,*** which it uses as shields, ***pressing hard against one another,*** so that the end of one overlaps the beginning of the next, of course. And these scales signify his defense having been joined together against plans (*rationibus*) [against him] from all sides, so that he may be everywhere invulnerable to the plans of those attacking and laying hold of him, of course. The same thing is signified under another metaphor in 1 Sm 17,[37] where it is said that Goliath *was clothed with a coat of mail having scales,* so that, to be sure, he would be everywhere invulnerable to David.

And expanding on this, God adds: [7] ***One is joined to another,*** through convergence, of course, ***and not even,*** that is, so much as, ***air can come between them,*** by which they may be separated, of course. Ps:[38] *They came together as one against the Lord and against His Christ.*

And expanding on this further, He adds: [8] ***One,*** that is, the defending of one vice, ***will adhere to another,*** that is, the defending of another vice, ***and holding*** [***one another***], to be sure, as hooks[39] mutually connected to one another and joined together with glue, ***they will by no means be separated,*** that is, be able to be separated, so that, protected on all sides, he may never be able to be touched by the arrows of the truth, of course; for in such a way impiety is armed against the truth. Hos 13:[40] *The iniquity of Ephraim has been bound together; his sin has been hidden.*

[9] ***His sneezing.***

Here God describes the frightful appearance [of the serpent]

35. 1 Sm 17.6.
36. Namely, Goliath: see 1 Sm 17.4–11.
37. 1 Sm 17.5.
38. Ps 2.2.
39. Here I read *ansae* with MS E rather than *ansis* with Weiss's edition.
40. Hos 13.12.

in five ways, namely: with regard to what proceeds from his inmost parts, with regard to his eyes, with regard to the smoke of his mouth, with regard to the air (*spiritu*) of his nostrils, and with regard to his breath or exhaling. And that is: ***His sneezing***. "Sneezing" is the [expulsion of the] refuse of the brain, when vapor or ventosity that has been lifted up from the deepest parts to the top of the head, with clumps in the head being brought together with one another and bound up and suddenly expanding, is cast out through the nostrils. And this signifies the indignation that Leviathan suddenly casts out and blows forth against the human race; hence, God says: ***is like the splendor of fire,*** for he breathes out fire and blows it forth among those who are good. 2 Mc 9:[41] *Moreover, being filled with pride, he was breathing out fire in his rage against the Jews.*

And God adds the description with regard to his eyes: **[*and*] *his eyes,*** gleaming with anger, of course, ***like the eyelids of dawn***. For at "dawn," light mingled with darkness twinkles; in the same way, in one who is enraged the fury of his face flashes under the darkness of obscurity. Est 15:[42] *When he* [*King Ahasuerus*] *had lifted up his face and with fiery eyes had shown the fury of his heart, the queen collapsed, and her color turned pale, and she rested her fallen head on her handmaid.*

And concerning his mouth, God adds: **[10] *Out of his mouth proceed lamps* (lampades)**. *Lampas* in Greek is the same as *flamma* in Latin, and by these words is understood anger set ablaze, and by others[43] are understood things burning up completely in the midst of anger, so that of God Himself it can be said: *His wrath burns and is heavy to bear,* according to Is 30,[44] and that place in Song 8:[45] *His lamps are lamps of fire and flames.* And this is what follows: ***like torches of kindled fire***. "Torches" are pieces of burning wood, because by means of fire, which he has conceived in his heart, he launches them[46] against others through words, so that

41. 2 Mc 9.7.

42. Est 15.10.

43. That is, by other related words, such as *ardens,* which appears in Is 30.27, quoted by Albert immediately below.

44. Is 30.27.

45. Song 8.6.

46. That is, torches.

by a similar fire those having been enraged may set the innocent on fire and burn them up. Hos 7:[47] *They are all adulterers, like an oven that has been kindled by the cook.* And a little beyond this:[48] *He slept all night and was baking them; in the morning he himself was kindled as a flaming fire. They were all heated like an oven.*

And concerning his nostrils, God adds, and that is: [11] ***Out of his nostrils proceeds smoke,*** and He explains the manner: ***like that of a pot heated and boiling.*** "A pot heated and boiling" holds heat in its innermost parts and exhibits it through smoke and in vessels bubbling up higher. In the same way, raging Leviathan, as long as he conceives within himself anger against good people, displays this anger outwardly through the smoke of evil contrivance and in vessels of cruel words. Jer 1, where the anger of the king of Babylon against the people of God is described, signifies this very well, saying:[49] *I see a heated pot, and its face from the face of the north.*

And concerning his exhaling, God adds: [12] ***His breath,*** supply: blowing, ***makes coals burn.*** Here the sending forth of evil counsels is called "breath," and "coals" are the evil counselors whom Leviathan sets on fire and "makes burn." Now his breath, by the fire of his own heart, inflames evil counselors for the purpose of contriving most wicked counsels, by which he is able to harm those who are just. Is 54:[50] *Behold, I have created the smith who blows the coals in the fire.* And expanding on this, He adds: ***[and] a flame comes forth out of his mouth,*** that is, anger similar to a flame. Is 30:[51] *He will show the terror of his arm in the threatening of fury and the flame of an engulfing fire.*

And God adds concerning his neck and the harmfulness of its effect, and that is: [13] ***In his neck,*** erect and proud and stubborn, to be sure, ***strength,*** that is, inflexibility with regard to humbling, ***will dwell,*** namely, by reason of a habit, not by reason of the light touch of temptation. Jb 15:[52] *He has run against God with an erect*

47. Hos 7.4.
48. Hos 7.6–7.
49. Jer 1.13.
50. Is 54.16.
51. Is 30.30.
52. Jb 15.26.

neck, and with a fat neck he is armed. ***and poverty goes before his face.*** For his presence leads to poverty. Jl 2:[53] *Before its face a devouring fire, and after it a burning flame: the land is like a garden of pleasure before it, and behind it a desolate wilderness.*

And God adds concerning the joining of his members, which move all things and inspire them to harm; these members are either particular evil ways, or wicked people of the same mind as one another. And that is: **[14]** ***The members of his flesh.*** "Flesh," as the natural philosophers (*physici*) say, is the medium of touch, and it signifies those who, by the gentle inspiration and animation of Leviathan, take on his disposition (*sensum*), and they are supple to his every impression. Concerning these, it is said in Jn 6:[54] *The flesh profits nothing.* These people are called animals, because brute animals perceive (*sentiunt*) nothing but those things that are of the flesh. 1 Cor 2:[55] *The natural man* (animalis homo) *does not perceive the things that are of the Spirit of God.* And this is what He adds: ***are joined together with one another,*** that is, acting together, just as the throat with drunkenness, and the throat and drunkenness with fornication. Ex 32:[56] *The people sat down to eat and drink, and they rose up to play,* that is, to fornicate, as the Gloss says on that passage.[57] Dn 13:[58] *We eagerly desire you; on account of this, comply with us and have sexual intercourse with us.* And He adds:

Against him.

And God says this concerning the hardening of his heart; and He speaks of two things, namely: against what it is hardened, and the hardening of his heart. And that is: ***He,*** namely, God, ***will send lightning bolts,*** as threats of terror, of course, ***against him, and they will not be carried,*** for God does not threaten good people, but rather the wicked, ***to another place,*** supply: except over him.

53. Jl 2.3.

54. Jn 6.64.

55. 1 Cor 2.14.

56. Ex 32.6.

57. See PL 113:287 and *Biblia Latina cum Glossa Ordinaria: Facsimile Reprint of the Editio Princeps,* vol. 1, p. 191, neither of which contains the specific gloss on Ex 32.6 that Albert indicates here.

58. Dn 13.20.

Wis 5:[59] *Bolts of lightning will go straight out of the clouds, and they will be shot out as if from a well*—that is, strongly—*bent bow, and they will fly to a fixed place,* so that they may certainly hit the mark of the one who shoots the arrows, of course. As a result of these [lightning bolts], however, he neither repents nor is softened.

And this is what follows: [15] ***His heart will be hard.*** Ex 7:[60] *Pharaoh's heart was hardened,* so that threats would not heal it. ***as a stone,*** which cannot be softened. Ex 10:[61] *I have hardened his heart, and that of his servants, so that I might work these my signs in him.* ***and it will be firm as a smith's anvil,*** which, the more it is hammered, the more it is hardened and blunts the hammer that strikes it; and this signifies the hard hearts possessed by Leviathan, which, the more they are beaten, the more they are hardened in hatred of the one who beats them. Jer 7:[62] *They have hardened their necks, and they have done worse than their fathers,* for the words of the Lord are most threatening, like a hammer. Jer 23:[63] *Are not my words, says the Lord, like a burning fire and like a hammer that pounds the rock to pieces?* The "anvil," moreover, is a hard heart, on which the hammer of God's word forges; and the more it forges in a hard human, the more it is pressed together, so that it does not receive the form of God's word. Sir 38:[64] *The blacksmith, sitting by the anvil and considering the ironwork,* but the anvil does not receive that work.

[16] ***When he will be destroyed.***

Here God shows how in His awe-inspiring judgment Leviathan will be swept away, and two things are spoken of, namely: His judgment; and the strength of him against whom His judgment is brought forth, in that place:[65] *When the sword will have overtaken him.*

And that is: ***When he will be destroyed,*** in accordance with God's awe-inspiring judgment, of course, when he will lose his power, ***the angels,*** that is, the holy ones who see his condemnation, ***will***

59. Wis 5.22.
60. Ex 7.13.
61. Ex 10.1.
62. Jer 7.26.
63. Jer 23.29.
64. Sir 38.29.
65. Jb 41.17.

fear, and, being terrified, when his condemnation has been seen, of course, ***they will be purified,*** if, in fact, what is able to be purged in them will be purged by this fear. Is 33:[66] *Behold, those who see will cry out; the angels of peace will weep bitterly.* Sir 1:[67] *The fear of the Lord drives out sin.*

And God adds a description of his power and strength, by which he sets himself against every good thing. And this part is divided into two. First, He sets forth this description in particular; and second, in general, in that place:[68] *There is no power on earth.* In the first of these subdivisions, there are again two things. For first God shows how Leviathan attacks the arms of the holy ones; second, how he attacks the holy ones themselves, in that place:[69] *The archer will not put him to flight.* And that is:

[17] ***When [the sword] will have overtaken.***

And this is a continuation of the foregoing, as if it were saying: "Certainly by an awe-inspiring judgment Leviathan will be swept away, and it will be reserved for him because he wished neither to be terrified nor corrected by the judgment of the holy ones."

And that is: ***When,*** namely, before the judgment, ***the sword,*** of the attack of the holy ones, of course, ***will have overtaken him, it will not be able to stand firm,*** the sword, of course, for it repels all the blows of such a sword. Ps:[70] *Gird your sword on your thigh, O most powerful.* Song 3:[71] *Behold, sixty strong men from the most powerful of Israel surround the bed of Solomon, all holding swords and most skilled in warfare.* The sixty strong men are those who refer all things that were made in the world during the six days to the Decalogue, and, fortified in this, they assail Leviathan with the sword of God's word. Eph 6:[72] *And the sword of the Spirit, which is the word of God.* ***nor a spear,*** supply: will be able to stand firm, for he turns aside from and does not care about a spear. But a spear is power striking from long range, and it is said to strike from

66. Is 33.7.
67. Sir 1.27.
68. Jb 41.24.
69. Jb 41.19.
70. Ps 44.4.
71. Song 3.7–8.
72. Eph 6.17.

long range because it strikes according to eternal truth. Jb 39:[73] *Above it the quiver will rattle; the spear and seething shield will glitter.* 2 Sm 1:[74] *His spear has not turned back.* ***nor a breastplate,*** supply: will be able to stand firm. The "breastplate" signifies the justice of the holy ones. Wis 5:[75] *He will put on justice as a breastplate.* And the sense is that neither is Leviathan wounded by the sword of God's word, nor does he feel contrition by the spear, nor is he turned back by his breastplate to penance, from which place he should be spared the most extreme judgment. Jb 21:[76] *The wicked man is preserved for the day of perdition, and he will be led to the day of wrath,* and Jb 18:[77] *On this day the youngest will be amazed, and horror will fall upon the foremost ones.*

And God adds the reason for this: **[18]** ***For he will count iron as chaff,*** that is, he regards all laws and authorities that aim to subdue as weak chaff that is easily combustible and consumable, and therefore he does not care about them. ***and,*** supply: he will regard ***brass as rotten wood,*** that is, resounding in the eloquence of the holy ones, since nevertheless it has been written of the saints in Dt 33:[78] *Let him dip his foot in oil. His shoe will be iron and brass.* For holy men soften with oil the foot of rectitude on which they stand, so that it may not be unnecessarily heavy, and they have an iron and brass shoe in the strictness of judgment and truth because they establish justice in the truth of authority, which tames them, and in the resounding of preaching, exhortation, and disputation. But Leviathan considers these as "chaff" and as "rotten wood" and as nothing that can prevail against him.

And God adds how Leviathan withstands the saints: **[19]** ***The archer will not put him to flight.*** The "archer" is a virile and vigorous man, shooting sharp arrows from the hidden senses of Scripture and puncturing the hearts of sinners; these archers have been given to the Church against the deceitful tongue of

73. Jb 39.23–24.
74. 2 Sm 1.22.
75. Wis 5.19.
76. Jb 21.30.
77. Jb 18.20.
78. Dt 33.24–25.

Leviathan. Hence in a Psalm it is said:[79] *What will be given to you, or what will be assigned to you, to a deceitful tongue? The sharp arrows of the Mighty One.* 2 Sm 1:[80] *The arrow of Jonathan never turned back.* These archers do not put Leviathan to flight, but rather he always rages and attacks.

to him the stones of the sling have been turned into stubble, so that he does not care about their blows. A "sling" is drawn around in a circle by two cords, and, when one cord is released and the other is held back, it casts out a stone and strikes. And this signifies knowledge greatly strengthened by reasoning and being drawn around by investigation, which comes about by two cords, namely, by the character of Scripture and by the reasoning of investigation. Once Scripture is uttered, it casts out the stone of clear and shattering truth and strikes accurately. Jgs 20:[81] *Slinging stones so accurately that they could strike even a single hair, and by no means miss by going to either side.* With a sling of this kind and such stones David struck down the Philistine, according to 1 Sm 17,[82] but such a sling and its blow Leviathan does not regard, except as stubble easily blown away: **[20]** ***He will consider the hammer as stubble.*** The "hammer" is the powerful word of the Lord's threat. Jer 23:[83] *Are not my words a fire and like a hammer that pounds the rocks to pieces?* But Leviathan rejects this as "stubble" because he perceives its blow very little; for he has been hardened against all truth, because, as it is said in Is 28:[84] *He has put his hope in lies, and he has been protected by falsehood,* and in Jn 8:[85] *He is a liar and the father of lies.*

and he will mock the one brandishing the spear, that is to say, the divine wrath threatening him. Wis 5:[86] *He will sharpen his awful wrath into a lance.* 2 Sm 23:[87] *All transgressors will be rooted out like thorns, which are not removed with the hands. And if anyone wishes to*

79. Ps 114.3–4.
80. 2 Sm 1.22.
81. Jgs 20.16.
82. 1 Sm 17.49.
83. Jer 23.29.
84. Is 28.15.
85. Jn 8.44.
86. Wis 5.21.
87. 2 Sm 23.6–7.

touch them, he must be armed with iron and the shaft of a lance; but, having been set on fire, they will be burned to nothing.

And God adds how Leviathan holds himself with respect to the examples of the saints: **[21]** ***The rays of the sun,*** that is, the examples of the saints, ***will be under him,*** supply: having oppressed him. Mt 5:[88] *So let your light shine before men that they may see your good works and glorify your Father who is in heaven.* Leviathan suppresses those rays so that they are not able to shine forth with unimpeded light. Is 13:[89] *The stars of heaven and their brilliance will not distribute their light; the sun has been made dark in its rising, and the moon will not shine with its light.*

And because someone could say that this vexation will be redeemed by a smaller price, God excludes this, adding: ***and he will strew gold under himself like dirt,*** that is, in comparison to following his own will, he considers gold to be dirt. Wis 7:[90] *I declared riches to be nothing in comparison to her.* And after a few words:[91] *All gold in comparison to her is but a little sand, and silver in view of her will be considered as dirt.*

God adds, moreover, how strong Leviathan is in his raging: **[22]** ***He will cause the deep sea,*** that is, the depths of the heart's bitterness, ***to grow hot like a pot,*** which contains heat in its depths. Is 57:[92] *The heart of the wicked person is like the raging sea, which is unable to be at rest.* Jb 30:[93] *My inner parts have begun to boil without any rest.* For Satan, when his own spirit has been ignited, so sets fire to the tinder (*fomitem*) that the whole heart grows hot within for evil.

And expanding on this, He adds: ***and he will make it,*** the depths of the sea or of the heart, ***as when ointments boil,*** which, when they "boil," breathe out widely. And God intends to say that just as ointments soften and, when they are boiling hot, seize the body by its spirit and turn the body's members to itself, in this way the wickedness established in the tinder (*in fomite*)

88. Mt 5.16.
89. Is 13.10.
90. Wis 7.8.
91. Wis 7.9.
92. Is 57.20.
93. Jb 30.27.

softens all the strength of man and possesses it and turns it to itself. These are the ointments of harlots, among which Asa died according to 2 Chr 16.[94] For "Asa" means raising up a creature (*facturam*), because he raised and lifted up concupiscence, in which he was made (*factus est*), to greater strength.

Moreover, concerning the strength of Leviathan, God even adds: **[23]** ***A path will shine,*** that is, will appear, ***after him.*** Indeed, through whichever paths he crawls, he leaves his poison behind him, causing the paths to shine. Jl 2:[95] *They will advance on their roads, and they will not deviate from their paths.*

And God speaks of the instruments of Leviathan: ***he will consider the abyss,*** that is, the depths of the human heart, ***as growing old,*** that is, failing and raving. For Leviathan enters and deceives those who are profound in heart and astute. Dn 13:[96] *Unfairness came forth from the older judges, who seemed to rule the people.*

Then, to this [description of Leviathan's power and strength] through so many separate particulars, God adds in general: **[24]** ***There is no power on earth,*** that is, earthly power, ***that may be compared to him,*** that is, that may be able to be compared to him, for he is stronger than all earthly powers. ***who,*** that is, because he ***was made to fear no one.*** Hab 1:[97] *He is horrible and terrible, and from his very self,* that is, from his free will, *judgment and burden will come forth.* **[25]** ***He sees every lofty thing,*** for the face that is proud rises up to lofty and high things. Is 2:[98] *The lofty eyes of man are humbled.* Is 10:[99] *I will punish the fruit of the proud heart of the king of Assyria, and the glory of the haughtiness of his eyes.*

he is king, as if a lord who both rules and is preeminent, ***over all the children of pride.*** They are called "the children of pride" in whom nothing but pride has been born, and who have been formed entirely according to the pattern of pride, concerning whom it is said in the Psalm:[100] *The pride of those who hate you rises*

94. 2 Chr 16.12–14.
95. Jl 2.7.
96. Dn 13.5.
97. Hab 1.7.
98. Is 2.11.
99. Is 10.12.
100. Ps 73.23.

up continually. The king of these is Leviathan; hence Is 14 says:[101] *I will ascend into heaven, I will exalt my throne above the stars of heaven; I will sit on the mountain of the covenant; on the sides of the north I will be like the Most High.*

But from all these words God intends to prove nothing except that the infection of the first serpent is so great that no pure human (*homo purus*) will be able to be clean, and so a great part of the disputation has been determined.[102] For Eliphaz and Bildad and Zophar and Elihu said these things and therefore affirmed that blessed Job, as unclean, had been stricken for sin. Job also, above in chapter 9, said:[103] *Indeed, I know that this is so, and that man cannot be justified in relation to God;* but he added that he did not have such great sin that, according to the order of human justice, it ought to have been punished by such great misfortune, and therefore [he concluded] that human life is not governed according to the order of human justice. It was determined, therefore, by the word of the Lord that no one is clean from filth, which was introduced, as it were, as a middle course and as evidence that the rule of divine providence is similar to the rule of human providence (nothing remains to be determined except whether the rule of divine providence is similar to the rule of human providence). This Job denied and his four friends affirmed, for then it was responded both to those arguments proposed earlier, which the four friends introduced, and to the conclusion that they intended to prove. And in this the whole disputation will have been determined. Toward this end, therefore, the next chapter is introduced.

101. Is 14.13–14.

102. On the "pure human," see the commentary on 40.20 above, p. 272, n. 102.,

103. Jb 9.2.

CHAPTER 42

HEN JOB *responded to the Lord and said.* Here the principal question is determined as well as those things relevant to the question, and therefore the chapter is divided into three parts. In the first of these, what was principally being inquired about is determined. But because a true solution is, as Aristotle says,[1] a manifestation of what is false according to which it happens to be false, therefore in the second part [God] makes clear the false that is related to the question, in that place:[2] *And after the Lord had spoken.* Because Bildad had said—and Zophar had agreed about this, and Eliphaz and Elihu as well—that if a just person is ever permitted to be punished, he is compensated for this with a reward, this is shown to be true in the third part, in that place:[3] *And the Lord added.*

In the first part, there are three things: for in the first place, the outstanding wisdom of God is made clear; second, Job's penance concerning imperfect expression; third, the true determination of the question.

And that is: ***Then Job,*** in the nominative case,[4] ***responded to the Lord and said.*** Indeed, already having been instructed by the Lord concerning the ways of His providence, Job was able to respond, which he could not do before he was instructed. There is a parallel in Dn 10, where Daniel said to the angel:[5] *Speak, my Lord, because you have strengthened me,* as if he were saying: "If you

1. Aristotle, *SE* 18.
2. Jb 42.7.
3. Jb 42.10.
4. Because the name Job is indeclinable in Latin (*Iob*), Albert helpfully specifies that "Job" is the subject of the action here.
5. Dn 10.19.

had not strengthened me, I would not have been able to hear your words, nor to respond."

And Job confesses the omnipotence and wisdom of God, adding: [2] ***I know that you can do all things,*** and therefore also with regard to human affairs you can do what you will. Est 13:[6] *O Lord, Almighty King, all things have been established in your power, and there is no one who can resist your will, if you determine to save Israel.* On account of this, your governing [of all things] is ordered according to your will. Rom 9:[7] *Why do you seek to know more? Does He not have mercy on whomever He wills, and harden whomever He wills?*

And concerning God's wisdom, Job adds: ***and,*** supply: I know that ***no thought is hidden from you.*** Hence the Gloss on that place in Rom,[8] *God delivered them over to a reprobate sense,* says:[9] God works in the hearts of humans to bend their wills to whatever He wills. Heb 4:[10] *All things are naked and manifest to His eyes, to whom we must give an account.* Sir 23:[11] *All things were known to the Lord God before they were created; so, too, after they were perfected, He beholds all things.* Ps:[12] *He who has formed their hearts one by one, and who understands all their works.*

When the truth has been confessed, God expresses his anger at those denying it, for what follows must be read with contempt: [3] ***Who is this.*** Jer 49:[13] *Who is that shepherd and rustic?* ***who conceals,*** that is, who thinks to conceal from me, ***counsel,*** that is, the hidden determination of his own heart, ***without knowledge?*** my knowledge, of course; that is: as if I were ignorant of the counsel of his heart. Sir 23:[14] *The eyes of the Lord are far brighter than the sun, looking around and seeing all the ways of men.* Therefore,

6. Est 13.9.

7. Rom 9.18–19.

8. Rom 1.28.

9. The following gloss appears not in the *GO* on Rom 1.28 (PL 114:474), but rather on Rom 1.24 (*Tradidit illos Deus in desideria cordis eorum . . .*; PL 114:473).

10. Heb 4.13.

11. Sir 23.29.

12. Ps 32.15.

13. Jer 49.19.

14. Sir 23.28.

he who says that the Lord is ignorant of human deeds must be despised.

Then, concerning penance, Job adds: ***Therefore, I have spoken foolishly,*** in this: of course, that I said that I had been afflicted with a judgment that was not fair; but, in fact, whatever you do, O Lord, you who can do all things and know all things, you do with a fair judgment. Is 32:[15] *The fool says foolish things.* Ps:[16] *You are just, O Lord, and your judgment is right.* ***and things that exceeded my knowledge beyond measure,*** for divine things exceed our knowledge beyond measure. Rom 11:[17] *O the depth of the riches of the wisdom and the knowledge of God! How incomprehensible are His judgments, and how unsearchable His ways!*

And, concerning the determination of the question, Job adds: **[4]** ***Hear,*** that is, declare judgment according to your truth, which you have taught me, ***and I will speak,*** because I am not able to speak otherwise. Gn 18:[18] *I will speak to the Lord, although I am dust and ashes.*

He adds, moreover, how he is able to speak: ***I will question you,*** by seeking the truth from you yourself, of course, so that you may illumine me. Nm 22:[19] *Will I be able to speak anything other than what God puts in my mouth?* And that is what follows: ***and you respond to me,*** through illumination, of course. 1 Sm 3:[20] *Speak, Lord, for your servant is listening.*

And Job determines the question according to what he has heard from the Lord. Is 50:[21] *He awakens in the morning, in the morning He awakens my ear so that I may hear Him as a master.* **[5]** ***With the hearing of the ear,*** that is, with the hearing of a general narrative by means of tradition (*per famam*), ***I have heard you,*** at first, of course, when I murmured[22] about my scourges, supposing that you governed human affairs according to the order of

15. Is 32.6.
16. Ps 118.137.
17. Rom 11.33.
18. Gn 18.27.
19. Nm 22.38.
20. 1 Sm 3.9, 10.
21. Is 50.4.
22. Here I follow MSS TEFM, which add *sc. quando murmuravi sc.,* instead of Weiss's edition, which reads simply *primo de flagellis.*

human justice and therefore that I had been stricken unjustly. Jb 36:[23] *Remember that you do not know His work, about which men have sung.* Jb 28:[24] *We have heard of His fame* (famam). ***but now,*** after your instruction, of course, ***my eye,*** intellectual, of course, ***sees you,*** in the clear truth, of course; supply: and therefore, I now recognize that your governing is dissimilar from every mode of human government, considering that, in governing, you look to nothing except the order of [your] wisdom and purpose. Hence, Dionysius also in his letter to Apollophanes says:[25] You have given your hands to the truth, and you have been freed from the darkness of falsehood.

And Job revokes what he had spoken imperfectly, and that is: **[6]** ***Therefore, I blame myself,*** by revoking what was spoken foolishly, of course, ***and I do penance,*** inflicting punishment on my very self by means of satisfaction and compunction because I have failed. Hence, he said above in chapter 39:[26] *I, who have spoken thoughtlessly, how can I answer?* ***in dust and ashes.*** Indeed, "ashes" and a hair shirt are the armor of penance. Jon 3:[27] *The penitent king of Nineveh dressed himself in sackcloth and sat in ashes.*

[7] ***And after.***

Here God begins to make clear the false, which was contained in the accusations of Job's friends. But because [to speak] what is false is a sin in three ways,[28] therefore three things are spoken of here, namely: the condemnation of the false; the commanding of penance for the sin, in that place:[29] *Therefore, take;* and the satisfaction for the offense by fulfilling the penance commanded, in that place:[30] *So they departed.*

And that is: ***After the Lord had spoken,*** through inspiration, of course. Hos 2:[31] *I will lead her into the wilderness, and I will speak*

23. Jb 36.24.
24. Jb 28.22.
25. Dionysius, Epistle 11 *Ad Apollophanem.*
26. Jb 39.34.
27. Jon 3.6.
28. Here I read *in tribus modis* with MS E, rather than *moribus* with Weiss's edition.
29. Jb 42.8.
30. Jb 42.9.
31. Hos 2.14.

to her heart. ***these words to Job,*** concerning the doctrine of His own governing and providence, of course. Nm 12:[32] *I speak to him mouth to mouth.* **He said to Eliphaz the Temanite.** God speaks to Eliphaz because he was the principal [interlocutor], so that His words may pass over through him to the others. Mk 13:[33] *What I say to one, I say to all.* ***My fury is raging against you,*** for the truth rages against falsehood and condemns it. Prv 8:[34] *I detest arrogance and pride, and a perverse way, and a double-tongued mouth.* Ps:[35] *You will destroy all who speak a lie.* ***and against your two friends,*** who agreed with you, of course.

And God adds the reason: ***because you have not spoken what is right before me,*** that is, what is true concerning my providence, ***as my servant Job has,*** who alone is a witness to the truth. Wis 1:[36] *He who speaks unjust things is not able to hide, neither will the rebuking judgment of God pass him by.* Rv 3:[37] *He says these things: Amen, the faithful and true witness.* But because God wills that no one should perish, but return to life through penance, He therefore commands penance for such sins, adding: [8] ***Therefore, take for yourselves,*** that is, for the remission of your sin, ***seven bulls,*** by which is signified the slaughtering of stiff-necked pride among the seven [deadly] sins, ***and seven rams.*** "Rams," which strike with their horns, signify the violent and obstinate justification of falsehood against the truth, [justification] which also must be slaughtered; and God designates "seven" because four people were attacking Job,[38] and they were attacking him in three ways, namely, by assertion, by reasoning, and by reproach. Dn 3:[39] *In a contrite soul and a spirit of humility may we be accepted by you, as in holocausts of rams and bulls.* ***and go to my servant Job,*** because you are unworthy to present the offering. Sir 34:[40] *The Most High does not approve the gifts of the wicked.* ***and offer for yourselves,*** to Job himself, of course,

32. Nm 12.8.
33. Mk 13.37.
34. Prv 8.13.
35. Ps 5.7.
36. Wis 1.8.
37. Rv 3.14.
38. Namely, Eliphaz, Bildad, Zophar, and Elihu.
39. Dn 3.39–40.
40. Sir 34.23.

a holocaust, that is, the matter (*materiam*) of the holocaust, because you are unworthy to present the offering. Sir 34:[41] *God will not consider the oblations of the wicked, nor will He be appeased for sins by the multitude of their sacrifices.* ***And my servant Job will pray for you.*** Jas 5:[42] *The constant deprecation of a just person accomplishes much.* Jn 9:[43] *We know that God does not hear sinners; but if anyone is a servant of God and does His will, God hears him.* And that is: ***His face,*** offered to me in prayer, of course, ***I will accept.*** Gn 4:[44] *The Lord considered Abel and his offerings.* Jn 11:[45] *I knew that you always hear me.* **so that folly may not be imputed to you,** as punishment and condemnation, of course. Ex 32:[46] *The Lord was appeased from* [*doing*] *the malice that He said He would do to His people.* He says "folly," suggesting that they sinned out of ignorance, and therefore are more readily received back by penance. Gn 20:[47] *Will you really destroy a just and ignorant people?*

And God repeats the reason, so that the penance commanded may seem more just: ***for you have not spoken what is right in my presence,*** although it appeared to be right in the presence of men. Jas 3:[48] *If anyone does not offend in speech, he is a perfect man.* ***as my servant Job has,*** supply: spoken what is right. Jb 1 and 2:[49] *In all this, Job did not sin with his lips, nor did he say anything foolish against God.*

And God adds concerning the obedience of Job's friends, and the satisfaction for their work, and their undertaking penance. And that is: **[9]** ***So Eliphaz the Temanite,*** when the contempt of the Lord, which his name means, had been set aside, ***and Bildad the Shuhite,*** when the old age of ancient error had been cast down, ***and Zophar the Naamathite,*** not scattering the slight hope of truth any further, ***departed.*** He says nothing about Elihu because he added nothing new, but he delimited the positions of the others.

41. Ibid.
42. Jas 5.16.
43. Jn 9.31.
44. Gn 4.4.
45. Jn 11.42.
46. Ex 32.14.
47. Gn 20.4.
48. Jas 3.2.
49. Jb 1.22 and 2.10.

and did as the Lord had spoken to them. Ex 24:[50] *All the things that the Lord has spoken we will do, and we will be obedient.* ***and the Lord accepted the face of Job,*** by hearing him favorably, of course; it says "accepted," moreover, because the Lord accepted the offerings presented on their behalf. Is 56:[51] *Their holocausts and their victims will please me upon my altar.*

[10] ***The Lord also,*** by the intercession of Job, of course, ***was converted,*** namely, from anger to placation. Ps:[52] *Convert, O Lord, just a little, and be persuaded in favor of your servants.* ***at the penance of Job,*** undertaken on behalf of his friends, of course; and that is: ***when he prayed for his friends.*** Wis 18:[53] *A man without blame, hastening to pray for the people, bringing forth the shield of his ministry, prayer, and by incense making supplication, withstood the wrath and put an end to the calamity.* At the end of Hos:[54] *I will love them freely, because my wrath has been turned away from them.*

And the Lord added.

Here Job's recompense is specified by a double reward. And four things are said here, namely: how God restored things twofold; how Job's opponents returned to friendship; how his property came forth doubled and God restored his children; and how Job finished his life in joy. And these four things are clear according to the letter.

And that is: ***And the Lord added*** beyond the first things that Job had lost, of course, ***double to all the things that Job had before,*** supply: which had been destroyed. Ps:[55] *According to the multitude of my sorrows in my heart, your consolations have delighted my soul.* Jas 1:[56] *He gives to all abundantly, and He does not reproach.* Sir 42:[57] *In his land he will possess double.* Double, however, are the things that they will lay hold of in body and in soul, on the inside in the joy of the heart and on the outside in the enjoyment of bounty.

And concerning the conversion of Job's friends, God adds:

50. Ex 24.7.
51. Is 56.7.
52. Ps 89.13.
53. Wis 18.21.
54. Hos 14.5.
55. Ps 93.19.
56. Jas 1.5.
57. See Sir 42.25; cf. Is 61.7.

[11] ***And all his brothers,*** that is, those related to him by blood, ***and all his sisters,*** that is, those related to him by blood, ***and all,*** supply: his friends, ***who,*** by the acquaintance of friendship, of course, ***knew him before, came to him,*** as friends, who were his opponents before. Prv 16:[58] *When the ways of man will be pleasing to the Lord, He will convert even His enemies to peace.* Sir 25:[59] *With three things my spirit is pleased, which have been approved before God and men: peace among brothers, and the love of neighbors, and a husband and wife who are in harmony with one another.* ***and they ate bread,*** by which all sumptuous refreshment is understood, ***with him in his house,*** so that the abundance of his house may be indicated. Lk 15:[60] *It was fitting that we should dine sumptuously and rejoice, because your brother was dead and has come to life again; he was lost and has been found.* Ps:[61] *With the voice of joy and praise, the sound of one dining sumptuously.* ***and they moved their heads over him,*** which is a sign of admiration while comforting good people; hence above Job said:[62] *And I would comfort you with words, and I would move my head over you.* ***and they,*** namely, his friends, ***comforted him about all the evil that,*** in the past, of course, ***the Lord had brought upon him,*** so that the multitude of present goods would make Job forget the past evils. Is 54:[63] *In a moment of indignation I have hidden my face from you for a little while, but with everlasting compassion I have had mercy on you.*

And lest there be no joking around, God adds: ***and each one gave him one ewe,*** which was a sign of innocence and simplicity more than a gift. Jn 10:[64] *My sheep hear my voice, and I, the Lord, know them.* ***and one gold earring,*** which, when given to a wise person, signifies obedience to God more than it is a gift. Gn 24:[65] *I placed earrings to adorn her face, and I put bracelets on her wrists.*

And concerning the doubling[66] of Job's possessions, God

58. Prv 16.7.
59. Sir 25.1–2.
60. Lk 15.32.
61. Ps 41.5.
62. Jb 16.5.
63. Is 54.8.
64. Jn 10.27.
65. Gn 24.47.
66. Here I read *duplicatione* with MS TEFM rather than *duplicitate* with Weiss's edition.

adds: [12] ***And the Lord blessed the latter days,*** that is to say, times, ***of Job more than his beginning,*** twice as much, of course, just as Zophar said above:[67] *When you will have supposed that you have been consumed, you will rise as the morning star.* For in the end the Lord repays. Is 58:[68] *You will be like a well-watered garden, and like a spring of water whose waters never fail.*

And He enumerates them: ***And there arose for him fourteen thousand sheep,*** although from the beginning he had only seven thousand, which represent, as Gregory says, the perfection of the four cardinal virtues and of the teaching of the four Gospels and of the Decalogue all drawn together into one—that is, into the length of perseverance and the width of charity and the depth of wisdom.[69] For 1,000 is a cube number arising from 10, as from a root.[70] ***and six thousand camels,*** which signify the cubed perfection of works, which were completed in six days, according to Gn 1. ***and a thousand yoke of oxen,*** which signify the perfection of labor and of obedience, ***and a thousand donkeys,*** which signify the perfection of simplicity and of carrying the burdens of neighbors. Gal 6:[71] *Bear the burdens of one another.*

And He adds concerning the restoration of Job's children: [13] ***And he had seven sons,*** just as at the beginning, of course; they signify, as Gregory says, the seven gifts of the Holy Spirit.[72] ***and three daughters,*** which, as Gregory says, signify the three theological virtues: faith, hope, and love.[73]

And concerning the names of his daughters on account of their preeminent dignity and beauty, God adds: [14] ***And he named one Dies,***[74] because of the brilliance of her charity in accordance with her dignity. Jdt 15:[75] *You are the glory of Jerusalem, you are the joy of Israel, you are the honor of our people.* ***and the second***

67. Jb 11.17.
68. Is 58.11.
69. Cf. Gregory, *Mor.* 35.16.42.
70. See also *On Job* 1.3 (vol. 1, pp. 56–57).
71. Gal 6.2.
72. Cf. Gregory, *Mor.* 35.16.42.
73. Cf. ibid.
74. *Dies* means "day" or "daylight."
75. Jdt 15.10.

one Cassia[76] on account of the aroma of her fame. Ps:[77] *Myrrh and stacte and cassia,* supply: come forth, as the Gloss says,[78] *from your garments.* ***and the third one Cornustibii.***[79] The Hebrew word that is translated as "horn" (*cornu*) is ambiguous, meaning both "according to brilliance" and "horn." Hence, Ex 34,[80] where one translator rendered it, *The face of Moses was made brilliant,* whereas another said, *horned.* But "antimony" (*stibium*) is an herb with which women beautify and paint their faces. Hence Ezek 24:[81] *You painted around your eyes with antimony, and you were adorned with women's ornaments.* And 2 Kgs 9:[82] *Then Jezebel, having heard Jehu come in, painted her eyes with antimony, and adorned her head, and looked out the window.* And the sense is that, given the degree to which Job's daughter was beautiful, she did not need antimony for her complexion. Ps:[83] *With your splendor and your beauty, set out, proceed successfully, and reign.*

And He adds in general: **[15]** ***And there were not found women as beautiful*** in dignity, grace, and excellence ***as the daughters of Job.*** At the end of Prv:[84] *Many daughters have gathered riches; you have surpassed them all.* Jdt 10:[85] *The Lord bestowed beauty on her, because all this dressing up did not proceed from desire, but from virtue. And therefore the Lord increased this beauty in her, so that she appeared to the eyes of all incomparably beautiful.* And this is what follows: ***in all the earth,*** for all people were admiring their beauty. Song 4:[86] *How beautiful you are, my dear, how beautiful you are.* ***and their father,*** Job, of course, ***gave them,*** already married, ***an inheritance among their brothers,*** so that they would not be grieved by exile. Nm 27:[87] *Give them possessions among their father's kinsmen, and let them suc-*

76. *Cassia* means "cinnamon."

77. Ps 44.9.

78. See *GO* on Ps 44.9 (PL 113:910), which appears not to contain the brief gloss Albert references here.

79. *Cornustibii* means "horn of antimony."

80. Ex 34.30.

81. Ezek 23.40.

82. 2 Kgs 9.30.

83. Ps 44.5.

84. Prv 31.29.

85. Jdt 10.4.

86. Song 4.1.

87. Nm 27.6.

ceed him in his inheritance. This was said well enough concerning his daughters.

Then God adds how Job's life ended in joy: **[16]** ***And after these things,*** scourges, ***Job lived,*** with the Lord extending life for him, just as He did for Hezekiah according to Is 38,[88] ***one hundred forty years,*** so that, indeed, insofar as he lived among punishments, he might be restored. For the lifespan of a human is one hundred and twenty years, as the Philosopher[89] and Gn 6[90] say; hence, if Job calculates beginning from this time, twenty years were added beyond the length of a human life. ***and he saw his children,*** supply: his own, of course, seven sons and three daughters, ***and his children's children,*** namely, his grandchildren, ***all the way to the fourth generation,*** that is, all the way to his great-great-grandchildren. And the very same thing is said of Tobit, that he saw the children of his grandchildren, and that he lived the rest of his life in joy and, with a good increase of the fear of God, he departed in peace.[91] ***and he died,*** to the world, of course, but not to God, that is to say, he died in the Lord. Gn 49:[92] *Having fulfilled the commandments, by which he was teaching, he put his feet up on the bed and died.* ***an old man,*** with the hoariness of the mind more than of age, ***and full of days,*** with no night of darkness interposed. 1 Thes 5:[93] *All of you are children of the light and children of the day; we are not children of the night or of darkness.* At the end of Is:[94] *An infant who has not completed his days will not be in you, since a child who is a hundred years old will die.* Ps:[95] *They will still increase in a fruitful old age.* Amen.[96]

88. Is 38.5. See also 2 Kgs 20.5–6.
89. See Aristotle, *GC* 2.10.5.
90. Gn 6.3.
91. Tb 14.1, 4.
92. Gn 49.32.
93. 1 Thes 5.5.
94. Is 65.20.
95. Ps 91.15.
96. MSS TEFM add the following Explicits. T: It ends. E: It ends. The literal exposition *On Job* of Master Albert ends. F: The written work *On Job* of brother Albert the German of the Order of Friars Preachers ends. M: The written work *On Job* of brother Albert the German, formerly bishop of Regensburg, of the Order of Preachers, which was compiled, read, and written in the year 1274 in the German city of Cologne, ends.

INDICES

GENERAL INDEX

INDEX OF HOLY SCRIPTURE

Old Testament

New Testament

RECENT VOLUMES IN THE FATHERS OF THE CHURCH, MEDIAEVAL CONTINUATION

RUPERT OF DEUTZ, *Commentary on the Songs of Songs,* translated by Jieon Kim and Vittorio Hösle, Volume 22 (2024)

BL. HRABANUS MAURUS, *On the Formation of Clergy,* translated by Owen M. Phelan, Volume 21 (2023)

ST. ALBERT THE GREAT, *On Resurrection,* translated by Irven M. Resnick and Franklin T. Harkins, Volume 20 (2020)

ST. ALBERT THE GREAT, *On Job, Volume 1,* translated by Franklin T. Harkins, Volume 19 (2019)

ST. HILDEGARD OF BINGEN, *The Book of Divine Works,* translated by Nathaniel M. Campbell, Volume 18 (2018)

ALBERT THE GREAT, *On the Body of the Lord,* translated by Sr. Albert Marie Surmanski, OP, Volume 17 (2017)

WORKS OF ST. ALBERT THE GREAT IN THIS SERIES

Questions Concerning Aristotle's On Animals, translated by Irven M. Resnick and Kenneth F. Kitchell, Jr., Fathers of the Church Mediaeval Continuation 9 (2008)

On the Body of the Lord, translated by Sr. Albert Marie Surmanski, Fathers of the Church Mediaeval Continuation 17 (2017)

On Job, Volume 1, translated by Franklin T. Harkins, Fathers of the Church Mediaeval Continuation 19 (2019)

On Resurrection, translated by Irven M. Resnick and Franklin T. Harkins, Fathers of the Church Mediaeval Continuation 20 (2020)